Language Variety
in the South

Language Variety in the South

Perspectives in Black and White

Edited by

Michael B. Montgomery
and Guy Bailey

Foreword by James B. McMillan

The University of Alabama Press

Library of Congress Cataloging in Publication Data

Main entry under title:

Language variety in the South.

  Bibliography: p.
  Includes index.
    1. English language—Southern States—Variation—
Addresses, essays, lectures.   2. English language—
Dialects—Southern States—Addresses, essays, lectures.
3. Black English—Southern States—Addresses, essays,
lectures.   4. Afro-Americans—Southern States—Language—
Addresses, essays, lectures.   I. Montgomery, Michael,
1950–   . II. Bailey, Guy H., 1950–   .
PE2922.L36   1986   427'.975   84-16396
ISBN 0-8173-0244-1

To John H. Fisher and
    James B. McMillan,
    the inspiration behind this work

Contents

Foreword

James B. McMillan

Southern American English has been studied more intensively, over a longer period of time, than any other North American dialect, but has not been described systematically or accounted for historically. Dozens of valid studies report dozens of facets of this variety of English, and some of its obscure history has been dug out piecemeal, but the known data do not yet justify a comprehensive descriptive grammar or a coherent account of its evolution.

Many reasons for this state of affairs are obvious. "Southern American" is not a homogeneous dialect, but too often has been approached as if it were; disparate studies of different populations of informants are rarely interlocking; only after LAGS and DARE are completed will systematic reports cover the whole geographical South, and neither of these enterprises will treat syntax exhaustively; caste and class differences vastly complicate the subject; the relationship between black and white English has occasioned polemical attacks and defenses that have perverted objective analysis; the notion of "socioeconomically comparable blacks and whites" has obscured the realities of side-by-side white and black speech communities; written records of eighteenth- and nineteenth century Southern speech are rare and of uneven quality; too many sentimental notions have become theories before adequate analyzed data justified theorizing; the data have not included many segments of free speech uninterrupted by interviewers; the processes of pidginization, creolization, and decreolization have only recently received needed attention.

What seems to be needed are more common assumptions and methodologies of investigators, more comparable and interlocking studies, and more efforts to relate independent investigations. The fact that a number of specialists got together in 1981 to read papers and exchange views on Language Variety in the South is an encouraging sign of increased commonality of interest, and the resulting papers (making up this volume) show positive steps

James McMillan

toward correcting divergencies of the past and toward accurate description of the evolution and present state of the dialects that make up "Southern American."

Acknowledgments

This book is based on a three-day research conference of the same name held at the University of South Carolina in Columbia on October 1-3, 1981. The editors of this volume wish to thank the following for their generous support of the meeting: the National Endowment for the Humanities (grant number RD-*1899-81), the Department of English at USC and its chairman, George Geckle, and the College of Humanities and Social Sciences at USC and its dean, Chester Bain. Twenty-one of the papers in this volume were presented at the conference; two others, those of Dorrill and Sommer, were solicited. We wish to thank the contributors for their patience and cooperation in the production of this collection. We also want to thank student assistants Rosa Costa, Yadira Diaz, and Michael K. Smith for their logistical help at the conference.

We thank John Fisher, Professor of English at the University of Tennessee, for the idea to organize a conference focusing on recent research on language patterns in the South.

In particular we wish to express our gratitude to the many members of the University of Alabama Press staff for their cordial and patient guidance through every stage of the complex process of converting this collection of papers into a publishable manuscript. In particular, we wish to mention Malcolm MacDonald, Elizabeth May, Michael Burton, Daniel Ross, and Anna Jacobs.

Invaluable assistance in preparing this manuscript was rendered by Bill West, Roger Blau, and John Powers in showing how to put this material on word processor, Angela Bailey and Thomas Hayes in proofreading, Adrienne Chingkwei Lee in drawing the phonetic detail, and Daniel McCarthy in his expert copyediting.

Language Variety
in the South

Introduction

Michael B. Montgomery and Guy Bailey

In a 1967 article entitled "Needed Research in Southern Dialects," the late Raven I. McDavid, Jr. listed seven broad areas in which research on the English language in the Southern United States was lacking, among them the speech of Southerners who had migrated north, the speech of relic areas such as the Delmarva Peninsula and Appalachia, and nonverbal communication. The area which he emphasized most, however, was the speech of blacks in the South. McDavid noted that "as important as . . . the study of the speech of relic areas, and especially Appalachia [is], the study of Negro speech is far more urgent for teaching programs in all parts of the United States" (1967c:121).

Since 1967, sociolinguistic research has made it even clearer that no question in the study of American English is more crucial or more controversial than that of how the speech of blacks and whites in the South is related. Answers to this question not only have far-reaching pedagogical implications, but also can tell us much about the origin of language differences in the United States (whether they derive primarily from the British Isles, from language contact situations, especially in the Caribbean, or from both), about how the English language and its cultural reflexes have evolved and been transmitted in this country and about language change. In addition, judgments about the relationship between black and white speech have been critical in making decisions about basic literacy issues of teaching reading and writing, as shown especially by the recent Ann Arbor decision.[1]

Despite the accumulation of a large body of pertinent literature, scholars in the field are still a long way from a consensus on this important question.[2] This is the result of several factors, the most important being the paucity of comparable data-based studies. More large-scale studies of black speech have been undertaken outside the South than in the South; the comparable material about white speech and black speech in the South has until recently been largely anecdotal. As a result, many recent studies compare black to white speech in the North, where they certainly diverge more than in the South. Wolfram (1974:498) attributes the difficulty of comparing existing studies of Southern speech to "non-comparable data bases, different elicitation strategies, non-comparable informant selection, and different analytical models of description." Moreover, it is clear, as both Wolfram 1973b and Traugott 1972 suggest, that sociopolitical considerations have often played a role in judgments about black-white speech relations.

All of these problems are compounded by the failure of many scholars to recognize the geographical, historical, and social complexities of the South and the ethnography of speech in the region, factors which make any unqualified statement of black-white speech relationships in the South impossible. Extending from Maryland to Texas, the South, according to Gastil 1975, actually comprises two broad subregions, each of which is, in turn, composed of many "districts" and "subdistricts" (see map 1). This regional diversity reflects not only physiographic differences, but also differences in social and ethnic composition. The proportion of blacks in the population varies greatly from district to district, with many counties in upland regions having no blacks at all. Even within subdistricts, the social relations between whites and blacks may vary substantially. Furthermore, as McMillan has noted, to understand language variation in the South, it is always of utmost importance to know who talks to whom, when, and where.[3] Ultimately, then, only detailed ethnographic studies will enable us to describe the speech of blacks and whites in various parts of the South.

The most unfortunate reason for the lack of consensus about black-white relations in the South, however, involves the temper of the field in the 1960s and 1970s. During these years, many researchers and students of language variation in the United States tended to split into several camps having different approaches and different goals, the two most prominent being dialect geographers, whose primary scholarly forum was the American Dialect Society, and sociolinguists, whose major forum for presenting and discussing research was the NWAVE (New Ways of Analyzing Variation in English) conferences. Dialect geographers have been primarily interested in variation in vocabulary and pronunciation, while sociolinguists have been concerned with systematic grammatical and phonological variation. These two camps became identified with opposing views on the origin of language differences in the South (more on this below) and on the significance of these differences, especially in the classroom.

The two groups also differed significantly in their methodology: the dialect geographers worked within the framework of the regionally based, broad-scale linguistic atlas investigations (see Atwood 1963 for background); the sociolinguists worked within the

Map 1 Districts and Subdistricts of the South
(from Gastil 1975:174)

framework developed for quantitative analysis of variation as a
function of social stratification within individual speech communities by Labov, Wolfram, Fasold, and others. There was therefore
little communication between these groups and often less than
mutual respect. More significant, however, were the strident
polemics of much of the work during this period (see, e.g., Stewart
1972b, a review of Wolfram and Clarke 1971, and Dillard et al.
1979), in addition to the tenuousness of the data often presented.
Assertion and polemics often replaced detailed analysis of carefully gathered linguistic data.

To say that the question of black-white speech relationships in
the South has not been answered is not to say, however, that no
relevant research exists. This introductory essay documents what
seem to be four distinct stages in the study of language patterns
as they relate to the question of how similar or different white
and black speech are in the South. These stages have supplemented, rather than superseded, each other; each has been characterized by different approaches and analytical tools, different
methodologies, and different goals. Consequently, each stage has
produced quite different claims and conclusions.

Proponents of each approach continue to work, to write, and

to publish, but they have not reached a consensus. In fact, much of the recent work shows that the original question of how black speech differs from white speech is far too simple and that differences across social class, region, sex, and generation are as important as racial differences.

Virtually no one has said that no differences exist between black and white speakers at least somewhere in the South. The real issues concern the range and the source and of these differences and their linguistic, cultural, and pedagogic significance. In documenting the principal research on language variation in the South here, we skip the numerous largely impressionistic studies published before World War II and the studies of literary dialect. References for these are among the more than eleven hundred in McMillan's Annotated Bibliography of Southern American English (1971).

The systematic investigation of black and white speech began with the editing of the field records for the Linguistic Atlas of the Middle and South Atlantic States (LAMSAS), two-thirds of the fieldwork for which was done before World War II and one-third after. As the second phase of the Linguistic Atlas of the United States and Canada, directed by Hans Kurath, LAMSAS followed the tradition of broad-based direct field investigation begun by Gilliéron in France and developed by Jaberg and Jud in Italy and Switzerland.[4] Unlike in the European atlases, Kurath expanded his sample to include common informants (usually with a high school education and less restricted social contacts) and cultivated informants (usually college educated, with extensive social contacts) as well as folk speakers (usually with a grade school education and few social contacts), so that he was able to provide some indication of both the social and the regional distribution of forms. In addition, in the South Atlantic states of Maryland, Virginia, North Carolina, South Carolina, and Georgia, forty blacks were interviewed. The completed LAMSAS sample consists of interviews with 1,216 informants, nearly all of whom were over fifty at the time they were interviewed. These informants were natives of their communities and provide a data base with which research on the speech of subsequent generations can be compared. So far, three summary volumes based on LAMSAS have appeared: Kurath's Word Geography of the Eastern United States (1949), Atwood's A Survey of the Verb Forms of the Eastern United States (1953), and Kurath and McDavid's The Pronunciation of English in the Atlantic States (1961). Two of a projected sixty fascicles of LAMSAS have appeared recently from the University of Chicago Press (McDavid et al. 1980-   ).

In the subset of the lexicon investigated in LAMSAS, Kurath finds no significant differences in the range of responses of blacks and whites in the South Atlantic states and suggests that there are no categorical differences between black and white speech: "The speech of uneducated Negroes . . . exhibits the same regional

and local variation as that of the simple white folk" (1949:6).
Kurath explains differences that do exist as the result of cultural
lag: The speech of blacks is "more archaic or old-fashioned, not
un-English, but retarded because of less schooling" (1949:6). In his
study of verb morphology, Atwood (1953:41) further refines
Kurath's observations, noting that differences between black and
white speech are statistical--that is, differences in frequency of
occurrence--rather than categorical:

> Some items . . . (particularly frez, cotch, he do, and
> gwine) are considerably more frequent among Negroes than
> among white informants. A larger sampling of Negro usage
> might enable us to classify these and other forms as
> "characteristically Negro," but the difference would again
> be one of frequency. I cannot point to any form that is
> widely current among Negroes that is not in use among the
> more rustic of the white informants.

In addition to these two works, several studies smaller in
scope but either based on LAMSAS materials or making use of
linguistic atlas methodology have addressed the question of black-
white speech relationships. The earliest and perhaps most important of these is McDavid and McDavid's, "The Relation of the
Speech of American Negroes to the Speech of Whites" (1951).
Written primarily to debunk the racially ethnocentric myths that
black speech is the product of physiology and that the "Negro contributed nothing of himself from his African heritage except a few
exotic words" (p. 6), this study documents some two dozen words
of African origin (including such common words as okra, gumbo,
goober, and badmouth) which have been taken over by whites. The
McDavids further suggest that African influence might extend
beyond the lexicon to include grammatical forms such as for, as
the particle with the infinitive of purpose (as in he come for tell
you), and phonological tendencies such as the higher frequency of
consonant cluster simplification than among white Southerners.

This important article also discusses the problems which at
that time faced scholars, especially white scholars, who studied
African survivals in black speech: "The scholar who accepts the
theory of Negro inferiority tends to explain any apparent differences between Negro and white speech on the basis of the Negro's
childlike mind or imperfectly developed speech organs. Or if he
tries to be fair, he will probably deny that there are any essential
differences" (p. 5).

Since 1951, Raven McDavid has expanded these observations
on black-white speech relationships (1965a, b, 1966a, b, 1967a, b,
c, 1968, 1973a, b; McDavid and Austin 1966; McDavid and Davis
1972). While continuing to assail racially ethnocentric myths,
McDavid emphasizes that, in the absence of other firm evidence,
we can assume only that "the range of variants is the same in

Negro and white speech, though the statistical distribution of variants has been skewed by the American caste system" (1965a: 258n). He also discounts the notion that "'racial' dialects, independent of social and cultural experiences" exist (1966a:8).

Although their data come from LAMSAS, the McDavids' emphasis on African survivals owes much to Turner's study of Gullah (1945, 1948, 1949). Turner was able to show that African languages have significantly influenced not only the lexicon of Gullah but also its grammar and phonology. Equally as important, Turner's work initiated black speech as a legitimate subject of investigation in and of itself.

Among noteworthy other studies of black speech using linguistic atlas methodology are Williamson's investigations of Negro speech in Memphis (1961, 1968). Williamson compares her data with white speech sampled in LAMSAS and finds that her informants generally use the same morphological forms as those in Atwood 1953, although Type I Memphis blacks tend to use the uninflected third person singular somewhat more frequently. She also indicates that the phonological systems of black and white Southerners are generally the same, with the distinguishing features of black speech primarily at the subphonemic level.

In later studies (1969, 1970, 1972), responding primarily to those who argue that black speech has a creole origin (discussed below) and that certain structures are characteristic of black speech, Williamson continues to maintain that the linguistic system of blacks is essentially the same as that of whites. She points out that many supposed black features (including existential it, zero copula, and gonna) occur in Southern white speech and that discussion of any differences between black and white speech exaggerates those differences at the expense of innumerable similarities. Much of Williamson's evidence, however, is from literary dialogue and random personal observations rather than from systematic collection or fieldwork.

Joy Miller 1972, also a response to creolists, uses similar evidence in attempting to show that finite be and zero copula are features of white as well as black speech. While several of her literary examples of the invariant be are ambiguous in their semantic force, all of the examples taken from speech seem to have resulted from will or would deletion and thus do not counter the claim that the feature is unique to black speech. Miller's examples of copula deletion are somewhat more convincing.

The most explicit attempt to refute the creole theory, however, is a series of essays by Lawrence Davis (1969, 1970a, 1970b). Davis argues that the claim for "Black English," a racial dialect, is in part a result of the fact that most people who make the claim are Northerners:

> To most Northerners the notion of the difference between
> Black and White speech was accepted as a matter of

course, and there was an obvious reason for this easy acceptance. The Northerners came from the cities where patterns of settlement had resulted in large Black ghettos, and, since the Blacks were the largest southern group in the northern cities, the vast majority of the southern speakers heard by northern linguist(s) were Black; in the North, in other words, there was de facto Black English [1970a:59].

Davis 1969 argues that the creolists emphasize particular features of black speech, rather than treat the system as a whole, and that they ignore the numerous similarities between black and white speech. In a study of the speech of three Kentucky counties, Davis 1970b finds no systematic differences between the speech of his single black and eleven white informants. (In an earlier study of the speech of Louisville, Kentucky, however, Howren 1958 found that the phonology of white speech is typical of the South Midland area, while that of black speech is typical of the Southern dialect.)

In recent years, two theses and one dissertation have used LAMSAS data, pairing black and white informants by locality, age, education, and socioeconomic status. Greibesland 1970 compares the phonology of three pairs of informants in Virginia and Maryland and finds two features (the pronunciation of /w/ and the "standard English labiodental fricatives" /f, v/ as bilabial fricatives) in the speech of the black informants only; one feature, final consonant cluster reduction, more frequent among blacks; but most features, including postvocalic /r/ and all vowel features, not correlatable with race. Dorrill 1975 examines the LAMSAS records of two pairs of comparable black and white informants from South Carolina communities, also to compare phonological features. With respect to final consonant cluster reduction, the realization of final [θ] as [f], and the appearance of postvocalic /r/, he finds no significant differences, but only differences "of a minor statistical nature" (p. 58).

Dorrill 1982 studies patterns of stressed vowels in the speech of sixteen pairs of comparable black-white LAMSAS informants from Maryland, Virginia, and North Carolina. He examines fifteen different vowel nuclei in five different phonological environments and establishes systematic phonetic differences, but no phonemic differences, between the vowels of his sixteen black and sixteen white informants:

The greatest single difference between black and white speech found in this study is the greater tendency for blacks to have monophthongal pronunciations of stressed vowels. Whites have a corresponding greater tendency for upgliding diphthongs. This pronunciation difference is more marked among free vowels than among checked vowels. It

is most apparent among the mid vowels, particularly /e/
and /o/, and reaches near-categorical proportions in
certain environments. It may be that this feature is one of
those used by listeners in determining the race of the
speaker.

Another important difference between black and white
speakers found in this study is the greater tendency for
homogeneity in black speech . . . the use of . . . sub-
dialectal areas seems to be more valid for the white
speakers than for the black speakers [p. 94].

During this first stage of research, linguistic geographers contributed significantly to the understanding of black-white relations
in the South, but linguistic atlas evidence, as McDavid and Davis
1972 point out themselves, is not sufficient to answer the question
once and for all:

First of all, the Linguistic Atlas project is preponderantly
concerned with white speech; even in the Old South there
were interviews with Negro informants in only about a
fifth of the communities selected. There are valid reasons
for this decision--notably the notorious lack of funds for
field work, and the lack of Negro scholars who were
interested in field work. Still, one would like to see more
data, even though there is no reason to distrust the reliability of that which we have.

Furthermore, the methods of the Linguistic Atlas exclude certain kinds of evidence that are of concern to
those who desire to make cross-racial comparisons. Like
its predecessors in France and Italy, the Atlas has concentrated on short-answer questions, of vocabulary, pronunciation, and morphology, syntactic items are few,
because it is difficult to frame questions that would give
an unequivocal response. And in the absence of mechanical
aids, it was hard for even the best investigator in the
1930's to record extended phrases from free conversation
[p. 307].

Critics of atlas methodology, though, note that substantial
amounts of tape-recorded data from comparable black and white
informants are precisely what is needed to answer the question,
since, as Fasold (1981:166) says, "the genuine differences between
black and white language are in part statistical and are sensitive
to aspects of the surrounding linguistic environment." More recent
work in linguistic geography and regional lexicography may well
overcome these problems. The Linguistic Atlas of the Gulf States
(LAGS), with fieldwork completed in 1983 and editing now in
progress, includes more than 240 black informants, over 20 percent
of the more than 1,100 interviews from Georgia, Florida, Alabama,

Tennessee, Arkansas, Mississippi, Louisiana, and eastern Texas. All LAGS field records were tape recorded in their entirety (in fact, the tape-recorded interview is the field record), and many contain large amounts of free conversation (see Bailey and Bassett, this volume, for a study based on LAGS records). The Dictionary of American Regional English (DARE) also includes many black informants from the South (almost 15 percent of its sample from the region); many of these informants were tape recorded while reading a set passage and also in undirected conversation (see Joan Hall, this volume, for a study based on DARE records).

The second stage in the study of black and white speech relationships in the South was not a response to the shortcomings of linguistic atlas methodology, even though its conclusions were remarkably different. Rather, this stage was prompted by increased research in the 1960s on the structure of pidgin and creole languages, especially in West Africa and in the Caribbean. In light of this research, a number of scholars (Stewart, Dillard, Loflin, and Beryl Bailey chief among them) have made two far-reaching claims about the speech of blacks in the United States: It has a different "deep structure" and is therefore only superficially related to the speech of whites, and it derives not from seventeenth- and eighteenth-century Anglo-American dialects but from a Plantation Creole.[5] Although these scholars have produced few direct, data-based comparisons of black and white speech in the South, they have influenced profoundly later views of the relationship.

Both claims of the creolists derive primarily from the work of William Stewart (1964, 1965, 1966, 1966-67, 1967, 1968, 1970a, b, c, 1971, 1972a), although Robert Hall 1950 suggested the possibility of a creole substratum for black speech a decade and a half earlier. Stewart's work has been primarily a response to educational problems that black children face, problems which Stewart believes are a result of

> a disturbing correlation between language behavior on the one hand and socio-economic and ethnic stratification on the other. The correlation is particularly controversial insofar as it involves the speech of large numbers of American Negroes. . . . Yet the fact is that Negroes account for most of the most pedagogically problematic non-standard dialect speakers of the most radically non-standard dialects of natively spoken English in the entire country [1967:22].

The speech of many blacks is so radically different from that of whites, even in the South, Stewart asserts, because it has a different origin and history: "With very few exceptions the form of English which [Africans who became slaves] acquired was a pidginized one, and this kind of English became so well established as the principal medium of communication between Negro slaves in the British colonies that it was passed on as a creole language to succeeding generations of the New World Negroes, for whom it was their native tongue" (1967:22). This "pidginized form of English," Stewart believes, was learned not in the New World, but in West Africa, where it "originated as a lingua franca in the trade centers and slave factories" (1967:24), and it was spread throughout the Caribbean and the United States through the importation of slaves and became a creole. The plantation system led to cleavages in the black population, with the result that domestic servants often learned the English of their masters while fieldhands preserved the creole. Furthermore, since the eighteenth century this English creole has gradually become decreolized, more like the language of whites, with the breakdown of the plantation system and increased education for blacks; but that decreolization, Stewart contends, is still incomplete.

As a consequence, the nonstandard speech of blacks differs structurally, in kind, not just quantitatively, in degree, even from that of Southern whites. Illustrating these differences, Stewart points to a number of features as characteristic of nonstandard black speech, including the grammatical and semantic contrast between zero copula and "durative" be, the zero possessive, and undifferentiated pronouns (among others). He concludes that "nonstandard features in the speech of [Negroes] may be due in part to the influence of the non-standard dialects of whites with whom they or their ancestors have come in contact, but they also may be due to the survival of creolisms from the older Negro fieldhand speech of the plantations" (1967:26).

To develop his creole hypothesis, Stewart relies primarily on attestations of speech from novels, plays, and other literary works, a very different kind of evidence from that which linguistic geographers used. While the creole hypothesis continues to be a matter of considerable controversy, Stewart has expanded the range of data available for studying how black and white speech are related by his use of literary sources. Even more important, Stewart has redirected the focus of research from morphology and vocabulary to syntax, semantics, and phonology, and to systematic structure, rather than the incidence, of linguistic features. Finally, the work of Stewart and other creolists has brought about increased discussion of the educational implications of language differences.

Of the scholars who have followed Stewart's lead, J. L. Dillard is the most prolific. He further develops the creole hypothesis and its educational implications in articles (1964, 1967, 1968, 1971, 1973) and books (1972, 1975, 1977), the most important of which is Black English: Its History and Usage in the United States (1972). Dillard not only rejects the notion that seventeenth- and eighteenth-century British regional dialects are the source of any distinctive black speech but also the claim that white colonists in the eighteenth century spoke distinctive regional dialects. He attributes this to "dialect leveling, a very well-known phenomenon in migration which means that even the white residents of colonial America did not speak or transmit British 'regional' dialects" (1972:73), and sees language contact situations as the primary source of variation in American English.

In hypothesizing that a Plantation Creole was the basis of present-day black speech, Dillard emphasizes three points. First, like Stewart, he contends that this Creole was a development of a pidgin that originated not in the United States, but in West Africa.[6]   Second, Dillard suggests that, before the Civil War, there was a great deal of diversity in black speech:

> For an indeterminate period--but one which lasted nearly two hundred years--there were three language groups among slaves:
>   (1) Those who learned the English of their masters. Most of these were either house servants or the mechanics who were allowed to work in the towns, the wages usually being retained by the owners. The language of the freemen and of their descendants was more or less of this type.
>   (2) The great mass of native-born field workers, who spoke Plantation Creole.
>   (3) Recent imports from Africa, some of whom brought Pidgin English with them. The others must have faced a difficult language-learning problem [1972:98].

Finally, Dillard maintains that while it is clear that the speech of slaves varied socially, "there was one life style and dialect for the vast majority of them" (1972:99). Even after the Civil War the Plantation Creole continued its spread, so that the features came to characterize black speech throughout the South.

Dillard devotes considerable attention to the relationship between black and white speech in the South, asserting that they "are generally distinguishable but that some Southern white dialects have been strongly influenced by Negro dialect [as] . . . the prime fact about Southern white dialect . . ." (1972:216). In addition, he claims that black speech is "likely to have produced some--not all--of the differences between Southern white dialect and Northern white dialect" (1972:191).

Relying on the comments of eighteenth- and nineteenth-century travelers and observers of Southern culture, Dillard suggests that social relations between blacks and whites resulted in substantial influence on white speech by blacks and in white bidialectalism, especially among upper-class white males. However, the social situation, particularly the "pull of the rules of conduct," did not favor such bidialectalism or even the use of "standard English" among blacks (1972:207). According to Dillard, then, black speech

was the "creative and innovative" force, white speech the "imitative" (1972:189). He illustrates this relationship by suggesting
Afro-American origins for such Southernisms as carry, meaning "to
conduct someone"; evening, referring to any time of day after
noon; perfective done; and tote. Dunn not only echoes Dillard's
emphasis on black influences, but attributes the denial of black
influence by earlier scholars to an attempt to "soothe the wounded
egos of the middle and upper classes [of Southern whites] who were
. . . seeking some manner by which to restore their pride" (1976:
117).

Stewart and Dillard concentrate most of their research on
sociohistorical factors which they believe make the creole hypothesis the most likely explanation for present-day distinctive black
speech. Later creolists, however, have become increasingly concerned with linguistic change. Rickford 1977, for example, considers the origins of "black English" in terms of four linguistic
criteria for prior creolization: simplification, admixture, divergence from other dialects, and similarity to other creoles. After
evaluating features of black speech (including consonant cluster
simplification, r deletion, intonation, stressed been, copula absence, and invariant be [among others]), Rickford concludes that
"the linguistic evidence [for a creole background] satisfies the
criteria . . . often enough to make the prior creolization of BE
[Black English] very likely indeed" (1977:215). Elsewhere, Rickford
1974 details possible steps in the decreolization of invariant be.

Traugott 1976 takes a very different approach in concluding
that "aspects of VBE [Vernacular Black English] can best be explained in light of centuries of linguistic change, and development
from a pidgin to a creole, through various stages of decreolization,
to a point where VBE, though largely assimilated into the various
English vernaculars, still has features which clearly distinguishes it
from them" (p. 93). Traugott examines a series of passages from
West African Pidgin, Tok Pisin, Jamaican Creole, Gullah, and VBE
to demonstrate both the features which characterize creoles and
their similarities to features in black speech.

Whereas Traugott maintains that black speech has been largely
assimilated into the various English vernaculars, other scholars
claim that the speech of blacks is only superficially related to
that of whites. Thus Beryl Bailey suggests that "the southern
Negro 'dialect' differs from other Southern speech because its
deep structure is different, having its origins as it undoubtedly
does in some proto-creole grammatical structure" (1965:172). She
illustrates this deep-structure difference with phrase-structure
rules for nonverbal predications in English (no particular variety is
specified), in Jamaican Creole, and in the speech of the character
Duke, a Southern black in Warren Miller's novel Cool World.

Loflin 1967, 1969, 1970, Loflin, Sobin, and Dillard 1974 and
Fickett 1970, 1972 have developed in greater detail the hypothesis
that black speech has a unique deep structure. For example, using

data elicited from a single fourteen-year-old male from Washington, D.C., Loflin claims that the deep structure of the "nonstandard Negro English" (NNE) verb system differs from that of "Standard English" in at least four ways: NNE has no category of perfect in its base; the contrast between be and am/is, and are requires an addition to the Tense category; there is no agreement between subjects and verbs other than be; and unmarked verbs, traditionally identified with the "Standard English" present, may be neutralized (1970:28). Fickett makes even broader claims about the structure of black speech, maintaining that "Black English has five aspects, four relative past tenses, two relative future tenses, and a true present tense. It has a combination of tense and aspect, but only one tense may appear as a predicator" (1972:19). Luelsdorff 1975 suggests that the phonological system of black speech is also significantly different from that of whites and has constructed a generative phonology of "Black English."

While scholars during this second stage have redirected the research on black speech and have opened up new sources of data, they, like the linguistic geographers before them, have for several reasons not provided a very thorough description of how black and white speech are related. The most important of these reasons involves research strategies. Initially, most creolists concentrated on sociohistorical factors which make the creole hypothesis plausible. As a result, the history of black speech which they reconstructed is essentially "external" rather than "internal," with the "emphasis on reconstructing historical developments and contacts rather than linguistic forms as such" (Wolfram 1973c:675). Although more recent work (especially that of Rickford 1977, and Rickford's essay in this volume), has done much to rectify the situation, much remains to be done.

The linguistic data used by the early creolists and others who claimed that black speech has a radically different deep structure also present problems. Many of their claims about contemporary black speech are based on small amounts of data, small samples (single informants in the case of Loflin and Luelsdorff), or anecdotal evidence such as that used by Dillard (see Wolfram 1973c and Fasold 1975b), although Rickford 1975 is a notable exception. Further, these scholars have often compared black speech not to white vernaculars, but to "Standard English," a variety which they neither define nor describe. Using literary attestations and the comments of early travelers and other nonlinguists has both opened new avenues of research and posed new difficulties. Dillard recognizes that there are problems in using literary sources (e.g., he points out that white authors provide little lexical evidence), but he maintains that "many white writers, especially those who grew up on Southern plantations and were bidialectal, have managed the grammar of Black English rather well and have, insofar as ordinary orthography will permit, done a reasonably good job of indicating pronunciation" (1977:155). Weaver 1970, however, has demonstrated that writers of fiction are unreliable in their treatment of variable phenomena, and most of the features usually associated with black speech are variable rather than categorical.

Using the observations of laymen creates even greater difficulties, some of which can be seen in Dillard's handling of two articles by Read. In "The Speech of Negroes in Colonial America," Read 1939 examines newspaper advertisements describing runaway slaves and concludes that slaves brought up in this country usually spoke "good English." Read's evidence for his conclusion, then, is the observation of slave masters, the writers of the advertisements. Both Stewart 1968 and Dillard 1972, however, point out that such evidence cannot be taken at face value:

> It is necessary to evaluate the evidence in terms of what the owners meant by the term good English. It is quite possible that they meant something like "English which can be understood" or even "good English--for a slave." Since the frame of reference of comparison to other slaves had already been established by the advertising medium itself, there is no chance that anyone would make the mistake of interpreting the phrase to mean the English of the fugitive slaves was being compared to that of non-slaves [Dillard 1972:83-84].

Elsewhere, Dillard is not so cautious. In "British Recognition of American Speech in the Eighteenth Century," Read 1933 examines the observations of British travelers, who comment on the absence of dialect differences among Americans. Dillard (1972:73) accepts these observations at face value, but surely one must ask what British travelers meant by "uniformity" or the absence of dialect and what their frame of reference was. Quite possibly, these observers meant that American speech was uniform in comparison to British speech or, as Read suggests, that they "failed to find dialectal variation partly because of a lack of intimacy with the country" (1933:325). Inconsistency in handling observations of such laymen, along with the difficulties in using literary sources, is a major problem in creolists' reconstruction of the history of black speech.

The third stage in the study of how black and white speech in the South are related has directly addressed the problems of reliable research design and the conflation of synchronic and diachronic issues, but it has not developed in reaction to inadequacies of earlier research. Rather, this stage of research has been largely a consequence of new directions in sociolinguistics, including an interest in quantifying linguistic variation and incorporating it into a grammar, and also a consequence of attempts to provide linguistic descriptions of nonstandard speech for educators. Sociolinguistic researchers in this stage have concentrated on Northern urban areas such as Detroit and New York, and, therefore, they have produced limited data useful for direct comparisons of black and white speech in the South. But they have significantly influenced the methodology of some studies in the South, and much of our knowledge about the structure of black speech in the United States is due to their efforts. More important, they have redirected the focus of research to the intensive study of speech in its social settings.

The new directions in sociolinguistics follow largely from the work of Labov on Martha's Vineyard (1963), in New York City (1966; Labov et al. 1968), and in Philadelphia (1972d). In these studies, Labov made use of new sampling procedures, formulated the concept of the "linguistic variable," developed techniques to measure the quantitative nature of linguistic variation, and created a formalism, the variable rule, which allowed him to incorporate "free variation" into linguistic theory. These technical innovations have made possible detailed descriptions of black speech, with emphasis on linguistic systems rather than on individual linguistic features, and on quantitative as well as qualitative differences between systems.

Besides providing the theoretical base and the technical apparatus which underlie much sociolinguistic research, Labov and his associates have produced extensive studies of black speech (Labov et al. 1968, Labov 1972a). Labov's work in New York City was designed primarily to serve three functions: to demonstrate the internal cohesion of vernacular black speech, to provide a linguistic description of that variety, and to compare that variety systematically to "Standard English." To examine the structural and functional differences between "Negro non-standard English" and "Standard English," Labov and his associates interviewed three groups of New Yorkers: "(1) a geographically random sample of fifty individual preadolescent speakers in Vacation Day Camps; (2) six preadolescent and adolescent peer groups in South Central Harlem, studied in individual interviews and group sessions; (3) a random sample of one hundred adults, in a middle-class area and the two working-class areas of the peer group studies" (Labov et al. 1968:I:v). After analyzing a number of sociolinguistic variables, including the absence of postvocalic /r/, consonant cluster simplification, the copula, remote present perfect <u>been</u>, perfective <u>done</u>, and multiple modals, Labov reaches the following conclusions:

1. BEV [Black English Vernacular] is a distinct system from other dialects in several important grammatical categories of the tense and aspect system.
2. BEV extends many of the rules of other dialects by including new environments and raising output probabilities in older environments. No new transformations are required to account for the special forms of BEV involving negation, quantifiers, modals, and other functional elements of the grammatical mechanism.

3. BEV shows its systematic character in a set of interrelations between rules of types 1 and 2 such that
they operate jointly to preserve the major grammatical and semantic functions of language [1972a:61].

Despite the internal consistency of black speech and its systematic differences from "Standard English," Labov concludes that
black speech "is best seen as a distinct subsystem within the
larger grammar of English" (1972a:63-64). In other words, unlike
many creolists, Labov asserts that black and white speech differ in
"low-level rules which have marked effects on surface structure"
(Labov et al. 1968:I:v), rather than in deep structure. The functional relations between black speech and white speech, however,
are more complex. Labov et al. 1968 isolate several speech events
(e.g., toasts and "rifting"), which are unique to black speech and
conclude that nonstandard black speech is valued positively by its
speakers.

In addition, Labov and his associates (Labov et al. 1968; Labov
1972a) demonstrate the social and stylistic stratification of black
speech. In particular, they note three sharp cleavages in the
population: middle class vs. working class, "lames" vs. club
members, and adults vs. adolescents. The grammar of middle-class
adults most closely resembles that of the white middle class, while
some features (such as invariant be, and ain't used for didn't) are
restricted to adolescents. Lames, preadolescents and adolescents
excluded from their peer groups, tend to resemble adults in both
their grammar and their values. These social cleavages are further
complicated by differences in style shifting, with teenage working-
class club members, unlike adults, showing little style shifting
except in the most formal contexts.

As Labov's methodology has been extended to other studies of
black speech, especially in Northern cities, these findings have
been replicated, amplified, and in some cases modified. The most
important of the studies is Shuy, Wolfram, and Riley 1967, a large-
scale survey of Detroit speech consisting of tape-recorded interviews with over 700 residents, both black and white, speaking in
at least three styles: conversational style (largely from narratives and descriptions), single response style, and reading style.

The most important interpretive study based on the Detroit
data is Wolfram 1969, which examines the sociolinguistic structure
of the black community by correlating eight linguistic variables
(consonant cluster simplification, morpheme medial and final /θ/,
syllable final /d/, postvocalic /r/, zero copula, invariant be, suf-
fixal -z, and multiple negation) with five social variables (social
status, racial isolation, age, sex, and style). Wolfram concludes
that all of these social factors, except racial isolation, correlate
strongly with linguistic differences: members of lower social
classes, teenagers and preadolescents, and males tend to use more
nonstandard forms while all speakers use more nonstandard forms

in more informal styles. Wolfram also points out a difference in the way that phonological and grammatical variables are stratified: "Phonological differences between social groups tend to be quantitative whereas the grammatical differences are often qualitative" (1969:217). Although Wolfram's analyses sometimes differ from those of Labov (cf. the analysis of invariant be in each), the Detroit findings generally confirm the results of Labov's work in New York.

As other surveys of urban areas (e.g., Legum et al. 1971; Mitchell-Kernan 1970) confirmed the early work of Labov and Wolfram, sociolinguists began to speak of a "Black English," a dialect transcending geography, with caste and class its significant social correlates. The most important sociolinguistic analysis of the grammar of this "Black English" is Fasold 1972, a detailed study of tense marking in the dialect, based on interviews conducted in Washington, D.C., in 1968-69. After examining the absence of the past tense suffix, the absence of the third singular present suffix, and "distributive be," Fasold indicates that no single phenomenon accounts for all three. While "the absence of -ed is due to rules of phonology which operate on the phonetic segments representing -ed almost without regard to syntactic function" (1972:218), the absence of -s is a grammatical difference between black speech and other English dialects, with some black speakers apparently having no concord rule at all. An even more divergent feature of black speech is "distributive be," or unconjugated be referring to objects or events distributed intermittently in time, a verb which is tenseless. Despite the differences between black speech and other English dialects, Fasold suggests that "Black English" does not have a radically different tense structure.

The early work of Labov, Wolfram, Fasold, and others provides much information about black speech in Northern cities, but it has little to say about how black and white speech are related in the South. However, in the late 1960s and early 1970s, seven studies in the South conducted using the sociolinguistic framework, have a direct bearing on the issue: Anshen 1969, Houston 1969, 1970, 1972, Summerlin 1972, Fetscher 1971, Dunlap 1973, Graves 1967, and Wolfram 1971, 1974. Each of these is an intensive study of one group or community of speakers that investigates the patterning of a small number of linguistic variables.

Concentrating on phonological variables, Anshen analyzes the sociolinguistic structure of the black community in Hillsborough, North Carolina. He then compares his findings to those of Levine and Crockett 1966, a study of white speakers in the same town. From significant quantitative differences in the realization of word-final /r/, /ɪn/, and /θ/, and initial /ʒ/, he concludes that "the two groups of speakers speak different varieties of English" (1969: 101).

Summerlin's research seems to confirm Anshen's contention. After looking at consonant substitution and deletion in the speech of black and white grade schoolers, high schoolers, and teachers in northern Florida and southern Georgia, Summerlin asserts that racial, as well as educational, differences in phonology are statistically significant. She also says that significant differences are not limited to nonstandard speakers; the speech of blacks and whites who use "regional standards" is also significantly different.

Houston's studies of black school children in north Florida treat many of the same phonological features analyzed by other sociolinguists, but she offers a very different explanation for idiolectal variation. Whereas Labov, Wolfram, and Fasold all treat such variation as inherent, the result of linguistic and social factors, and as a normal part of an individual's grammar, Houston attributes such variation to shifts in "register," a kind of code switching. Houston asserts that black children have a "school register" and a "non-school register," with each containing "features appropriate to the particular situation and no other" (1969: 600), and that the children's communicative abilities are superior in the latter. Finally, Houston suggests that "the difference between black and white English in the South happens to be far less than in the North . . . ; but even in the South the difference is evident, and it is of course inaccurate to state that Black English is equivalent to general Southern English" (1969:600).

Fetscher's study of thirty-six Atlanta fifth graders (divided equally between upper middle class and lower class and between white and black) finds that differences in vowels, especially front vowels, reflect social class for both races. Variation in consonants is, however, more common among blacks.

Dunlap explores agreement, contraction, and deletion of the copula and the incidence of "invariant be" for ninety-six Atlanta fifth graders (unequally divided among upper middle, lower middle, and lower class, but equally divided between black and white). He finds that the zero or deleted copula correlates most closely with social class, with middle-class whites never deleting the form and upper-middle-class blacks deleting it only once. On the other hand, lower-class blacks deleted the copula 27 percent of the time, lower-middle-class blacks 9 percent, and lower class whites 1 percent. Dunlap also points out that discussions of copula deletion are often misleading, since researchers fail to specify what counts as a full, contracted, or deleted form when postvocalic /r/ is realized as [ə]. Unlike copula deletion, invariant be is used by only his black informants, and Dunlap suggests that it might be "the one grammatical marker which distinguishes the speech of blacks from that of whites" (1977:77-78); among blacks, it is sharply graded by social class. Perhaps Dunlap's most provocative finding is that the use of invariant be by his Atlanta informants differs from that described by Wolfram and Fasold; he finds that be is used for constant states, momentary occurrences, and even past occurrences, as well as for events distributed in time.

Graves interviewed and took short writing samples from eighty eighth graders in east-central Alabama (equally divided between upper and lower class and between black and white) to study selected grammatical features. He finds some features (third person singular don't and the double negative) characteristic of lower-class informants of both races, one feature (ain't) characteristic of lower-class white informants, and several features (invariant be, zero copula, and absence of the third singular present -s, plural -s, and past -ed) characteristic of lower-class blacks. He also finds, however, that certain features, including absence of the plural -s, possessive -s, past tense -ed, and hypercorrect plural -s and possessive -s, are far more common in writing than in speech. His study thus reveals a new dimension to the variation in these forms. Whiteman 1976 pursues oral-written dimensions further and is able to account for many black-white differences in writing in developmental terms.

The most important sociolinguistic work on the South in this third stage, however, is that of Wolfram 1971, 1974, who tries to resolve the disagreement between linguistic geographers and creolists over how black and white speech are related. Based on fieldwork in Holmes and Franklin counties, Mississippi, and making use of analytical techniques developed in Northern urban surveys, these two studies systematically compare the speech of black and white school children of similar socioeconomic backgrounds, concentrating on diagnostic variables isolated in earlier work. In his study of Holmes County school children, Wolfram 1971 notes that linguistic geographers were right to claim that many processes in black speech are present also in white speech, but he suggests that they often operate differently and apply with significantly different frequency. For example, he finds that while the third person singular marker is absent in both black and white speech, it is absent 85 percent of the time for blacks but only 13 percent of the time for whites. As a result, Wolfram says that

> in the case of White children, the alternation [between absence and presence of the third singular marker] is obviously an integral part of the system (i.e., we have inherent variability). But in the case of the Black informants, we may rightly ask if -z third person can be considered an integral part of the system. That is, this form is not an integral part of the system, and its infrequent occurrence may be attributed to "dialect importation," a language contact phenomena in which a non-indigenous form is borrowed from another dialect without its syntactic incorporation into the target dialect [1971:145].

Wolfram cites frequent hypercorrection as additional support for his hypothesis. However, he concludes in general that the speech of his white and black informants differs superficially, not in "deep structure," as Dillard and Loflin would claim. Consonant cluster deletion and deletion of possessive -z distinguish Wolfram's speakers on the basis of race, but copula deletion and "distributive be" are different matters. In his study of Franklin County school children, Wolfram concludes "that there are some Southern white dialects in which copula deletion does operate qualitatively much as in VBE [Vernacular Black English]. From this point, there is a continuum of Southern white varieties which progressively diverge" (1974:516). On the other hand, he concludes that "'distributive be' is typically NOT [emphasis Wolfram's] found in Southern white speech, though it is an integral aspect of all VBE varieties studied" (1974:524).

After making these synchronic generalizations about two aspects of copula use in black and white speech, Wolfram speculates about how this use came about. He suggests that both copula deletion and "distributive be" may have arisen in black speech through a process of decreolization. However, while copula deletion was assimilated by whites from a late stage of decreolizing black speech, when assimilation would not require serious syntactic modification, "distributive be" was not assimilated because it would have required significant modification in the grammar.

Much of the important sociolinguistic research on how black and white speech in the South are related is summarized in Fasold 1981--an attempt, based primarily on Fasold 1972 and Wolfram 1971, 1974, to synthesize previous research and come to some reasonable conclusions. While sociolinguists have often differed in their analyses, Fasold's "moderate" conclusions on both the synchronic and diachronic issues are fairly typical and nicely illustrate the sociolinguists' position in relation to that of both the linguistic geographers and the creolists:

> To the question of whether or not there exist significant differences between black and white languages in the South, I would answer, "Yes, to some degree, for some features." When the relevant data are investigated sufficiently carefully, it appears that some aspects of some variables show significant differences in the speech of blacks from what is to be found in the speech of whites. These differences are of sufficient theoretical interest that they should not be ignored, but they by no means indicate widespread deep differences in grammar and phonology.
>
> As far as history goes, the conclusion I have come to is that the creole hypothesis seems most likely to be correct, but it is certainly not so well established as Dillard (1972), for example, would have us believe. Decreolization, however, seems to have progressed so far as to have obliterated most of the original creole features [1981:164].

The sociolinguists, then, generally stand between the linguistic geographers and the creolists in their views on both synchronic and diachronic issues. Their studies have not answered definitively questions about how black and white speech are related in the South, but their real importance lies in their contributions to methodology and to our knowledge about the structure of black speech. As yet they simply have not done enough work in the South, especially with Southern white speech, which is virtually undescribed. Comparisons of black speech to "Standard English," a variety neither defined nor described, and to middle-class Northern white speech merely obscure, rather than clarify, black-white speech relations. Wolfram's work is an excellent beginning, but his research is limited to two Mississippi counties; it is impossible to know how general or typical his findings are.

The most serious problem with sociolinguistic research in the South, however, involves the populations which have been sampled. Almost without exception, sociolinguistic researchers in the South have concentrated on the speech of children, occasionally comparing it to the speech of middle-class adults. Researchers have restricted their samples in such a way for good reason--to provide information for educators, to overcome possible effects of age grading, and to obtain speech untainted by sociolinguistic aware-ness--but their findings about black and white speech are never-theless limited. These investigations ignore that variety, white folk speech, most likely to be similar to black speech (cf. Bailey and Bassett, this volume). Moreover, since the children recorded in these studies are classified by the socioeconomic status of their parents, the failure to interview their parents brings into question the validity of comparing the children's speech.

To make generalizations about and to speculate on diachronic relations between black and white speech based on the speech of children is to assume that these speech varieties have always had fairly stable relationships and have responded to linguistic changes in the same way, as well as to ignore possible generational dif-ferences. Recent work by Labov 1980b suggests that, in Philadel-phia, blacks are not undergoing incipient sound changes which affect white speech. This kind of information is crucial to under-standing the development of black and white speech in the South, but we cannot obtain it without research on older as well as younger speakers.

Over the past decade, a fourth stage has developed in the study of language relationships in the South. Research in this stage is plentiful and eclectic and explores new aspects of the problem, analyzing old data in new ways, discovering new data sources, and using more varied approaches. It is the result of scholars in the South often combining, but working outside, the frameworks established in the first three stages and addressing unresolved questions from those stages. These scholars have also begun to acknowledge the influence of field methods, field instruments, analytical models, speech situations, and types of data (oral/written, free conversation/one-word response, etc.) on a study's findings and to qualify their findings in these terms. While much of the research in the fourth stage either directly or by implication addresses diachronic questions, like that in the first two stages, an increasing amount explores strictly synchronic questions, often in a broader way than sociolinguistic studies in the third stage, by using new sociolinguistic and ethnographic models. The new synchronic studies should prove especially useful in sorting out the educational implications of language differences.

As a consequence of this new research, the relationship between black and white English in the South seems much less simple than it once did. It clearly includes an entire range of questions involving demography, social dynamics, community relations, and educational experience. While the new research adds greatly to what we know, it vividly shows what we do not know, and it challenges many earlier assumptions and conclusions.

Many of the representative researchers in this fourth stage have conducted intensive studies in Southern communities for their dissertations, some in white communities, some in black communities, and some in both. O'Cain 1972 and M. Miller 1978, for example, are intensive studies of black and white informants in Charleston, South Carolina, and Augusta, Georgia, respectively.

While using linguistic atlas collection techniques, such investigators examine large, stratified samples and focus on a handful of crucial variables in concluding that education, age, and social class influence linguistic choices as much as race does. Hopkins 1975 investigates for Savannah the same phonological features O'Cain does in Charleston, but concentrates on the white middle-class population. He finds that Savannahans share many speechways with Charleston, but that some prestigious variants in Charleston are stigmatized in Savannah because they are associated with Irish and Jewish speakers there. Feagin 1979, on the other hand, uses a variety of field techniques and analytical tools, to explore the verb usage of white upper- and lower-class speakers in Anniston, Alabama, and to describe the range of patterns within that one community. Schrock 1980 and Nix 1980, sociolinguistic studies of stylistic variation of black speakers in Pope County, Arkansas, and Wilmington, North Carolina, respectively, are aimed at replicating the Northern urban studies of Labov, Fasold, and Wolfram. Both find substantially less use of nonstandard forms than have been found in the North.

At the same time, three large-scale projects, LAMSAS, LAGS, and DARE, have begun or will soon begin publication. In addition, the basic materials of another project, the Linguistic Atlas of the North Central States (LANCS), were published several years ago (R. McDavid et al. 1976-1979) and include data from one Southern state, Kentucky. For an analysis of some of the Kentucky data, see McDavid and McDavid's essay in this volume. Two fascicles of

LAMSAS (McDavid, O'Cain, and Dorrill 1980-   ) have appeared; a third and a fourth had been edited by the summer of 1981. Protocols (equivalent to the field notebooks of the other linguistic atlas projects) of LAGS (Pederson et al. 1981), which include data from over 1,100 interviews conducted in eight states between 1968 and 1983, have recently been published by University Microfilms. These LAGS records constitute the largest collection of data on Southern speech, a massive data bank for investigating generational as well as racial speech relationships.

The data from LAGS are complemented by the data from its pilot study, the Dialect Survey of Rural Georgia (DSRG). Developed explicitly as an exercise in biracial dialectology, the Georgia Survey pairs black and white native Georgians of comparable cultivation and social and educational background in a network of rural communities (with populations under 2,500) in grid squares across the state.

Pederson, Rueter, and Hall 1974, Pederson 1975, and Pederson, Dunlap, and Rueter 1975 describe the methods of the survey. With taped field records from over 300 informants, half of them black, in seventy-eight communities, DSRG provides a substantial body of data on comparable black and white speakers in several subregional contexts. Results of the survey have been reported in Pederson 1969, 1972, 1973, Rueter 1975, Hall 1976, and Rueter 1977. Perhaps the most significant findings involve the complex regional and social relationships between black and white speech. Pederson (1969:281) states that

> when the distinction between social castes (black and white) is recognized as a constant factor in the linguistic geography of north Georgia, dialect boundaries must be multiple because black speech and white speech have distinctly different patterns of regional distribution. Black folk speech extends the Upcountry Lower Southern dialect northward into the mountains where South Midland forms prevail among whites, and white folk speech extends the South Midland dialect into the plantation area where Upcountry Lower Southern forms prevail among all black and educated white speakers.

Pederson further notes that, while black speech differs from white speech in all of the north Georgia communities (1969:281),

> no variety of black speech can be characterized . . . as either uniform or exclusive in terms of its segmental units. The uniqueness of black folk speech seems to rest in the pivotal position it occupies in the rural community, sharing phonological features with cultivated blacks and whites, grammatical features with white folk speakers, and lexical forms with all members of both castes.

According to recent word from Frederic Cassidy, its editor, DARE will begin to appear in the summer of 1985. Joan Hall's paper in this volume indicates what DARE can show about lexical variation in the South, including the kinds of qualifications necessary in determining which terms are used only by blacks.

Until recently, the study of black speech in the South, except for the LAMSAS survey (which had forty black informants from Maryland to Georgia) and Williamson 1961 (a study in Memphis), has been limited primarily to basilectal forms, especially those on the offshore islands of South Carolina and Georgia (especially in the work of Turner). The speech of these islands, called Gullah or Geechee, has been considered an isolate. However, recent work by Rickford 1974, 1977 (and his essay in this volume), Cunningham 1970, Jones-Jackson 1978a, and Nichols 1976 (and her essay in this volume), of the less extreme forms in that region; by Vaughn-Cooke 1976, W. Sanders 1978, Schrock 1980, and Nix 1980 of black speech elsewhere in the South; and by the Linguistic Atlas of the Gulf States (over 200 of whose interviews are with black informants) has begun to provide the more extensive data needed for comparing black speech in different parts of the South. Work has barely begun, however, in determining whether Gullah is a locally creolized variety, a product of the isolation and other demographic factors peculiar to that area, or whether it represents an extreme form of creolized English different only in degree from varieties of black speech farther inland. Certainly the pronominal system in Gullah, with ee for the nominative and um for the objective (see Jones-Jackson in this volume), is different from any other thus far examined on the North American mainland.

Recent interest in other possible creole language communities in the South may also indicate whether Gullah and inland varieties are related. Hancock's work (1980a, this volume) on Afro-Seminole Creole in southwest Texas, apparently carried there by runaway Georgia slaves among the Seminoles, and Gilbert's study in this volume of a triracial isolate of mixed white, black, and Amerindian (Piscataway) ancestry in southern Maryland, which seems to use a remnant of a creole, suggest that creoles may retain features that reveal such influence. Other isolated groups, throughout the South, are as yet unexplored (cf. W. Gilbert 1946 and Beale 1956).

Also, research on subregional variation in black speech will have much to say about how language differences in the South arose and developed. Diachronic questions have preoccupied both the creolists and, to a lesser extent, the linguistic geographers (one of whose ultimate aims has been to connect New World linguistic patterns to those of the British Isles). But rather than rely heavily on external, anecdotal sources, as the creolists did in the 1960s, more recent investigators, like Rickford, Vaughn-Cooke, and Nichols, have explored internal evidence (i.e., variation within the language and between subgroups in specific speech communities) to reveal patterns of change in progress. These studies make it clear that tracing historical changes in the English of the South presupposes good sociolinguistic analyses of speech communities.

In addition to field research, two other sources of data have recently begun to answer diachronic questions about Southern English. One is early collections of letters, diaries, and other records of nineteenth-century white overseers, many of whom were only marginally literate and whose writing, therefore, often reflects their speech. Eliason 1956 discusses features from these records in a broad survey, but Hawkins 1978 and 1982 analyzes in detail four features of the language of these overseers, whose nonstandard speech may well be one of the "missing links" in the reconstruction of Southern English. In addition to studying the presence and absence of determiners, personal subject pronouns, and word-final syllables, Hawkins compares the use of the copula verb be to the Northern urban studies of black speakers by Labov, Fasold, and Wolfram; she finds similarities in how surrounding elements constrain copula absence but also finds that is and are are absent to the same extent, unlike the Northern urban studies.

Another source of data is the transcribed narratives of exslaves, collected in the 1930s by the Works Progress Administration, on which two scholars have based major studies (Brewer 1974 and Schneider 1981, 1982). Of considerable interest because they record speech of informants born in the mid-nineteenth century, these narratives also show how earlier linguistic patterns can shed light on those not made clear by contemporary sociolinguistic analysis. For example, Brewer's paper in this volume shows that an apparently synchronic, and in this case idiolectal feature (hypercorrect use of third person singular -s), was in fact a semantic feature for the ex-slaves, a marker of verbs of duration. After examining morphological and syntactic features in 104 interviews with ex-slaves from nine Southern states, Schneider concludes the following about mid-nineteenth-century black speech:

> It has to be concluded that the linguistic character of [early black English] is largely determined by its descent from the nonstandard English spoken in the colonial period, which can be established clearly for most of its linguistic forms and structures independently. There are no indications that a supra-regional uniform "Plantation Creole" throughout the American South has ever existed, and no clear signs of ongoing creolization. On the contrary, an even closer analysis of the material . . . reveals the existence of unmistakable patterns of regional distribution amongst a number of the linguistic items taken into account, and also discloses some influence by social factors [Schneider 1982:38]

Beyond these continuing diachronic studies of how English has developed in the South and the evidence that investigations of diachronic and synchronic questions can complement each other, the most productive recent research on linguistic variation in the South has been strictly synchronic studies. Many of them result from an increasing interest in different methodological approaches and from the availability of new analytical tools and new ways of assessing linguistic communities. Among these approaches are the quantitative study of speech variation by Feagin 1979 and Nichols 1976, who use implicational scale analysis, and Nix 1980, Butters and Nix in this volume, and Rickford in this volume, who use variable rule analysis. The use of other tools, such as acceptability questionnaires (Butters 1973 and Coleman 1975) and syntactic argumentation (Boertien 1979, Boertien and Said 1980, and Boertien in this volume), to determine the rules for negation and interrogation with multiple modal constructions provides evidence on language that cannot be gathered through conventional field methods.

Other, more recent investigations use models of speech communities different from the socioeconomic status models of urban sociolinguistic projects in the 1960s and early 1970s. Feagin's paper in this volume applies the network model of sociological analysis, which studies language variation in terms of the relationships of speakers to one another, a model developed by Milroy 1980. Feagin applies the network model to her data from white informants in Anniston, Alabama, to show the interplay of two speech norms, a prestige norm and a nonstandard norm, for people of all ages and social status in Anniston.

Other researchers use a broader, ethnographic approach to speech communities that emphasizes linguistic function rather than linguistic forms per se. These ethnographic studies are based on how speakers relate to one another within a speech community, rather than on the more "objective" socioeconomic measures used in some earlier studies. Two such efforts are Davis' report in this volume, a study of Charlotte teenagers, and Heath's 1983 ten-year study of how children in two South Carolina Piedmont communities, one black community and one white community, develop communication skills and language attitudes and how they adjust to teachers and school situations. To arrive at a broader social understanding of language diversity, such studies take into consideration which speakers talk to whom, about what, and under what circumstances.

As the result of a fruitful decade of fieldwork and research, we have much more information on language variation in the Southern United States. The polemics about differences between black and white speech, the most frequently addressed and the most crucial aspect of this variation, had largely subsided by the end of the 1970s. The increased interest in methodology as a key in detailing patterns of language variation complemented a renewed interest in conducting fieldwork and a blending of ideas from linguistic geography, sociolinguistics, and creole studies. It thus seemed an advantageous time to bring together significant research projects undertaken over the previous several years to establish the "state of the field" of research in the study of Southern English, to have researchers and scholars share ideas, and to stimulate further research. Therefore, with the cosponsorship of the National Endowment for the Humanities and the University of South Carolina, a three-day conference in October 1981 brought together twenty-five presentations of original, data-based, and in most cases primary, research. Twenty-one of the papers in this volume, all but those of Sommer and Dorrill, are revised versions of papers presented at that conference.

What does all of this research have to say about the general question of how black and white speech in the South are related? A great deal. The evidence presented at the conference, and in this volume, clearly indicates that the question of black-white differences can no longer be phrased in any simple way, because linguistic variation in the South seems no more dependent on race than on other social factors: the age, sex, and educational background of the speaker. This point has certainly been suggested elsewhere, but the many studies in this volume, especially those of Miller and of Bailey and Bassett, demonstrate it conclusively.

In examining plurals of nouns ending in -sp, -st, and -sk for Augusta, Georgia, blacks and whites, Miller finds that speakers of both races typically use (and probably always have used) unmarked plural forms. The secondary pattern for whites is triple cluster plurals (-sps, -sts, and -sks; Miller calls them "book forms"), while for blacks it is disyllabic plurals (e.g., waspes, testes). Miller shows that this difference in secondary patterning is closely related to the availability of schooling in the area over the past two generations.

Bailey and Bassett limit their study to one well-analyzed (cf. Fasold 1972, Dunlap 1974) feature, invariant be. They show that in eastern Louisiana and lower Mississippi it is, as investigators elsewhere have contended, significantly more common in black speech than in white speech, but they go on to show that to see invariant be only as a racially diagnostic feature would be seriously misleading. In both black and white speech, the use of invariant be is restricted in the same way: it is much rarer in the speech of the educated than of the uneducated, it is more common in speakers over sixty-five years old, and it is used less often by women than by men. In addition, the form has very similar functions and meaning for both blacks and whites.

Clearly then, taxonomies of features such as those by Fasold and Wolfram 1970 and Fasold 1981 of black speech are no longer realistic. On the one hand, they obscure and overlook much of the rich variation among both blacks and whites in the South. On the other hand, they overstate differences at the expense of important generalizations about similarities. As new research reveals that variation in Southern speech communities is more complex than supposed, researchers who seek to interpret that variation in a pedagogically useful way face an even greater challenge.

None of the evidence in this volume suggests that in the South the speech of blacks is identical to that of whites; wherever distinctive social communities exist, distinctions in speech will also occur. Looking closely at black-white speech relationships, as the papers in this volume do, is a kind of heuristic. It is a way of beginning to explore variation in Southern English, to understand the many other important ways in which Southern English varies, from one region of the South to the other, from one social group to another, and from one generation to another. All of these go to make up language variety in the South.

NOTES

[1] On July 13, 1979, U.S. District Court Judge Charles W. Joiner ruled that the Ann Arbor (Michigan) School District Board had denied access to equal educational opportunity for seven black elementary school children. For the text of the court decision and the school district's plan to comply with the decision, see Joiner 1979. For reactions to the decision, primarily by sociolinguists, see Whiteman 1980. For background reports, position papers, and task force reports at the February 21-23, 1980, symposium on the Ann Arbor decision at Wayne State University in Detroit, see Smitherman 1981.

[2] Fasold 1981, a paper originally read at the spring 1980 Southeastern Conference on Linguistics meeting in Memphis, Tennessee, is one recent attempt to synthesize several studies of black and white speakers in the South (primarily Wolfram 1974 and Fasold 1972) in order to address the question of black-white speech relationships. Fasold's primary purpose was the updating of the Fasold and Wolfram 1970 discussion of linguistic features that are more typical of black speakers. He reduces the list of features to seven (for a rejoinder, see Sledd 1980). Fasold's conclusion on black-white speech relations in the South takes a qualified middle ground (see above, pp. 20-21).

[3] In remarks responding to Fasold 1981 at the spring 1980 Southeastern Conference on Linguistics meeting in Memphis, McMillan called for more sensitive descriptions of speaker interaction in the South and for more extensive study of intonation patterns of Southerners.

[4] For a discussion of the background of the Linguistic Atlas project, see Kurath 1939 and Atwood 1963.

[5] Some scholars suggest that a more recent process of creolization has caused black speech to diverge. Dillard (1972:109) attributes this divergence to the increased isolation of blacks from whites after the Civil War. McDavid (1979:298) proposes that "neo-creolization" may have occurred in recent years in Northern inner cities, where blacks have little contact with white speakers.

[6] The debate over the genesis of this English pidgin is best found in Cassidy 1980a, who argues for a Caribbean origin, and Hancock 1980b, who argues for a West African origin.

Some Similarities between Gullah and Caribbean Creoles

Frederic G. Cassidy

The creole languages of the Caribbean area may seem rather marginal to the subject of language variation in the South. Yet the Gullah speech of the Charleston, South Carolina area, and especially the offshore Rice Islands, which is unquestionably creole, has more in common with the folk language of the Anglophone Caribbean than with any other kind of United States speech. Gullah, surviving on the North American mainland, is an anomaly which requires explanation. Its relationships with the basilects of the Bahamas, Jamaica, Belize, the Virgin and other Leeward islands, Trinidad, Barbados, Guyana, Surinam, and minor coastal settlements--even some creole languages of West Africa--cannot be left out of account if we are to understand the history and the extent of the black diaspora to the New World.

Gullah has another aspect that cannot be ignored: It is mainly because of the survival of Gullah that the theory, principally espoused by Stewart and Dillard, that all American black English passed through a creole stage, can be defended--insofar as it can be. Gullah is undeniably a basilect, even if other forms of American black speech are mesolectal or acrolectal, the latter two in those respects in which they coincide with American white speech. Gullah furnishes a fairly full repertory of features for comparison with other kinds of American black speech, showing where each type stands in a pattern of comparisons and where the types overlap.

The term "black English" has been used too often as if it names something monolithic or unitary or homogeneous. Especially in the 1960s, with the Black Power movement in full swing and a number of white academics with genuine sympathy for the cause, but little scholarly knowledge of the black scene, breaking into print, some silly assertions were made and hotly argued on the basis of the way one or two teenage informants in Washington or New York (or some other large city) spoke. Since then, better knowledge, real fieldwork (though by no means enough), and scholarly sifting have got rid of the least defensible claims. We all know now that black English is no more homogeneous than white English--if anything, less so--and that what is needed at this point is less speculation and more collection and analysis of data. Many theories have been proposed; now they need to be tested. This testing is going forward in some quarters, and enough has been done so that the field is now recognized as one in which scholarship can be respectable.

What is known about the history of Gullah? The geographical center is the area of Charleston, South Carolina, whence it has spread to some extent inland. But it is preserved especially as the folk speech of the Rice Islands, a group that stretches along the Atlantic Seaboard some 160 miles and includes some islands of adjoining Georgia. The climate and agricultural conditions lent themselves to rice growing, an important element in the antebellum plantation culture. The source of the name Gullah has been debated; even Turner, the first linguistically trained investigator, declined to choose between the two African possibilities: a Liberian people named Gola and the Congo people who gave their name to Angola. Other scholars since, so far as I know, have not made a firm choice. It seems, however, that despite the closeness of the forms linguistically, the Gola people were too obscure to have imposed their name upon their fellow slaves in America or upon the plantation owners and slave traders, whereas the Congo slaves, exported first by the Portuguese and later by the Dutch from the area of present-day Angola, outnumbered all others, as analysis of the possible sources of Turner 1949's list of surviving Africanisms will show (Cassidy 1980a:4-5). Aphetism is a very common characteristic of all forms of black English; so for Gullah to have come from Angola is more plausible, and I choose this origin.

The first planters of the Charleston area (1670) came from Barbados, bringing their slaves with them. These slaves, and others during the early years, are likely to have been from the Gold Coast (now Ghana) and Nigeria, but there was constant "recruitment" thereafter from widespread sources, all the way from Senegal down to Angola--virtually the entire West African coast--as well as the hinterland, into which the slave trade reached for increased supplies. Hancock has stated that Barbados was less a source of supply for other plantation areas, including the Carolina plantations, than a depot and distribution point, and he questions the full establishment of creole speech in Barbados that might have been passed on, with the slaves, to Jamaica, Surinam, Carolina, and other sugar colonies (Hancock 1980b). This would make Barbados an exception in the entire colonial picture--and I have expressed my doubts of that (Cassidy 1980a). Moreover, new evidence is coming to light on this point. In any case, however, the question cannot be settled here. Wherever it came from, and however it became established, it is certain that a form of Creole English, later called Gullah, was established well before the end of the seventeenth century around Charleston and that it is closely related to other Caribbean Creoles of today. From Charleston it spread inland, and later out to the islands, when rice growing began there. (It was at this later period, presumably, that blacks from the Guinea Coast, experienced in rice growing, were much sought after.)

The inland blacks came into frequent contact with whites of many kinds, but blacks on the islands were isolated from the general white community. It should also be mentioned that runaway slaves (like the Maroons of Jamaica, Surinam, and Guyana) joined forces with the Indians and ultimately went west with them. A remnant of such a group, of mixed Seminole and black origin, speaking a type of Gullah, still survives around Brackettville, Texas (Hancock 1980a). I contend that Gullah had the same origins as the Anglophone Caribbean Creoles, with a strong, early input from the Gold Coast, even if later that was overlaid with influences from the Guinea Coast. Gullah certainly preserves elements of both. In my opinion, Turner's book on Gullah is still the best around, if accurately used, but it has been treated hastily and offhandedly by some.

Now we will sketch, in the most general way, the features of nonnative languages which characterize pidgins and creoles created in connection with European languages, Portuguese, French, Dutch, Spanish, and of special interest to us, English. There are almost no records--the merest scraps only--of any English pidgin language in the Caribbean. What can be said of it must be worked out by inference from the presumably descended Creole languages. The best assumption still seems to be that a contact language, or pidgin, was developed initially between West Africans and the Portuguese, who got to Africa first more than a century ahead of other Europeans, and were trading there before America was discovered.

The other Europeans who followed them remade the Portuguese pidgin, or made similar ones of their own. Slavery, it must be remembered, was not imported to Africa by whites. It was an age-old institution of most peoples in Asia, the Near East, and Africa; and it was fully established in the Mediterranean and Northern Europe before the Christian era. Indeed, the modern objection to chattel slavery, and the attempt to dispose of it, is a European and Christian idea, a "Western" idea, now accepted nominally by the United Nations, though not universally put into practice even yet. Europeans did not invent the slave trade or bring it to Africa. They did put it on a fully organized, lucrative basis, as one of the sources of wealth that the New World made possible. It should also be noted that it was Europeans, revolted by the effects of the slave trade, who finally put an end to it.

The pidgin language was adequate as an interlingua for trade purposes. But when Europeans made settlements along the West African coast and Portuguese traders took African wives, the new generations, who fitted neither parental culture and learned neither parental language well, worked out a language of their own: a creole language. Presumably this was the natural, easy result or outcome. Adequate models of the parental languages were lacking and, especially, there was little community pressure to conform. Portuguese, of course, remained the official language of government, but once the Afro-Portuguese Creole became established, it would be learned by everybody, even though, as the word creole indicates, it was spoken mostly by servants and the common people. There was ample time for the Portuguese to develop such a lower-class, everyday, easygoing idiom before the rest of the Europeans came along and to spread it wherever the Portuguese sailed and formed colonies--India, Polynesia, China. Thus when the French, the English, and the Dutch followed this lead, they either availed themselves of the already established Portuguese Creole or imitated it, using features of French, English, Dutch, and so on. Exactly how this was accomplished is a matter of controversy.

It used to be thought that the creole languages were formed after the uprooted slaves had been brought to the New World. Present opinion favors, instead, the belief that they began in Africa and that enough slaves had picked up enough creole speech before they left Africa, or did so on the voyage, that simple communication was possible. Whichever way it happened, the fact of widespread similarities has to be explained. The old description of a creole language as a European lexicon hung onto an African syntactic framework is well supported by Alleyne's Comparative Afro-American (1980). It is the best thing there is so far, showing the deep likenesses of structure underlying the surface differences of the creoles.

Only a few features from a passage of Gullah, recorded by Turner about 1940 on Edisto Island, will be mentioned here: an old woman is recalling the earthquake of 1886 and the fear it caused in the people (Turner 1949:268). Creole features include the use of African [də], an auxiliary of continuing action [wi#də#gwʊɪn], "we are going." In [ʋɪ no də ʋgəs], "I know it was August," [də] takes the place of the verb. In either case, it is certainly of African origin (perhaps from Twi or Ewe), and it is also found in Jamaican, Guyanese, and Belizean Creoles.

In the seventeenth century, when, as is well known, the English pronoun thou was replaced by you in the singular, a contrast with plural you was lost. Since that time, many attempts have been made by speakers of English to repair this deficiency. Some make a plural of you: yous(e); some add a plural marker, you-uns, you-lot; and in the American South one hears you-all, or y'all, the only highly successful substitute. The creole response to this need was to adopt a plural pronoun from Ibo or a related African language. In Gullah it is [una], in Jamaican /unu/, and similar forms are found in the Bahamas, Belize, Nicaragua, Tobago, and else-where. The Gullah example from Turner's recording is [unə stan stɪl], "you stand still."

Creole verbs and pronouns regularly do without European morphology. Verbs are not inflected; they have only one form. Specifically, Gullah [mɛk] and [tɛk] continue the pronunciation they had in earlier Pidgin English, a pronunciation still current in Sierra Leone Krio, Cameroons Pidgin, and Surinam Creole. It was originally a pronunciation from the North and West of England. In the process of decreolization, the first inflectional suffix to be adopted has generally been -ing. Thus /mɪ da go/, "I am going," becomes in Gullah [ʊɪ də gwʊɪn] and, when the African auxiliary is replaced, I am going. This changeover is evident in the Caribbean Creoles and in Gullah.

Back to the earthquake. The word hear comes through as yeri [yu yɛrɪ dɪ pipl holərɪn], "you hear the people hollering." This word, interestingly, combines English with African features. The y- is another North and West Country English dialect feature (also preserved in Appalachian yearth, "earth," and yearly, "early"). In Gullah yeri, "hear," the -i is added to suit African phonotactic patterns, in which words cannot end in a consonant (except /n/). So yeri exemplifies the creole blend. It was formerly widespread in Jamaica, Belize, and Surinam, but is now archaic. A variant form in Gullah is yeddy.

Other Africanisms besides [unə] and [də] that turn up in the account of the earthquake are the words [bʌkrə], "white person," and [sa], "quickly." Buckra is from Ibo and Efik mbakara, literally, "he who surrounds or governs," but in plain English "master." The Jamaican form, backra, is closer to the African than Gullah buckra. This word was borrowed into English in the seventeenth century and is found throughout the Caribbean. Sa, on the contrary, from the Vai language, must have been borrowed much later, when slaves from the region of Liberia and Sierra Leone were sought because they were experienced at growing rice--and were therefore brought to the Rice Islands. Sa is not used in Jamaican Creole nor in Sierra Leone Krio. It was not spread through the Caribbean. This also implies its recency: the widespread Africanisms are generally those that were adopted early.

When Gullah is placed alongside its similarly structured Caribbean Creoles, then, there are three questions: How and under what circumstances was it formed? Why was it preserved? Why is it breaking down?

It is known that the Charleston colony began as the Caribbean ones had done; it was, so to speak, a colony of colonies. The first planters were resettled Barbadians, and some of their slaves already knew some form of English. Some were certainly creoles--that is to say, born in the New World, not in Africa. There is plenty of evidence that the creole blacks considered themselves vastly superior to those newly brought from Africa (in Jamaica they called them "salt-water Negroes" and were rather afraid of their "wildness"). The creoles made no real attempt to learn the African languages; under the conditions of slavery, it would have been futile. Some new loans were nevertheless introduced, or former ones reinforced. The English language of the planters was the accepted model, even though, under plantation conditions, field slaves had little opportunity to use the model: the overseers, bookkeepers, and lower-level whites under whom they worked were often speakers of regional dialects of English. The slaves' real language was, and had to be, creole, at least to begin with, and it underwent the usual developments of any language, adapting itself to and growing with the needs of the community it served.

Domestic slaves were considered a cut above field slaves. They had the best opportunity of any to learn upper-class language, and it is safe to say that decreolization must have begun with them. Nevertheless, on the whole, the creole language became established as part of the plantation system, and in places like Jamaica has outlasted the end of slavery by well over a century. As long as the plantation system lasted in the American Deep South, the social and linguistic differences continued with little change. In Virginia and Maryland, as has been shown, and on a much smaller scale in the Northern states (New Jersey, New York, New England), slaves were never as separate from the work and general life of their owners as in the South. Plantations or households were much smaller, and the numerical proportion of blacks to whites was never as high. Whether or not a creole language had been originally introduced, it could hardly have become established. The remnants of Creole that are found today in non-Gullah black speech could have come about in more than one way.

For the Gullah, the conditions of life were different, and here is my second question: Why was their language preserved? The answer is that on the Rice Islands and in similar mainland areas, where a limited, routinized agricultural life was the only one, the language too became stabilized, isolated from outside differences and pressures. Descriptions exist of the rarity of whites on some of the islands--of children being frightened the first time they saw a white man, his <u>buckra</u> reputation no doubt having preceded him. Under such conditions of isolation, there was little reason for the language to change. Any considerable language change takes generations to accomplish. Non-Gullah blacks have been gradually adapting their speech to surrounding and prevailing white speech; the Gullah continued in the traditional way into this century.

Decreolization had begun before the 1940s. Turner's recordings show that creole was much better preserved on some islands than on others, and in the speech of older people. Nothing is surprising in that, but it is the fact. It <u>would</u> be surprising if <u>no</u> elements or features of Gullah had been adopted outside the Gullah area. There is not time to go into that here, but I will give one example. Among upper laboring and lower middle-class white speakers in Memphis, Tennessee in the 1920s, and still to some extent today, the creole use of dem (from them), postposed to a name, designates a group (according to George W. Thompson, a Memphis native and a contributor to the DARE file for the period 1920-35). Thus, in Ambrose Gonzales' 1922 example from Gullah, Sancho dem means "Sancho and his companions." This is regularly used in Jamaican, in other Caribbean creoles, and in Sierra Leone Krio. It is probably not limited to Memphis. There is no proof that it got into white speech from Gullah, but that is the most likely possibility. Needless to say, whites who say it are quite unaware of it as possibly a black loan.

The third question is: Why is Gullah breaking down, being decreolized? Probably the chief reason is that the formerly tight agricultural communities, where cultivators had to accomplish their daily "tasks" of hoeing the crops (a "task" was a term of measurement: the amount of land that could be worked in a certain span of time) and where this kind of hand labor is used, are rapidly changing. The old isolation is gone. Bridges are being built to some of the islands (e.g., James Island). Better transportation is making the mainland more accessible; schools are being improved; white promoters are moving in; and radio and television are also introducing the outside world. Gullah's other function as an idiom which blacks could use among themselves--an in-group speech--has become less necessary, and conformity to the "outside" speech has obvious economic advantages. Gullah is apparently on the way to being an "old-timey" thing, which new generations may have no more than sentimental reasons to preserve.

The Caribbean islands, where Creole speech still flourishes, have been gaining independence and setting themselves up as new nations: mini-nations, one might say, hardly able to sustain themselves economically. For them, the preservation of creole is a mark of separate nationhood, although, ironically, fifty years ago it was roundly condemned as "bad English," and the schools fought it furiously. Now it is tolerated at the lower levels, though the schools still aim at an "educated" form of English, with local coloration, that can be used without disadvantage in the outside world. Even so, decreolization continues, slowly but surely. It is difficult to find speakers of the basilects. In the Caribbean, the sense of new nationhood may slow decreolization, but there is no possibility of that for Gullah.

In conclusion, let it be said that American English, both white and black, has historical connections of many kinds which cannot be ignored. In the seventeenth century a "colonial layer" of English included the entire English-speaking Atlantic world, of which the Caribbean was a part. Settlers moved back and forth, south and north, looking for the "main chance." At the time of the Revolution, Loyalists moved from New England to Canada, from Charleston to the Bahamas, and to other places where plantation life could be continued under the British flag. Nobody will question the value of studying Gullah in connection with the Caribbean Creoles, but I see good reason for widening our sights further. We will not understand American English fully until we take all its varieties into account. Gullah is an extreme variety, but it is a part of the whole, and should not be left aside.

Some Principles for the Study of Black and White Speech in the South

John R. Rickford

This paper is organized in the following way. I will share a few personal reminiscences about my first fieldwork experiences in South Carolina. Then I will present four principles which need to be followed whenever two or more language varieties are compared, but particularly in the case of black and white speech in the South, because these principles seem to be frequently neglected in this area. Then I will apply these principles to plural formation in Sea Island Creole, demonstrating that their application results in a different and richer view than would otherwise be obtained.

My reminiscences are from the first time I arrived in Savannah, Georgia, after a long bus ride from California, and then went over to Hilton Head Island, South Carolina. I will never forget how amazed I was to step on a fishing boat belonging to the Hilton Head Fishing Co-op and hear Americans who sounded strikingly like Guyanese. I had read about Gullah, or Sea Island Creole, in the works of Turner and other people, but it was quite a different experience to <u>hear</u> the speech, to hear people who sounded so strikingly like "back home." The variety I was hearing was not basilectal Gullah, but it was like music to my ears.

I have had two opportunities to hear this music again. The first was when I took down the dusty Sea Island Creole tapes which I had recorded in 1970 and 1972 and started to go through them to prepare this paper. The second was when I visited the Sea Islands in September 1981, using the opportunity to renew my friendships with the people who were still living (many, unfortunately, had died)[1] and to make some new recordings, including an important interview with a white Sea Islander ("Mr. King").

Turning now from personal to professional concerns, I was reminded, when I was on the Sea Islands, that it was there I first heard the work <u>juk</u> being used in the U.S.A. The word, which I was quite familiar with from my native Guyanese environment, means "pierce" or "poke at," and the context in which I first heard it on the Sea Islands was when a mother turned to her child, who was sitting on a verandah idly kicking at the meshed enclosure, and said something like:

1. Mind you don' juk yuh foot through dat mesh.
   "Take care not to poke a hole through that mesh with your foot."

The professional question I want to ask is whether whites also use the form. However, I need to apologize for asking this question, because such a question can lead one up the garden path. Experience reminds me that too often we approach the comparison of black and white speech by asking overly simple questions. This model, "Blacks use form x; do whites also use x?" is used again and again when discussions of black/white speech differences arise. But this model provides an accurate view of neither black nor white speech, and thus it provides an inadequate basis for comparison.

Four Principles for the Study of Black and White Speech

Instead of this single, simplistic question, I propose four principles which need to be considered when we compare a feature in one language variety to a similar or equivalent feature in another. The principles are not original (the first and the second should be basic to all linguistic description), and they certainly have more general application, but they are not always followed in American dialect research, especially where comparisons of black and white speech are concerned. The four methodological principles will be stated, therefore, in terms of things we need to "remember" to do:

1. We need to attend carefully to the form and meaning of the feature. Someone who answers my question about juk by saying that he or she has heard it as [jʊk] instead of [jʌk] is obeying this principle, as is someone who notes the occurrence of a similar (identical) form in juke-box.

2. We need to specify the linguistic environment in which the feature occurs. This is perhaps less critical for an isolated lexical item like juk, but it can be critical for the phonological and grammatical features with which we are often concerned.

3. We need to tabulate the frequency with which the feature occurs. It is of course in sociolinguistic work, of the the type exemplified by Labov, Wolfram, and Fasold, that this principle has been most carefully followed. These scholars (and others) have demonstrated the importance of considering not only what occurs

and where, but how often.

4. We need to consider the interrelation of the feature with other features in the grammar. This principle is articulated throughout Weinreich's classic 1953 monograph on languages in contact, and was rearticulated by his student Labov, in his 1971 discussion of what constitutes a "system." More than thirty years after the former and more than a decade after the latter, this remains one of the most neglected areas of dialect research.

With regard to the first principle, the need to attend carefully to the form and meaning of the feature, much of the literature on black English remote BIN seems to have suffered from a confusion of the stressed and unstressed versions of this form. In research I have done in the South Carolina Sea Islands and in Philadelphia (Rickford 1975), it is clear that the remote interpretation resides only in the stressed form, as in "She BIN married." Sometimes there is even implosive force to the initial b. The unstressed form, as in "He bin married," does not carry the remote interpretation, but simply describes a perfective or sometimes anterior state or event. Furthermore, in investigations we have conducted with black and white subjects on the meaning of stressed BIN (Labov 1972a, Rickford 1975), blacks regularly differ from whites in recognizing both the remote reference of BIN and the fact that the state to which it refers is still in effect at the moment of speaking, when it is used with a stative predicate. In a sentence like "She BIN married," for example, twenty-three of the twenty-five black respondents in one experiment (Rickford 1975:173) perceived the subject as still married, while only eight of the twenty-five white respondents did.[2]

With respect to the second principle, the importance of specifying the context(s) in which the feature occurs, we can again look at the case of stressed BIN versus unstressed bin. The latter can occur with time adverbials, as in "She bin married for twelve years," but the former cannot. A sentence like *"She BIN married for twelve years" is ungrammatical in black English--unless, of course, there is a pause after "married," in which case the pause represents an elliptical unstressed bin in a full sentence which might read: "She BIN married! (She bin married) for twelve years."

As a second example of how principle 2 might be important in the study of black or white speech, it is instructive to consider "He be miner," which McDavid (1973b:269) introduces with the observation that this use of an invariant be form "still flourishes in the west counties of England." In a paper urging us to "go slow in ethnic attributions," the implication seems to be that the much heralded invariant be of American black English is not as unique as has been previously supposed. But the precise meaning of the McDavid example is not specified, and the prenominal environment in which the be in this example occurs is not one in which the iterative or distributive be of black English usually occurs. Context, as well as meaning, will have to be carefully considered before this example can be accepted as a valid challenge to the uniqueness of invariant be in black English. (Contrast the more persuasive challenge posed in this volume by Bailey and Bassett's data on white Southern use of invariant be).

In relation to the third principle, concerning the frequencies with which the feature occurs, note that while both B. Bailey 1965 and Williamson 1970 pay attention to the following environments in which the inflected copula is absent in the speech of blacks and whites (respectively), neither gives us information about the frequency of this phenomenon in these environments. Labov 1969 first demonstrated that the copula was absent most often before gonna and Verb + -ing, less often before adjectives and locatives, and least often before noun phrases. The quantitative distribution of the copula in this study was in turn given a hypothetical explanation by Stewart 1970a and Bickerton 1973 in terms of differences in the order and ways in which predication in nominal, verbal, and other environments might have evolved in the course of the decreolization of black English, given comparable developments in Sea Island Creole (Gullah) and Guyanese Creole. Dennis and Scott 1975 have also suggested a diachronic explanation for the varying frequencies of copula absence in different environments, pointing to differences in the ways in which the copula is realized in equivalent environments in various West African languages. My interest here is not in assessing the plausibility of these hypotheses; it is in pointing out that they have been made possible by attention to frequencies in the first place and that, in the process, our actual and potential understanding of black speech has been considerably enriched.

I do not want to leave discussion of this principle without pointing to the fact that Wolfram 1974 has looked at the frequencies of are and is deletion in the speech of Mississippi whites and found the latter feature to be far less frequent than the former. This is a significant quantitative difference from the patterns of black English speakers, among whom is deletion is very high, as indicated in the research of Labov 1969 in New York City and Wolfram 1969 in Detroit.

The grammatical interrelations which principle 4 refers to are of two kinds. The first are the paradigmatic relations which a form has with alternatives which are available within the grammar. To the extent that one follows Labov's "principle of accountability" (1969) in adhering to principle 3--that is, reporting the number of occurrences of a feature out of the total number of cases in which it could have occurred--principle 4 will be satisfied, at least in part. For instance, in looking at copula absence, we also have to count cases of copula presence, as Labov 1969 and others have done for black English.

To take another example, not quantitative in approach, note

that in his analysis of the copula in Guyanese Creole, Bickerton 1973 considers the conventional English forms (waz, ɪz, etc.), as well as the creole locative and aspect markers ("He de home," "Me a waak"), as well as zero ("He ∅ sick"). The point is that in an accountable approach we cannot simply look at isolated forms, but must consider them in relation to the larger semantic or syntactic functions they mark and to the alternatives which are available for the expression of equivalent meanings or functions. We should not simply look at plural -Z, for instance, but at plural formation.

In considering the first kind of interrelations, we hold meaning or function constant and look for alternative forms, but in considering the second kind, we hold form constant and look at its behavior with different meanings or functions. Often this involves the search for a more general phonological process affecting a particular grammatical form. For instance, in looking at is deletion in black English, Labov 1969 is led to a more general examination of vowel reduction to account for the disappearance of the remaining vowel once contraction has occurred. And in looking at are deletion among Mississippi whites, Wolfram considers r desulcalization (or deletion) as a general process, not only as it affects the r in are, but as it affects the r's in noncopula forms like bear and mother. Looking at these kinds of interrelations may involve more than looking at the interaction of phonological and grammatical rules, however. For instance, Washabaugh 1975, attempting to replicate Bickerton's 1971 analysis of variation between Guyanese Creole fu and tu as infinitival complementizers, finds that replacement of the equivalent basilectal complementizer (fi) in Providence Island Creole correlates with replacement of a similar form that serves as both genitive and dative preposition. The following PIC sentences show the grammatically different but phonologically identical fi forms:

2. Complementizer: ai mek fi stan op, "I tried to stand up."

   Genitive Preposition: ai put fi mi haan pan it, "I put my hand on it."

   Dative Preposition: de de luk fi mi wid gon, "They are looking for me with a gun."

One could of course continue to discuss these principles with other examples from the literature; instead, we will examine plural formation in Sea Island Creole, beginning with the Sea Island data base.

Sea Island Data Base

   Sea Island Creole (or Gullah), spoken on the South Carolina and Georgia Sea Islands,[3] is the one variety of black American speech which everyone recognizes as creole or creole-derived (Davis 1969), and it is natural to expect significant differences between the Sea Island Creole speech of blacks and the southern speech of whites in the area. It is also natural to turn to African languages and other Atlantic creoles (Turner 1949) to look for analogues, although some scholars have also sought parallels in earlier varieties of British English (Johnson 1930). In either case, it is important to recognize that Gullah or Sea Island Creole is undergoing decreolization, a process in which the proportion of basilectal creole speakers is decreasing and the language is developing intermediate varieties closer to standard English.[4] As I have suggested elsewhere (Rickford 1974), this should not lead us to wring our hands in despair, but instead to follow the decreolization process carefully for insights into the way in which existing varieties of mainland Vernacular Black English might have evolved.
   The data in this paper are drawn primarily from a black woman from one of the South Carolina Sea Islands (not Hilton Head), whom I will refer to as Mrs. Queen. She was eighty-four years old when I recorded her in 1970, in the course of a sociolinguistic interview lasting more than an hour, designed to elicit conversational and casual speech (Labov 1972b). She was the oldest resident on the island at the time, and although her speech contained several of the classic basilectal creole features, its decreolized or mesolectal features were particularly revealing. It is not easy to place Mrs. Queen on existing multi-index scales of social stratification (Warner et al. 1960; Hollingshead and Redlich 1958), which seem to be better adapted to towns and cities than to the small, rustic island community where she lived. On these "objective" scales, she would undoubtedly rank at the bottom, since her main occupation had been subsistence farming, fishing, and shucking oysters in the local oyster factory, and since her education went no further than third grade:

   3. Dat's it. I stop right dey . . . I had to go on de farm,
      go to work an' help to make a living.

   But "objective" sociological classificaion might omit several relevant ethnographic details, like the fact that she served as one of a handful of midwives on the island for many years, delivering over one hundred babies in her time, while her husband served as undertaker (in addition to working as a farmer and fur trapper). In times of crisis, it was to the Queens' home that many an islander would turn for help, and this helped establish their status as a cut above the ordinary. Furthermore, like most of the blacks on the island, she owned the land she lived on and the house she lived in, and--unlike the average lower-class urban dweller--by no means considered herself downtrodden. On the contrary, she thrived on the life of fishing and farming and went to the cities on the mainland only when she had to shop or visit relatives. She had been active in the church and burial society for many years and was popular among the residents of the island, including the handful of whites.[5]

Mrs. Queen's status as the oldest resident also made her something of the matriarch of the island, one of the key individuals to whom visitors (researchers, reporters, tourists, educational and other administrators from the mainland) would be directed. I have never heard of her being anything other than welcoming to these visitors, and she seemed to have developed a polite and amiable style of sharing her reminiscences with strangers.[6]

I mention these details to establish that, contrary to what classification of Mrs. Queen as "lower class" might suggest, her education and primary occupation were no lower than those of 99 percent of her generation on the island, and her community status was more elevated than average because of her professional expertise and other factors. These details will facilitate comparisons between Mrs. Queen and other Sea Islanders, black and white, in terms of socioeconomic status and other potentially significant factors. In this paper, I will concentrate on her data alone because I wish to demonstrate how application of the four principles (outlined above) affects our perception of what her speech (or decreolizing Sea Island Creole, more generally) is like. This paves the way for future linguistic and sociodemographic comparisons.

Plural Formation (Mrs. Queen)

On the basis of what has been written about Gullah or Sea Island Creole (Turner 1949, Cunningham 1970) and other creoles (Alleyne 1980, Dijkhoff 1982), we expect to find two basic types of plural in the speech of Mrs. Queen, and we do:

4. Noun ǂ ∅ (i.e., no overt marking), especially when the noun is preceded by a plural numeral or quantifier, as in "I got two brother whole, y'know."[7]

5. Three varieties of Noun, preceded or followed by dem (a form identical with the creole third person plural pronoun; cf. nan in Papiamentu):

   a. Dem ǂǂ Noun, as in "It bin cheap in dem day."
   b. Proper Noun ǂǂ dem, as in "Da's where Viola dem live."
   c. Common Noun ǂǂ dem, as in "Yeah, buy it from de masa dem."

If we were to ignore the four principles (as is customary), we might proceed at once to comparisons with other language varieties and speculations about possible diachronic sources (as is customary).

The unmarked plural (type 4 above) is found to some extent in a number of English dialects. As noted by Wright (1905:263),

> Nouns expressing time, space, weight, measure, and number when immediately preceded by a cardinal number gen. remain unchanged in the plural in the dialects of Sc.[otland] and Eng.[land].

More recently, in relation to the United States, McDavid (1973b: 268) notes that:

> Even the uninflected plurals of nouns of measure (forty bushel, ten mile, five ton, and the like) are not solely identified with the South, for they occur widely in other regions.

That unmarked plurals were even more general in the English of earlier times is suggested also by the following words from an anthem written by King Henry VIII (1491-1547):

6. O Lorde, the maker of al thing, / We pray Thee nowe in this evening / Us to defende, through Thy mercy, / From all deceite of our en'my. / Let neither us deluded be, / Good Lorde, with dreame or phantasy, / Oure hearte wakying in Thee Thou kepe . . .

On the other hand, we might note, as Turner 1949 did, that several West African languages have no formal distinction between singular and plural in some of their noun classes. For example, in Tshiluba the class 3 noun n∫ila can be either singular or plural ("path" or "paths"). So this type of plural could have entered the creole from either an English or a West African source.

With respect to the plurals with dem, I have been informed that type 5a, in which the pronoun precedes the noun, is found in Somerset, England (Elizabeth Traugott, personal communication). Even though Turner 1949 provides comparable examples from Ibo and Yoruba (e.g., Ibo nwo_3ke_3, "man"; n_3di_3 nwo_3ke_3, "men"--the prefixed form, n_3di_3, meaning "these" or "people"), the question of an English or African etymology would again probably be moot. However, with respect to types 5b and 5c, which to my knowledge have no English parallels but do have parallels in some West African languages (e.g., from Westermann 1930, quoted in Alleyne (1980:151): Ewe ame, "man"; ame-wo, "men," where wo is the third person plural pronoun), the case for a distinct African (via creole) origin is stronger.[8]

Note that we have moved from the differences between black and white dialects to their origins--a mixing of issues which Wolfram 1974, Feagin 1979, and Fasold 1981 note is prevalent in the literature, but which they urge us to avoid. Instead of continuing with the preceding lines of discussion, let us therefore reexamine Mrs. Queen's plurals in the light of our four principles.

Following the principle of careful attention to form and meaning, we are forced, on reexamination, to deny separate status to the 5a type cases and to merge them with those of type 4. The reason is that the dem in "dem day" (type 5a) does not indicate only plurality, as it does in "de masa dem" (type 5c), but also deixis.[9] In all cases in which it occurs before the noun, dem is a plural distal demonstrative, equivalent to "those" (which doesn't seem to occur in Mrs. Queen's data), and in contrast with dese, "these" (as in "Oh dese chi'ren now, dey livin!"). We would therefore be no more justified in considering as a separate category of plural formation those cases in which the noun is preceded by dem than cases in which the noun is preceded by dese or any other modifier whose meaning includes, but is not limited to, plurality (e.g., three, some, many). That the prenominal dem belongs with these other modifiers, and not with the postnominal dem, is also suggested by the fact that like the former, but not the latter, it can be separated from the modified noun by one or more adjectival modifiers (as in "Some o' dem odda one" and "dem big old tree").

It is of course frequently asserted (e.g., by Bickerton 1981:24, Dijkhoff 1982:29) that, in creole systems, plural marking on the noun is rendered unnecessary when it is preceded by a plural numeral or any other modifier including the semantic feature of plurality. This is a hypothesis which we will pursue below, but its pursuit requires a grouping of prenominal dem with plural numerals and quantifiers and a merging of the unmarked nouns following dem with the category of unmarked nouns in general. As it turns out, some of the nouns following dem are marked with -Z (z ~ ɨz ~ s), as in "dem cars," "dem lil babies," and these will be merged with the Noun #Z category which has to be opened once we apply principle 3.[10]

The other category which is affected by close attention to meaning is type 5b plurals, which we have to set aside on the grounds that they do not mean "more than one" entity of the kind referred to in the noun, but the specific entity (usually a person) referred to in association with unspecified others. The distinctive character of these "associative" plurals is revealed more clearly in decreolized varieties in which they show up in the form Proper Noun and dem (e.g., "John and dem").

If we leave aside principle 2 for the moment and apply principles 3 and 4 simultaneously, reporting the frequencies of all means of expressing the plural for regular nouns in Mrs. Queen's speech which remain after principle 1 has been applied, we obtain the results in table 1.[11]

Table 1
Plurals of a Black Sea Islander (Mrs. Queen)

Total Sample Size (n)	Noun (#Z)## dem "De boy(s) dem"	Noun #Ø "De boy"	Noun #Z "De boys"
128	1%	76%	23%

The first striking thing about table 1 is the infrequency of the Noun (#Z) ## dem type, based on one example: "de masa dem."[12] Before applying our principles, we were attracted to this 5c type of plural in Mrs. Queen's speech because of its unusual character. Now, however, it appears to be marginal part of Mrs. Queen's grammar. But there are two qualifications in this assumption. First, despite its infrequency, this type may represent the residue of a system in which white speakers participated very little, if at all. I have seen no reports of white Southerners using this type of plural (as against types 5a or 5b). Second, although this type has clear creole roots (Alleyne 1980, Dijkhoff 1982), table 2, showing the distribution of plurals in eight speakers in the Guyanese Creole continuum, shows that its frequency remains low even for the most basilectal or least decreolized speakers, like Irene and

---

Table 2 Plurals of Eight Speakers
in the Guyanese Creole Continuum

Name	Sample Size (n)	Noun (#Z)## dem "De boy(s) dem"	Noun #Ø "De boy"	Noun #Z "De boys"
Irene	179	18%	73%	9%
Reefer	205	13%	68%	19%
Derek	80	9%	82%	9%
Nani	148	9%	74%	17%
Kishore	275	2%	42%	56%
Seymore	299	2%	6%	92%
Bonnette	163	1%	3%	96%
Katherine	150	0%	6%	94%

Reefer.[13] The highest frequency for this type in the subsample from the overall sample of 24 speakers (see Rickford 1979) is 20 percent.[14] Speakers like Nani, Kishore, and Bonnette chart the progressive diminution of this type which accompanies decreolization, its eventual demise being marked in the speech of Katherine.

To explain the low frequency of this type even among less decreolized speakers, we need to turn to principle 2, for plural dem does not co-occur with preceding plural numerals or quantifiers, with indefinites, and--at least in Sea Island Creole (Cunningham 1970), although not in Guyanese Creole--it is restricted to cases in which the noun is [+human]. This restricted set of potential environments accounts, to a large extent, for the low frequency of this type in tables 1 and 2.

With respect to the unmarked (Noun #∅) plurals, it is striking that this type accounts for fully three-quarters of Mrs. Queen's plurals, making her comparable to the most basilectal Guyanese speakers in table 2. (Her overall pattern is most similar to that of Nani.) That her speech is considerably less decreolized than that of Northern speakers of the Black English Vernacular (BEV) is clear from the fact that the mean frequency of plural absence reported among BEV speakers in New York City does not exceed 13 percent (Labov et al. 1968:I:161-62),[15] and in Detroit does not exceed 5.8 percent (Wolfram 1969:143).[16] McDavid 1973b reports some cases of plural absence in southern white English, and Wolfram and Christian (1975:169ff) report similar cases for white Appalachian English, but in neither case are details about their frequency provided. Both sets of authors describe plural absence as primarily limited to nouns of weight and measure, however, indicating that the phenomenon is highly restricted in these dialects.

By contrast, only seven of Mrs. Queen's table 1 plurals are with nouns of weight and measure (all with the lexical item acre, four marked by Z and three without). Plural absence is, for her, a much more widespread and differently conditioned phenomenon (as we will see below).

Given the distribution of Noun +∅ and Noun +Z cases in Mrs. Queen's data, two questions inevitably arise: whether the variation between these cases is phonologically or syntactically conditioned, and whether it should be treated in terms of the variable insertion or deletion of plural -Z. To investigate these questions, I looked first at Mrs. Queen's strong nouns (those with plurals involving a vowel change, like mouse/mice and man/men), hoping that they would provide some indication of whether the inflected standard English plural is an underlying part of her grammar. There are twenty-seven occurrences of a plural strong noun in Mrs. Queen's data, all duly inflected, but since they all involve a single lexical item, children, the evidence is less than decisive. Turner (1949: 223) in fact listed this item as one of two exceptions to his general observation that "practically all Gullah nouns have the same form in the plural as in the singular":

Among the few exceptions are 'čilən "children" and manz "men"; but the singular form of each of these is also used as a plural [p. 3].

It is true, however, that I have found no occurrences of the child and man plurals which Turner found over thirty years ago, and this, together with one hypercorrect reference to a "twenty-feet boat," might be taken as a weak, preliminary indication that Mrs. Queen's grammar might include a morphologically marked plural category. (Note that the syntactically marked case, "de masa dem," already establishes the existence of "plural" as an underlying grammatical category.)

Returning to the weak nouns represented in table 1 (i.e., those which require suffixation of -Z--phonemically /z/ or /s/ or /ɨz/--in standard English, as in boys, weeks, and places), I have coded each semantically plural noun (regardless of whether -Z was present or absent) according to the following potential conditioning factors. The first two are syntactically/semantically motivated and associated with creole languages; the latter two are phonologically motivated and associated with nonstandard dialects of English:

7a. Whether the Noun Phrase (NP) in which the noun occurs is existentially presupposed (typically associated with the occurrence of a definite article in creole languages, as in Guyanese Creole [GC] di buk, Papiamentu [P] e buki, "the book"), existentially asserted (typically associated with an indefinite article, as in GC wan buk, P un buki, "a book"), or existentially hypothesized (typically associated with zero, the creole "generic" and/or "nonspecific" article, as in GC buk, P buki, "a book/books"). These Noun Phrase categories, originally proposed by Bickerton 1975, 1981, have been argued by Dijkhoff 1982 to be intimately bound up with plural-marking in Papiamentu, the creole of Curaçao, Aruba, and Bonaire. Following Dijkhoff, I hypothesized that to the extent this "creole" system was carried over to -Z plural marking, -Z absence would be most likely with the existentially hypothesized NPs (which never take the pluralizing nan in P or dem in GC), less likely with the existentially asserted NPs (which are followed by the pluralizing nan in P only when "one cannot deduce from the context that a plural is meant"), and least likely with the existentially presupposed NPs (which are generally followed by nan in P).[17]

7b. Whether there is a plural quantifier (including numerals), a dem demonstrative, or neither of these plural modifiers preceding the noun. My hypothesis is that this syntactic factor group will show a strong favoring of -Z absence when either of the first two plural factors is present, since -Z marking in these cases is redundant.

7c. Whether the noun ends in a <u>nonsibilant consonant</u> (e.g., <u>shed</u>), a <u>sibilant consonant</u> (e.g., <u>box</u>), or a <u>vowel</u> (e.g., <u>tree</u>). My hypothesis is that to the extent this phonological factor group has any systematic effect, -<u>Z</u> absence will be favored after nouns that end in consonants, since consonant clusters (disfavored in many nonstandard dialects of English) are avoided in the process.

7d. Whether the noun is followed by a word beginning with a consonant or pause (e.g., <u>tree fall</u> or <u>tree</u> . . .) or by a word beginning with a <u>vowel</u> (e.g., <u>tree off</u>). My expectation with this phonological factor group is that if it has any systematic effect, -<u>Z</u> absence will be favored by a following consonant or pause and disfavored by a following vowel (cf. Labov 1972c:44-45).

To assess the independent effect on plural -<u>Z</u> absence of these factors, I used the multivariate analysis provided by the variable-rule computer program (VARBRUL) developed at the University of Montreal by Sankoff and his associates (see Cedergren and Sankoff 1974, Rousseau and Sankoff 1978). The program uses maximum likelihood methods to calculate an input probability (p_0), representing the tendency for the rule to apply regardless of individual factors, and a probability coefficient for each of the factors (p_1, p_2 . . . p_n), representing its independent contribution to the probability of rule application in any given environment (p). The variable rule model used in processing Mrs. Queen's data is the logistic one:[18]

8. $$\frac{p}{1-p} = \frac{p_0}{1-p_0} \times \frac{p_1}{1-p_1} \times \ldots \times \frac{p_n}{1-p_n}$$

In this model, probabilities above .5 favor rule application; those below .5 disfavor rule application; and those just around this central figure have no effect either way. By comparing the probability coefficients calculated for individual factors, we can assess their relative effects. The program also selects the factor <u>groups</u> which are most significant by comparing the log-likelihood figures which result when each factor group is used by itself to predict the variability in the data, in combination with two other factor groups, in combination with three other factor groups, and so on--up to the maximum number of factor groups available. Application of this multiple regression procedure in our case results in selection of the two phonological factor groups as significant and rejection of the two syntactic/semantic factor groups as insignificant.[19] The favored two-factor group analysis is shown in table 3.

Table 3
Probability Coefficients of Individual Factors in Favored
Two-Factor Group Analysis of Mrs. Queen's Plurals

Preceding Phonological Segment   Following Phonological Segment

Nonsibilant Consonant___: .654   ____ Sibilant Consonant: .609
Sibilant Consonant___:.587   ____ Pause: .604
Vowel___: .271   ____ Vowel: .297

Note: Input probability = .78, log. likelihood = -58.409,
                    significance = .032.

The effects of the following phonological segment, represented by the probability coefficients in table 3, are neatly illustrated in the following sample from Mrs. Queen, in which we find acre (phonetically [ekə], without final r) before a consonant or pause, but acres before a following vowel (note that the second was is phonetically [əz], without initial w):

9. See, da's de way it was. An den five acre (pause), ten acres was over here, on dis side, and dat ten acre divide up to two--five acres a piece!

They also agree with the findings of Labov et al. (1968:I: 160-64) on plural -Z absence among black teenagers and adults (for instance, the T-Birds show 13% -Z absence before consonant or pause, 9% before vowels in casual speech, while the Cobras show 30% and 0% in comparable environments),[20] and with Labov et al.'s findings on the deletion of final t and d in consonant clusters, which is also disfavored by a following vowel. It should be noted that Wolfram (1969:61) suggests that the major effect of the following segment on simplification of consonant clusters in BEV in Detroit is consonantal versus nonconsonantal; that is, that a following pause patterns with a vowel rather than with a consonant. But Fasold (1972:67), providing separate statistics on each of the three environments (something neither Labov et al. nor Wolfram does), finds that his Washington, D.C., BEV data support Labov et al. rather than Wolfram: a following pause patterns with a following consonant (favoring 73% and 76.2% simplification of bimorphemic consonant clusters respectively), while a following vowel is alone in disfavoring cluster simplification (28.7%).

Our results for the following factor group are in line, therefore, with previous studies. But beyond statistics there is a need for linguistic explanation (Bickerton 1971, Washabaugh 1975:109,

Fasold 1975a:37), and no one, to my knowledge, has attempted to explain why a following pause should pattern with a following consonant in favoring consonant cluster simplification and/or plural -$\underline{Z}$ absence. If the distinction is between consonantal/nonconsonantal environments, this can be explained as part of a general tendency to avoid consonant clusters, but this clearly will not work for a vocalic/nonvocalic distinction.

One possible reason for a following vowel favoring the presence of a preceding consonantal segment is the fact that the vowel may serve as a cliticizing environment for the consonant, the consonant becoming the onset of the following syllable rather than the coda of the preceding one. In the case of a preceding consonant cluster, the result would be to split the cluster between two syllables, which is productively/perceptually simpler than if the cluster remains in one (e.g., pastus$ rather than $past$us$ for "past us" or "passed us"). In the case of a consonant preceded by a vowel, this would have the effect of converting a (C)VC syllable into a (C)V syllable, or of preventing the creation of a (C)VC one (e.g., dez v$ rather than dez v$ for "days of . . ."). If (C)V syllables are accepted as "simpler" than (C)VC ones (and they certainly are commoner in baby talk and in pidgins and creoles), this might also be a productive/perceptual ease explanation. Since neither a following consonant nor pause can serve as a cliticizing environment for a word-final consonant, neither would offer the "simplification" which cliticization provides, and both would serve as disfavoring environments.

There are some wrinkles to be ironed out with this hypothesis (for instance, do following vowels have this cliticizing effect on the final consonant of a preceding word everywhere, or only in fast speech, or primarily when the final consonant represents a bound morpheme?).[21] Also, we would probably want to do some instrumental measurement, and perhaps some perception testing, to verify the impressionistic cliticizing effect, but this hypothesis at least takes us one step beyond the solid, replicable set of observations that we already have.

With respect to the effect of a preceding nonsibilant consonant, it is no surprise that this would favor -$\underline{Z}$ absence most strongly, because a consonant cluster would be prevented in the process (e.g., cats, dogs). The slightly favoring effect of a preceding sibilant is at first problematic, however. Since the shape of -$\underline{Z}$ after sibilants is - z, no consonant cluster would be created by its presence. If, however, the vowel of - z is generated by vowel insertion and the derivation of all plural suffixes begins with the suffixation of a sibilant (s in the example provided by Elgin 1981: 375),[22] then a consonant cluster would be created at this first stage in the case of word-final sibilant and nonsibilant consonants alike, and their almost identical favoring effect on -$\underline{Z}$ absence would be explained.

Up to this point we have shown that the primary constraints on -Z̲ absence in Mrs. Queen's speech are phonological rather than syntactic/semantic, and we have attempted to provide linguistic explanations for the statistical effects observed. What we have not done, however, is make a decision to treat -Z̲ absence as the result of a deletion rule operating on an underlying suffix, or as an insertion rule creating a plural suffix. It is to this issue that we now turn.[23]

The tendency in the literature on BEV is to treat the discovery of regular phonological constraints on the presence or absence of a grammatical variable as evidence in favor of the variable's being present in underlying structure and subject to a deletion rule in the course of derivation (cf. the standard variation treatments of the BEV copula and final t̲, d̲ deletion). The rationale for this is never spelled out, but since the phonological component in a generative grammar is interpretive, operating on the output of the syntactic component, it can be argued that while phonological processes can take grammatical information into account, the reverse is either theoretically more difficult or impossible. By this argument, we would have to presume an underlying grammatical -Z̲ suffix for Mrs. Queen, deleted by a phonologically conditioned rule which applies in the majority of cases, once the phonological component is reached.

Of course, it is precisely this last fact--the preponderance of -Z̲ absent forms in Mrs. Queen's speech--which makes us uncomfortable about suggesting that the suffix is underlying.[24] There is a tendency in the variationist literature to regard the statistically more frequent form as underlying. For instance, Wolfram's first reason for suggesting that third-present -Z̲ might not be underlying in BEV is the fact that it was "much more frequently absent than present" (1969:137) in the speech of his Detroit informants. The same argument had been given by Labov et al. (1968:I:164) for their New York City data. The explicit rationale for this approach is again not usually given, but it is presumably based on "economy" arguments: it is "cheaper" to account for the occasional occurrences of a feature by the application of a grammatical rule inserting it than to account for the nonoccurrences by the prior application of grammatical rule insertion, followed by the application of a phonological rule which has the effect of wiping out the newly inserted feature more often than not.

The only alternative to a phonological -Z̲ deletion rule, however, is a grammatical -Z̲ insertion rule with phonological constraints, and it is difficult to see how this is possible in any framework in which the phonological component is interpretive and subsequent to the grammatical one. For instance, one way of handling English plurals in a generative grammar is by means of a segment transformation which introduces a [-singular] affix segment following a [-singular] noun (see Jacobs and Rosenbaum 1968:89 for an early treatment). The rules in the subsequent phonological component specify the phonetic realizations of this affix in different lexical and phonological environments and, in our case, provide for its variable deletion. If we want to avoid a deletion rule, we have to suppose that at the stage in the syntactic derivation of a sentence at which this segment transformation were to apply, the grammar would look ahead to the phonological component and see whether there were favoring or disfavoring phonological factors there before applying. This might be possible in a "more sophisticated approach" in which, as suggested by Palmer (1971:186) we ought to be able to move in both directions between phonology and syntax and syntax and phonology; but it does not appear to be possible in any of the currently dominant models.[25]

It is thus theoretically difficult to account for the systematic phonological conditioning we observe by anything other than a -$\underline{Z}$ deletion rule, and the frequency with which it applies should not deter us from this solution. Within generative phonology there are deletion rules which operate 100 percent of the time, but are justified by the distributional facts of the language or the formal requirements of a generative system. Compare, for instance, the analysis in which the underlying adjectival forms in French [pɑti garsõ], "little boy," [gro garsõ], "big boy," contain final consonants ([pɑtit̲], [groz̲]) which are obligatorily deleted before a following consonant in the course of derivation (Schane 1973:75).

Accordingly, we will account for Mrs. Queen's plural absence with the following preliminary variable rule:[26]

10. Z ===> <∅>   <~V >   #⎯   ##<~V >
                    [+noun] [-sing.]

In prose terms, a plural -$\underline{Z}$ is more likely to be variably deleted if the final segment of the preceding noun is not a vowel and if the following segment is not a vowel.

We have now applied our four principles to the analysis of Mrs. Queen's plurals, except for the second half of principle 4, in which we look not at paradigmatic alternatives but at the behavior of similar forms elsewhere in the grammar. With respect to the postnominal dem pluralizer, we need to look at the other instances where this form is deployed. We have already noted that dem is unchallenged by those as a prenominal demonstrative modifier in Mrs. Queen's speech. In its role as a third person plural subject pronoun, however, dem is used rarely, only three times out of fifteen (the other occurrences being the standard English dey, "they") in Mrs. Queen's hour-long interview. The following are the actual occurrences:

11. An my granmudda an any odda dat bin to um ("her")--
    <u>dem</u> also was manacle.

12. <u>Dem</u> bin de people what own de slave, you see.

13. Robbie and Roosevelt, dey died . . . <u>dem</u> bin de two
    oldest one.

Even in these cases it is arguable whether the form should be classified as a personal or demonstrative pronoun (again equivalent to standard English <u>those</u>). In any case, Mrs. Queen's speech is certainly decreolized in this respect, and the diminution of <u>dem</u> as a personal pronoun subject may have heralded its diminution as a postnominal pluralizer. Why demonstrative <u>dem</u> has thus far been unaffected by decreolization is a source of great fascination to me, but I can think of no simple answers except that, unlike the other creole categories employing <u>dem</u>, it is found in a number of nonstandard English dialects.[27]

With respect to plural -<u>Z</u>, the other potentially related areas which have been considered in earlier studies of BEV (Labov et al. 1968, Wolfram 1969) are the third present ("He walk<u>s</u>"), the possessive ("John'<u>s</u> house"), adverbials ("sometime<u>s</u>"), and monomorphemic forms ending in a sibilant ("bo<u>x</u>," "place"). The third-present category is very difficult to assess in Mrs. Queen's speech, for most of her verb stem tokens are not present tense at all, but unmarked past, in accord with the system for nonstative creole verbs described by Bickerton (1975:28):

14. He <u>come</u> to the island, I don' know when--don' know
    what time now.

Some of the cases which would be past, according to this system, are open to classification as instances of the historical present, however (and thus countable in tabulations of third-present marking).

15. An I <u>say</u>, "Come an look at me; watch me plant dis
    potato." An he <u>come</u> in an <u>sit</u> right in dis yard and
    <u>start</u> talkin, an I <u>say</u>, "Oh, let's go now an get some-
    ting to eat." I <u>come</u> on in . . . .

Apart from the difficulty of determining what to count as cases of potential third-present marking, it is difficult to imagine that third-present marking could become well established in the grammar until the creole tense-aspect system had decreolized further. In any case, the evidence from this area is unclear. The frequency with which a final sibilant is absent in the remaining three categories in Mrs. Queen's speech is shown in table 4.[28]

Table 4
Final Sibilant Absence in Three Other Categories (Mrs. Queen)

	Before Vowel		Before Consonant		Before Pause		Total	
	No.	%	No.	%	No.	%	No.	%
a. Possessive	3	67	21	90	No Data		24	88
b. Adverbials	2	50	8	75	3	67	13	69
c. Monomorphe- mic Forms	3	0	8	12	12	0	23	4

Note: No. = Sample Size

Even though categories a and b show a conditioning effect of vocalic versus nonvocalic following segments similar to that observed with plural -Z, they do not appear to be governed by a similar deletion rule operating on a grammatically underlying segment. In the possessives, the three instances of -Z presence all involve proper names; one the name of an island organization ("Oyster's Union Society") and two the name of a point on the island ("Benjie's Point"). These could well have been learned as unanalyzed wholes, and once removed from the data pool, all we are left with is twenty noun possessives which show no possessive suffix whatsoever and no evidence of phonological conditioning, but which involve the process of syntactic juxtaposition which is common in creole systems. The adverbials, in turn, appear to show lexical rather than phonological conditioning, with oversea and sometime always without a final sibilant (1 and 5 cases respectively), and afterwards and a long ways always occurring with a final sibilant (1 case each). The only item with word-final variation is someway(s) (2 tokens with the final sibilant and 3 without).[29]

In the third category in table 4, the monomorphemic forms ending in a sibilant, the evidence is clear: the sibilant is present in the underlying form, and is not subject to the phonologically constrained deletion processes which plural -Z undergoes. This is true even when the final sibilant is part of a consonant cluster (as in box, six, grits, else). There are fifteen such cases in the data, and in only one of them--an occurrence of the proper name Haynes before a consonant ("Hayne die")--is the final sibilant absent. This clearly shows that whatever disfavoring effect preceding or following vowels have on processes that remove a word-final sibilant, it applies only when the sibilant represents plural -Z or a grammatical inflection (cf. footnotes 21 and 29).[30]

Having applied all four of our guiding principles, I hope I have demonstrated how different (and richer, more complex) our view of pluralization in Mrs. Queen's speech is as a result. The associative plurals and the prenominal demonstratives with <u>dem</u> have been set aside on semantic grounds, and it has been demonstrated that although one example still remains of the postnominal creole construction in which the third person plural pronoun serves as a pluralizer, the function <u>dem</u> as a third person pronoun has itself been weakened with its increasing replacement in subject position by <u>dey</u>. The plural -<u>Z</u> suffix has been shown to be absent, rather than present, in the majority of cases in Mrs. Queen's speech--a vast quantitative difference from the BEV speakers in the large Northern cities. But though syntactic as well as phonological constraints are carefully attended to, Mrs. Queen's plural absence appears to be qualitatively similar to that of Northern BEV speakers, insofar as it is best described as a deletion rule with phonological constraints. The fact that she is far less advanced on a decreolization trajectory, however, is clear from the fact that she appears to have no corresponding possessive -<u>Z</u> in her grammar, and that the phonological processes which affect the plural -<u>Z</u> do not appear to apply to all final sibilants, but are grammatically constrained. Elsewhere (Rickford 1980), I have shown that phonological and grammatical processes work closely together to facilitate decreolization. The examples in this paper constitute additional examples, although of a different sort.

With more detailed understanding of Mrs. Queen's system of plural formation and its interrelationships with other elements in her grammar, the stage is properly set for the kinds of comparisons which are critical for an understanding of black/white speech relations in the South, in the United States, and in the New World. We need comparisons of Mrs. Queen with other decreolizing black Sea Islanders, with less decreolized speakers of West African and Caribbean Creoles, and with more decreolized Northern speakers of BEV. We also need comparisons of her with whites of equivalent and different socioeconomic and settlement histories, on the Sea Islands, in the South, in other parts of the United States and the English-speaking world. These will allow us to answer not only the narrower questions about similarities and differences, but also the larger questions about linguistic constraints on decreolization and language change and about the sociolinguistic consequences of contact (or lack thereof) between socially/ethnically/culturally different populations. These are the ultimate edifices we want to build. I hope to have demonstrated in this paper that key elements in their construction are the four principles which we need to bring to bear on our analyses.

NOTES

[1]Since October 1981, two more of the elderly Sea Islanders have died, including one with whom I stayed during my last visit. As traditional exemplars pass on, traditional aspects of Sea Island language and culture are increasingly threatened.

[2]In a recent informal replication of this experiment with a class of Stanford students, however, a higher proportion of whites appeared to understand the meaning of stressed BIN. This might indicate diffusion of the form over the past ten years (parallel to the diffusion of black lexical items like hip and black kinesics like the multistage handshake), or an East Coast/West Coast regional difference which hadn't been detected before (only a few of my earlier informants were from the West Coast). I hope to do further investigation of these questions, including the relation of counter-negative stressed BEEN in the colloquial standard ("He's BEEN doing it" = "He HAS been doing it") to the remote BIN of the Black English Vernacular. The semantics of the two forms overlap, and in both cases the stress seems relatable to the loss of phonetic material by contraction or deletion--a process of compensatory strengthening parallel to the more familiar examples of compensatory lengthening (e.g., of a vowel following the loss of postvocalic r) in phonology.

[3]Hancock 1980c describes a form of Gullah extant in Texas, spoken by the descendants of Afro-Seminole scouts who migrated from Florida in the early nineteenth century.

[4]See Rickford 1983 for alternative models of decreolization as a general process.

[5]This fact, however, led her to be regarded as "white oriented" by some of the local black residents, a categorization which was mitigated only by the fact that she was old.

[6]It is quite likely that these interactions in themselves helped to increase her competence in mesolectal varieties of English. In the case of the recording I made with her, I attribute whatever success I had in getting beyond Mrs. Queen's formal transactional style (it is always difficult to gauge such success in absolute terms) to the fact that I differed from the average visitor or magazine writer who interviewed her, insofar as I had been living on the island for a while and had come to know her somewhat before the interview. Also, I came from the same ethnic background, interviewed her using a similar linguistic system (Guyanese Creole noninversion of questions and other creole features were as evident in my stretches of discourse as in hers), and got into topics which led to more involved and spontaneous speech. (For instance, her long narrative about the death of her husband led me, undesignedly, into an account of the death of my father, and was followed a little later by her narrative of the tornado which struck the island.) In these stretches of the interview, Mrs. Queen's vernacular came to the fore.

[7]The symbol ⫶ is used for an inflectional morpheme boundary. The symbol ⫶⫶ is used for a word boundary.

[8]That is, disregarding alternative explanations--like the
possible influence of a universal bioprogram in the formation of
creoles (Bickerton 1981).

[9]Alleyne (1980:100-01) suggests that dem is a plural marker in
the English creoles, whether it occurs before or after the noun,
and that it is only in Sierra Leone Krio and Guyanese Creole that
both positions occur. The latter claim is not quite correct (Gullah
is listed as having only prenominal dem, but both types are attested in this paper), and while it may be true that dem is a plural
form of the definite article in the Surinam creoles (Sranan, Saramaccan), it seems clearly to have demonstrative force in GC and
Gullah. Alleyne himself describes it as an "attentuated demonstrative" in Krio.

[10]This is a classic case of "elimination of redundancy," said to
be characteristic of pidgins and creoles; but note that it is similar
to what is reported for English and Scottish dialects by Wright
1905, on page 45.

[11]Nouns referring to frequently hunted animals (e.g., mink,
otter, coon) were not included in the count, because they appear
to take no plural inflection in this area (like deer), as in other
English dialects.

[12]There is also one example of de chilren dem, which is
excluded from the count because this table is restricted to data on
the regular or weak nouns. See the discussion of chilren as an
exceptional form (below).

[13]It should be pointed out that Irene, Reefer, and the other
speakers listed in table 2 and are Indo-Guyanese: descendants of
indentured laborers from India who (from the mid-nineteenth
century) have replaced African slaves as the main labor force on
Guyanese sugar plantations, and who seem to have inherited the
creole speech of the latter and preserved it quite faithfully.

[14]Note, however, that the statistics for the Guyanese speakers
are based on all semantically plural noun tokens, including weak
and strong nouns.

[15]This is the mean for the Thunderbirds and Oscar Brothers
(in New York City) over all styles and environments, which I was
able to calculate from the figures for the latter given by Labov et
al. (1968:I:161-62). The figures for the Aces and the Jets are even
lower, 5% and 6%--comparable to the 6% figure for the white
Inwood group. Equivalent figures for working-class black adults
range from 1% for a Northern lower-working-class group to 13%
for a Southern lower-working-class group investigated by the
authors.

[16]This is the figure reported for a lower-working-class black
group. The means in Wolfram (1969:143) for other black groups
are: UWC, 4.4%; LMC, 1.2%; UMC, 0.5%.

[17]Compare also Alleyne (1980:100): "In all the [Caribbean

English] dialects pluralization operates on definite nouns, but usually not on indefinite nouns."

[18]I wish to thank Shana Poplack for making a version of this program available and for discussing its novel features.

[19]Even though the first two factor groups were not found to have a significant effect on the observed variation, one run of the program gave probability coefficients for all four factor groups, and these are reprinted here because of their potential interest:

> Input Probability = 0.743, log. likelihood = 57.363
> Existentially Presupposed NP = .685, Existentially Asserted NP = .200, Existentially Hypothesized NP = .519
> Preceding Plural Quant. = .553, Preceding dem = .426, No Plural Modifier Preceding = .521
> Preceding Nonsibilant Consonant = .652, Preceding Sibilant Consonant = .564 Preceding Vowel = .291
> Following Consonant = .594, Following Pause = .633, Following Vowel = .284

Note that neither of the hypotheses for the first two factor groups was supported.

[20]Note, though, that Labov et al. did not give separate percentages for __C versus __## and that for one group of adults (lower-class South), the reverse effect is obtained, with a following vowel favoring -Z absence (__C = 10% vs. __V = 14% in Style A, __C = 12% vs. __V = 19% in Style B).

[21]Labov et al. do not suggest the cliticizing hypothesis, but note (1968:I:132), with respect to the simplification rule for sC clusters (e.g., test), that "word boundary has little influence but inflectional boundaries do: that is, we obtain testing quite often, but the effect of a following vowel across word boundary is not great enough to give us more than a small percentage of test about what? rather than tes' about what?"

[22]Elgin's sample derivation for beaches, beginning with s rather than z as the basic form of the plural, is as follows (1981: 375):

#biych - [+PLURAL]#	Deep Structure
#biych + s#	Add the plural ending
#biych + e + s#	Apply the vowel insertion rule
#biych + e + z#	Apply the voicing rule
beaches	Surface Structure

See also Labov et al. (1968:I:132-33) for a similar derivation beginning with -z.

[23]One other alternative is to treat Mrs. Queen as a perfect bilingual or bidialectal speaker, manipulating two separate linguistic systems (English when instances of plural -Z are observed and Gullah/SIC when instances of -Z absence are observed). It is probably true that her synchronic variation represents a tran-

sition point in Mrs. Queen's acquisition of English and her movement away from a -Z-less creole system. But the strict co-occurrence restrictions which help to demarcate separate "codes"
(Labov 1971, Gumperz 1967) are often missing--note the oscillation
between plural absence and presence with the same lexical item
and within the same sentence in example 9. Mrs. Queen is better
analyzed, for this reason, as exemplifying one inherently variable
linguistic system, even though this might have come about from
the merger of originally distinct rule-sets. Note that Fasold (1972:
133-47) considers the interference or cosystems analysis for BEV
third-present -s in some detail, and rejects it in favor of an inherent variability "variable rule" analysis (for speakers who vary
almost equally between -s and Ø). Note too that some kind of variable deletion or insertion rule for plural -Z is also needed in other
varieties of English in which no question of "mixture" with a distinct system is possible, neither as a descriptive device nor as a
diachronic explanation.

[24]Labov et al. (1968:I:164ff) use two other kinds of evidence
to argue that third-present -Z is not underlying in BEV: the
prevalence of hypercorrections and the absence of style shifting.
Mrs. Queen shows us two hypercorrections--twenty feet boat and
the thirteenth days of September--but these seem to involve
knowledge of subtle restrictions on the placement of the plural
suffix rather than a lack of the basic rule to insert the plural
suffix in a [+plural] environment. And with respect to style
shifting, note that in a typical expository stretch of the interview,
where Mrs. Queen explains how she became a midwife and what
the job entails, -Z absence rises to 94% (15/16). Ideally, we would
want to do a multivariate analysis of style in conjunction with the
other factors so far found to be significant, but preliminary indications are that it is significant.

[25]This is what Bickerton (1975:109-10) suggests for at least
some speakers' acquisition of past -ed in Guyana: "a rule which
permits -ed everywhere except before a following (perhaps
homorganic only stop)." Although Bickerton subsequently finds
other (grammatical) factors to be more significant, note that the
proposed rule would have been theoretically difficult for the same
reasons discussed in this paper (i.e., the interpretive status of the
phonological component).

[26]Preliminary because it can be more formally stated in terms
of features and because the possibility of collapsing this rule with
other consonant-removing processes remains to be investigated.

[27]One final potential constraint on the rule which we have not
mentioned is lexical conditioning. The 127 Ø and -Z tokens in Mrs.
Queen's data come from 51 different nouns. Many of these consist
of only one token each, and only seven have at least five tokens
each (which we might consider a baseline for reliability). Of these
seven, four displayed categorical -Z absence (slave, boat, oyster
without final r, and one) and could conceivably be lexical

exceptions to the segment transformation introducing the plural suffix. The other three nouns (thing, cent, and acre without the final r) show variable -Z absence. Interestingly enough, a white Sea Islander, comparable in social status to Mrs. Queen, appears to show no phonological conditioning, and more plausible lexical conditioning of -Z absence (which is far lower in his case than in Mrs. Queen's). His data were discussed in a follow-up paper to this one, presented at the eleventh NWAVE colloquium, held in Washington, D.C., October 21-23, 1982.

[28]Compare the following figures for dem vs. dey as third plural subject pronouns in the Guyanese speech of Reefer: dem (115), dey (34).

[29]There are ten apparently clear cases of third-present, however, all involving generics/habituals. Of these, only one case has a final -Z, and it is, interestingly, one of the two tokens before a vowel. The remaining preconsonantal and final cases all lack -Z, providing additional evidence for the favoring effect of a following vowel on inflected -Z.

[30]Mrs. Queen's possessive pronouns, however, show more evidence of morphological case marking, the only exceptions being you and dey, which can be treated as cases of r-deletion: my (17) / me (0), your (0) / you (2), his (3) / he (4), her (2) / she or he (0), our (1) / we (1), der (0) / dey (3).

On the Status of Gullah on the Sea Islands

Patricia Jones-Jackson

Gullah, also called Geechee, is the language of African-Americans residing on the offshore islands of Georgia and South Carolina.[1] Some linguists, such as DeCamp, believe that the language is dead or dying, precipitated by the influx of outside social forces: "Gullah, once widely spoken in Georgia, South Carolina, and the nearby Sea Islands, is now nearly extinct on the mainland and becoming rare on the islands" (1971:17). After more than seven years of study in the area, this writer agrees with residents of the islands, teachers, and administrators who feel that the language is endangered, but certainly not dead. The objectives of this paper are to discuss factors contributing to the continued growth and development of a variety of contemporary Gullah and to describe one class of features that is waging a strong battle to survive against standard English.

Demographic History

The Sea Islands were the home of Indians before Europeans came to this country; thus, the region is characterized by such names as Wadmalaw, Sampit, Santee, Yamassee, Pee Dee, Waccamaw, Yacamaw, and others. After the forced migration of the Yamassee and other Indians, the islands became the home of African slaves, ex-slaves, and their free ancestors (Christophersen 1976).

Few Europeans inhabited the islands during the era of the slave trade because of the heat and the threat of malaria, and few descendants of Europeans are permanent residents of the more secluded islands today. Federal census figures for the Sea Islands areas have historically shown high concentrations of African and African-American populations. The federal census for 1880, for example, showed that Charleston County, which includes many of the Sea Islands, contained 30,922 whites and 71,868 blacks. In 1940, the Sea Islands communities still maintained a majority black population. The federal census for 1940 for Johns Island showed that of its 3,534 residents, 2,623 were black. For Wadmalaw Island, the census showed that of the 1,607 inhabitants, only 251 were white.

The black to white ratio of Charleston County and the surrounding Sea Islands remained fairly stable until the 1930s. The Berkeley Charleston Dorchester (BCD) Council of Governments reported in 1979 that from 1930 to 1970 Charleston County had a 145 percent growth in population, between 1970 and 1978 adding approximately 4,200 persons per year. Much of the population growth was a consequence of industrialization and commercialization, brought on by bridges connecting many of the Sea Islands to the coast. This change, in turn, led to the development of exclusive resort areas, such as Kiawah and Seabrook islands. Most immigration to the areas since 1930 has been by whites. The 1970 census indicated that blacks were only 31.4 percent of the population of Charleston County, as opposed to more than 50 percent in 1930.

While this distribution reflects a major change in racial composition, especially in Charleston County during the last 100 or more years, the social structure of the Sea Islands is somewhat obscured by these figures. For example, only a few of the Sea Islands are experiencing major shifts in population and industrialization, and these are not the remote and economically distressed areas. Unemployment and population lags seem to be related to the distance and poor accessibility of an island from the mainland. Islands such as James and Johns in South Carolina are connected with bridges and paved roadways, providing excellent access to and from the Charleston area, and they are experiencing more population growth than other islands in the area. For example, whereas blacks comprised approximately 80 percent of the population of Johns Island Township in 1940, only 41 percent of the island residents were black in 1970 (BCD Council of Governments 1979).

The remote islands, such as Wadmalaw and Edisto, have not shown any significant population changes. The 1980 BCD Council of Governments Report on Less Economically Developed Areas in Charleston County reveals that Edisto Island has historically had a slow population growth with little in- or outmigration. The report estimated that the 1980 census would reveal a population of 1,120, which would be a decrease from the 1,374 reported in 1970. Edisto's population remains predominantly black (81%).

The 1980 BCD Report also shows Wadmalaw Island to be sparsely settled. Approximately 43 square miles in area and situated between Johns and Edisto islands, it is rural and, like Edisto, has had very little in- or outmigration in its history. Eighty-five percent of its native-born inhabitants are black. While 30 percent of the housing is occupied by owners, Wadmalaw's economic and demographic characteristics are such that the island is ranked second in the region in terms of economic distress. It has no water or sewer services, and its only corporation is Metal Trades, which provides services primarily for ship repair. Most of the inhabitants are laborers, farmers, and fishermen, though an increasing number of people have returned home to the island to work in professional capacities, rather than find employment, more convenient modes of transportation, and residence in the cities.

The demographic information suggests that remote islands such as Wadmalaw and Edisto will remain immune to most outside social forces. Likewise, other islands, such as Yonges, St. Helena, Daufuskie, and Sandy, show that the influx of whites is not precipitating a deterioration of the traditional social and racial composition of the remote Sea Islands communities. Census projections for the area through 1995 indicate that little population change and few (if any) industrial changes will occur, except on the islands closest to the shore. If these projections for the social and racial environment are true, it is unlikely that acculturating forces will greatly modify the language and culture of the remote Sea Islands communities in the near future.

Methodology

The fieldwork for this paper was more than seven years of research, primarily on Wadmalaw Island, South Carolina. The corpus included twenty speakers from the island, ranging in age from ten to ninety-six years (see table 1). The use of third person singular pronouns for each speaker was surveyed to test the hypothesis that contemporary Gullah speakers still maintain an unspecified system for differentiating gender. Nine consultants were selected from the twenty, on the basis of such factors as range of pronouns used, length of speech sample, interaction within the community, and, of course, willingness to tolerate the investigator.[2] The consultants were asked questions designed to elicit specific, lengthy responses concerning their mother, father, sisters, and brothers, as well as neutral subjects such as the ocean, since the islanders love fishing and netting.

The Gullah-speaking community still adheres very closely to the concept of the extended family. Thus active older members of the family are the heads of the household until they can no longer perform that function. The older consultants in this survey lived in the community, had children in their care or around them on a daily basis, and thus had ample opportunities to pass the language on to the younger generations.

Table 1   Consultants

Consultant	Approximate Age	Sex	Status in Community*
2	96	M	2
3	65	M	1
4	76	F	3
5	45	M	1
6	66	M	1
8	68	M	2
10	70	F	2
23	68	F	2
24	65	M	1

*1. Very active, 2. Active, 3. Not very active

Pronoun Variants

Gullah is in a state of flux on the Sea Islands, and a number of variants are used within a community (see Cunningham 1970). The pronominal survey was therefore designed to determine which variants were used most frequently. Such a determination would reveal the contemporary status of Gullah pronouns in relation to English pronouns. The variants are shown in figure 1 and their frequency of occurrence is shown in table 2.

Nominative   Possessive

Masculine i hi ɪt   Masculine i hi hɪm hɪz
Feminine i hi həɪ ʃi   Feminine i hi ʃi hɪz həɪ
Neuter i hi ɪt   Neuter i

Objective

Masculine əm ɪt hɪm
Feminine əm ʃi həɪ
Neuter əm i ɪt

Figure 1   Gullah Third Person Singular Pronoun Variants

It is interesting that the Nichols 1976 study, though undertaken on a different island in Georgetown County, revealed similar variants for contemporary Gullah speakers.

Table 2 Third Person Pronouns with Variants

Pronouns			Usage of Forms								
Person	Gender	Case	Basilect		PreMesolect		Mesolect		Acrolect		Total
			Form	%	Form	%	Form	%	Form	%	Occurrences
3rd	Fem	Nom	ɪm	0.0	i	55.2	hi	16.4	ʃi	28.4	67
3rd	Mas	Obj	əm	71.5	i	4.5	ɪm	21.0	hɪm	3.0	61
3rd	Fem	Obj	əm	74.2	i	3.2	ʃi	12.9	haɪ	9.7	31
3rd	Mas	Pos	ɪm	13.8	i	62.1	iz	20.7	hɪz	3.4	29
3rd	Fem	Pos	ɪm	0.0	i	83.8	ʃi	16.2	haɪ	0.0	6
3rd	Mas	Nom	ɪm	3.6			i	77.6	hi	18.8	165
3rd	Neu	Nom	ɪm	13.2			i	84.2	ɪt	2.6	38
3rd	Neu	Obj	əm	96.0			i	2.0	ɪt	2.0	51

Fem = Feminine　　　　Nom = Nominative
Mas = Masculine　　　Obj = Objective
Neu = Neuter　　　　　Pos = Possessive

Table 2 shows the distribution and frequency of each pronoun variant for the speakers surveyed. It is necessary to provide a category for those forms which appear without aspiration, such as /i/ and /hi/, because valuable information concerning language change may be lost if they are treated otherwise. For example, the /hi/ variant shows up, under primary stress, as a feminine referent, as in My mother, he was in church, which suggests that /i/ and /hi/ may be more than just phonological variants.

The findings for the group are interesting. Some English pronouns are largely absent, and among these are the feminine pronoun her, the subject and object pronoun it, and the whole category of possessive case pronouns, such as her, his, its, and others.[3] In a more recent survey (1980), these same pronouns were found to be infrequent in the speech of school-age children.[4] For example, observe in the following excerpt from a speech sample from a sixteen-year-old schoolgirl how standard masculine pronouns are used to refer to her mother.

Mae stay home all day . . . and that's all /i/ do . . . when we come home from school /i/ play like /i/ don wash two piece of clothes out and play like him don wash all day . . . /hi/ de say /im/ done wash. /i/ don't wash nothing . . . (laughs) . . . get big stick at we, run we in wood (laughs).

Of the 67 times the Gullah speakers in the survey used a third person feminine pronoun in the nominative case, the form e, /i/, was selected 37 times, she, /ʃi/ 19 times, and he 11 times. Speakers who alternated between e and he for feminine references (these forms are also used for masculine references) seldom, if ever, used she. This is significant because such usage shows that these speakers do not formally distinguish between masculine and feminine gender with separate pronouns such as he and she, as speakers of American English do.

In speech, there is no confusion when gender is unspecified in certain contexts. When a female is the subject of a conversation, /i/, e or he, is often used as an appositive to specify the previously named person. This is illustrated in the historical account The Storm of 1883 (Jones-Jackson 1978a), where the speaker says "My mother, he was in church." Later in the same narrative, the speaker is consistent in using English masculine pronouns to refer to his mother. Note the following:

Me ma, he was in church . . . just after Yatta get home, I call me ma Yatta. He name Liza. But then, ha! you know, I raise up with the old people then when the mother was call so in so. I can't bring that up now. I call em /əm/ Yatta. Well he get home a little before the old man.

While she is heard less frequently than e or he in contempo-

rary Gullah, it is most often used as a substitute for her, a pronoun usually absent in Gullah. Her is rare in the nominative case,
and even rarer in the possessive and objective cases.

Characteristically in contemporary Gullah, one hears she substituted in syntactic positions where standard English usage would
require her. An interesting fact is that speakers who use the
English feminine pronouns she and her, as opposed to the unspecified creole /i/, e, use them to refer to males as well. Such usage
shows that Gullah speakers are waging a strong linguistic battle to
maintain the grammatical structure of their creole system.

While they are indeed acquiring English pronouns, they are
adapting them into a system of unspecified gender, as is characteristic of creole language and languages of Africa and Asia,
whence many creole languages are derived. Thus one hears masculine pronouns used to refer to females and, in rare cases, vice
versa. Furthermore, when an English pronoun such as she is acquired to distinguish formally between masculine and feminine
gender, this pronoun is also adapted to fit the existing creole
grammar, and is often used without regard to nominative, possessive, or objective case. Note the following:

Did you know she? Well she bin kill sheself. (Gullah)

Did you know her? Well she killed herself. (English)

Like most languages, Gullah is constantly changing, but because of rapid commercialization on the islands, better educational
facilities, and the resulting superimposition of standard English,
Gullah is changing more rapidly than most languages that follow a
normal language life. Given the pressure now exerted on the Sea
Islands inhabitants to learn standard English, that some speakers
use she and her for males as well as females is an expected stage
in the change from Gullah to English. In Gullah, one pronoun can
perform a range of functions in a number of syntactic positions,
including reference to males or females. This is characteristic of
the system of unspecified gender of Atlantic Creoles and their
African parent languages, such as Igbo, Yoruba, Ibebio, and Efik.

In addition to her, other English pronouns appear to be almost
nonexistent in contemporary Sea Islands speech. Some of these
include the English nominative and objective it, as well as the
possessive case pronouns its, hers, and his. However, few of these
pronouns appear in the speech of the consultants for this study.
The Gullah pronouns e and em, /əm/, replace standard English it 97
percent of the time that a neuter pronoun is needed in subject
position, as in The rain e de come, "It is raining." The same data
reveal that em, /əm/, the historical creole marker, is substituted
for the pronoun it in the objective case 96 percent of the time
that it would be expected in American English. There is a 2 percent occurrence of /i/ and 2 percent of /ɪt/. Note the following

examples:

> E miss em clean. (Gullah)

> He missed it completely. (English)

> E know em, but e can't call em. (Gullah)

> She knows it, but she can't remember it. (English)

In a 1980 survey, Jones-Jackson found that some speakers apparently had no rule for the use of standard English it. In sentences where the pronoun would be expected, it consistently failed to appear, as in the following example.

> So, my daddy say, "Well, I got to take this boy to the hospital." I say, "Papa, look a here! Well, that hospital, why, I mean something what the horse eat and they call em /əm/ bittle?" He say, "Yeah." And I didn't know no better until later on. Say, he was a hospital. I thought he was the same food my grandmother used to say. Cause she always call me, "Come on boy and get your bittle."

Taken in context, most English readers can make sense of the excerpt even without the English pronouns marking the objective and nominative cases. Most probably, it is for this reason (that the standard English neuter pronoun it is not necessary for making oneself understood) that it is slow to be acquired by Gullah speakers today, even under outside social pressures.

It is important to note that the objective case pronoun em, /əm/, appears frequently in Gullah and should not be confused with, or thought to be a contracted form of, either them or him. As Bickerton 1973 points out with regard to Guyanese Creole, a language similar to Gullah, any etymological connection between English him or them and V-em is questionable because em has no preaspirated allomorphs like him, his, or her. In Gullah, these pronouns often occur without aspiration, thus producing /im/, /iz/, and /ər/. The objective case pronoun em, /əm/, is a morpheme in itself and has no other variant. It does not contract to produce 'em, a variant of English him or them, and semantically the words are different.

Observe, in the following excerpt from Ber Rabbit and Ber Partridge Kill a Cow, how them and em are completely opposite in meaning. In a narrative on stealing, the speaker says a man's cow was stolen:

> Thief the man cow and kill em. (Gullah)

> Stole the man's cow and killed it. (English)

Rendered in English, this story will lead readers to understand that at least more than one cow has been stolen, if em is interpreted as a contracted form of them. In Gullah and other creole languages, em is not a contracted form, and it is substituted and understood as any of the objective case pronouns her, him, them, or it. The exact gender and the number of em are usually signaled by the context or other markers within the sentence. For example, when this investigator asked "Can anybody see ghosts?" one consultant answered, using em as a plural marker:

No everybody can't see em (them). But if you got feeling you can see em (them). The Soul and The Spirit (from Jones-Jackson 1978a)

Another category of pronouns that is missing in contemporary Gullah is the possessive case. This category was excluded from Nichols 1976 because of their infrequency in her data. It is probable, however, that if pronouns such as her and it do not appear in the nominative or objective cases, they will not appear in the possessive or genitive case. Not only are feminine possessive pronouns such as her or hers rare, but the masculine pronoun his is also rare. This is not to say that possession is not marked in Gullah; it is marked, but the speakers appear to avoid constructions in which English possessive pronouns must be used. They either use the creole pronoun e for masculine, feminine, and neuter (sometimes she for feminine) or they substitute, in place of his, hers, and its, the definite article the, either alone or in conjunc- tion with the word own (the own), as in The own husband ben shoot she, "Her own husband shot her" (see Cunningham 1970 for more de- tailed variation).

The wife aint de home. (Gullah)
My wife is not home.   (English)

E hurt e foot. (Gullah)
It hurt its foot. (English, meaning dependent on context)
She hurt her foot.
He hurt his foot.

She can cook she own.   (Gullah)
She can cook her own (hers).[5] (English)

Conclusion

The pronominal features outlined here are recognized as characteristic of creole languages, but not as characteristic of inland black speakers or speakers of other varieties of American English.

The demographic data show that native-born African-American inhabitants remain in the majority in the Sea Islands, and even with television and better educational facilities, a variety of contemporary Gullah speech remains the language of the home and the language of familiarity. While Gullah may be in danger of becoming extinct, it is safe to say that, at the present time, certain pronominal features of contemporary Gullah are holding their own against English.

NOTES

[1]This paper is an excerpt from a forthcoming book on Gullah. The research resulted from approximately seven years of study on the Sea Islands and in Africa. The project was funded in part by Howard University Faculty Development Grants and by an award from the National Endowment for the Humanities.

[2]"Consultant" is used instead of the traditional "informant" because it is a more positive term for the people who help us with our work.

[3]It is interesting that plural pronouns, such as us and our, are also infrequent in Gullah. We is still the primary pronoun used to mark first person plural subject and object, as in:

      This is we book.   (Gullah)
      This is our book.   (English)

      Come, go for hunt crab with we. (Gullah)
      Come, go to hunt crab with us. (English)

[4]The data are yet to be completed with the children. However, this account was taken in July 1980 from a 16-year-old girl who was angry with her mother.

[5]I am grateful to John Rickford for commenting on portions of this paper. Any misrepresentations, of course, are my own.

Prepositions in Black and White
English of Coastal South Carolina

Patricia C. Nichols

The language experience in South Carolina is well worth scholarly attention. From the beginning of the first successful European settlement in 1670, the colony was multilingual; it almost certainly had as much linguistic diversity as the new nation as a whole. Because certain portions of the state have been isolated from much mainstream activity until very recently, it provides an opportunity to study reflections of its early language situation as well as processes of contemporary language change.

For understanding the speech of the Southeastern United States, the speech of South Carolina is especially important, since many of her early settlers and their children formed the nucleus of later settlements in Georgia, Alabama, and Mississippi. The prosperous plantation system, based on the slave labor of West Africans, spread throughout the South, accompanied by speech patterns established in the Carolina colony. These patterns grew out of language contact between settlers and indentured servants from all parts of the British Isles, Germany, Switzerland, and France, and slaves from the Windward and Leeward coasts of West Africa, the Bight of Biafra, and Angola. Today, the lowlands and the highlands of South Carolina still retain faint echoes of the first languages of these Europeans and Africans, as well as many river and place names given by the first native North Americans.

For addressing one part of the complex interaction between the various linguistic groups, the Waccamaw Neck, between the cities of Myrtle Beach and Georgetown, provides an area long isolated from the rest of the state and an area which has sustained speech communities from the beginning of colonization (see map). In this spit of land between the Waccamaw River and the Atlantic Ocean, we find many reminders of the native Americans who once fished and hunted there. In addition to place names like Santee, Winyah, Waccamaw, and Wampee, these early inhabitants left traces of their time in the arrowheads and pieces of flint which small boys now find in abundance as they follow the tractors at planting time. None of the descendants of the original native Americans now live on the Neck. They have been replaced by two major ethnic groups that have occupied the Neck for almost 200 years: blacks of West African descent and whites of North European descent.

The black and white speech communities of the Waccamaw Neck have maintained separate social institutions and distinctive speech patterns since the area was settled by colonizers during the eighteenth century. Until the rapid development of the resort industry around Myrtle Beach following World War II, portions of the Neck were accessible only by water; the river and the ocean were the major highways. The first paved highway on the Neck was not built until 1935; a bridge to Georgetown was not completed until 1939. Older residents of the inland town of Marion tell of two-day journeys to the coast in their youth, over sandy roads and on ferries through the swamps. In this isolation, separate speech communities of blacks and whites grew up in the Upper and the Lower Waccamaw Neck.

Blacks came to the Lower Neck as chattel. They were bought and sold in the markets of Charleston, or sometimes in the ports of West Africa and brought directly to Georgetown, to work as laborers in the increasingly prosperous rice fields between river and ocean. By the mid-1700s, the West Africans far outnumbered their European masters in the region where this labor-intensive crop flourished. Wood 1974, a study of black life and cultural backgrounds in colonial South Carolina, maintains that the slaves from West Africa were highly valued and deliberately chosen for their knowledge of this subtropical crop. Though widely grown in the regions of present-day Gambia and Senegal, along the Central Niger Delta, and along the Gold Coast, rice was a crop about which most Europeans knew little. The tidewaters of the Waccamaw and the rich swamplands of coastal South Carolina were uniquely suited to one type of rice cultivation, if sufficient labor and expert knowledge of its culture were available. According to Wood, West African slaves provided both. More recently, D. C. Littlefield has uncovered evidence that South Carolina planters preferred slaves from the rice-growing region of Gambia, even though they imported more Angolas (1981:21). From an analysis of runaway slave records in South Carolina, Littlefield further concludes that a large proportion of Ibo women from the Bight of Biafra were imported to the state (1981:143-45). This recent study suggests that captives from Senegambia, Angola, and the Bight of Biafra made up the bulk of South Carolina's black population, and a large porportion of Gold Coast slaves went to Jamaica. Work on these locations is of potential importance in tracing the African-language backgrounds of colonial blacks in South Carolina.

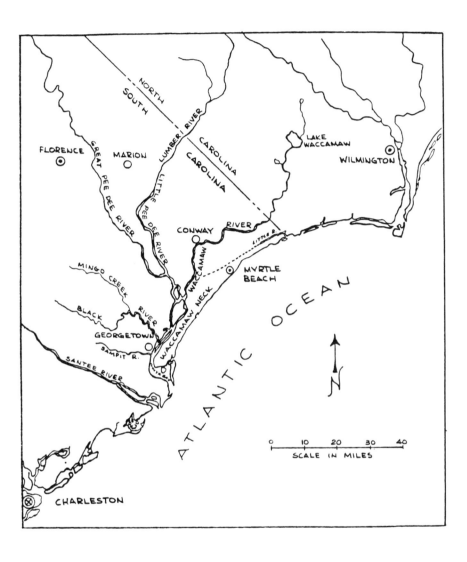

Coastal South Carolina (Northern Portion)
(Map drawn by Frank H. Nichols, Jr.)

Most whites came to the Upper Waccamaw Neck as small
farmers. Just outside the prosperous rice-growing area, this section also had rich farmland; lacking the extensive tidal flow of the
Lower Neck, it was better suited to cotton and, later, tobacco.
Rice was grown on a small scale, and older residents remember the
good taste of home-grown rice, but few large plantations existed
in this section. Most of these farmers came to the Upper Neck in
response to offers of free land and sometimes even tools and pro-
visions. As the frontier area of the colony in the late 1700s, land
of the Upper Waccamaw Neck was offered to "poor Protestants" of
Europe in return for their providing balance to the increasingly
black population of the colony and a buffer against the ever-
present threat of Indian uprisings.

Most of these settlers seem to have been of Scotch-Irish origin,[1] though some came up the coast from older French Huguenot
settlements in Georgetown and Charleston. The county of Horry,
where Myrtle Beach is located, was named for one of these Hugue-
nots, who fought in the Revolutionary War with another famous
French Huguenot, Francis Marion. A few German families were in
their number. Some of these settlers came south from sparsely
settled North Carolina; others came north from the more crowded
territory along the southern coast of South Carolina; still others
came from colonies farther to the north or directly from Europe.

The original, unsuccessful settlement of what is now Conway
contained a Presbyterian church founded by Scotch-Irish settlers,
with an early record of preaching in 1734 (Quattlebaum 1954).
Poor drainage and soil delayed development of this portion of the
Carolina colony, however. What is now Horry County did not split
off from the old Georgetown District until 1785.

Some 200 years after the original settlements were established, today's population distribution in the Waccamaw Neck
reflects the original settlement pattern: whites of European descent own small farms and have developed the beachfront in the
upper part of the Neck, while blacks inhabit much of the lower
part. Many blacks now own small parcels of the land which was
worked by their African ancestors as bondsmen and bondswomen.
The folklore, music, and speech patterns of the two parts of the
Neck preserve some distinctions and reflect some assimilation
between the two cultural groups, as Joyner has documented in his
work on South Carolina music and on Waccamaw Neck slave folk-
life (1971, 1984).

Language of the Waccamaw Neck

Seven years ago I began a systematic study of a black speech
community of the Lower Waccamaw Neck, and five years ago a
comparative study of a white speech community in the Upper Neck.
These communities have existed for some 200 years along the Wac-

camaw River, about 15 miles apart as the crow flies. On the Lower Neck, the original West Africans, who far outnumbered Europeans on the plantations, probably spoke either an African-English pidgin as their second language or the English Creole Gullah, which developed from an earlier pidgin (Nichols 1981a). Turner documented a number of African vocabulary items still in use in the Gullah spoken along the coast of South Carolina and Georgia as late as the 1930s (1949). Also in the 1930s, on the Lower Neck, Chandler collected narratives from ex-slaves (for the Federal Writers' Project) that contain evidence that Gullah syntax was still widely used (Rawick 1972, 1978, 1979).

Cunningham provides an analysis of the grammar of Gullah as spoken on Sea Islands to the south of Georgetown (1970), and several other linguists provide descriptions of portions of its phonology, syntax, and use in specific social situations (Rickford 1975, Nichols 1976, 1981a, Stewart 1977, Jones-Jackson 1978a, Hancock forthcoming). Today, many older speakers of the Lower Neck use some of the old creole features in social settings; middle-age and younger speakers use relatively few of them in interaction with outsiders, but far more within the home and community setting. Very young children, often cared for by the very old, use creole speech patterns until they begin formal schooling. Most speakers show a wide range of language use, which varies between the creole and the regional standard variety of English.

Elsewhere I have compared certain aspects of the verbal and pronominal systems of the two speech communities (Nichols 1981b, 1981c). I have reported that important differences between the black and white communities remain in the tense marking for strong or irregular verbs, while older white speakers sometimes show earlier English dialect forms for the same verbs in past tense. The verb bring, for example, will have the form bring as past tense for many black speakers, but brung as past tense for some white speakers. Significant differences in the pronominal system also show up for black and white speakers. Many black speakers do not make gender distinctions for third person singular pronouns; a single form, ee, can indicate either "he," "she," or "it." Many black speakers make a distinction, on the other hand, between subject and object forms of the third person neuter pronouns, a distinction not made in any contemporary dialect or at any historical stage in English. For such speakers, ee is used for subject "it," while um is used for object. Many white speakers retain the older English form hit (which has a continuous history from Old English) for subject "it," and some retain it for object as well. This form is almost never heard in the speech of blacks in the Lower Neck.

For comparisons of black and white speech, I have chosen morphosyntactic forms, such as past tense marking in the strong verbs and realization of the neuter singular pronouns, because they are, first of all, relatively free from phonological problems. The vowel change maintained for the strong verbs in standard English is easier to perceive than the regular past tense formation, which is conditioned by the phonological environment. The absence of this vowel change is equally easy to perceive. Similarly, the difference between the standard form it for neuter pronoun and the variants ee [ɪ] and um [əm] or hit [hɪt] are also relatively easy to perceive. Second, by choosing to study widely different forms from both the verbal and nominal portions of the grammar, I have been able to conclude that differences between the two speech communities are not just incidental but reflect fundamental or deep differences at the syntactic level.

This paper presents yet a third morphosyntactic difference between the two communities, one somewhat more complicated than the other two. It provides further evidence that, while both groups are moving toward a regional standard English, they are moving toward this target from different grammatical bases and along slightly different paths. These communities, because of their long isolation and different linguistic origins, provide a case study of language change in progress, and may serve as an illustration of similar changes which took place earlier, in less isolated circumstances, for black and white speakers of the Southern United States.

The portion of the grammar under examination here is the part of the prepositional system which indicates the location "position at" for the following nominal. In standard English, at is the preposition which performs this function. It can indicate either spatial or temporal relationships, as in the following examples:

John is at his office.

I'll pick you up at three o'clock.

For nonstandard speakers in both the white and black communities of the Waccamaw Neck there is alternation between the forms to and at for the meaning "position at." Black speakers sometimes use the null [∅] form, particularly before temporal static locatives. White and black speakers both use the null form before a spatial locative like home.

Table 1 shows the prepositional forms used for this category for male and female speakers of three different age groups (15-25, 25-65, 65-90) in both communities. These speakers were recorded in home interviews which lasted from 20 to 90 minutes each. The interviews were analyzed for presence and absence of the forms in positions where one would expect to find at in standard English. The absence of either form was noted because previous analyses of such morphosyntactic features had indicated that the null form often occurs at a transition stage for speakers who are moving from creole or nonstandard language varieties to a more standard variety (Nichols 1976). I have divided the speakers into "lects,"

Table 1
Static-Locative Preposition at in Black and White Speech
of the Waccamaw Neck, South Carolina

B = Black	o = old	M = Male	1 = at
W = White	m = middle-aged	F = Female	2 = Ø
	y = young		3 = to

Speaker

Speaker				
1B - oF			3	Lect I
13B - yF			3	
2B - oF		123		
5B - oF		123		Lect II
6B - oF		123		
8B - oM		123		
3B - oM		13		
4B - oM		13		
7B - oM		13		
11B - mM		13		Lect III
12B - mM		13		
15B - yM		13		
20W - oM		13		
21W - oM		13		
22W - oM		13		
23W - oF		13		
24W - oF		13		
9B - mF	1			
10B - mF	12 *			
14B - yF	1			
16B - yM	1			Lect IV
25W - mM	1			
26W - mM	1			
27W - mF	1			
28W - mF	1			
29W - yF	1			
30W - yF	1			
31W - yM	1			
32W - yM	1			

*Deviation.

groups of speakers who show similar usage of the variant to, Ø, or
at to mean "position at." Lect I shows two speakers using to categorically, as in examples 1-2:

Speaker 1B -oF:
1. I born to Clifton ("I was born at Clifton").

Speaker 13B -yF:
2. Some of um stay to the schoolhouse.

Lect II shows variable usage between to, ∅, and at, as in examples 3-10:

Speaker 2B -oF:
3. But now she duh work now to Brookgreen.
   "But now she is working at Brookgreen."
4. They been right there where you got at the river.
5. You ain't know where they make um at.
6. They be home 0 four clock.

Speaker 8B -oM:
7. I used to work down there to Waverly Mill.
8. Don't hardly salt um down--cure um ∅ home--at home no more now.
9. It wouldn't burn but so much at a time no way.
10. I just work for one place; I had work ∅ Conway Lumber Company.

Lect III shows the usage of the variants to and at by almost an equal number of black and white speakers. Speakers from the two communities appear to share the same usage for this lect; I argue (below) that they arrive at this similar usage via very different paths. Examples 11-18 show these variants:

Speaker 3B -oM:
11. He live down there to the All Saints Church.
12. He used to preach down there at the All Saints Church.

Speaker 4B -oM:
13. He used to stay up there to Woodville.
14. You'll see one of he daughter at Mary Village right there.

Speaker 20W -oM:
15. And they had one down there to Klondike, they called it, down there at Port Harrelson.
16. He'd go to the camp I's at.

Speaker 23W -oF:
17. He had the--had somebody to farm and him work to the sawmill down at Enterprise part the time.
18. They had a lot houses at Enterprise at that time.

Lect IV shows categorical use of at by young and middle-age blacks and whites. There are twice as many whites as blacks who share this Lect. Examples 19-22 show this usage:

Speaker 14B -yF:
19. My mother fears me driving on the water; even at day she does this.
20. I feel like if I'm not out there already, like at the club or something, I'm not gonna go out there after nine o'clock.

Speaker 29W -yM:
21. At the time they had a little small landing down at Peachtree.
22. Mr. Wilson's the one that give um the land to put the landing in at the end of the road, to get the highway paved.

Two of the examples are more adverbial than prepositional uses of at (examples 5 and 16). I have included them because they may be transitional features of Lects II and III, for speakers who show categorical use of neither to nor at. Further study may show that speakers who are moving from categorical to to categorical at make use of this adverbial at at the transitional stage (the evidence on this point is inconclusive as yet). There is evidence, from Turner's texts of Gullah (1949), collected during the first half of this century, that Gullah speakers at an earlier stage than the present study used to categorically to mean "position at," except for precisely the adverbial use of example 5. Turner's only examples of the variant at are of this kind.

I propose that Gullah earlier had only the preposition to to indicate both "movement toward" and "position at," as part of a basic set of six locative prepositions like that in figure 1. This set of six compares with the nine used for the same semantic space by standard English and with the single preposition used by West African Pidgin English (WAPE). Further discussion of these locatives is provided by Agheyisi 1971 for West African Pidgin English, Traugott 1974 for pidgin and creole locatives and markedness theory, and Nichols 1976 for Gullah.

While the West African Pidgin English spoken in contemporary Nigeria is not the most likely precursor of the creole Gullah, we may posit that a Pidgin English, similar to it, was. The use of a single preposition, fo, by such a pidgin to express all the meanings indicated by the nine locative prepositions of standard English is typical of a pidgin language. As the pidgin develops into a creole and acquires native speakers in a setting like that of the early colony of Carolina, the lexicon expands in a fashion similar to that of contemporary Gullah, which has six locative prepositions for this semantic category (Cunningham 1970, Nichols 1981a) The

	Dimension							
Direction	0-3	0-1	1-2	2-3	0-1	1-2	2-3	
Positive		to	on	in	at	on	in	
					to	onto	into	
	fo							
Negative		from	off	out	from	off	out	of
	Pidgin WAPE	Creole Gullah			Standard English			

Figure 1   Locative Prepositions in West African Pidgin
English, Gullah, and Standard English (from Nichols 1976:68)

black community of the Waccamaw Neck contains speakers who use
to categorically, as we would expect speakers of the creole Gullah
to do. It also contains speakers who use to and at and ∅ variably,
as well as to and at variably. Some speakers also use the standard
English at categorically, as we might expect in this community,
which has undergone recent social change associated with jobs and
education.

Lect III contains a number of white speakers who use to and at
variably. Because of the different linguistic histories of the two
communities, however, we might ask if assigning white and black
speakers who show this usage to the same lect is justified. On the
surface, their use of these morphosyntactic forms is the same. The
speakers of the white community, however, appear never to have
passed through the stages represented by Lects I and II. The variation between to and at to mean "position at" dates back at least
to A. D. 925 for some English dialects, according to the Oxford
English Dictionary. The early colonial settlers from northern England and Scotland probably came to the Upper Waccamaw Neck
using these forms variably in the eighteenth century.

Virginia McDavid, in a valuable survey of the records of the
Linguistic Atlas of the United States and Canada on the use of to
as a preposition of simple location (1963), finds that to is widely
used with proper names and place names all along the Atlantic
Coast and, sporadically, throughout South Carolina, North Carolina, and Georgia, as well as in New England, New York State, and
Pennsylvania--all early settlement areas. Since only about 3 percent of the atlas records for the Middle and South Atlantic states
(LAMSAS) are of black speakers, we must treat the atlas data for
South Carolina as primarily that of white speakers. We can, however, posit that such usage throughout this region by many white
speakers may have been reinforced and prolonged by use of the

creole to in the speech of blacks who formed the majority of the
population in the old plantation belt.

Wolfram and Christian have studied the contemporary speech
of similar white speakers (in two counties in West Virginia) who
retain many older British dialect features. Although they do not
give quantitative data, they list (1976:127-28) at as the form
typically used in dynamic locative constructions, such as:

I just go at my uncle's and fool around.

They find some deletion or null forms in constructions, such as:

I lived Coal City. (Pp. 127-28)

They find little or no contemporary use of to as a preposition of
static location in that section of the country, whose original settlers were of similar background to those of the Upper Waccamaw Neck. Their findings give additional support to my suggestion that the widespread use of the creole to by the black speech
community of the Waccamaw Neck may have reinforced the continued use of British dialect to for the white speech community in
this part of coastal South Carolina. Though similar, white and
black usage in Lect III has important historical and community
differences.

If we observed only isolated black and white speakers in the
Waccamaw Neck, without systematically examining the range of
usage in their communities, we might conclude that black and
white speakers are identical in their use of this preposition. Only
open-ended interviews which include all ages of the adult community and both sexes in fairly natural conversational settings can
show the full range of variation characteristic of these speech
communities. Older speakers in both communities tend to show the
variation between to and at, while the young and middle-aged are
moving toward the categorical use of standard at. Only black
speakers, however, have any categorical use of to and any variable
use of the null form [∅] for temporal-static locatives. There are
slight differences in male and female use of these variants, but
there are no conclusive trends.

I suggest that the different patterns of usage for the black
and white speech communities, as well as the coming together in
Lects III and IV, reflect ongoing processes of linguistic change--
processes which may have gotten under way in similar fashion, but
much earlier, in other parts of the Southern United States settled
by people of similar social and linguistic backgrounds. In less isolated areas, black and white speech communities whose language
was different from standard English may have had earlier opportunities and incentives to adopt the forms of standard English. In
the two communities of the Waccamaw Neck, segregated housing
patterns along racial lines were still the norm when I began my

study in 1974. Young adults, however, began to attend nonsegre-
gated schools in the 1970s, and far different social contacts have
been the norm for this generation than for their parents and
grandparents. Jobs have become increasingly less segregated for
middle-age adults in the two communities, as adults in both groups
moved from subsistence farming to the construction and seasonal
jobs associated with the tourist industry of the Grand Strand.
Where a dynamic social situation exists, as has been the case for
both communities since World War II, it is not surprising to find
the dynamic processes of linguistic change at work. What is happening for both groups' use of the static locative preposition is
only one small portion of the ongoing linguistic change.

NOTE

[1]According to Stephenson 1971, "Scotch-Irish" is the American name given to these settlers, while "Ulster-Scots" is the Irish
name. Mostly Presbyterian by faith, these settlers had lived in
northern Ireland for one or two generations. In the early 1600s,
when the Irish were suppressed under James I, English and Scottish
settlers were "planted" on confiscated lands in Ulster; under Cromwell in the mid-1600s more land was confiscated. The settlers
typically did not own the land they farmed in Ulster, and when
English trade policies severely depressed the Irish farm economy in
the late 1600s and absentee landlords raised rents to a level few
could bear, such settlers were receptive to the generous offer of
land in the Carolina colony.

While many immigrants went to other American colonies in the
early 1700s, many more came after the famine years in Ireland,
later in the century, and both groups of settlers ended up in South
Carolina in large numbers. One scholar gives them credit for
doubling the colony's white population: "Scotch-Irish immigrants,
both from Ireland and, more particularly, from North Carolina and
Virginia have been given, with German immigrants, the credit for
being mainly responsible for the doubling of South Carolina's white
population to 70,000 in the period between 1763 and 1775" (Dickson 1966:56). They came as settlers, fully able to pay their own
passage, to take up the offer of free land in the new colony; as
indentured servants, who sold their labor for a number of years in
return for their passage; and as convicts, deported from Ireland, to
work as servants in the colony (Dickson 1966, Smith 1961).

On the Classification of
Afro-Seminole Creole

Ian Hancock

The language of the Afro-Seminoles is an English-related creole, the origins of which go back 400 years to the West Coast of Africa. Afro-Seminole Creole (usually called [sɪmɪ'noːl] by its speakers) is spoken today by fewer than 500 people in communities in Oklahoma, Texas, and northern Mexico, who also speak English (in Oklahoma and Texas) and Spanish (in Texas and Mexico). It is giving way to the latter languages and may not survive until the end of the present century.

Most of the speakers in Texas were born in the closed environment of the Fort Clark Indian Reservation, and since 1917 their families have been living in the town of Brackettville in close contact with other Americans. Few people younger than about fifty are fluent in the language. In Oklahoma it survives even more tenuously among some families along the Canadian River (several miles south of Wewoka), in Seminole County, and among others along Salt Creek (west of Okmulgee) in Okmulgee County. Because of the strong sense of independence among the Afro-Seminoles and because of their earlier geographical and cultural isolation from the larger society, however, their language has preserved far more of its original character than has Sea Islands Creole of the Atlantic seaboard, from which Afro-Seminole separated over two centuries ago.

The process of creolization, which has produced Afro-Seminole (and many related languages spoken elsewhere), is a linguistic phenomenon whereby a new language is born out of the coming together of speakers who cannot initially communicate because they have no language in common. Such a contact situation is traditionally described as resulting in a mixture of two languages, called a pidgin, though in fact there is no verifiable instance of a pidgin resulting from contact between only two languages, and the "mixed" nature of such languages must also be questioned. The contact which ultimately produced Afro-Seminole was between

British sailors and West Africans on the Upper Guinea Coast.

Although every language has its own grammatical rules, which produce surface structures different from those of any other language, at a more fundamental level all languages share some of their characteristics. There is no language which does not have nouns, for instance. When groups of speakers, such as the European seamen and the Africans already mentioned, found themselves together and had to communicate, it seems that the structural features shared by the different languages fell together to form a kind of "lowest common denominator" grammatical base. Such a base is so elementary, however, that it must become more elaborate before it can begin to be the framework for a "full" language, and the brain generates new rules in order to expand this base.

Significantly, such initially reduced languages have gone on to expand themselves into full languages in very similar ways wherever they have developed anywhere in the world--a property of creolization which has become central to the research currently dealing with the origin and acquisition of language generally. Creoles come into being only when certain social factors are present (Whinnom 1981), and while a stabilized and well-established pidgin might eventually acquire native speakers (the traditional definition of a creole), many pidgins have never done so and have disappeared once their speakers went their separate ways.

In situations where such a language does not die out, but continues to be used and becomes the primary language of new generations within the community, the mechanisms of lexical and grammatical expansion will also continue. If for some reason the lexifier language is removed from the environment, the developing creole will become more innovative and "typically creole" (Sranan, Saramaccan, and Papia Kristang have expanded under such circumstances), and the same factor has helped shape the growth of Guinea Coast Creole English, the protocreole from which the creole component of Afro-Seminole descends.

If the lexifier language and the creole continue to be spoken in the same environment, however, metropolitanization is likely to occur because of linguistic and social pressures. As with creolization, certain social factors must exist for metropolitanization to occur. It is something like a swinging pendulum, although the lexifier the creole moves away from is quite different from the form it moves back toward.

The English which gave rise to Afro-Seminole grew out of many social and regional British dialects, it was nautical, and it was spoken nearly four centuries ago--far removed from modern American English. Sea Islands Creole, which has the same immediate origin as Afro-Seminole, has been spoken alongside English for a long time and is slowly metropolitanizing out of existence. Afro-Seminole is also disappearing, but not because of a shift toward English; it is simply not being transmitted by its almost-all-elderly speakers to the younger generations. And while Sea Islands Creole speakers are aware of speaking English, Creole, or various registers in between, Afro-Seminole speakers make no mistake about what language they are speaking--English or Creole--at any given time.

Afro-Seminole is only one of a large group of related languages spoken today in Africa, North and South America, the Caribbean, and the Pacific Ocean islands, all of which share input from a common earlier ancestor which we may call <u>Guinea Coast Creole English</u>. The latter is no longer spoken, nor do we have extensive records of it, but on the basis of its modern descendants and the historical facts we have gathered, we are to some extent able to reconstruct the circumstances of its origins and even to know what it may have sounded like. To illustrate, the equivalents of the sentence "Where did those women hear that you didn't want to go to John's house with us?" are given here in several members of this group, in English-based impressionistic spelling, in order to show the etymologies more clearly:

Afro-Seminole: Duh wisseh de ooman dem bin yeddy seh hunnuh nuh bin wan' fuh go tuh John House long wid we?

Jamaican: Duh which-pa't de ooman dem ben yerry seh unu no ben wan' fi go a fi John house wid we?

Guyanese: Uh wissie de ooman dem bin herry seh all-you nah bin wan' fu go a John house wid we?

Sierra Leone Krio: Nuh usie de ooman dem bin yerry seh una no bin wan' foh go nuh John ho'se wit we?

Cameroonian: Nuh husie de woman dem bi' hear seh wuna no bi' wan' foh go foh John y'i house witti we?

Suriname Sranan: Nuh usie de ooma' dem ben yerry ta'kee unu no ben wan' fu go nuh a ho'so fu John 'lang o' we?

Pitcairnese (South Pacific): Side 'em ooman bin hear tell y'alli no bin wan' fuh go a house fuh John 'long fuh ucklun?

There are records from 1553 onward of groups of Britishers who went to live on the West African Coast more or less permanently (Hancock 1976:25). Some of them were criminals, some political exiles, and still others were simply attracted to life on the African littoral. Whatever their reasons, these settlers were all male and nearly all between the ages of fifteen and thirty. They are referred to in modern writings as Lançados (Boxer 1969,

Rodney 1970, Nolasco da Silva 1972, Hancock 1972, 1975, 1976, 1980b), a Portuguese word meaning people who were "thrown" from the ships (Portuguese, because the first Lançados, and indeed the first Europeans, to take up residence in Africa were from Portugal). The Lançados in the present situation came from all parts of Britain and spoke a great many different dialects of English. There was as yet no established standard, and of course no media communication. Literacy and schooling were privileges of the wealthy, and contacts with speakers of other dialects were few. Rural life in Britain, even in the early part of the present century, must have differed little from that experienced by villagers in 1600:

> They lived in a small world, my mum and the old lady; a world bounded by an imaginary line which encircled their homes--a line with a radius of about half a mile. The little world that encompassed them was one of . . . the Church and nearly every soul who lived in what was then a mining village. They were married there, and gave birth to their children under the very roofs of their present homes . . . their children were wedded from there, and they themselves were destined to die there [Fletcher 1972:106].

Young men from homes like this, joining a ship in port for the first time, would have presented problems of communication to their new shipmates, and in the course of time they developed a variety of English which they could all understand (Reinecke 1938, Hancock 1976). They did this by retaining those words and constructions they had in common and by discarding whatever extreme dialect features might have hampered communication. This leveling process shares some characteristics with creolization, although the achieved "common denominator" would have differed far less in its structural characteristics from any one of its input dialects than it would have in a truly multilingual situation.

This "leveled" English was further distinguished because it was used onboard ship and, as a result, had an extensive nautical component. Each sailor who spoke this "Ship English" could of course also speak his native regional British dialect, which was drawn upon once the sailors took up residence on the coast. This seems to have taken place between about 1580 and 1630 under circumstances described by Rodney 1970. The Europeans took African wives, and in the lançado-African households they established the Guinea Coast Creole English gradually developed.

This kind of domestic social arrangement was able to continue as long as the Portuguese and the Dutch confined their slaving activities to Lower Guinea and the Congo-Angola coast, and as long as the English purchased their slaves from other Europeans in the West Indies. But when this became too costly, and the English too began taking slaves directly from the African coast, they were no longer welcome in the same way. Englishmen who wanted to live and trade in West Africa had to build castles and forts to protect themselves.

By this time, two or three generations of Afro-Europeans, the first Creoles, had grown up, and their new language and new society had become established. We can guess that the sailors were obliged to continue speaking Ship English, adding to it from their home dialects, because they were no longer at sea, and adjusting it to the speech of their wives (who may have spoken Wolof, or Serer, or Mandinka, or Dyola), who were also learning to speak like their men. The vocabulary of the men's speech supplied the lexical base of the emerging Creole, despite the great discrepancy in numbers between African and European, because creolized English was useful along the coast from settlement to settlement, unlike any single African language. Although universal grammatical structures provided the framework out of which the Creole grew, there was no corresponding universal lexicon; this was based on just one of the input languages.

The phonology of the English spoken by the seventeenth-century sailors has been examined by Matthews 1935 and discussed by Hall (1966:117-21), who was the first to attempt a few sample reconstructions of "Proto-Pidgin-English." This was further examined by Gilman 1976, who arrived at some phonological rules for what he calls "Creole A" (from which the Atlantic anglophone creoles descend) and for which he suggested a few protoform grammatical features.

A Portuguese creole was also spoken along the same coast, descendant forms of which are still spoken there in places. The social background to the Portuguese Lançados has been dealt with by Rodney 1970 and by Nolasco da Silva 1972. While inhabitants of the Afro-European settlements may well have been familiar with both Portuguese and English Creole, only the latter had a domestic social function in English-settled areas and became for its speakers a native language. Africans from outside these communities, who were drawn to them--people called Grumettos or Grumetes in the literature--also acquired a knowledge of Creole and were often eventually absorbed into the Creole population, especially as the number of incoming white settlers decreased. It was the Creoles and Grumettos, too, rather than the Europeans, who tended the slaves held captive on the coast while they awaited shipment, and it was Creole, not English, which these slaves learned to speak. It was essential that they knew some of that language because, whenever possible, slaves who spoke the same African language were kept apart from each other (although the efficacy of this technique has probably been overestimated). Creole was all they had in common.

In the early years of the slave trade, such slaves were kept on the coast for a year (or even longer) before they were transported across the Atlantic--a voyage that could last a further four or five months. This gave the earliest arrivals sufficient time to acquire a knowledge of Creole, and even when the volume and the efficiency of the slave trade increased, so that newly arriving slaves did not have so much time to acquire Creole in Africa, they learned it from other slaves with whom they were put to work in the Americas. Since they also worked with indentured whites--especially in Barbados and North America: bond servants, who were usually Scottish or Irish or Gypsy and spoke their own varieties of regional British English--and since metropolitanization already had an effect on the Creole taken across the Atlantic, it is probably safest to say that Black English--which that speech has become today in the United States and Canada (Dillard 1972:114)--never had a wholly Creole origin.

The opposite view from that of Dillard, Wood, Stewart, Hall, and others, who hold that "the original English of the Negro slaves seems to have been a creolized variety" (Hall 1966:15), has most recently been taken by Schneider (1981:358), who states categorically that

> there is no doubt that a supra-regionally uniform creole language spoken by Black slaves all over the South has never existed, and Black English is derived almost completely from the originally British-English folk speech of the early American colonists.

Because of the geographical isolation of the Sea Islands between Carolina and Florida, because of the continual (and illegal) arrival of Creole-speaking Africans into the area into the late nineteenth century, and because all slaves who arrived on the Atlantic Seaboard were not sent to other parts of the United States, Gullah does not have the same history which has produced black English elsewhere in the country.

Beginnings of Gullah

In this paper, "Gullah" refers to the earlier North American Plantation Creole out of which both Sea Islands Creole and Afro-Seminole Creole have grown. In this respect, my use of the term differs from the established one.

The English took most of their slaves to Barbados, which they settled in 1627, before distributing them to their other colonies. By 1695, well over half of the approximately 2,000 blacks in Carolina (which was founded in 1670) were from Barbados--though after 1698 they were increasingly brought directly from Africa. Carolina originally covered a huge area, which included some of what is today Florida; Georgia was Creek Indian country and considered free territory. When Georgia became a colony (by charter) in 1732, it immediately tried to prohibit slavery, but because of pressure from Carolina it was unsuccessful. Until 1749, Georgia received its slaves from Carolina, but after that date began importing them from other sources. Unlike Carolina, Georgia continued to bring slaves in from the West Indies, and until the importation of West Indian and African slaves was halted in 1770, they arrived from Jamaica, Antigua, Barbados, St. Croix, St. Kitts, St. Martin, St. Vincent, Montserrat, Nevis, Martinique, Guadeloupe, Grenada, and Cuba--a pattern of settlement quite different from that in South Carolina.

It is possible that Barbados, because of its history of settlement, never developed its own dialect of Creole English, or, if it did, it was highly anglicized (Niles 1980). Arguments for existence of a Barbadian Creole have been made by Cassidy 1980a, 1982 and Burrowes 1980. The other islands, however, did have their own creoles, and slaves from Nevis, St. Kitts, and elsewhere must have had little difficulty in communicating with each other on the North American plantations in the 1700s, since these dialects differ inappreciably even today. Gullah appears to have grown out of a leveling of all of these, and of the Leeward Islands dialects in particular. In some respects, this leveling was not unlike the leveling which produced Ship English: Gullah--or rather, its modern descendants--has characteristics that are found in several Caribbean creoles, but isn't exactly like any of them.

Development of Afro-Seminole Creole

During the seventeenth and eighteenth centuries, Florida, bordering Georgia on the south, was Spanish territory. Little love was lost between the English and the Spanish, the latter being happy to offer refuge to Georgian and Carolinian Indians fleeing from British slavery. These runaway Indians were called Cimarrónes in Spanish, a word meaning "fugitives" or "wild ones." (Virgin Islands Dutch Creole, but not Dutch itself, has maroon, "wild" [Magens 1770:6].) The Indians pronounced the Spanish word as cimalón or cimanól; hence the name Seminole.

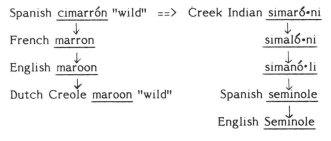

Spanish cimarrón "wild"   ==>   Creek Indian simaró•ni

French marron   simaló•ni

English maroon   simanó•li

Dutch Creole maroon "wild"   Spanish seminole

English Seminole

Although the first Africans in Florida were slaves of the Spanish, British slaves also fled south whenever they could; in fact, they were encouraged to do so by the Spanish. A royal decree from Spain, dated 10th October 1699, promised protection "a todos los desertores negros de los ingléses que huyeron a San Augustin y que se convirtieron al catolicismo" ["to all Negro deserters from the English who fled to Saint Augustine and who became Catholics"]. Porter (1971:164) writes of two Spaniards who were caught in Georgia and imprisoned for enticing slaves to leave Carolina and go to Florida.

The maroon slaves, however, did not generally ally themselves closely with the Indians, although some did, especially in the later years, when aggression from across the border became more severe. "As late as 1774, blacks were apparently not living among the Seminole [Indians]" (Littlefield 1977:5).

The migration of blacks into Florida ceased by the mid-1760s. "Spanish power in Florida, moribund for a score of years, had been extinguished . . . the British were at last in control and runaway Negroes from South Carolina and Georgia could no longer find refuge under the walls of St. Augustine" (Porter 1971:171). Thus these black maroons, the Afro-Seminoles, were finding refuge in Florida between about 1690 and 1760. That they were probably all from Georgia and that most Georgian slaves were West Indian, rather than directly African, supports the hypothesized Caribbean origin for Gullah.

By 1819, Florida had become part of the United States. With the importation of slaves now made illegal, Florida came to be seen as a likely source of slaves, and troops were sent in from time to time to try to capture the renegade Afro-Seminoles. These attempts were not successful, and in 1816 the United States government had made a final effort to destroy the Afro-Seminole settlements. This started a period of fighting which caused so much loss of life on both sides that a decision was made to relocate the black and Indian Seminoles farther west, which took until 1837 (after two Seminole wars and a great deal of killing). In that year, a group of Seminoles resettled in Indian Territory (now Oklahoma), but this was not far from the border with Arkansas, a slave state, and continual slave raids upon their settlement made life miserable.

In the first half of the nineteenth century, groups of Seminoles left Florida for other places as well. Some left for the Bahamas, some reportedly for Cuba, and others were invited to live with the Cherokee. Still others decided to remain in Florida.

In 1849, some of the Oklahoma settlers applied to the Mexican government for permission to go to live in Mexico, possibly because they felt more at home in a Spanish-speaking environment (Johnson 1980). Those who left Oklahoma and settled in Coahuila were nearly all black. Except for one family, the Indian Seminoles who had left decided to turn back before they crossed the Mexican border near Eagle Pass. About 300 Afro-Seminoles settled in Musquíz, and soon moved a few miles away, to El Nacimiento.

In Mexico, they met another Gullah-speaking group that was

already there: the Black Creek, who until 1837 had been part of the general Afro-Seminole population in Florida. In that year, General Jessup had captured 80 prisoners of war. They had been taken by Georgian Creek mercenaries, who had been promised they could keep them as slaves--a tactic employed to ensure their cooperation. Jessup reneged on this promise and gave the Creeks $20 apiece for the Afro-Seminole captives, debating whether to send them to the colony of Liberia in Africa or to Indian Territory out West. He finally decided upon the latter because it was less expensive. Unlike the other group, which left Florida by boat at the mouth of the Mississippi, the Black Creeks were marched overland to the Oklahoma Territory, and left there for Mexico in 1843. (Today, the Brackettville community remains aware of which families are "Seminole" and which are "Creek," but is apparently less aware that both groups are essentially the same, separated for only thirteen years of their common history.)

In 1870, the U.S. government asked the Mexican government if the Seminoles, with their reputation as fighters, could help the U.S. Army drive the Plains Indians out of southwestern Texas so that settlement there would be safer for whites. The Seminoles agreed and garrisoned themselves in Fort Duncan and Fort Clark (in Eagle Pass and Brackettville respectively). They were successful, and they continued to serve the United States until 1914, when they were discharged (Warrior 1982, McCright 1981). For three years more they lived on their own reservation, on the grounds of Fort Clark, but this was taken from them, and since 1917 they have lived across the highway in Brackettville. Some returned to Nacimiento, but only about five families live in that community now, on widely separated ranches. Others have gone to live in neighboring towns, such as Ozona, Del Rio, and San Antonio, and still others have moved farther away, to New York, St. Louis, and California. Everyone, however, makes an effort to return to Brackettville, especially at New Year's.

Descendants of the Oklahoma Afro-Seminoles who did not move to Mexico in 1849 lost communication with the Texas and Mexico groups after separation, but this was reestablished in 1981 (Tijerina 1981) when a number of people from Wewoka attended the Brackettville Juneteenth celebration.

The Seminoles were never informed of their rights as American Indians, and their attempts to be included on the Seminole Register and to obtain land of their own were ignored. The dispute over Florida land-sale reparation is still proceeding in Oklahoma, where the Bureau of Indian Affairs is reluctant to include the Afro-Seminoles in the general Seminole Indian population and, consequently, is withholding several million dollars from them.

Afro-Seminole Migrations

(Numbers refer to map on opposite page.)
1. Carolina, founded in 1670, extended much farther south then. Georgia was founded in 1732, but relied upon Carolina as a source of slaves until 1749, when it began to import them from the Caribbean.
2. The city of St. Augustine was a haven of refuge for runaway Africans from British North America (Deagan 1983). The Spanish officially offered them protection in 1699, though probably to serve as a "buffer" between Spanish and English territory, rather than from any humanitarian motive.
3. From 1818 until the mid-nineteenth century, numbers of Afro-Seminoles took residence on Andros Island in the Bahamas (Porter 1945, Goggin 1946). Their descendants live there today at Red Bay.
4. In 1816, Fort Nichols, the "Negro Fort," was attacked by the U.S. Army with the help of 500 Upper (Georgian) Creek. The possibility of relocation to Indian Territory began to be discussed at this time.
5. Another group of Afro-Seminoles reportedly landed at Guanabacoa (near Havana), about 1820, but nothing more is known of them.
6. Numbers of Afro-Seminoles and Black Creeks settled for some years in Indian Territory, before some of them moved across Texas to northern Mexico. Their descendants live today in Okfuskee, Seminole, Okmulgee, and Hughes counties in Oklahoma.
7. In 1850, the Afro-Seminoles reached Santa Rosa (now Musquíz), and shortly thereafter moved to El Nacimiento, about 10 miles away. There they were joined by the Black Creek and a few others. The Kickapoo Indians, also relocated from the United States, live in another village, about 5 miles from El Nacimiento.
8. In August 1870, about 100 Afro-Seminoles became army scouts for the U.S. government and were based at Fort Duncan and Fort Clark.

Afro-Seminole and Other Creoles

Changes which have occurred independently in each Creole since their separation from each other must be considered before we can determine the relationship between Afro-Seminole Creole and other members of the same language family. Lack of documentation makes determination problematical, and conclusions must be arrived at on the basis of linguistic and external historical criteria. Where available, early samples of the various Creoles may oblige us to modify conclusions, based on contemporary data. While prepositional na occurs today only in the West African and Surinam groups and in the "spirit language" of Jamaican maroons (Bilby

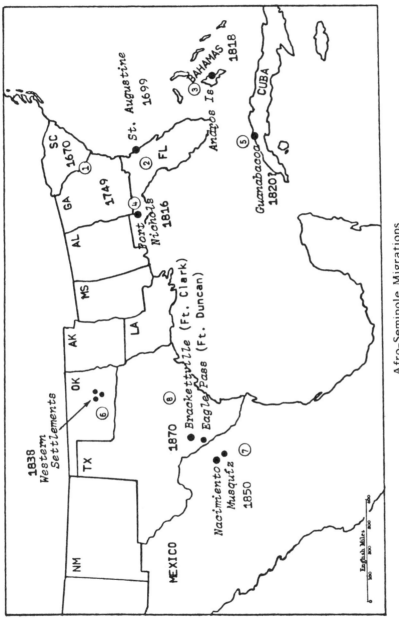

Afro-Seminole Migrations

1983), elsewhere, the corresponding forms are da and a. Na is recorded several times in a text dated 1793 from St. Kitts (Day 1852:II:121-22): a' cum na mi house, "Your run na Basseterre," etc. Similarly, na, with its verbal function, now exists only in West Africa, Suriname, and the maroon spirit language (and in Virgin Islands Creole Dutch). The equivalent forms da and a are used elsewhere; but an Afro-Seminole text, dated 1799 (Kloe 1974:82), includes the line "nusso grandy hungry do you" (cf. Sranan naso gran angri du yu, "That's how great hunger afflicted you").

Afro-Seminole and Sea Islands Creole

Afro-Seminole Creole and Sea Islands Creole share a common origin in an earlier speech, for which the name Gullah is retained here. This dates back to before 1760, when Creole speakers from British territory stopped fleeing south into Florida. The name Gullah (and Geechee) may not have existed at that time, as neither is known to speakers of Afro-Seminole. Also, there is no evidence that there was an unbroken continuum of Gullah from Carolina into north-central Florida, and movement between these areas was dangerous. It may be assumed, therefore, that Sea Islands Creole and Afro-Seminole diverged and began to develop independently no later than that date. Nevertheless, despite over 200 years of separation, the two dialects (or, more accurately, groups of dialects) remain in essence the same thing. Differences are intonational and lexical, and to a far lesser extent grammatical. Recordings of conservative Georgia SIC (such as those made by Stoddard or Reeves from the works of Gonzales) are readily understood in Texas, while more decreolized varieties (e.g., those recorded by Stewart in South Carolina in 1976) were almost completely unintelligible. This may suggest a predictably closer link with Georgian, rather than Carolinian, SIC--apart from factors due to decreolization.

Most of the grammar is shared by ASC and SIC. Differences include:

ASC	SIC
General negation with no Negation with ain't rare	Negation with no becoming obsolete General Negation with ain't
Future marker en (gwen, gwine) No future with go	Future marker go (gwine) No future with en
Negated future with nen	Negated future with ain't gwine

<±Animate> plurals with <u>dem</u>	Animate-only plurals with <u>dem</u>, except in old texts
Comparatives with <u>more</u> + adjective-<u>er</u> + <u>than</u> No comparative with <u>pass</u> or <u>more</u> <u>nor</u>	Comparative with <u>pass</u> recorded, but becoming obsolete; now with (<u>more</u>) + adjective-<u>er</u> + <u>than</u>, or adjective + <u>more</u> <u>nor</u>
No habitual/progressive using <u>does</u>	Habitual/progressive using <u>does</u> becoming more common <u>the</u> more recent the sample
No instrumental construction with pattern <u>take</u> + NP + VP Instrumental <u>with</u> <u>with</u> only	Instrumental construction with pattern <u>take</u> + NP + VP; also with <u>with</u>
Front-focusing with nominals only: <u>dǝ rice e wan' eat</u>	Front-focusing with nominals and verbals: <u>dǝ rice e wan' eat</u>; <u>dǝ tief e tief ǝm</u>

Phonological differences include [šɛm], "saw it," and [kæːm], "take it," in ASC, where SIC also has [šʌm] and [cʌrǝm], as well as [siɛ̃m] (Hopkins 1982:24) and [carǝm] (Turner 1949:251); an unrounded vowel in, for example, [flɒɪ], [krɒɪ], "fly, cry," ASC [flʌɪ], [krʌɪ]; and lack of a bilabial fricative in, for example, ASC [we], [wɪsɛ], "which, where," SIC [ße], [ßɪsʋɪ], etc.

The lack of the bilabial fricative and other West African phonemes, such as [kp], [gb], [c], [ɟ], etc. (Turner 1949:240-48), found in SIC, together with the corresponding lack of African-derived vocabulary, confirms the period of West African influence upon the coastal dialect. Sea Islands Creole contains, via Sierra Leone Krio, a great number of Mende words, expressions, and even a few songs. Mende did not reach the coast, and consequently begin to influence Krio, until after about 1800, so the presence of words from that language in SIC must date from the nineteenth century--long after the split with ASC.

Items shared by Krio and SIC, but not by any other Creole, including ASC, are <u>poŋ</u>, intensifier of distance; <u>dʒadʒa</u>, "to nag"; <u>muskyat</u>, "muskrat"; <u>blan(t)</u>, habitual aspect marker; <u>bumba</u>, "lift up"; <u>sayfa</u>, "ponder"--and possibly <u>noto</u>, prenominal negator (S. E. Stewart 1919:394 has <u>notta me</u>, "not me" [Krio <u>noto mi</u>], although William Stewart has pointed out to me the alternate possibility of this being ultimately <u>no dǝ mi</u>, which would mean "It isn't me." See also SIC <u>yent dǝ mi</u>, "It isn't me.").

Items which are shared by Krio and both ASC/SIC include <u>fambul</u>, "family"; <u>fenč</u>, "fence"; <u>ɔt</u> (ASC <u>hɔč</u>), "to extinguish"; <u>ɛnti</u>, "indeed"; <u>ram</u> as variant of <u>am</u> (third person object pronoun) after certain preceding word-final vowels; <u>wikade</u>, "weekday"; <u>bɔbɔ</u>, "small boy"; kin, "can, be able"; NP + yon, possessive construction; neva, negated completive marker; lilibit, "a little"; papisho, "extravagant behavior," etc.

Afro-Seminole Creole and Caribbean Creoles

Gullah has been linked by writers to the Caribbean for a good many years, back to the time of Herskovits 1936 and beyond. Wood (1974:173-74) writes of an early, though unspecified, Caribbean basis for Gullah, while others, such as Bailey 1966, Lee 1972, and Cassidy 1980a, 1980b, have drawn specific parallels with Jamaican. In an article dealing with what may be the earliest available text in Afro-Seminole Creole, Kloe 1974 in fact refers to it as "Gullah-Jamaican dialect." He and other writers have emphasized Jamaican because several sources are available for that language, including an extensive dictionary, and because very little other than unpublished theses has appeared on the so-called "small island" creoles.

There is reason to link Gullah more closely to the dialects of the Lesser Antilles than to Jamaican, which should be grouped under a separate Western Antillean branch. Cassidy and Le Page (1967:xl-xli) originally argued for a Leeward Islands origin for Jamaican:

> St. Kitts, Nevis and Barbados had been settled since the 1620's, and it is likely that by the 1650's the patterns of Creole speech in these islands had already started to form . . . these colonies continued to supply settlers, and some slaves, for the new colony in Jamaica.

Cassidy (1980a:6) later recanted this position, saying that "the Leeward Islands were too small and too remote to play a strong role"--at the same time developing arguments against my proposals regarding the early linguistic situation in Barbados (Hancock 1969). In a more recent publication on the subject, Cassidy (1980a:8) lists only Barbados and Jamaica as sources of the first slaves brought into Carolina.

Cooper (1979:125-26) has taken issue with Cassidy's position on two grounds:

> First, geographical size could not have been terribly significant in the seventeenth century when settlers and slaves inhabited very limited areas of the land on the different islands. Secondly, even if one granted that geographical size was in fact important, the argument would still prove self-contradictory: the Leewards (taken as a group) are still geographically larger than Barbados. For the sake of consistency, therefore, Cassidy would be obliged to deny, or affirm, the importance of both Barbados and the Lee-

wards, but not one to the exclusion of the other.

Cassidy (1980a:14) places Gullah "in the same line of derivation as Sranan and Jamaican Creole, all three beginning in Barbados and going their separate ways," thus:

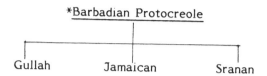

I have elsewhere (Hancock 1980b) given my reasons why I
don't believe this genetic relationship is the true one. Like
Cooper, I believe that the Leewards and Barbados were indeed
important as sources of slaves, but I see only the former as linguistically significant. Le Page and Tabouret-Keller (1985:55) also
conclude that

> the linguistic outcome in Jamaica is clearly distinguishable
> from that in Barbados, and the demography of a commu-
> nity in its formative years is clearly an important factor
> in determining such an outcome. It may be that it is more
> misleading than helpful to speak of a "Creole English" in
> anything more than a minor role in forming the way Bar-
> badians developed their local English dialect.

I do not wish to pursue here the issue of a specifically Barbadian Creole as the progenitor of Gullah. I believe Cassidy is wrong
in suggesting either a Jamaican link (in his earlier writings) or a
Barbadian one (as he has more recently posited); my arguments
against the latter have been presented elsewhere. My arguments
against a Jamaican and for a Lesser Antillean origin are supported
by a number of lexical, phonological, and grammatical characteristics which each shares and, at the same time, cast doubt on a
shared, immediate origin for Jamaican and Lesser Antillean Creole
(which Cassidy represents by Barbadian).

The weakest arguments are lexical. In terms of the Caribbean
(excluding the Bahamas), more shared forms have been found with
Jamaican than with Lesser Antillean; but this cannot be taken as
indicative of more Jamaican influence until an exhaustive study of
Lesser Antillean lexicon has been made. While the Dictionary of
Jamaican English was consulted for items from that language, no
corresponding source is yet available for the other Caribbean
creoles. Also, there is no way to be sure that such words as kaŋki,
"steamed cornmeal pudding," or šiši (-tʌk), "female chatter," were
not at one time also found in Jamaican; but it is significant that
no items have thus far been found in both Gullah and Jamaican

which are not also present in one or more of the Eastern Antillean creoles. Suggestive, but not conclusive, is the preference for certain forms over others; thus Gullah generally prefers lɛf to the commoner Jamaican liːv, "leave," and lɛ wi, "let's," to mek wi. Although some of these are also found in Jamaican, they are less common there. This is also true of certain phonological forms; thus Gullah hənə, second person plural pronoun; fə, preverbal marker; and bin, anterior marker, are closer to Eastern Caribbean (w)ʊnə, fu, and bin than Western Caribbean unu, fɪ, and ben.

Grammatically, Gullah belongs to the go group of creoles, that is, those forming the future construction with go or its derived forms ('o, gwine, gwen, wen, en, etc.). This also occurs in some Western Caribbean creoles, but not in Jamaican (which has wi), except in the periphrastic a guo, "am going to." Use of done in preverbal position is common throughout the Leeward and Windward dialects, but not in Jamaican, although it exists there. Bailey (1962:11) includes both mi don iit and mi iit don, "I have finished eating," but omits discussion of the first possibility in her later grammar (1966). The possessive absolute construction in Gullah makes use of own most commonly, as in the Eastern Caribbean and Krio; elsewhere this is constructed with one, as in Guyana, or with for + NP, as in Suriname, Jamaica, Liberia, and Pitcairn.

SIC: That house is Bee own ("that house is Bee's own").
ASC: Da house de Bee own.
GUY: Da house a Bee one.
SUR: A oso dati na fu Bee.
JAM: Dat house a fi Bee.

Cunningham (1970:41), however, includes one example from SIC which appears to be constructed on the Jamaican model: That house is for Mrs. Washington, which she translates as "That is Mrs. Washington's house"; and Tometro Hopkins informs me (in personal communication) that constructions of the type dat (d)ə for Bee house are not uncommon in the same dialect. These would not be possible with the same interpretation in ASC and may be postseparation acquisitions in SIC.

Taylor 1971, in a brief but important article dealing with linguistic characteristics typical of creolized languages, includes the presence or absence of a particle indicating progressive aspect only or both progressive and habitual. Jamaican, Haitian, and some others indicate habituality by zero; Krio, St. Kitts, Nevis, and some others indicate it with the same particle that is used for progressive aspect. In this respect, Gullah matches Eastern Caribbean, not Jamaican:

Gullah: Ah də go də school   a)   "I am going to school (right now)."

	b)	"I am going to school (these days)."
Jamaican: Mi a guo a skuul	a)	"I am going to school (right now)."
Mi guo a skuul	b)	"I am going to school (these days)."

Similarly, Gullah, like Krio and the Eastern Caribbean creoles--but unlike Jamaican--may use the progressive/habitual to express intended action:

Gullah: Ah də sing fə we chuch	a)	"I'm singing for our church (now)."
	b)	"I'll sing for our church (next week)."

Jamaican: Mi a sing fi wi choch	a)	"I'm singing for our church (now)."
Mi wi sing fi wi choch	b)	"I'll sing for our church (next week)."

Gullah has also introduced a habitual marked by <u>does</u>, found in Guyana, the Windwards, the Leewards, and some of the Western Caribbean creoles, but not Jamaican. Since this is found in SIC only, however, and not ASC, it may represent a recent feature resulting from metropolitanization.

Gullah appears to be most closely related to the creoles of the Eastern Caribbean--in particular, those of the Leeward Islands. It does not seem to be especially close to Jamaican or any other Western Caribbean dialect, nor do its creole characteristics appear to be of Barbadian origin. Further research will allow us to define these relationships more accurately. Although they share a common origin in pre-1760 Gullah--in particular, the varieties spoken in Georgia--modern Sea Islands Creole and Afro-Seminole differ in a number of respects, the most important being the impact of metropolitanization on the former and the nineteenth-century influence upon the same dialect from Krio and other West African anglophone creoles.

The English of the Brandywine Population: A Triracial Isolate in Southern Maryland

Glenn G. Gilbert

The Brandywine population--also called Wesorts, Piscataway Indians, or Creoles--includes about 5,000 people who live primarily in Prince Georges and Charles counties in southeast Maryland, in Baltimore, and in Washington, D.C.[1] The people are of mixed black, Amerindian, and white descent. They are staunchly Catholic, socially isolated, and highly inbred; most probably they represent an old indigenous element dating back to the late seventeenth century in its present location. Before the War Between the States, people of this group were "free people of color" who often owned small parcels of more or less fertile tobacco land and occupied a caste-like position separate from the white slave owners and the black slaves.

The Brandywine people have been studied by anthropologists (Mooney, Speck, W. Gilbert, and Porter, among others), sociologists (Harte and his students), and geneticists (Witkop and his associates and students). Because of the intensive inbreeding over many generations and the apparent introduction at an early date of certain genetically transmitted anomalies (e.g., lop ears, albinism, heart valve defects, Albers-Schenberg disease [a nervous disorder], kidney and pancreas diseases, and others), geneticists have made important contributions to the genetics of human groups in the course of several large-scale investigations of the Brandywine population in the last twenty years. Dentinogenesis imperfecta (a dental defect affecting the enamel) has been documented by Witkop and his associates as more common among the Brandywines than in any other known human group. Albinism is also exceptionally frequent.

Piscataway, an Algonquian language closely related to the Nanticoke and Delaware languages, was spoken by the Indian ancestors of the Brandywine people, but it apparently died out by the beginning of the nineteenth century. Up to that time, the language repertoire of the Brandywine community probably included

Piscataway (only among family and friends?), Creole English (most domains), standard English (school, church, government, outsiders), and Latin (church). Even after Piscataway was largely given up in the family domain, certain individuals seem to have retained a residual knowledge of it, especially in the domain of herbal medicine and healing. The twenty-seventh chief of the Piscataway tribe, Turkey Tayac (Philip Sheridan Proctor), told me, in a tape-recorded interview on March 21, 1978, that he had learned some of the language from his grandmother around the turn of the century.

His obituary (Anonymous 1978a) describes Tayac as having patients "all over the Eastern seaboard" whom he treated with Indian herbal medicine. Just after his tribe acquired a 285-acre tract of land, he is quoted as saying: "All my life, I've wanted a place to teach the Piscataway language to children, Indian ceremonies, herb medicine, nature. That's my plan." Another obituary (Anony- mous 1978b) reports that "Turkey Tayac . . . apparently was the last to speak the Piscataway tongue. Language recordings that he made for the Smithsonian Institution before World War II were given to the Library of Congress and apparently can no longer be located, according to a local Indian historian."

Even though very little is known about Piscataway syntax and lexicon (the main source is a catechism of the seventeenth century), a pamphlet--distributed at Indian Day, July 11, 1981, in Prince Georges County, Maryland (Maryland Indian Heritage Society 1981)--still proposed to teach it to Indians as part of a language revival movement. Thus it is difficult to determine even approximate dates in describing the death of the Piscataway language, if it can indeed be called dead. For many Brandywines, their identification with the Piscataway language is a unifying force, which is more a matter of one's positive attitude toward the language than being able to speak it.

Following Turkey Tayac's observation, in the interview of March 1978, that there are systematic differences among English speakers in Charles County ("I can tell each family by the way they talk"), my initial hypothesis was that since the Brandywine people make up a caste which is separate from both whites and blacks, their English would differ systematically in the survival of creole features which were formerly much more frequent and widespread on the Atlantic Coast. One of two situations could be anticipated:

1. When matched for age, sex, socioeconomic class, and religion, the Brandywines would be intermediate in frequency of creole features[2] when compared to whites and blacks; or

2. The Brandywines would be more conservative even than blacks, both in retaining these features and in their frequency of use. This conservatism would distinguish them from both blacks and whites. (A possible explanation of such a finding would rest in the different model for English and the different process of learning

the English pidgin and creole which may have distinguished African slaves from the free, racially mixed population. An additional, or alternative, explanation would be the Brandywines' social isolation for the last 300 years.)

Exploratory interviews were conducted in March 1978 and March 1981 with eight subjects, yielding approximately 10 hours of tape-recorded speech. The interviews consisted of "directed conversation," eliciting a type of speech corresponding to Labov's Style B: formal interview speech (Labov 1966:90-135). Style A, casual speech, was also obtained, in short passages, when a family member present in the room was addressed or when a topic became "emotionally loaded."

Part of the recorded material is of striking historical and folklore interest, as well as highly revealing linguistically (with respect to the unexpected survival of creole features reminiscent of Gullah or Liberian Creole English). The subjects ranged in age from 18 to 78. Six were female and two male; four were Brandywines, three were black, and one was white. All but the white informant belonged to the working class. All were Catholic.

The remainder of this paper reports the preliminary findings of the linguistic analysis that has been made so far. No definitive answers to the initial research question are as yet available. Nevertheless, there are indications that the Brandywines may be indeed more conservative in retention of creole features than are either blacks or whites. The strikingly frequent deletion of final consonants is reminiscent of Liberian English (personal communication from Ian Hancock). This is no surprise since the Liberian colony was originally called "Maryland," after the place of origin of many of the repatriated slaves. According to William Stewart (personal communication), a dialect geographer, if pressed to place the Brandywines on speech alone, might place them in interior South Carolina or Georgia. The retention of such a wide range and frequency of creole features is surprising both for the relatively northern location of the area and for its proximity to Washington, D.C.

The speech of the Brandywines provides an important insight into the nature of the contact pidgin that was once used among Europeans, Africans, and Indians in the Southern coastal areas (Dillard 1972, 1975; Hancock 1982). It also suggests the value of sociolinguistic studies of other isolate triracial groups on the East Coast, especially in the Lower Chesapeake area (including the peninsulas of eastern Virginia) and in coastal and inland North Carolina. Blu, in her study of the Lumbees of Robeson County, North Carolina, has noted that their speech differs systematically from that of whites and blacks and calls for further linguistic study.[3] Stewart suspects systematic differences among the Brass Ankles of the Charleston, South Carolina, area as well (personal communication). Many other cases can be cited (see W. Gilbert 1956).

Farther to the north, in the Northern Chesapeake region and beyond, there may also have been an English creole, as Dillard (1972:103-14) has suggested. Its relation to Delaware Pidgin English (Thomason 1980) and to Gullah has yet to be determined. Today, the best conservators of this Chesapeake-oriented creole may well be the triracial isolates of mixed descent, not the descendants of the slaves.

The following list of possible creole features is based on a tape-recorded interview with informant JSS, who (with his sister, informant MSP) shows the greatest number and frequency of such features.[4] The other six informants exhibit some or all of these features, but less frequently.

JSS, a Brandywine male, born in 1910, has lived in Charles and southern Prince Georges counties all his life; he is a farmer (tobacco sharecropper) and is Catholic. His appearance is white, with fair complexion; his eyes are gray-blue, and his straight dark-brown hair is now mostly gray. One and a half hours of directed conversation on various folkloric and local-activity topics were tape recorded.

Phonology

1. Simplification of final consonant clusters; devoicing and/or deletion of final consonants (frequent):[5]
   L. 553, [kɔ a dɔ̃ lɔː hɛᵊβələˀ]
   "'course I done lost hell of a lot [of hair]."
   L. 138, [æ̃ hyɛ kɔ̃ᵐ ə doᵖ kə̃ dæ̃ᵘ]
   "And here come a dog come down." (And then a dog came downstairs.)
   L. 530, [lʊæɪ heːⁱ] "Look at his head!"
2. Deletion or aspiration of s̱ preceding a consonant (frequent):
   L. 528, [mɔ́ːtliː] "mostly"
   L. 551, [bɪ́fn̩ɨˢ] "business."
3. Dental affricates [t̪θ, d̪ð] and stops [t̪, d̪], instead of [θ, ð] (frequent).
4. Alternation of the alveo-palatal affricate [ǰ] with the voiced palatal slit fricative [j] (frequent):
   L. 407, [siː dɪshya yʊŋ ǰɛ́n̠ éːṣn̩ ɪᶻ ɔ' deː wɔ̃nduː ɪᶻ leː dæ̃ⁿ ɔl deː]
   "See, this here young generation, is all they want to do is lay down all day."
5. Deletion of word boundaries with unusual and extensive sandhi (frequent):
   L. 523-24, [kɔː yu teːk miː, aᵊwʊɡ́aᵊtɪ̃nᵊpleː ɾə deːædəmáɾəæ̃ noːbədiədnoːmi̥]
   "'Cause you take me, I would go right in E Plata, day after tomorrow, and nobody'd know me."[6] (JSS is talking about his ability to pass as a white in La Plata, county seat of Charles

County. Either he must change his speech, the differences aren't noticed, or the whites he associates with talk the same.)

6. Use of pitch 3 (high) where standard English has pitch 2 (mid) or pitch 1 (low) (frequent):
    [³yú: bɛ́dná˨ b↗ɛ́ŋnə̃n²dɛ́m ²blǽčíln hyə̃³]
    "You better not bring none of them black children here."
    (Talking about his parents' attitudes toward black playmates when he was a child.)

7. Syllable timing (frequent in Style A; infrequent in Style B).
    See the example under 6, above.

Syntax

1. Very frequent deletion of final consonants removes any overt marking of noun plural -s, possessive -s, third person singular present -s, -'s (contracted copula and has), past tense -ed, contracted had, would, have, will, etc.

2. Prominence of aspectual distinctions over tense distinctions in the verb system (especially in Style A).

3. Past completive (?) tEkEn [təkən] (several occurrences):
    #200, And when I tEkEn come home, I met this same girl. (Coming home from a fortune teller who described his future wife to him).
    #258, Once, I tEkEn plant corn.

4. Standard English past tense form of strong verb used in the present (once):
    #432, You come out there and hit a bush couple time, E handle broke, "You come out there an hit a bush a couple of times and the handle breaks." (Talking about the poor quality of handles on today's store-bought axes.)

5. Existential it's (categorical):
    #347, It's a heaven, and a hell, and a purgatory.

6. Complementizer fE (infrequent)
    #471, They wudn't no law fE make Em come there, you know, see you, "There wasn't any law to make them (or him) come there, you know, to see you" (talking about medical doctors' not making home calls when he was young).

7. Zero complementizer (infrequent; see 6 above):
    #267, I had pay [hæpe:] for the labor.[7]

8. Locative into, inE (frequent):
    #121, People couldn't stay into [íntù:] it (a haunted house) and moved out.
    #183, Well, I believe in, uh, inE fortune teller. "Well, I believe in fortune tellers."
    #222, I believe into them people.
    #409, All they want do is . . . get ready for the next day, and be up into a beer joint or a good-time place (talking about the

lazy younger generation).

9. Zero preposition (where standard English has at, of, to, with
   . . .) (frequent). See above.[8]
   #291, He was living over ∅ here Mulberry Grove.
10. In for standard English on, to (infrequent):
    #283, And sent it up here in Baltimore (to Baltimore), 'Bacco
    Growers 'Sociation.
    #332, Well, I went t', uh, in the eighth grade . . . (to the
    eighth grade).
    #392, In, uh, fifth o' November . . . (on the fifth of Novem-
    ber).
11. Indefinite article one, "a, an" (once):
    #126, One man went there fE tE stay all night, "A man . . ."
12. Zero definite article (infrequent):
    #125, And ∅ fellow look around . . . ("And the fellow looked
    around . . .")
13. Nominative personal pronoun, masculine third person singular
    (categorical), feminine third person singular (infrequent), and
    third person plural (several examples) he, ee:
    #203, And ee [ɪː] ("she") said that, uh, she told me that . . .
    #321-325, In our book, church, they wouldn't marry our first
    cousin, two first cousin. The second cousin or third cousin,
    then they marry . . . They, they two first cousin, ee ("they")
    won't marry Em; but now, they marry Em, "In our book,
    church, they [the priests, the officials] wouldn't let us marry
    our first cousin, two first cousins. [If they are] the second
    cousin or third cousin, then they marry . . . [if] they, they are
    two first cousins, they won't marry them; but now, they marry
    them" (talking about the church's former prohibition on first-
    cousin marriages--which seems, by the way, to have been
    largely ineffectual).
    #170 . . . And ee ("they") say, you follow that rainbow to the
    end . . .
14. Nominative and accusative personal pronoun, third person sin-
    gular neuter it [ɪ] or [ɪˀ] (categorical):
    #207, And so, the same thing that the man told me, the for-
    tune teller, it [ɪ] come true. Note: This [ɪ] is usually attached
    to a preceding word, as a suffix, by a sandhi rule.
15. Noun plural marker and them, [ǽdɛ́m] or [ǽdɛ́]:
    #105, I and my father and they [ǽdɛ́ː] ("and the others"?)[9] were
    talking about it. [tɔkɪ̃nbaᵘdɪ] (ɪ),"it," is attached by the sandhi
    to a preceding word; see 14, #207 above.
16. Possessive pronoun with inalienable body parts (once):
    #192, And read the lines in my (the) palm of my hand . . . (a
    fortune teller was reading his palm).

In the study of the phonology is further information on linguistic change in the pronunciation of the dental fricatives [θ,ӡ̆] and
postvocalic r. Koiter 1978 analyzes these phonemes in the speech

of the three subjects recorded in March 1978: Turkey Tayac (83),
MSP (c. 62), and William Tayac (43). Although the three subjects
represent roughly three successive generations, they have led very
different kinds of lives. Nevertheless, they are all members of the
"core" group, related to each other by blood, and share common
attitudes toward the Brandywine group and its relations with
whites and blacks. Postvocalic r is shown by Koiter to be more
affected by greater geographic mobility than [θ,ӡ̌] (see figures 1
and 2).

	Strong Retroflexion	Weak or No Retroflexion
Turkey Tayac (83 years)	28%	72%
MSP (c. 62 years)	18%	82%
William Tayac (43 years)	60%	40%

Figure 1 Postvocalic r Variants for Three Brandywine Subjects
(Source: Koiter 1978)

	Fricative	Affricate or Dental Stop
Turkey Tayac (83 years)	25%	75%
MSP (c. 62 years)	37%	63%
William Tayac (43 years)	49%	51%

Figure 2 Dental Fricative Variants for Three Brandywine Subjects
(Source: Koiter 1978)

It appears that although Turkey Tayac came from a highly
r-less area, he traveled a good deal during his lifetime and has
more retroflexion of postvocalic r than MSP, who stayed in the
"core" Brandywine area. On the other hand, the increased use of
the fricative variants of [θ] and [ӡ̌] seems to be a function of age
rather than geographic mobility. This latter change appears to be
below the level of consciousness; that is, it is largely immune to
stigmatization and conscious correction. Lack of postvocalic r is
more noticeable, stigmatized, and subject to conscious correction.

The original research question concerning the existence and
direction of systematic dialect differences between Brandywines,
whites, and blacks in Charles County has only begun to be addressed in this paper. Further investigation will address this question.[10]

NOTES

[1]This research was carried out under a grant from the American Philosophical Society (Hays 29, 1980), whose support is gratefully acknowledged.

[2]"Creole features" are defined as those aspects of phonology (segmental phonemes and prosody), syntax, and lexicon which are descended from Plantation Creole (Dillard 1972:22, etc.) and are not yet completely decreolized. Some of these features may have a dual origin (British dialects and Plantation Creole), having merged by a process which Herskovits 1941 called European/African syncretism. The research hypothesis deals with the unequal distribution and unequal frequency of occurrence of socially diagnostic features of phonology and syntax for which a Plantation Creole origin is likely. (For a discussion of "socially diagnostic" variation, see Wolfram and Fasold 1974.)

[3]Following Blu's suggestion, Brewer and Reising 1982 clearly show the effect of "covert prestige" (Labov 1966) in Lumbee lexicon and phonology, a phenomenon not unlike what Labov observed in the early 1960s on the island of Martha's Vineyard. Unfortunately, Brewer and Reising have not yet been able to provide a direct comparison with the speech of whites and blacks presently living in Robeson County. Also, they are primarily interested in the social significance of variation in the community, rather than in the historical provenience of the variants. Nevertheless, it seems that the same research questions posed in the Charles County, Maryland, study could be investigated in Robeson County (and vice versa).

[4]The tape recorder was a Sony TC-D5M stereo recorder with two Sony ECM-16 clip-on electret condenser microphones. The tape was TDK SA-C90 chrome-dioxide tape with Dolby B noise reduction. The technical quality of the recording was good, suitable for phonological as well as syntactic and lexical analysis.

Also present during the interview was MSP, the principal informant's sister, who was approximately 65 years old--a nurse's aide at the Charles County hospital in La Plata and widow of a tobacco farmer. Her appearance was Indian, with swarthy skin, dark eyes, and straight black hair. The fourth person in the room was my father, W. Gilbert, an anthropologist. In 1945 he published, in collaboration with Turkey Tayac, the first ethnographic description of the Brandywine population, and he has maintained a continuing interest in this and similar groups in the Eastern United States.

[5]Indications of frequency of occurrence are impressionistic. The examples are for illustrative purposes only. "L." refers to the written line number of the transcription from the tape; # refers to the location on the tape, indicated by the tape counter.

[6]The symbol E represents shwa [ə], a mid-central vowel. When it functions as a hesitation marker in discourse, it is represented

by "uh."

[7]The "zero complementizer" may well alternate with tE, fE tE, and fE. (Cf. 11 #126; 6 #471.) Up to now, however, the zero variant has been observed only in the modal have to; thus it may be a lexical and not a syntactic feature, or it may be the result of a phonological reduction. It is of course very common in Southern speech.

[8]Noted by Wolfram and Christian (1976:127) for Appalachian English as well.

[9]Possibly a hypercorrection of the creole pluralizer -dem. (And them, attached to a [+human] noun, is of course common in many varieties of American English; it may well represent a linguistic syncretism, as discussed in note 2, above.) Holm (1982:9) has noted another kind of hypercorrection of the same creole construction in Gullah and Bahamian English: "Personal names can be followed by and those to indicate the person's relatives, friends, or usual associates. This appears to be a hypercorrection of the creole pluralizer -dem (same position and meaning) by analogy with the demonstrative dem (as in dem people) becoming those."

[10]As this paper was being revised for publication, preliminary results from a second study in Charles County became available. In the first week of January 1982, 29 second graders in four public schools were interviewed and tape recorded. Fourteen students were black, six were Brandywines, and nine were white. Quantification of the results for final consonant cluster simplification and for postvocalic r "deletion" shows that whites simplified (or deleted) the least, blacks the most, and Brandywines showed intermediate values. Analysis of variance indicated the results to be significant beyond the .001 level. Details of this study are forthcoming.

Although these findings seem to support the first alternative hypothesis one (see page 103), many longtime residents claim that older Brandywines (such as JSS) differ markedly in their speech from both blacks and whites. This points to a research procedure which holds socioeconomic class constant but which varies ethnic group and age. In addition to the phonological variants mentioned in this paper, the centralized variants of the diphthong /ai/ may well be socially diagnostic, as in the case in Robeson County, North Carolina.

Lexical Diffusion: Evidence from a Decreolizing Variety of Black English

Fay Boyd Vaughn-Cooke

Supportive evidence for the theory of lexical diffusion has been steadily accumulating from languages throughout the world. So far, evidence has come from Chinese dialectology, English, Dravidian, German, Nootka, Tibetan, Nitinat, Swedish, and Canadian French. This evidence, drawn from historical changes that span generations and, in some cases, centuries, stands in contrast to microchronic evidence from language acquisition studies (Ferguson and Farwell 1975 and Hsieh 1972). The goal of this paper is to test the theory of lexical diffusion further by using data from the intriguing linguistic process of decreolization. Specifically, I show that the concept of lexical diffusion can best account for a phonological change in progress in a decreolizing variety of black English. Before describing the data and methodology, I will review the tenets of the theory of lexical diffusion.

Lexical Diffusion

To account for phonological change in linguistic systems, the theory of lexical diffusion was first advanced by Wang 1969 and later elaborated by Wang and his associates (Chen 1972, Chen and Wang 1975, Wang and Cheng 1970, and Cheng and Wang 1977). According to these investigators, a sound change "spreads itself gradually across the lexicon," operating "on words or groups thereof one after another" (Chen 1972:469). The theory holds that "words change their pronunciations by discrete, perceptible increments (i.e., phonetically abrupt) . . . severally at a time (i.e., lexically gradual) rather than always in a homogeneous block" (Wang and Cheng 1970:553).

Two concepts are fundamental to the theory of lexical diffusion: the temporal and the lexical dimensions of a phonological process. I will first examine the temporal dimension, of which there are two aspects: the internal and the external. The external time dimension concerns the time sequence relation of rules, while the internal time dimension concerns the chronological profile of a single phonological process. For example, the study of this latter aspect involves an examination of the gradual evolution and the expansion or regression of a particular phonological change.

The second dimension is the lexical one. In the words of Chen and Wang, "a phonological rule gradually extends its scope of operation to a larger and larger portion of the lexicon, until all relevant items have been transformed by the process" (1975:256). Chen and Wang note that a phonological innovation can turn out to be completely regular, that is, it can affect all relevant lexical items, given the time to complete its course. They note further that in many cases a phonological rule peters out before all the relevant lexical items undergo change, or that the innovating rule can be thwarted by another rule competing for the same items. This latter notion of competing sound changes provides a very credible way of accounting for exceptions--items which do not change but which belong to the "phonologically definable lexical category" (Hsieh 1972:90) of words which should change. It is the inability of the Neogrammarian view of sound change to account for the exceptions to sound laws (words which should change, but do not) that has motivated the search for the alternative explanation put forth by the lexical diffusionists.

Data and Methodology

As noted earlier, this paper tests the theory of lexical diffusion further with data from black English, a decreolizing dialect. Diachronic and synchronic evidence indicates that this language variety has passed through the stages of pidginization and creolization and that some of its structures are probably undergoing the last stages of decreolization. This last linguistic process, a form of language change, is achieved by introducing marked and complex structures (relative to the structures in the creole) into speakers' grammars. Decreolizing language varieties like black English can provide an exceptional investigative opportunity for students of language change because they represent time that has been greatly compressed by powerful external factors. This compression or shrinkage of time can expose the full cycle of certain changes and allow the analyst to observe, in a relatively short period of time, a complete process of linguistic evolution.

The specific sound change that I attempt to account for within the framework of lexical diffusion is a resyllabification process that is diffusing across the lexicons of three generations of working-class black speakers in Franklin County, Mississippi. Resyllabification, in its most radical form, is a phonological process which increases or decreases the number of syllables in a lexical item. A less radical operation of this process results in the redistribution of syllable segments in a lexical item.

This paper focuses only on that process of resyllabification which expands or reduces the number of syllables in a word. The reduction process is achieved by the deletion of entire syllables, as in <u>invaded</u> being realized as 'vaded, or by the deletion of one of the segments of a syllable, as in <u>believe</u> being realized as /bliv/. The expansion process is achieved by opposite means, that is, entire syllables are added or individual vocalic segments are. inserted after consonants. For example, if historically, 'vaded instead of <u>invaded</u> is the lexical variant for certain speakers, such speakers must add the initial syllable in- in order to resyllabify 'vaded. To resyllabify monosyllabic /bliv/, speakers will have to insert a vowel between the first two consonants of /bliv/. As the examples indicate, both the addition and the insertion increase the number of syllables in a word. Below, I consider the details of the linguistic sample in which resyllabification is operating.

One way to study a linguistic change in progress is to study samples of speech from at least two successive generations of speakers with comparable social characteristics (Labov 1972a). Following this requirement, the primary investigation of resyllabi-fication is based on 40 one-hour tape-recorded samples of sponta-neous conversation from three generations of working-class infor-mants. The generations include speakers in the following age groups: 8-20-year-olds (29 speakers), 40-59-year-olds (6 speakers), and 60-92-year-olds (5 speakers). In keeping with the principles of major sociolinguistic empirical studies (Labov 1972b, Wolfram 1969, Fasold 1972, Baugh 1979), information about the informants' social class, sex, age, level of education, and occupation is viewed as a critical component of the data. The diffusion of the resyllabifica-tion process is systematically affected not only by internal linguis-tic constraints, such as phonological environments, but by powerful external social constraints as well.

This investigation of resyllabification is restricted to those words that have initial or potential initial unstressed syllables. For example, it is concerned with the variants of lexical types like <u>invaded</u>, <u>because</u>, <u>around</u>, and <u>pretend</u>. Lexical items like <u>probably</u>, with noninitial unstressed syllables, can be resyllabified by dele-tion of the unstressed syllables (e.g., resyllabification of <u>probably</u> yields /prabli/) and are excluded from the analysis. The set of lex-ical variants ultimately selected as the focus of this study includes 1,536 occurrences of 101 different lexical items. These items are extracted from the spontaneous conversations of the 40 infor-mants.

The extraction involved recording, for each informant, all words with initial unstressed syllables and their alternate forms without such structures. For example, all occurrences of <u>because</u> and 'cause were recorded. After extraction, all lexical variants were categorized according to the phonological shapes of the ini-

tial unstressed syllables of the marked variant.[1] The categorization yields five groups of variants. These include variants which
have, or with the potential to have, initial V-shaped syllables (e.g.,
across and 'cross), initial VC shaped syllables (e.g., until and 'til),
initial CV1-shaped syllables (e.g., because and 'cause), initial
CV2-shaped syllables (e.g., suppose and 'spose), and initial CCV-
shaped syllables (e.g., pretend and 'tend). The percentage of alternates that contain the initial syllable is calculated for each category within each age group.

Evidence for the Resyllabification Process

Evidence from the Major Categories. The evidence for resyllabification comes from the five groups of alternating variants that
emerged from the categorization process. The first and largest
category of variants is presented in table 1.

Table 1
Lexical Variants Comprising the Category of V Types

about	~ 'bout	especially	~ 'specially
around	~ 'round	emergency	~ 'mergency
along	~ 'long	alive	~ 'live
afraid	~ 'fraid	another	~ 'nother
across	~ 'cross	attending	~ 'tending
enough	~ 'nough	associate	~ 'sociate
imagine	~ 'magine	allowed	~ 'lowed
away	~ 'way	afford	~ 'ford
allow	~ 'low	according	~ 'cording
arithmetic	~ 'rithmetic	America	~ 'merica
appendicitis	~ 'pendicitis	Elizabeth	~ 'lizabeth
agreed	~ 'greed	approve	~ 'prove
attend	~ 'tend	approven	~ 'proven
attention	~ 'tention	eleven	~ 'leven
approved	~ 'proved	occasionally	~ 'casionally
alone	~ 'lone	occasion	~ 'casion
asylum	~ 'sylum	agree	
electric-	~ 'lectric	adjust	
election	~ 'lection	eloped	
appendix	~ 'pendix	accept	
attempt	~ 'tempt	again	
ahead	~ 'head	admit	
eleventh	~ 'leventh	appointed	
appreciate	~ 'preciate	accumulated	
awhile	~ 'while	above	
against	~ 'gainst	imagination	
assignment	~ 'signment	established	

equipment	~	'quipment
elect	~	'lect
elected	~	'lected

Table 1 contains variants with initial unstressed syllables of a V syllabic structure. While most words in this table have alternate forms (e.g., about ~ 'bout, some items never have such alternation. For example, again occurred more than 16 times in the data, but *'gain was never recorded as an alternate form. Consider now the items in table 2.

Table 2
Lexical Variants Comprising the Category of VC Types

until	~	'til	unless	~	'less
expect	~	'spect	excuse	~	'scuse
experience	~	'sperience	exactly	
instead	~	'stead	investigate	
except	~	'cept	extent	
invaded	~	'vaded	unlessen	

Table 2 shows the variants with initial unstressed syllables of a VC syllabic structure. Like the V types, some forms in this category show alternation (e.g., invaded ~ 'vaded), but other forms never do (e.g., exactly).

The third category of items is presented in table 3.

Table 3
Lexical Variants Comprising the CV1 Category

because	~	'cause	divorced	~	'vorced
before	~	'fore	banana	
behind	~	'ahind	beginning	
molasses	~	'lasses	retired	
remember	~	'member	depression	
beside	~	'side	together	
relation	~	'lation	between	
depend	~	'pend	remembered	
become	~	'come	decided	
discrimination	~	'scrimination	potatoes	
participate	~	'ticipate	pertaining	
decide	~	'cide		

This table contains lexical types with initial syllables characterized by the CV1 syllabic structure (the difference between CV1 and CV2 structures is described shortly). As for the V and the VC types, many of these items have variant forms (e.g., <u>molasses</u> ~ '<u>lasses</u>); however, in keeping with a lexicon undergoing change, <u>other</u> items within this cateory (e.g., <u>together</u>) never show any variant forms.

The fourth category of items is displayed below in table 4.

Table 4
Lexical Variants Comprising the CV2 Category

suppose	~	s'pose	believed
believe	~	b'lieve	balloon
belong	~	b'long	supporting
believing			below

Table 4 contains lexical items with initial syllables of a CV2 syllabic structure. This group differs from the items in table 3 because CV1 and CV2 items are resyllabified differently. In the CV1 items, both segments of the initial syllable are involved in the addition or deletion process, while in the CV2 items only one segment is involved. The first segment of the initial syllable in the CV2 items can cluster with the first segment of the second syllable, which produces unmarked variants like /bliv/ and /spoz/. As with the other three categories, some CV2 lexical items never show alternate forms (e.g., <u>below</u>). While this item occurs six times in the data, no examples of *<u>blow</u> are recorded.

Words comprising the final category of lexical items are listed in table 5.

Table 5
Lexical Variants Comprising the CCV Category

pretend ~ pətend ~ 'tend
pretending ~ detending ~ 'tending

This last category of items shows initial unstressed syllable with a CCV shape. While it contains only two lexical items, alternate forms are recorded for both. For example, the unmarked variants '<u>tend</u> and '<u>tending</u> occur in the data.

To summarize, within each of the five categories, some items have alternate forms and some never have such forms. Following the basic premise of the theory of lexical diffusion, I propose that a resyllabification rule is gradually spreading across the lexicons of the black English speakers and correctly resyllabifying those lexical items which fit its structural description. The rule has not begun its operation on some items (e.g., <u>because</u>) for some speakers (oldest and middle-age informants); it operates variably on the great majority of lexical items in the five categories for all speakers; and it operates categorically on some items (e.g., <u>below,</u> <u>together</u>) for some speakers.

This characterization of the rule's operation corresponds exactly with three stages of lexical diffusion through synchronic variation described in Wang 1979. Wang proposes that during a typical sound change words appear in three states: (1) the unchanged state, represented by the archaic variant; (2) the synchronic variable state, represented by alternation between the archaic (e.g., <u>'vaded</u>) and the innovative (e.g., <u>invaded</u>) variants; and (3) the changed state, represented by only innovative variants. As noted above, the lexicons of the informants have words in all three of these states; however, most lexical items that could be affected by the change have synchronic variation.

I will now demonstrate how the resyllabification rule is spreading across the lexical items presented in tables 1 through 4 (the two items in table 5 are not included because the few tokens are not distributed across the three age groups). This is done by first examining the percentage of items that show marked syllabification for all categories of lexical variants at three different periods in time, represented by the three age groups. The relevant percentages appear in table 6.

Table 6
Percentage of Marked Syllabification for the Four
Major Categories of Lexical Variants by Age

	Time Age Groups	T^1 60-92	T^2 40-59	T^3 8-20	Total
V Types					
MS/total		32/201	105/356	135/349	272/906
% MS		15.9	29.4	38.6	30.0
VC Types					
MS/total		0/12	10/24	16/24	26/60
% MS		0	41.6	66.6	43.3
CV1 Types					
MS/total		4/42	42/109	104/167	150/318
% MS		9.5	38.5	62.2	47.1
CV2 Types					
MS/total		7/31	8/53	21/41	36/125
% MS		22.5	15.0	51.2	28.8

At time 1, represented by the speech of the 60-92 age group, table 6 shows that for the V types, only 15.9 percent of this groups' 201 tokens appear as marked forms. At time 2, represented by the speech of the 40-59 age group, 29.4 percent of the V types appear as marked forms. Another increase in the percentage of marked forms occurs at time 3: the 8-20 age group produces the marked syllabification for 38.6 percent of its 349 tokens. Note that the percentages show a steady increase of marked forms over apparent time and, further, that precisely the same pattern occurs for the VC and CV2 types. This pattern is violated only once in table 6, at T^2 for the CV2 types. Unexpectedly, the middle-age speakers produce a lower percentage of marked forms than the old speakers. The percentage for the young speakers, however, conforms to the pattern observed for the other three categories. Their percentages are always higher than those for the middle-age and old speakers.

Analysis of external (social) factors (e.g., level of education,

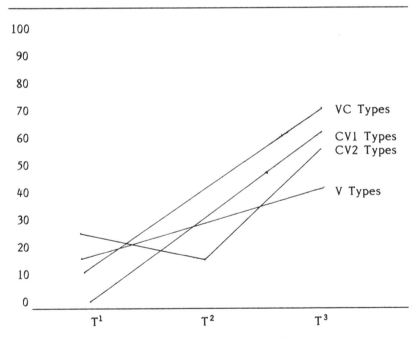

Figure 1 Increase in Marked Syllabification over Time
Across Four Categories of Lexical Items

age, sex, and social class) reveals that the relatively higher level of formal education of the younger speakers plays a major role in stimulating their greater preference for the marked and innovative variants. [2] The consistent rise in marked forms over apparent time for the four types of lexical items is shown in figure 1. The figures in table 6 show another feature worth noting. The total percentages for the four categories of lexical items vary, indicating that, overall, some categories are changing faster than others. VC and CV1 types have higher percentages of marked forms than V and CV2 types. This variation in the overall percentage of marked syllabification by category is shown in figure 2.

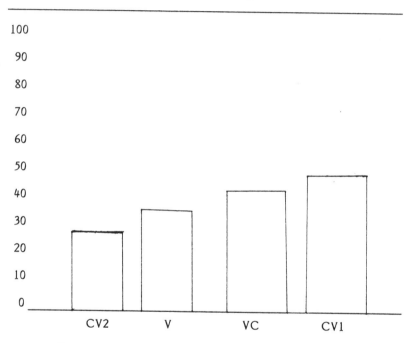

Figure 2   Variation in the Occurrence of Marked
Syllabification for the Four Categories of Lexical Items

Evidence from Words within the Major Categories. Specific lexical items within the four categories have been examined to determine whether the pattern observed in figure 1 is repeated. The illustrative items from the V types provide evidence that the increase in marked variants over time is a striking feature of the data, even at the level of individual words. Consider the frequencies in table 7.

The lexical items in table 7 exhibit a highly regular pattern in the frequency of marked forms. This pattern emerges clearly when the oldest informants are compared with the youngest. Note that a significant rise in marked forms across the two age groups occurs

for every lexical item except <u>again</u>. The percentages for this item
show that only the marked variant occurs for both age groups.

Table 7 Increase in Marked Syllabification over Time
for a Subset of V Types

Time Age Group	T^1 60-92	T^2 40-59	T^3 8-20
Lexical Item			
about ~ 'bout	17/111 15.3%	47/172 27.3%	68/221 30.7%
around ~ 'round	8/38 21.0%	18/79 22.7%	35/77 45.4%
along ~ 'long	0/8 0%	3/10 30%	3/6 50%
across ~ 'cross	0/3 0%	1/8 12.5%	3/8 37.5%
enough ~ 'nough	2/3 66.7%	8/11 72.7%	1/1 100%
away ~ 'way	3/8 37.5%	2/8 25%	12/14 85.7%
another ~ 'nother	2/4 50%	5/6 83.3%	14/14 100%
ago ~ 'go	-- --	9/11 81.8%	2/2 100%
eleven ~ 'leven	0/4 0%	-- --	4/7 57.1%
again	4/4 100%	-- --	8/8 100%

This is strong evidence that <u>again</u> no longer alternates with
*<u>gain</u> and that the use of the marked variant has become categori-
cal for the speakers in the sample. When the older speakers are

compared with the middle-age speakers, substantial increases in the frequency of innovative variants are observed for all words except two, around and away. With respect to around, table 7 shows that the oldest and middle-age speakers have only negligible differences in their percentages of marked variants. For the other item, away, the frequency of marked forms is lower for the middle-age speakers than for the oldest speakers.

Finally, when the youngest speakers are compared with the middle-age speakers, substantial increases in marked variants are recorded for all items except one: about. For this item, table 7 shows only a minimal increase in innovative variants across the two generations. This retention of unmarked forms for the youngest group could be related to the fact that 'bout is not stigmatized in casual speech and that it is used frequently by middle-class speakers.

Further examination of the items in table 7 reveals another notable characteristic: the different rates at which the unmarked variants are transformed into marked variants. Compare, for example, the frequencies across the three age groups for along and

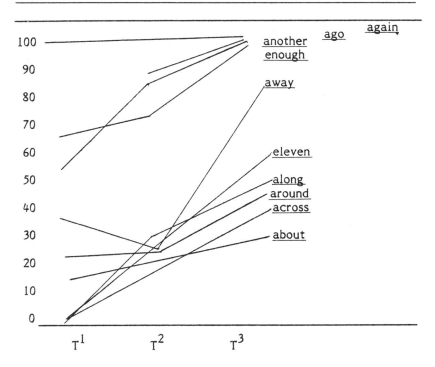

Figure 3 Variation in Transformation to Marked Forms
for a Subset of V Types

another. This latter item shows much higher frequencies of the innovative variants than the former. While both show consistent increases over time, the transformation of 'nother to another is nearer to completion than the transformation of 'long to along. Figure 3 captures the variability in the rate of change for V type items.

Internal Factors Affecting Spread of the Resyllabification Rule

In this section I examine some of the internal factors which affect the spread of the resyllabification rule. The final phonological segment of words which precede the lexical variants in each of the four categories has been inspected to determine whether the percentage of forms having the marked syllabification increases or decreases in a particular phonological environment. I hypothesize that the spread of resyllabification across a particular group of lexical items will be slower if the addition of the initial syllable complicates the syllabic structure. The results of the analysis of the phonological environments which precede V type lexical items support this hypothesis well.

When a vowel precedes the marked variant of a V-type lexical item, the syllabic structure is complicated by the clustering of vocalic segments. The following sentence shows such clustering (the relevant segments are underlined):

105:12, I didn't know what to tell you about it. (V#V)

The informants in the sample strongly object to such clustering by resisting the addition of V-shaped initial syllables in the environment of a preceding vowel. Consider the low frequencies of V addition recorded in table 8.

The percentages in table 8 show that when consonants precede the V types, resyllabification occurs faster for all age groups. The oldest speakers exhibit the characteristic resistance to marked forms, even in the more favorable environment of a preceding consonant. However, as table 8 shows, their output of marked innovative forms is higher than in the less favorable environment of the preceding vowel. A similar comparison can be made for the middle-age and youngest informants. Figure 4 captures the different effects of preceding vocalic and consonantal segments on the resyllabification of V-type lexical items.

Systematically and consistently, consonants and vowels also affect the phonological environments which precede the other three categories of words involved in the change. For a detailed discussion of these effects, see Vaughn-Cooke 1976.

Table 8 Effect of a Preceding Vowel and a Preceding Consonant
on Resyllabification of V Types

Preceding Phonological Environments

Age	V-	C-
60-92		
MS/Total	3/64	29/137
% MS	4.6	21.1
40-59		
MS/Total	15/93	90/263
% MS	16.1	34.2
8-20		
MS/Total	13/70	122/279
% MS	18.5	43.7
Total	31/277	241/679
	13.6	35.4

Historical Aspects of Resyllabification

The central proposal of this paper is that the variety of English spoken by the informants in the sample has undergone the
processes of pidginization and creolization, and that this variety is
presently undergoing what are probably the last stages of decreolization. At this point, it will be helpful to consider some of the
historical evidence that the early forms of black English spoken in
the United States were pidginized and creolized versions of English, characterized by linguistic rules that generate natural structures. The major evidence comes from early literary records which
include examples of black speech. These records include evidence
for rules that generate the unmarked syllabification for multisyl-
labic items. Consider the example recorded by J. F. D. Smith in "A
Tour of the United States of America" (quoted in Dillard 1972:87):

Now, massa, me know me deserve flogging, cause if great
fish did jump into de canoe, he see me asleep and I no
catch him.

Note deletion of the unstressed syllable in because, to yield
the unmarked syllabification 'cause. Other examples of this deletion process are presented in Starnes' "The Slaveholder Abroad"

(quoted in Stewart 1972a). Below are the relevant passages.

>They didn't seem to talk good English talk, nohow; an 'peared like they couldn't adzactly onderstand me. [1972a:69]

>Uncle Cudjer, he looked at his hands, then he drawed back one of um cross his mouth, then he put both of um upon his stomach. [1972a:70]

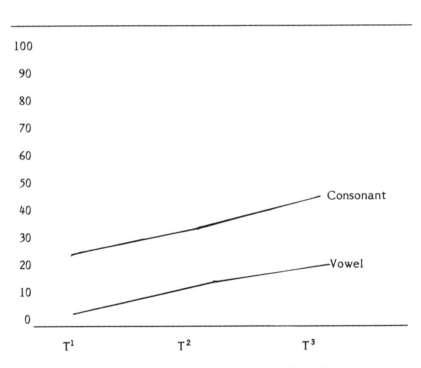

Figure 4 Comparison of Effects of Preceding Consonant and Vowel on Resyllabification of V Types

The underlined items 'peared and 'cross are additional examples of the rule generating the unmarked syllabification for standard English appeared and across. These items exhibit the more marked syllabification characterized by the presence of both the unstressed and stressed syllables.

On the evidence examined so far, and specifically the examples which have been resyllabified, it would seem that the first generations of black English speakers (slaves and their immediate descendants) probably used exclusively a rule generating the unmarked syllabification for the lexical items in tables 1-5. It seems reasonable that the early speakers of black English used a deletion-type syllabification rule resyllabifying the relevant portion of their lexicons by deleting the initial syllables of items like those in Tables 1, 2, 3, and 5, and by deleting the second members of the initial syllables of items, like those in table 4. The resyllabification of the oldest group of speakers strongly supports this proposal. Eighty-five percent of their lexicon shows the unmarked syllabification.

At this point we should note that two resyllabification rules have operated in the history of black English. The early and natural rule began during the pidginization process. The rule's input consisted of standard English lexical items exhibiting the marked syllabification, and its output was the unmarked variants without the initial unstressed syllable. In accordance with the creole hypothesis, I propose that the unmarked variants used by the pidgin speakers were acquired by the immediately succeeding generations; therefore, these variants were part of the lexicon of their first language.

In keeping with the Creole hypothesis, I propose further that use of the pidgin as a mother tongue marked the beginning of creolization. During creolization, the natural syllabification rule generating unmarked forms was passed on to later generations of speakers. But, as I have argued, the data from our oldest informants provides evidence for a second syllabification rule. The job of this unnatural, context-sensitive rule was to reverse the effects of creolization. Its input consisted of the unmarked creole forms, like 'bout, 'cause, and 'cross (mentioned above), and its output was the marked variants, about, because, and across.

Table 9 shows that for the oldest speakers in the sample, only

Table 9 Percentage of Forms Showing Marked Syllabification for Three Generations of Working-Class Black Speakers

Age	60-92	40-59	8-20
Initial Syllables Present/Total	43/286	165/542	276/581
% Present	15.0	30.4	47.5

15 percent of their 186 unmarked variants have been transformed

by the innovative, late syllabification rule. The limited operation of this rule for the members of the oldest generation strongly suggests that their parents, or the generation which preceded them, did not use the late rule at all. If such is the case, the low output of marked forms for the speakers over age 60 signals the beginning of decreolization and the loss of the earlier natural syllabification rule.

The times at which the two syllabification rules began to operate can be more clearly seen from the outline below. The proposed time frame, 1600-1975, begins with the century during which slaves first came to the United States and ends with the decade in which the data for this study were collected.

Figure 5 is constructed from the outline on table 10 and the frequencies from table 9, which show a consistent increase of marked forms across age groups. It shows the rise of marked sylla-bification as a function of time.

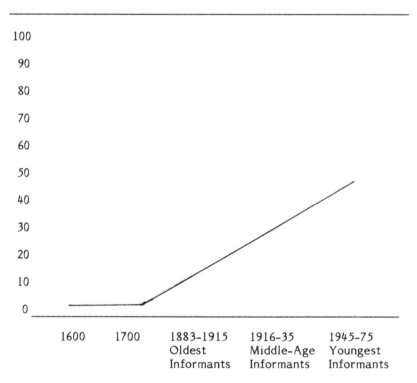

Figure 5 Resyllabification: Increase in Marked Forms
as a Function of Time

Two final issues should be examined. One involves the characterization of resyllabification as a process complicating the phonological systems of the informants, and the other considers some of the ways the present analysis differs from the major variation studies on black English. The former issue will be considered first.

Complexity of the Resyllabification Process

I have proposed that sound change by resyllabification complicates the informants' linguistic systems because structures are being <u>added</u> to the speakers' grammars, and the rule responsible for these additions is a fairly complex one. Let us reconsider what resyllabification involves. A speaker acquiring the resyllabification rule must learn that certain CV-shaped syllables (e.g., <u>re</u>, <u>be</u>) can be added to certain unmarked variants (e.g., '<u>member</u>, '<u>cause</u>) and that certain V-, VC-, and CVC-shaped syllables can be added to specified subsets of unmarked variants. During acquisition of this rule, a speaker might hypothesize that <u>any</u> initial CV-type syllable can be added to any unmarked variant. Such an unconstrained hypothesis could result in resyllabifying an archaic variant with the wrong initial syllable. A number of examples of incorrect resyllabification are observed in the data. Consider the following:

I was /ditɛːnɪn/ I was the clown. (57-1:773)
"I was pretending I was the clown."

They would /pətɛn/ they was monsters. (57-1:308)
"They would pretend they were monsters."

These examples indicate that speaker 57-1 knew that /tɛn/ and its related form /tɛndɪn/ should be preceded by an unstressed syllable. However, her use of /di/ and /pə/ shows that she was not certain, at this stage, <u>which</u> CV syllable should be added.

An example involving another lexical item was recorded for speaker 92:

I can't think of the name of that /kəstɪfɔkɔt/. (92-026)
"I can't think of the name of that certificate."

In this example, the syllable /kəs/ was added, instead of the target syllable /sə/.

Two additional examples, from informants 28-2 and 96-1, were recorded:

He could go to the <u>department</u> with his girl. (28-2:661)
"He could go to the apartment with his girl."
(It is clear from the context that <u>apartment</u> was intended.)

He went /əhaɪn/ the curtain. (96-1:557)
"He went behind the curtain."

These examples, and those recorded for speakers 57-1 and 92, show that sometimes the added initial syllables do not have the same phonological shape as their target counterpart. For example, the initial syllable of apartment is a V-type syllable, but speaker 96-1 added a CV-type syllable. It appears that speakers who add incorrect syllables know the main function of the resyllabification rule. They know that it is supposed to generate initial syllables for a certain set of items in the lexicon, but they have not learned which initial syllables are to be generated for the specific items within the set.

Two examples of incorrect syllable addition, which can be added to the ones cited above, are mentioned by Dillard (1972:249). He notes the use of remorial for "memorial" and revorce for "divorce."

Present Analysis Compared with Other Studies of Black English

The analysis undertaken in this paper differs from some major language variation studies utilizing data from black English. These studies include Labov 1972a, Wolfram 1969, and Fasold 1972. Comparison of these studies with the present study reveals a major difference in analytical goals and the theoretical frameworks employed. In the former studies, synchronic variation, evidenced by alternating linguistic structures, is analyzed within the framework of what is now known as variation theory. A major tenet of this theory is that the ability of speakers to produce alternate forms of linguistic structures should be attributed to their linguistic competence and not to unsystematic performance. Optional rules (a feature of standard generative theory) are eschewed by variation theorists, and the notion of variable rules has been introduced. The latter are formal expressions of a speaker's knowledge of the linguistic and social constraints which affect the frequency of occurrence of alternating linguistic structures.

Unlike the variation studies, arguments regarding the nature of a speaker's competence are not central to my analysis. The present study has sought to demonstrate that observed synchronic variation represents a sound change in progress. To demonstrate this, I have introduced the dimension of time by analyzing a three-generation sample of language within the framework of lexical diffusion, a theory of phonological change.

In my view, the type of analysis described in this paper builds on the work of variation theory and enhances our knowledge of black English and of sound change. Research has revealed that the variable nature of many structures of black English is an outstanding feature of this dialect; however, an explanation for the more

Table 10 Proposed Time Frame Indicating Centuries in Which Natural and Unnatural Resyllabification Rules Began

Time	Process	Rule Operating	Input	Output
1600 (?)	Pidginization	Natural Syllabification	around because about	'round 'cause 'bout
1700 (?)	Creolization			'round, 'bout, and 'cause are monosyllabic members of the lexicon
1800 (?)	Creolization			'round, 'bout, and 'cause become firmly established monnosyllabic members of the lexicon
1800 (?)	Decreolization	Variable operation of unnatural syllabifica- tion rule (late rule)	'round 'cause 'bout	around ~ 'round because ~ 'cause about ~ 'bout
1900	Decreolization	Variable operation of unnatural syllabifica- tion rule		Higher frequencies of occur- rence of around, because, and about
1975	Decreolization	Variable operation of unnatural syllabification rule		Frequencies for around, because, and about continue to increase as evidenced by data from youngest speakers

than average number of fluctuating variants in black English was not systematically presented in the earlier studies. This study provides an explanation for the variation that characterizes the resyllabification process. Following other scholars, I have proposed that such variation is the principal indicator of a sound change in progress. The inability of a study to reveal this fundamental role of variation represents a major shortcoming of its analytical framework.

With regard to sound change, this study has enhanced our knowledge by providing a detailed investigation of a change in a decreolizing variety of language. Since decreolization is a mechanism of linguistc change, a theory of language evolution must be able to account for it. Thus the rich bodies of data from creoles and decreolizing varieties of languages must be utilized as testing grounds for hypotheses about language change. The analysis in this paper is a step in that direction.

NOTES

[1]The Praguean notions, marked and unmarked, are used in a general evaluative sense; thus lexical items which exhibit the initial unstressed syllable (e.g., invaded) are considered marked while their alternate forms, without the unstressed syllable (e.g., 'vaded), are considered unmarked. I propose that the marked syllabification is more complex perceptually than the unmarked one; evidence for this position can be found in the experimental works of Lehiste 1972 and Bond 1971. As the presentation of the details of the resyllabification process will show, the direction of the change in progress in black English is from unmarked to marked; that is, the unmarked variants are the archaic structures while the marked variants are the innovative structures. The introduction and integration of marked structures into a language variety is a principal feature of the general process of decreolization.

[2]For a detailed examination of the effect of external factors on resyllabification, see Vaughn-Cooke 1976.

Durative Marker or Hypercorrection?
The Case of -s in the WPA Ex-Slave Narratives

Jeutonne P. Brewer

Researchers have long noted the presence or absence of the suffix -s in the speech of blacks, and their findings may be classified in four groups:

1. The third person singular present tense -s occurs with all persons in the present tense. The regularized present tense -s forms alternate with unmarked forms. For example, I loves or I love (Harrison 1884).

2. The third person singular form is uninflected; the suffix -s occurs with all other forms in the present tense. For example, he take but I takes (Putnam and O'Hern 1955).

3. The suffix -s is not part of black English grammar. Suffix -s forms, which occur rarely, are examples of hypercorrection or performance errors (Labov et al. 1968; Fasold 1972; Wolfram 1969).

4. The verb -s form indicates habitual or durative aspect, rather than denoting concord or indicating hypercorrection (Scott 1973, Jeremiah 1977).

Many blacks today report that verb -s form still survives, and explain its meaning this way: "If I live in Boone, I may have just moved there. If I lives in Boone, I have lived there for a long time and still live there." This view of the verb -s form in black English, which supports (at least in part) Scott's and Jeremiah's findings, has not been supported in studies of the English of urban blacks, either in Northern cities such as Detroit and New York or in Washington, D.C.

The purpose of this study is to analyze the use of the verbal -s in early black English. The data are taken from interviews with

ex-slaves, collected in the 1930s by the Federal Writer's Project
(FWP) of the Works Progress Administration (WPA).

Analysis of this material shows that the verb -s form in early
black English is not restricted to third person singular subjects in
the present tense. Furthermore, it can occur with any person, but
it is not used as a regularized present tense marker with all persons. The frequent occurrences of -s forms in early black English,
the fact that it is not used as a concord marker, and the fact that
the -s can occur with all persons in the present tense bring us to
the question stated in the title of this paper: Are the -s forms
hypercorrect forms, reflecting a black English speaker's adopting
the standard English third person singular present tense -s, or are
the forms examples of the use of early black English -s as a durative marker? Both functions have been proposed in the literature.
The WPA ex-slave narratives provide an important and quantitatively sufficient source of data with which to try to answer these
questions.

WPA Ex-Slave Narratives

During the 1930s, a massive government relief project, known
as the Federal Writers' Project of the Works Progress Administration, collected reminiscences from ex-slaves about their experiences during slavery. Under the direction of John A. Lomax, the
WPA workers interviewed ex-slaves in 17 states. At the end of the
project, over 2,000 narratives (Yetman 1967) were deposited in 17
volumes in the Library of Congress.

This effort, generally called "The Slave Narratives," provides
the data for this study. These materials, collected about seventy
years after emancipation, reflect the grammar of black speech
from the middle of the nineteenth century and include interviews
from a wide geographical area. Because the ex-slave interviews
were collected before mechanical recording machines were readily
available, WPA interviewers had to write information by hand or
make shorthand notes for later use. Also, the interviews typically
contain only examples of a careful style of speech, rather than a
variety of speech styles characteristic of recent synchronic studies
(Brewer 1973). Even with these limitations in mind, it is well to
remember that these interviews contain the most extensive source
of data available about the speech of blacks a century ago.

The archival materials indicated that the Washington WPA
office was concerned primarily with collecting slave narratives in
the words of the ex-slaves, as true to the then current idiom as
possible. The correspondence of the Washington office, the direc-
tives and questionnaire issued from that office, and the correspondence of the state offices indicate the WPA interviewers tried
to record the words and idiom of the ex-slaves (Brewer 1979,
1980). The data in the interviews demonstrate that the WPA work-

ers recorded examples of such features as invariant be and remote past been, shown to be significant features in sociolinguistic studies of blacks (Fasold 1969, Labov et al. 1968, Labov 1972a, Rickford 1975, Wolfram 1969, 1974).

The Sample

The sample for this study consists of WPA interviews collected in South Carolina and Texas. Photocopied typescripts of these ex-slave narratives were published in Rawick 1972.

On the basis of region (or subregion), age, and sex, I have selected a stratified sample of 69 interviews for each of four age categories: 60-69, 70-79, 80-89, and 90 or older. The typescript narratives include only three interviews with subjects in the 60-69 age group. (I do not include additional interviews in which the subjects related stories of other ex-slaves, but only those in which the subjects related their own experiences.) These three interviews were collected from individuals who were not actually ex-slaves, but were born after emancipation. The Texas interviews of females 90 or older include six interviews, while the 80-89 category contains only four interviews because study of the text of the interviews reveals that the phrase "about 90" was intended to mean "at least 90 or older" rather than "almost 90."

In South Carolina, the WPA interviewers collected two interviews with four ex-slaves (SC 6, 28, 30, 38) and three interviews with one ex-slave (SC 86). The Texas typescript narratives include the one interview for each ex-slave.

Data Extraction and Analysis

Each occurrence of the verbal suffix -s was entered into a file on a TRS-80 microcomputer. In addition to the example in context, items such as the narrative number, a co-occurring adverb and its category, and a coding for grammatical context were typed into the file. The examples were then sorted and searched for instances of -s in relation to grammatical and social factors. Each instance of the absence of the verbal suffix -∅ has been tabulated and analyzed in terms of the number of instances that could have been used with third person singular pronoun subjects. Also, the uses of -s with subjects other than third person singular subjects have been analyzed in relation to these third person singular uses. Only clear examples of present tense uses of the -∅ variant are included in the analysis; -∅ examples occurring with past adverbs in the immediate or limited larger context are excluded from the analysis.

These interviews contain 331 examples of the reported use of the nonconcord verb -s. Almost two-thirds of the ex-slaves inter-

viewed (40 ex-slaves or 63.49% of the sample) used nonconcord -s;
23 of the ex-slaves (36.51%) did not use nonconcord -s. Furthermore, nonconcord -s accounts for half or more of the present
tense examples in 31 narratives.

Analysis of the data will demonstate that the suffix -s is
regularly used with subjects other than the third person in the
present tense, and that it functioned as a grammatical marker in
an earlier period of black English. This different distribution and
function will be compared with the findings in studies of present-
day black English and historical studies of black English grammar
(see table 1).

Table 1
WPA Ex-Slave Narratives
Primary Sample of 63 Narrators

| | Texas | | South Carolina | |
	M	F	M	F
60-69	145	0688	046	
70-79	056 077 067 109 069	029 116 047 122 051	011 036 028 040 034	008 035 018 039 032
80-89	001 014 006 017 013	004 012 011 016	002 010 005 013 009	006 022 012 026 016
90+	002 009 003 015 005	008 030 010 041 026 064	015 082 019 086 073	004 065 030 092 038

Concord of -s

In standard English, the third person singular in the present
tense is marked by the redundant suffix -s. Recent sociolinguistic
studies of present-day black English have demonstrated the characteristic absence of the -s suffix (Labov et al. 1968, Fasold 1972,
Wolfram 1969, 1971). For example, in his study of Southern children of comparable socioeconomic classes, Wolfram 1971 finds that
the white subjects use the suffix -s 85 percent of the time, the
black subjects only 13 percent. The use of -s in the slave narratives is quite different: the suffix -s is regularly used with personal pronoun subjects other than the third person singular. Examples 1 to 10 show the use of -s in the ex-slave narratives:

1. My folks allus belongs to the Calvins and wore their name till after 'mancipation (TX 1:1).[1]

2. I lays in de bunk two days, gittin' over dat whippin' (TX 5:15).

3. I stays with mamma till I get married in 1871 to John. Armstrong, and then we all comes to Houston (TX 8:30).

4. I sits 'round and hurts all de time (TX 14:46).

5. I 'member when I's lil' us goes visit my uncle, Major Scott (TX 47:164).

6. De first time I was married was to Phillis Read . . . and we jes' jumps over de broom (TX 77:272).

7. Dis livin' on liberty is lak young folks livin' on love after they gets married (SC 2:5).

8. My white folks comes to see me pretty often, though they lives way up dere (SC 65:299).

9. You knows it was hard times when dere wasn't no salt to season the vegetables (SC 35:153)

10. Dey never had no ice in dem days as you well knows; but us had a dry well (SC 86C:60, part 2).

Sentences 2 to 4 illustrate the use of -s with the subject I; sentences 3, 5, and 6 with the subject we/us; sentences 7 and 8 with they; and sentences 9 and 10 with you. Plural NP subjects also occur as subjects of verb -s; see sentences 1 and 8. These sentences clearly show that the suffix -s form is not an agreement marker.

In fact, the occurrence of the -s form with non-third person singular subjects is the rule rather than the exception in the ex-slave narratives. As table 2 shows, more than half the examples of -s occur with the subject I. The ex-slaves of both South Carolina and Texas use -s most frequently with I. Third person singular subjects account for almost 15 percent of the -s forms; the ex-slaves from Texas account for most of these uses (53 of 58 uses), while the South Carolina ex-slaves use -s with third person singular subjects very infrequently. The third person plural subject they accounts for 12 percent of the -s forms, the first person plural we, we'uns, or us almost 11 percent, and the second person subject you almost 7 percent.

The figures in table 2 clearly show a pattern of use in which the -s form occurs frequently with subjects other than the third person singular. Further analysis of the data will indicate a distinctive function for suffix -s in early black English.

Analysis of Verb -s

The occurrence of the suffix -s is so frequent in the early black English recorded in the ex-slave narratives that it can be neither ignored nor relegated to performance error. Its use is not

Table 2
Suffix -s Occurrences with Pronoun Subjects

	I N/%	+3rd Sing N/%	You N/%	+1st Plur N/%	They N/%	Total
SC	80/65.04	5/4.06	27/21.95	2/1.63	9/7.32	123
TX	135/50.75	53/19.92	0/0.0	40/15.04	38.14.29	266
Total	215/55.27	58/14.91	27/6.94	42/10.80	47/12.08	389

dependent upon agreement with a third person singular subject. Furthermore, it is necessary to take into account not only the variants -∅ and -s in relation to third person singular subjects, but also all pronoun subjects.

If we take into account only agreement and nonagreement (that is, -s and -∅) with third person singular subjects, we find a pattern similar to that reported in recent studies of black English (Wolfram 1969, 1971, 1974, Fasold 1972). Table 3 shows that for the ex-slaves in both South Carolina and Texas the variant -s with the third person singular pronoun subjects occurs less frequently than the absence of -s, that is, the variant -∅. As a group, the ex-slaves use the -∅ variant 134 of a possible 192 times (69.79%) and the -s variant 58 of a possible 192 times (30.21%). Both groups of narrators use the -∅ variant more than half the time; in fact,

Table 3
-s and -∅ with Third Person Singular Pronoun Subjects

	-s N/%	-0 N/%	Total
SC	5/7.04	66/92.96	71
TX	53/43.80	68/56.20	121
Total	58/30.21	134/69.79	192

the South Carolina ex-slaves use the -∅ variant categorically (almost 93% of the time).

However, this kind of analysis would eliminate from consideration 85% of the verbs with the -s suffix. As noted in table 2, only 58 of 389 occurrences of the -s variant (14.91%) occur with third person singular pronoun subjects.

Analyzing the use of nonconcord -s only in relation to the total number of -s forms is also inadequate. This approach would demonstrate that the ex-slaves used nonconcord -s 85% of the time (331 of a possible 389 uses). However, this approach does not take into account the occurrence of the -∅ variant with third person singular subjects.

Nonconcord -s, then, must be examined in relation to both variants: -∅ used with third person singular subjects and -s with other pronoun subjects. In this way, the apparent third person form is compared with the variants occurring with the third person singular pronoun subjects. Table 4 ranks the 63 ex-slaves in decreasing frequency of use of -s with the third person singular. Even with this conservative measure, it is clear that nonconcord -s is a characteristic feature of early black English. In 33 of the interviews, nonconcord -s occurs at least half the time. This level of variation substantiates the claim that -s functions neither as a third person singular marker nor as a regularized present tense marker.

Table 4
Nonconcord -s with Pronoun Subjects
in Relation to -∅ and -s Variants

State and Narrator	Sex and Age	Verb -∅ +3rd Sing	Verb -s Total	Total Verbs	Verb -s -3rd Sing	Verb -s -3rd Sing %
SC 46	M 62	0	5	5	5	100
TX 68	F 67	0	16	16	16	100
SC 35	F 75	0	2	2	2	100
TX 56	M 77	0	2	2	2	100
TX 122	F 78	0	1	1	1	100
SC 34	M 79	0	2	2	2	100
SC 5	M 82	0	5	5	5	100
TX 6	M 80	0	1	1	1	100
TX 13	M 84	0	10	10	10	100
TX 14	M 89	0	8	8	8	100
SC 73	M 90	0	1	1	1	100
SC 2	M 85	0	20	20	19	95
SC 16	F 83	0	10	10	9	90

TX 51	F 78	2	16	18	16	88.89
TX 67	M 75	0	17	17	15	88.24
SC 86B		1	5	6	5	83.33
SC 86A	F 97	2	9	11	9	81.82
TX 17	M 84	3	33	36	29	80.56
TX 77	M 79	0	40	40	31	77.50
SC 8	F 75	2	6	8	6	75
SC 65	F 106	2	6	8	6	75
SC 11	M 77	6	13	19	13	68.42
TX 69	M 78	0	6	6	4	66.67
SC 4	F 83	1	2	3	2	66.67
TX 15	M 90	2	7	9	6	66.67
TX 8	F 91	4	35	39	26	66.67
SC 82	M 96	1	5	6	4	66.67
SC 86C		9	14	23	14	60.87
TX 26	F 90	8	10	18	10	55.56
SC 10	M 81	4	4	8	4	50
SC 12	F 82	2	6	8	4	50
SC 13	M 87	5	5	10	5	50
TX 9	M 94	1	1	2	1	50
TX 5	M 94	6	15	21	10	47.62
TX 16	F 80	8	9	17	8	47.06
TX 47	F 78	5	4	9	4	44.44
TX 10	F 93	1	4	5	2	40
TX 116	F 79	10	6	16	6	37.50
TX 12	F 84	0	3	3	1	33.33
SC 26	F 87	4	2	6	2	33.33
TX 2	M 93	10	16	26	6	23.08
SC 36	M 90	8	1	9	1	11.11
TX 145	M 67	0	0	0	0	0
SC 40	M 73	0	0	0	t	0
TX 29	F 75	2	2	4	0	0
SC 32	F 76	2	0	2	0	0
SC 39	F 77	0	0	0	0	0
TX 109	M 78	0	0	0	0	0
SC 28A	M 79	0	0	0	0	0
SC 28B		1	0	1	0	0
SC 18	F 79	8	0	8	0	0
TX 1	M 80	0	0	0	0	0
SC 22	F 80	0	0	0	0	0
TX 4	F 80	1	0	1	0	0
SC 6A	F 83	0	0	0	0	0
SC 6B		0	0	0	0	0
TX 11	F 87	2	0	2	0	0

SC 9	M 88	0	0	0	0	0
SC 30A	F 90	0	0	0	0	0
SC 30B		8	0	8	0	0
SC 38A	F 90	0	0	0	0	0
SC 38B		0	0	0	0	0
SC 19	M 92	0	0	0	0	0
TX 3	M 93	0	2	2	0	0
SC 92	F 93		0	0	0	0
TX 30	F 94	0	0	0	0	0
TX 41	F 100	3	0	3	0	0
SC 15	M 104	0	0	0	0	0
TX 64	F 112	0	2	2	0	0
South Carolina		66	123	189	118	62.43
Texas		68	266	334	213	63.77
Total		134	389	523	331	63.29

We should also note that the 27 interviews in which noncon-cord -s does not occur include very few present tense examples. Only 27 of the 134 examples of the -∅ variant (20.15%) and 6 of 389 examples of the -s variant (1.54%) occur in these 27 narra-tives; the past tense was most frequently used.

The tabulation of the 331 uses of nonconcord -s in figure 1 shows the percentage of use and the number of examples in the 42 narratives in which nonconcord -s occurs. There is no sharp divi-sion between narrators who rarely and those who always use non-concord -s. There are two narratives in the lowest 10-20 percent range; they account for a total of 7 nonconcord -s examples. The remaining 40 narratives indicate an increasing percentage of non-concord -s in both the variable 30-70 percent range and in the categorical 80-100 percent range, even in the cases in which there are only two or three narratives in a group.

The distribution of -s and -∅ with pronoun subjects differs from the use reported for white Southerners. For example, in her study of white Alabama speech, Feagin 1979 found significant patterns in the use of -s with nonpronominal third person plural subjects, no instances of -s with we and you, and minimal use (1.4% for the urban working class) with I. She also found rare nonagreement with third person singular, that is, the variant -∅ (2.7% for urban working class, 4% for rural working class).

We can also note that the ex-slaves use the suffix -s with a large number of different verbs. That is, the use of -s is not re-stricted to a limited number of verbs or a limited group of verbs used in set phrases. The 14 verbs with which the narrators use -s 10 times or more are listed below:

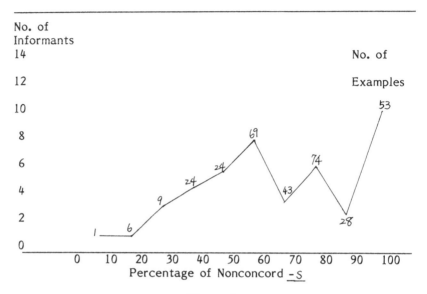

No. of
Informants

Figure 1
Frequency of Nonconcord -s with Non-Third Person
Singular Pronoun Subjects in 42 Narratives

Table 5
Frequent Verbs

get	45	go	18	start	11
know	26	tell	18	like	10
want	24	take	14	live	10
come	21	say	13	work	10
do (Aff.)	20	marry	11	Total	251

These verbs account for 251 of 331 examples (75.86%) of non-concord -s. The suffix -s is used with both stative and nonstative verbs (live, come), performative verbs (say), and perceptual verbs (know). Get, the verb with which suffix -s occurs most frequently, typically has the meaning "acquire" or "arrive."

Thus it is clear that the suffix -s is a feature of the early black English recorded in the ex-slave narratives; its use differs from that of white Southerners. The ex-slaves vary in their use of verb -s, but close analysis of their use of the form will demon-strate that the variation is accounted for by grammatical and social factors, rather than by hypercorrection.

Hypercorrection

With the exception of Putnam and O'Hern 1955, Scott 1973, and Jeremiah 1977, recent studies of black English have argued that the use of nonconcord -s is an example of hypercorrection. Arguments have been based on the use of -s with subjects other than the third person singular and with nonfinite verb forms.

In New York City, Labov et al. (1968:I:163-64) report a tendency to "hyper-Z"; that is, -s occurred in "odd, unpredictable and idiosyncratic positions." They also report that some speakers use "it a great deal, and others hardly at all." However, they also note that one speaker from South Carolina uses -s extraordinarily often.

Wolfram finds that -s occurs "over three times (233 out of 304 instances) more often with third person singular than with other persons" (1969:138). Only three of 24 working-class subjects use -s more frequently with subjects other than the third person singular. He concludes that, typically, -s "is absent on all forms; sometimes it may occur on third person singular forms; it also occurs on non-third person forms as a type of hypercorrection" (p. 138). In his "hierarchy of hypercorrection," Wolfram proposes that as speakers move closer to standard English, they will use verb -s more frequently with the third person singular.

Fasold finds that -s is used more frequently in the Washington data with third person singular subjects than with other subjects; -s occurs very rarely with nonfinite verbs. His analysis of "hyper-s" shows that the use of -s is "slightly more frequent with non-third person subjects" than with third person plural subjects (1972:132).

In the early black English recorded in the ex-slave narratives, the situation is quite different. The suffix -s occurs infrequently with the third person pronoun subjects. Furthermore, -s rarely occurs with nonfinite verbs; these are the only examples that occur in the narratives included in this study:

11. My marster had a driver . . . so he makes dat driver reports to him (TX 77:270).

12. Does you remembers that day? (SC 11:34).

13. I do not knows when er whar I was born. (SC 86A:43, Part 2).

If we compare the findings of this study wih Wolfram's "hierarchy of hypercorrection," we can note a quite different status of nonconcord -s in the ex-slave narratives. As figure 2 shows, the suffix -s is used more frequently with non-third person pronoun subjects in the narratives, while the converse is true for the Detroit study. There is little difference between the third person singular and plural uses in the narratives, but a significant differ-

ence in the Detroit study. In both studies -s is used more frequently with finite verbs than with nonfinite verbs.

The situation in early black English is somewhat similar to
Fasold's findings in Washington, but quite different from Wolfram's
Detroit findings. Also nonconcord -s occurs most frequently in
ex-slave narratives collected from individuals who are not approaching standard English. The two narrators who approach standard English (SC 28, TX 29) do not use noncondord -s. For example,
the Texas narrator uses are, a rare form in the ex-slave narratives
I have studied.

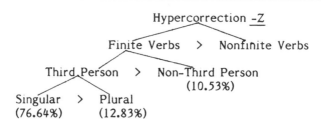

Black English in Detroit
(Adapted from Wolfram 1969:139)

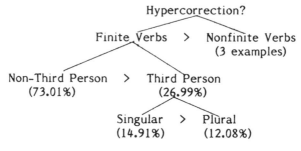

> = greater than

WPA Ex-Slave Narratives
(-s Based on Table 2)

Figure 2
Hierarchy of Hypercorrection

If the use of -s is an example of hypercorrection in early
black English--that is, if it is an overgeneralized rule--then we
expect the form to occur more frequently on nonfinite verbs,

including modal verbs which occur with third person singular subjects. The former happens very rarely, the latter not at all in the
narratives in this study. The pattern of nonconcord -s use is explained by its occurrence with adverbs and its interaction with
social variables.

Co-Occurrence with Adverbs

Adverbs that co-occur with verb -s indicate that the meaning
of nonconcord -s involves events that extend over a period of
time. This is the meaning that we would expect if nonconcord -s
functions in early black English as a durative marker.

Sentences 1 to 10, which illustrate the use of nonconcord -s
(above), also illustrate the use of the form with durative adverbs.
Sentences 1 and 4 describe events that extend over a long period,
as indicated by the adverbs allus and all the time. The adverb
until (till I get married in 1871) in sentence 3 is related to an
event for which the end point is known. Sentence 7 describes an
event for which the beginning point is known. However, sentence 6
is an exception; jumping over the broom is an event that does not
extend over a period of time.

Using the classification of time adverbs developed by Crystal
1966, I have analyzed the use of time adverbs that co-occur with
verb -s forms. Table 6 shows that the 153 examples with adverbs
in the same sentence or immediate context represent almost 40
percent (153/389, 39.33%) of the verb -s occurrences.

Table 6
Cooccurrence of Nonconcord -s with Adverbs

Class	Meaning	Adverbs (Examples)	Total in Class	% Total
Frequency				
A2	Single	one night once one time	13	8.50
A5	Occasional	sometimes	3	1.96
A7	Usual	on Sunday in spring most times	6	3.92

A8	Regular	every time at night during day	5	3.27
A9	Continuous/ Durative	always never now (nowadays) when (whenever) anytime	22 15	14.38 9.80

Duration

B1	Limit Known	until . . . all the year during dis period for five years two days	38	24.84
B2	End-Point Known	finally soon as . . .big enough	4	2.61
B3	Contem- poraneous	still	1	0.65
B4	Beginning Known	when I starts after she marries	20	13.07
B5	Limit Not Known	from way back	4	2.61

Explicit Time

		yesterday right now	22	14.38
		Total	153	

Clearly, most of the events with which nonconcord -s is used describe continuous or durative events. Categories A9 through B5 contain 70 percent of the examples with co-occurring adverbs (104/153). These are Crystal's Continuous/Durative categories. The separate category in the middle of table 5 contains 15 examples (9.80%) that are ambiguous in terms of frequency or duration of events. Also of interest is the fact that the single-event and explicit-time categories contain almost 25 percent of the examples.

Nonconcord -s as a durative marker can also occur in past contexts, as sentence 14 illustrates:

14. I lef' . . . and marries and made a livin' from public
    work in Marshall all my life (TX 56:192).

Perhaps, then, nonconcord -s itself indicates durative meaning
in these sentences:

15. She kep' sweet, Scotch snuff and sometimes I takes a
    pinch out (TX 26:84).

16. Course de white folks I b'longs to, had more slaves
    than I got fingers and toes (SC 16:52).

(That is, the occasional instances of taking a pinch were extended
over a period.)

The use of nonconcord -s in early black English supports Jeremiah's (1977:126-27) claim that -s functions as a durative aspect
marker in black English. Based on his study of letters, diaries, and
recollections by travelers, plantation owners, and missionaries
about slave speech in the South and Antigua, Jeremiah claims that
-s indicates habitual or durative aspect. He also reports finding
parallel uses of verb -s in present-day black English in Baltimore.

Social Factors

Earlier studies of nonconcord am (Brewer 1973, 1979) demonstrate that nonconcord am functioned as a morphosyntactic marker
of habitual or continuative action in early black English. Its use
may have preceded the introduction of invariant be. Furthermore,
the narrators from South Carolina and Texas tended to use different forms, and males used nonconcord am more frequently than
females.

In the case of nonconcord is, we find no dialectal split such as
that characteristic of nonconcord am. South Carolina narrators use
nonconcord -s 62.43% of the time (118 of 189 possible uses); the
Texas narrators used nonconcord -s 63.77% of the time (213 of 334
possible times). As a group, all the ex-slave narrators used nonconcord -s 63.29% of the time (331 of 523 times).

The male ex-slave narrators, however, used nonconcord -s
more frequently than did the female ex-slave narrators. Table 6
shows that the males used nonconcord -s nearly 70% of the time,
while females use the form slightly more than half the time. Sociolinguistic studies have shown that males tend to use stigmatized
variants more frequently than females. Females are more aware of
standard or prestige forms and tend to use stigmatized forms less
frequently than males. This suggests that nonconcord -s was a
stigmatized form in early black English grammar.

Although all the ex-slaves were elderly at the time they were
interviewed in the 1930s, an age range of approximately one gene-

ration is represented by the informants. Some of the informants were adults at the time of emancipation, some were young adults, and in the case of the 60s age group, they were born after emancipation. Therefore I have chosen to analyze the data in relation to four age groups, because the generations may reflect different time levels in black English.

The use of nonconcord -s by each age group in each state is shown at the top of table 7. The pattern of use is the same in

Table 7
Nonconcord of -s with Pronoun Subjects

State	Age Group	Verb -∅ +3rd Sing	Verb -s Total	Total Verbs	Verb -s -3rd Sing	Verb -s % -3rd Sing
Male Narrators						
SC Total	M60-69	0	5	5	5	100.00
TX Total	M60-69	0	0	0	0	0.00
SC Total	M70-79	7	15	22	15	68.18
TX Total	M70-79	0	65	65	52	80.00
SC Total	M80-89	9	34	43	33	76.74
TX Total	M80-89	3	52	55	48	87.27
SC Total	M90+	9	17	26	15	57.69
TX Total	M90+	19	41	60	23	38.33
Total Male		47	229	276	191	69.20
Female Narrators						
TX Total	F60-69	0	16	16	16	100.00
SC Total	F70-79	12	8	20	8	40.00
TX Total	F70-79	19	29	48	27	56.25
SC Total	F80-89	7	10	17	8	47.06
TX Total	F80-89	11	12	23	9	39.13
SC Total	F90+	22	34	56	34	60.71
TX Total	F90+	16	51	67	38	56.72
Total Female		87	160	247	140	56.68

Total by Sex

	Male	47	229	276	191	69.20
	Female	87	160	247	140	56.68
	Total	134	389	523	331	63.29

both states; the youngest narrators are categorical users of nonconcord -s while the oldest narrators use nonconcord about half the time (see table 8). For the middle-age groups, we find that the 70-79 age groups use the form 71% of the time--the converse of what we might expect in a consistent pattern of decreasing use of nonconcord -s with an increase in age. Nevertheless, the overall pattern of decreasing frequency of use of nonconcord -s by narrators in the older age groups suggests the possibility that the form may have been an innovation in this period of black English.

Table 8
Nonconcord of -s with Pronoun Subjects
Age Groups by State

State	Age Group	Verb -∅ +3rd Sing.	Verb -s Total	Total Verbs	Verb -s -3rd Sing.	Verb -s % -3rd Sing.
SC	60-69	0	5	5	5	100.00
TX	60-69	0	16	16	16	100.00
Total	60-69	0	21	21	21	100.00
SC	70-79	19	23	42	23	54.76
TX	70-79	19	94	113	79	69.91
Total	70-79	38	117	155	102	65.81
SC	80-89	16	44	60	41	68.33
TX	80-89	14	64	78	57	73.08
Total	80-89	30	108	138	98	71.01
SC	90+	31	51	82	49	59.76
TX	90+	35	92	127	61	48.03
Total	90+	66	143	209	110	52.63
Total		134	389	523	331	63.29

One caution should be kept in mind. Only three narrators are included in the 60-69 age group, while the other age groups are represented by 10 narrators each. Only two of the three narrators in the 60s (SC 46, TX 68) use the verb -s form. Nevertheless, the results of analyzing nonconcord -s by age suggest that future studies should consider age as a factor.

Conclusion

Nonconcord -s occurs in British English dialects and American English dialects, although it is typically more restricted, less systematic, and evidently less frequent than that recorded in the ex-slave narratives. For example, Wright (1968[1905]:296-97) reports:

reports:

1. Occasional use with first person singular and plural pronoun subjects in Yorkshire, Lancaster, and Lincoln;

2. -s with first person singular in "some of the southern and southwestern dialects";

3. -s for plural subjects in "most of the south-midland, eastern, southern and south-western dialects";

4. General use of -s for second person singular;

5. -s for third person singular, although often dropped in south midlands, eastern, and southern dialects.

In his American Dialect Dictionary, Wentworth (1944:526) records the absence of -s with third person singular in New York and Newfoundland and the use of -s with first person singular by blacks in eastern Virginia and Mississippi. Atwood (1953:26-27) notes that only in New England is "the first person singular form (I say) . . . recorded as a narrative form in reporting conversation." He suggests, tentatively, that "we works is fairly common in Type I in the S.A.S. [South Atlantic States], that I works occasionally occurs, and that both are in pretty general use among the more old-fashioned Negroes." Finally, he notes that all but one of the black informants use uninflected do with the third person singular.

Analysis of the ex-slave narratives demonstrates that verb -s occurs regularly and frequently in a significant number of narratives. However, it does not function as a regularized present tense marker; it can occur with all persons. It rarely occurs with nonfinite verb forms, indicating that the use of -s in early black English cannot be adequately accounted for as hypercorrections. Its co-occurrence with durative adverbs in early black English recorded in the ex-slaves narratives provides an indication of its function as a durative marker in the grammar.

British dialects of the eighteenth and nineteenth centuries are probably the source of nonconcord -s. However, the significance of the nonconcord -s is not its historical source, but its distinctive use. The English redundant third person singular form was adopted as a durative aspect marker in early black English grammar.

NOTE

[1]The sentences are presented as they appear in the typescript copies of the narratives. Numbers in parentheses indicate the narrative number and the page on which the sentence occurs. For example, "TX 1:1" indicates the first narrative in the Texas volume, that is, volume 4, page 1. "Part 2," added after the page number, indicates that the narrative is included in the second part of that volume (the two parts are paginated individually). The narratives are listed by name in the slave-narrative volumes; I have numbered the narratives consecutively in each volume for easy reference.

A Comparison of Stressed Vowels of Black and White Speakers in the South

George Dorrill

In a recent article in <u>Language in Society</u>, Labov states that after a decade of heated controversy a consensus has emerged concerning the nature and origin of the speech of American blacks (1982: 184). This paper attempts to contribute to this consensus by reexamining some of the data obtained by one of the parties of the controversy, the dialectologists associated with the Linguistic Atlas of the United States and Canada. The position that most members of this group have taken follows from the statement of Kurath, the director of the LAUSC, in his <u>Word Geography of the Eastern United States</u>: "By and large the Southern Negro speaks the language of the white man of his locality or area and of his level of education. But in some respects his speech is more archaic or old-fashioned, not un-English, but retarded because of less schooling" (1949:6).

Kurath 1949 does not present any data on black speech, nor does Kurath and McDavid 1961, <u>The Pronunciation of English in the Atlantic States</u>--other than a few scattered references to the substitution of /a/ for /æ/ among low-country blacks in South Carolina and Georgia. There is, however, a substantial amount of data on black speech in the unpublished archives of the various linguistic atlases. This paper reports on some findings of an investigation in the archives of the Linguistic Atlas of the Middle and South Atlantic States (LAMSAS). There are interviews with forty blacks, thirty-one of them complete, in this archive. Lowman conducted twenty-one of the interviews from 1933 to 1939. McDavid conducted ten interviews a decade later and transcribed tapes of another nine interviews conducted by Pederson or his students in the late 1960s and early 1970s. These interviews lasted approximately four to six hours each. They are recorded in fine phonetic notation and contain responses to over 800 questions concerning pronunciation, grammar, and lexicon.

To avoid possible problems of differing transcription practices, only Lowman's interviews are used in this study: sixteen pairs of black and white informants, comparable in age, education, and social class, living (with one exception) in the same county. Two pairs live in Maryland, seven each in Virginia and North Carolina (see map). The informants are located in the following counties (LAMSAS community numbers in parentheses): Maryland: Somerset (9) and St. Marys (22); Virginia: Prince William (N4), Fauquier (5A), Westmoreland (12), Essex (15), Charles City (21), Cumberland (43), Campbell (46), and Albemarle (59); and North Carolina: Martin (8), Craven (14), Brunswick (24), Sampson (25), Scotland (36), Franklin (38), and Anson (52).

In this study (reported more fully in Dorrill 1982), pronunciation is studied, since each atlas record has a great deal of phonetic data and the work of Kurath and McDavid 1961 needs to be supplemented. The fifteen stressed vowel nuclei that Kurath and McDavid have determined to be crucial for variation in the United States are examined. Reported here are results for five of the free vowels: /i/, /u/, /e/, /o/, and /ɔ/. These vowels are analyzed in six different environments: before pauses, voiceless obstruents, voiced obstruents, nasals, /l/, and /r/. Wherever possible, Kurath and McDavid's target words are used, so that in some cases there is a single target word in an environment and in some cases two. The target words are monosyllabic where possible. Approximately 3,000 tokens of the stressed vowels have been examined.

Table 1
Percentages of Monophthongal, Upgliding, and Ingliding
Pronunciations of Five Stressed Vowels

		Monophthongal	Upgliding	Ingliding
/i/	Black (N = 93)	83% (N = 77)	12% (N = 11)	5% (N = 5)
	White (N = 88)	36% (N = 32)	52% (N = 46)	11% (N = 10)
/u/	Black (N = 106)	79% (N = 84)	16% (N = 17)	5% (N = 5)
	White (N = 118)	58% (N = 68)	37% (N = 44)	5% (N = 6)
/e/	Black (N = 145)	56% (N = 81)	29% (N = 42)	15% (N = 22)
	White (N = 147)	17% (N = 25)	71% (N = 104)	12% (N = 18)
/o/	Black (N = 139)	71% (N = 99)	14% (N = 19)	15% (N = 21)
	White (N = 135)	36% (N = 49)	58% (N = 78)	6% (N = 8)
/ɔ/	Black (N = 98)	61% (N = 59)	21% (N = 21)	18% (N = 18)
	White (N = 98)	52% (N = 51)	31% (N = 30)	17% (N = 17)

One of the major findings is the greater tendency for blacks to pronounce vowels monophthongally, corresponding to an upgliding pronunciation by whites, as can be seen in table 1. The N's indicate the number of tokens of each vowel type.

For the vowel /i/, the target words chosen are three, week, grease, beans, and field. The tendency for blacks to have monophthongal forms of this vowel is very strong, with 83 percent of the tokens for /i/ being monophthongal (see table 2). The black informant from Somerset County, Maryland (MD N9), has five of the eleven tokens with upgliding forms heard among the black informants. Whites have a corresponding tendency to upgliding forms, although it is not nearly so pronounced as the monophthongal tendency for blacks--52 percent upgliding forms versus 36 percent monophthongal forms.

The target words for the vowel /u/ are two, tooth, dues, shoes, room, school, and bureau. Some of the forms include on-glides. Again, there is a marked tendency for blacks to have monophthongal forms (see table 3). There is also in this vowel a greater tendency for whites to have monophthongal forms than with any other vowel studied here. In certain environments, however, upgliding forms are more frequent for whites, as before a pause; ten of the sixteen whites have upgliding forms in this environment.

The vowel /e/ is recorded from the target words day, April, eight, bracelet, ways, strain, pail, and Mary. There is also a strong contrast in the pronunciation of this vowel, although the contrast is more in the strong tendency for whites to have upgliding pronunciations (see table 4). Although strong in all environments, this tendency is strongest in the word ways, where fifteen of the sixteen white informants had upgliding varieties. The white informant from Sampson County, North Carolina (NC 25A), has no examples of upgliding varieties in his speech at all, a situation similar to the case of the Maryland black, with no monophthongal examples for /i/.

For the vowel /o/, the target words chosen are ago, know, coat, road, home, old, four, and hoarse. In the pronunciation of ago, the performance of the black speakers comes as close to being categorically different from the white speakers as in any instance in this study (see table 5). All sixteen blacks have monophthongal pronunciations. Otherwise, the percentages are similar to those found for /i/ and /e/.

For the vowel /ɔ/, the target words are law, frost, dog, swamp, salt, and horse. For this vowel, the differences between blacks and whites are much less apparent, both blacks and whites tending to have monophthongal pronunciations (see table 6). The principal difference observed in the data is a somewhat greater tendency for blacks to have higher pronunciations of the vowel.

Examination of linguistic atlas data on comparable black and white speech in the South reveals systematic differences in the pronunciation of the stressed vowels. The differences, however, are at the subphonemic or phonic level; that is, the differences are systematically phonetic. This is the same type of variation that is used to characterize dialect differentiation in regional dialects in the United States (Kurath and McDavid 1961:2).

The differences, although systematic, are not categorical; that is, there are no features of speech that exist solely for blacks or whites. The fact that the differences are quantitative rather than qualitative may have led Kurath and McDavid not to consider them, but as Labov (1982:180) points out, "We must shift our methods as often as possible to undercut the tendency to keep proving ourselves right by making the same mistake over and over again."

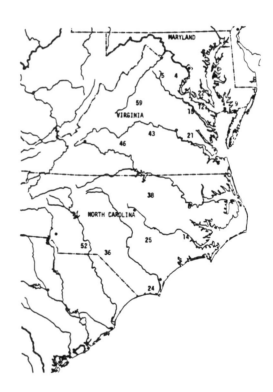

Location of Informant Communities

Table 2 Pronunciation of /i/

Community	_# bl.	_# wh.	_vl. obs. bl.	_vl. obs. wh.	_vd. obs. bl.	_vd. obs. wh.	_/n/ bl.	_/n/ wh.	_/l/ bl.	_/l/ wh.	_/r/ bl.	_/r/ wh.
MD 9	iʲ	Iˆi	iʲ	i·i	iʲ	Iˆiv	iʲ	i·i	iʲ	i·ᵊ	—	—
22	iᶻ·	r·i	i	r·i	iᵖ· i>	izi	iᶻ iᶻ	rʲ iʲ	i·	izʲ	—	—
VA 4-5	i	iᶻ·i	i	iʲ	i· iv·	i··	i· i	i·· i·ᵊ	i·	i·ᵊ	—	—
12	i·	izi	i·	i·	i·	i·	iᵊi iz·	i·· i·	i·ᵊ i·	i·ᵊ	—	ᶠ··
15	i·	Iˆiv	i·	i·i	i·	iv·	i·	i·i	i·	i·ᵊ	—	—
21	iᵖ·	izi	i	Iˆiv	i	izi	i·i	izʲ	i·	iv·	··	—
43	iᶻ·	iᶻ	i·	i	i·	i	i·	iĩ i	i·	i·	—	—
46	iv·	izi iv·	i·	i i·	iv·	iv·	i·	i·	i·	i·ᵊ	—	—
59	i>i	Iˆiv	i	i·i	i· i>·	i·	i· ᵗ·	i·	i·ʲ	i·ᵊ	—	—
NC 8	i·	izi	i·	i·ᵛ	i·	i·i	i·	i·i	i·ᵛ	i·ᵊ	—	—
14	i>i	ɟi	i	r·i	i·	Iˆiv	i·	i·i	i·ᵊ	iv·i	—	—
24	i·	izi	i·	i·ᵛ	i	i	iᵖ· ᵗ·	i·	i	i·	—	—
25	iv·	i>·	i·	i>·	i·	i·	i·	i i·	i·	i·ᵊ	—	—
36	iᶻ·	izʲ	iᶻ·	i·ʲ	iˆ	i>	iᵖ·	iᶻʲ iᶻʲ	iˆᵊ	i·	—	—
38	iᶻ· i·	i·i	iʲ i>·	iv·	i·	r·i i· ᵗ·	r·i	i·ᵊ	i·ᵊ	—	—	—
52	i>·	izi	iʲ	izʲ	iᵖ·	izi	i·	izʲ	i·	i·	—	—

Table 3 Pronunciation of /u/

Community	# bl.	# wh.	_ vl. obs. bl.	_ vl. obs. wh.	_ vd. obs. bl.	_ vd. obs. wh.	_ /n/ bl.	_ /n/ wh.	/l/ bl.	/l/ wh.	_ /r/ bl.	_ /r/ wh.
MD 9												
22												
VA 4-5												
12												
15												
21												
43												
46												
59												
NC 8												
14												
24												
25												
36												
38												
52												

Table 4 Pronunciation of /e/

Com- mun- ity	_ # bl.	wh.	_ vl. obs. bl.	wh.	_ vd. obs. bl.	wh.	_ /n/ bl.	wh.	_ /l/ bl.	wh.	_ /r/ bl.	wh.
MD 9	e / e˅ɪ	ɛᴧɪ˅ / ɛᵃɪ	eᵌ˅ / e·ᴵ	ɛᵃɪ / eᵛɪ	eᶻ	ɛᴧɪ	e·ᴵ	ɛᴧɪ	e·ᴵᴰ	e›ᴵ	ɛᴧ / eᴵ	ɛ›ᵌ / ɛ›
22	e· / e·	e·ᵀ˅ / eᵌ	e· / e·ᴵ	eᴵ / e·ᴵ˅	eᴧ· / e·	e›ᵗ	e·	e·ᶠ˅	e·	eᴵ˅	ɛᴧ / ɛ	eᴧᵌ / ɛᴧᵌ
VA 4-5	e·ᶠ / e·	e·ᴵ˅ / ɛ·ᵌ	eᶻ / eᴵ	e· / e·	e·	e·ᶻ	e·ᶠ˅	eᶻ	eᶻᵌ	e·	eᴵ / eᴵ˅	eᶻ / eᵌ
12	e· / e·ᵛ	eᴧ· / c·ᵌ	e· / e·	e·ᵌᴧ / e·ᵌ	eᶻ· / e›·	e·ᴵ˅	e›·	e›·	eᴵ˅	eᵌ	e / e·	eᴵ / e
15	eᶻ· / e›ᵌ	e·ᶻ / e›·	e›˅ / e··	e·ᴵ˅ / eᶻ	e: / e›:	eᶻ / eᵛɪ˅	e·	eᴵ	e›ᵌ	eᶻ	– / e	e / eᶻɪ˅
21	eᴧ·ᶻ / eᴧ·	ɛᴧᶻ / e·ᵌ˅	eᴧ· / eᴧᶻ	ɛᴧᶻ / e·ᶠ	eᴧᵌ˅ / eᶻ	ɛᶻᶠ	e·ᶠ	ɛᴧᶻ	eᶻ	ɛᶠᶻ	eᴧ· / eᴧ	eᵛᶠ / ɛᴧᶻ
43	e· / eᴧ·	eᶻ / eᵌᴧ	eᴧ· / e›·	e·ᵌ˅ / e·ᵌᴧ	e·· / eᶻ·	e·ᶠᵢ	~e·	e·ᶠ	e·ᵌᴧ	e·ᶠ	eᶻ / e·	eᶠ / eᵌ
46	e·ᶠ / eᵛᶻ	eᴧ· / eᵌ	‾eᶻ	e·ᶠ / e	e·	e· / e·ᶻ	e·	eᴧ·	eᴧᵌ	e·	– / e·	e· / e·
59	eᵛᴧ· / eᴧ·	eᶻ / e·ᶻ˅	eᴧ· / eᴧ	e·ᶻ / eᵛᶠᴧ	eᴧ·	eᵛᵀ˅ / eᶻᵛ	e›ᵌ	e·ᶠ	eᴧ·ᵌ	eᵛᶠ˅	eᶻ / e / eᴧ·	e· / eᶻᴵᵛ
NC 8	eᵛᴧ· / eᴧᵌᵛ	eᵛᶻᴧ / eᵛᶠ / e	eᴧᶻ / ɛᵃᴵ	eᶠɪ / ɛᵃᴵ	eᴧᶠ	ɛᴧᶻ	c·~ᶻ	eᵛᶻ	eᴧᵌ	eᵛᶻᵌ	eᶠᵛ / ɛ	ɛ / eᵛᶻ
14	e· / e·ᶻᵛ	ɛᶻ / ɛᶻ	eᶠᵛ / eᶻ	ɛᶻ / ɛᶻᵛ	e·ᶻ	ɛᵛᶻ / e›ᵌ·	ɛᶻ	e·ᴰ	ɛ·ᶻ	eᵌ / ɛᵌ	eᶻ / ɛᶻ
24	eᴧ· / e·ᵌᶻ	eᶻ / e·ᶻᵛ	eᴧ· / eᴧ·	eᶻ / e›ᶻ	eᴧ·	eᶠᶻ	eᴧ·	eᶻᵛ	eᴧᵌ	eᵌ	eᶻᵛ / e	eᶻ / e·
25	eᴧ· / e·	e·· / e·ᵌᶻ	eᶻ / e·	e›ᴧ / e	eᴧ·	eᵌᵌ	eᴧ·	e·	eᴧ·ᵌ	eᴧ·ᵌᵛ	e / e	eᵌ / e·
36	eᴧ· / eᵌᵌᴧ	e·ᶻ / e·ᴵ	eᴧ / eᴧ·	e·ᶻ / eᶻ	eᴧᵛᶻ	eᴧ·ᶻ / e›·ᵌᴧ	e·ᶠ	e·ᵌ	eᵛᶻ	eᴧ· / eᵛ·	eᶻ / eᶻ
38	eᵛ / eᵛᵞ	eᶻ / ɛᴧᶻ	e· / e·	– / ɛᴧᶠ	eᵛᶠᵛ	eᵛᶻ / ɛᴧᵢᶻ	eᵛᵌᴧ	ɛᶻᶻ / eᶠᵌ	ɛᶠᶻᵌ	eᵛ· / eᵛ·	eᵛᶠ / eᵛᶻ
52	eᴧ· / e	eᶻᶻ / eᵌɪ	e· / e·	ɛᶻᶠ / e›ᶻ	eᴧ·ᵌᴧ	eᶻɪ / eᴧ·ᵌᴧ	eᶻɪ	eᴧᵌ / ɛᶻᵌᵌ	eᶻ / e·ᵌ	eᶻ / eᵛᶻ

Table 5 Pronunciation of /o/

Com-mun-ity	__ #		__ vl. obs.		__ vd. obs.		__ /n/		__ /l/		__ /r/	
	bl.	wh.	bl.	wh.	bl.	wh.	bl.	wh.	bl.	wh.	bl.	wh.
MD 9	o· oʋ	oʋʋ oʋʋ	oʌᵊ	Ͻʋ	oᵊ oʋʋ	oᵛ o·ᵛ	oᵛ	oːʋ	oᵛ	oʋʋ	oᵊ o·ᵊ	o·ᵀ o·ᵀ
22	o· o·	o· oᵛ	oᵋ·	oᵛ	oᵋ·	oᵛ	oᵋ	o·	oᵋ·	oᵛ	Ͻᵊ o	Ͻᵊᵊ oᵛ
VA 4-5	oᵋ· o·	o·ᵛ —	o·	oᵋ·	o·ᵛ	o·	oᵋ	oᵋ·	oᵛ	oᵛᵛ	o o·	o· oᵊ· o·o
12	o· o·	o· oᵛ	o·	o·	oː	o·	õᵛ·	o·	oᵛ·	oᵛ	o· o·ᵊ	o· oᵊ
15	oᵋː o·	o·ᵛ o·	o·ᵊᵋ	oᵛ	o· oː	oᵛ o·ʋ	oᵋ· o·	oᵛ	o·	o·ᵛ	oᵊ o·	o· o·ᵛ
21	o· o	oᵛ oᵘ	o·	oᵛʋ	oᵛ o·ᵛ	oʋ	õ	oʋ	o·ᵛ	oᵛᵛ	oᵊ oᵊ	Ͻᵊᵛ oᵛᵛ
43	o· oᵋ	o· oᵛ	oᵊᵛ	oᵊᵋ	oᵋ·	oᵛ o·ᵛ	oᵋ·	õ·	oᵋ·	o·	oᵋ oᵋ·	o· o·
46	oᵋ o o·	oᵋ o·	o	oᵋ oᵛ	o·	oᵋ·	oᵋ	o· oᵊᵋ	o·	oᵊᵊ oᵋ·	o o·	oᵋ· oᵊ o·
59	oᵋ oᵋ·	ǫ· o·	Ͻ oᵋ	ǫ· ǫː	oᵋ·	ǫ·	õᵋ oᵋᵊ	̄oᵛ	oᵋ	ǫ·	oᵋ· oᵊᵊ	o·ᵛ oᵛ
NC 8	oᵛ· oᵛ	oᵋᵛ o·ᵛ	oᵛ	oᵛᵛ	o·	oᵋᵛ õ·	ɔᵋᵛ	oᵛ	o·ᵛᵛ	o·ᵊᵛ o·ᵛᵛ	oᵛᵛ oᵛᵛ
14	o· oᵛ	oᵊᵛ oᵋᵛ	o·ᵛ	oᵊᵛ o·ᵛ	oᵋ·ᵛ	õᵋ·	oᵛ	o·	oᵋᵛ	oᵛᵊ oᵛ oᵊ	oᵛ oᵛᵊ oᵛᵊ
24	oᵋ· oᵋ·	oᵛ oᵛ	oᵋ·	o·	oᵋ·	o·ᵛ	oᵋ·	oᵛ	o·	oᵛ	oᵋ oᵋ·ᵊ	oᵋᵊ oᵛᵊ
25	oᵋ oᵋ	o· o·	o·	oᵋ·	oᵛ oᵋ·	oᵋ·	o·	oᵛ·	oᵊᵊ	o·	o·ᵊ oᵊᵛ	oᵛ·ᵀ oᵛᵊ
36	oᵋ· oᵋ	o·ᵛ oᵛ	oᵋ·	oᵛ	oᵋ·	o·	oᵋ·	oᵛ	oᵋ·	oᵊᵛ	oᵋ· oᵋ·	oᵛᵀ oᵛᵀ
38	oᵛ· oᵛ·	oᵛ o·ᵛ	oᵛ·	o·ᵛ	o· oᵛ·	o·ᵛ õ·	oᵛ o·	o·	oᵛ	oᵛᵛ oᵛ·ᵊ oᵛᵊᵊ	oᵛᵊ o·ᵛ
52	oᵋ· o	oᵛᵛ oᵛᵛ	oᵋ·	oᵛ·ᵛ	o· oᵋ·	oᵛᵛ	oᵋ·	oᵛ	o·	oᵛᵛ oᵛ o·	o·ᵊ o·ᵊ

Table 6 Pronunciation of /ɔ/

Com-mun-ity	_ #		_ vl. obs.		_ vd. obs.		_ /n/		_ /l/		_ /r/	
	bl.	wh.	bl.	wh.	bl.	wh.	bl.	wh.	bl.	wh.	bl.	wh.
MD 9	ɔᵂᵉʳ	ɒᴬ·	ɒᴬˑᵌ	ɒᴬˑ	ɒᵃˑ·ᵛ	ɒᶠˑ·	ɒᴬˑᵌ	ɔᵛˑ	ɔᵛ·	ɒᶠᵌ	ɒᵃˑᵌ	ɒᶠᵈ
22	ɔᵛˑᵌʳ	ɒᴬˑ	ɒᴬˑᵌ	ɒᴬˑ	ɒᵃˑᶠ	ɒˑ·	ɒᴬˑᵌ	ɔᵛˑ·	ɔᵛ·	ɒᴬᵌ	ɒᴬˑᵌ	ɒᶠᵈ
VA 4-5	ɔᵛˑ	ɔː	ɔᵛˑᵌ	ɔᴬˑᵌ ɔˑᵌ	ɔᵛᶠ	ɔᴬ	ɔˑ·	ɔˑɔᶠ	ɔᵛᵌ	ɔˑᶠ	ɔᵛˑ	ɔˑᵌ
12	ɔᵛˑᶜ	ɔᵛˑ	ɔˑ	ɔᵛˑᵌ	ɔᴬˑ	ɔˑ·	ɔˑ	ɔˑᶠ	ɔˑ·	ɔᵛˑ	ɔˑ	ɔᵛˑ·
15	ɔ··	ɔᵛˑ	ɔ··	ɔᵛˑᵌ	ɔᴬˑ	ɔᶠᵌ	ɔˑ·	ɔˑ·	ɔᵛˑ	ɔˑ ɔᵛˑ	ɔᶠ	ɔˑ·
21	ɔˑ·	ɔᵛˑᵌ	ɔˑᵌ	ɔᵛ·	ɔˑ·	ɔᵛˑᶜ	ɔˑ·	ɔᵛˑ	ɔˑᵌ	ɔᵛˑ·	ɔᵛˑ·	ɔᵛˑ·
43	ɔˑ·	ɔᵛˑ	ɔˑ·	ɔˑᵌ	ɔᵛᵛ	ɔˑᶠ	ɔᴬˑ	ɔˑ	ɔˑ	ɔᵛˑ	ɔˑ·	ɔˑ
46	ɔᵛˑᶜ	ɔˑ·	ɔᵛˑ	ɔᵛˑ·	ɔˑɔ	ɔᶜɔ	—	ɔˑ·	ɔᵛˑ·	ɔˑ·	ɔˑɔᴬ	ɔᵛˑɔ
59	ɔᴬˑ·	ɔˑ·	ɔˑᵌ ɔˑ·	ɒᴬˑ	ɔˑ·	ɔˑᶠ	ɔˑ·	ɒᶠˑᵌ	ɔᴬ	ɔᵛˑɔ	ɔᴬˑ· ɔˑᵌ	ɔˑ·
NC 8	ɔˑ·	ɔᵛɔ	ɔˑ·	ɒᴬᵛᵌ	ɔɕ	ɕɕ	ɔˑ	ɔᵛɔ	ɔɔᴬ	ɔᵛɔ	ɔᶠᴬᶜ	ɔᵛɔᴬ
14	ɔᵛˑ·	ɔᵛˑ·	ɔᵛˑ·	ɒᴬᵛᵌ	ɔɔᴬ	ɒᵛ	ɔˑ·	ɔᵛˑ	ɔᵛˑ	ɒᴬᶠ	ɔᵛɔ	ɔˑᴬ
24	ɔˑ·	ɔᵛˑ	ɔˑ	ɔ	ɔˑ	ɔˑ	ɔᶠˑ	ɔˑ	ɔˑ	ɔᵛˑ	ɔᵛˑ·	ɔˑᵌ
25	ɔˑ·	ɔᵛˑ·	ɔᵛɔ	ɔᵛˑ	ɔᵛᵌ	ɔᵛˑ	ɔᴬ ɔˑ	ɒᶠˑ	ɔᵛᶜ	ɔᵛˑ	ɔˑᵌ	ɔᵀ
36	ɔˑ·	ɔᵛˑ	ɔˑ·	ɔᵛˑ·	ɔɔᵛ	ɔɔɔ	ɔᵛˑ·	ɔˑ·	ɔˑ·	ɒᴬᵛᵌ	ɔᵛɔ	ɔᴿ
38	ɔᵛˑ·	ɔᵛɔᴬ	ɔˑ·	ɔˑɔᴬɔ	ɔˑ·	ɔᵛᵌ	aᴬᵌ	ɕᶠᵌ	ɔˑᵌ	ɔᵛɔ	ɔᵛᵌ	ɔɔᵌ
52	ɔᵛˑ·	ɒᴬᶠ	ɔᴬˑᵌ	ɒᴬˑᵛ	ɔᵛˑ	ɒᴬᶠ	ɔˑ·	ɕᶠ	ɔᵛɔ	ɒᴬᵛ	ɔᵛˑ	ɒᵛᵛ

Invariant *Be* in the Lower South

Guy Bailey and Marvin Bassett

Unconjugated or invariant be is among the features most often discussed in the literature on the speech of blacks and whites in the South.[1] Generally, discussions of the feature involve three issues: its functions and meaning, its racial distribution, and its origin. In studies based both on fieldwork done in Washington, D.C., and on experiments designed to elicit subjective reactions, Ralph Fasold 1969, 1972 has distinguished two types of invariant be which do not occur in "Standard English." One results from the deletion of an underlying will or would (appendix B, no. 6: "If we'd get out working and be dirty on that old farm, we'd wash"). The other indicates an iterative or distributive aspect (appendix B, no. 41: "When it clabbers, it don't always be sour"). The latter, Fasold suggests, is tenseless and is unique to black speech. However, a number of people (including Labov et al. 1968, Dunlap 1974, and Brewer 1979) have provided data that appear to make Fasold's semantic analysis untenable. All three find that the second type of be is used by blacks to mark extended and continuous, as well as iterative, actions, while both Labov and Dunlap find examples of be that are used to specify instantaneous or definite time. In addition, Brewer and Dunlap provide examples of be occurring in past contexts.

Although Fasold's analysis of the function and meaning of the second type of be has been challenged, no one has presented convincing evidence that the form is used in Southern white speech. On the basis of speech samples from black and white school children in Atlanta, Dunlap (1974:77-78) suggests that "the use of invariant be might be the one grammatical marker which distinguishes the speech of blacks from that of whites," while Wolfram (1974:524), on the basis of fieldwork in Franklin County, Mississippi, indicates that "distributive be" is typically not found in Southern white speech."

Because no one has produced convincing evidence of the

second type of invariant be in Southern white speech, and because various creole languages have structures that are similar in function and meaning, if not in phonetic form, scholars such as Dillard 1972 and Stewart 1967, 1968 have argued that so-called distributive be has its origin in a plantation creole. Rickford 1974 has detailed the probable steps in the development of be from a creole. While indicating that the origin of "distributive be" is open to question, Wolfram (1974:524) says that "it does not appear unreasonable to suggest that it involved the relexification of be to align (but not necessarily match) with an aspectual category." However, a number of people, including McDavid 1965b and Dunlap 1974, have cautioned that any difference between black and white speech may well be the result of skewing caused by the system of racial caste.

The Linguistic Atlas of the Gulf States provides data which have a direct bearing on the first two of these issues concerning invariant be and which may have some importance for the third.[2] The LAGS data are useful for several reasons. First, LAGS scribes were instructed to record all instances of invariant be, along with an indication of where they occur in the field record, at page 26.1 of the protocol. Instances entered elsewhere are cross-referenced to 26.1. Second, because all LAGS field records were taped in their entirety and because the protocols preserve only tape-recorded data, investigators can easily recover the semantic contexts which are crucial in determining the meaning and function of invariant be. Third, LAGS field records generally, though not always, contain a fair amount of free conversation. Fieldworkers were instructed to try to get at least an hour of free conversation at the beginning of the interviews, which average about five hours in length.

Further, both McDavid's advice to the fieldworkers[3] and Van Riper's 1972 proposals for shortening the Atlas interview suggest conversational contexts in which much data can be elicited. As a result, the straight question-answer format was generally used to supplement directed conversation, and many of the worksheet items occur in free conversation. Two articles by Pederson, "Tape/Text and Analogues" (1974) and "Grassroots Grammar in the Gulf States" (1977), demonstrate the LAGS use of conversational material. Finally, the LAGS sample of more than 1,100 informants includes a broad range of social and racial coverage. Type I informants comprise about 40 percent of the sample, with Type II and Type III making up 35 and 26 percent respectively.[4] More importantly, the sample is over 21 percent black.[5]

Within the LAGS territory, the sectors of East Louisiana, Gulf Mississippi, and Lower Mississippi are particularly fruitful for the study of black-white speech relationships. The region provides a variety of economic and social structures. For example, in the sugar-producing counties of southern Louisiana and the cotton-producing counties along the Mississippi River, plantations were

among the largest in the South. Further, a number of slaves in
East Louisiana were imported either directly from West Africa or
from the Caribbean, rather than from states to the east. In many
counties in this area, blacks remain in the majority, and plantation
agriculture is still an important economic resource, with tenantry
replacing slavery. The piney woods regions of southeast Mississippi
and north Louisiana contrast sharply with the plantation areas.
The piney woods counties have always had much smaller black
populations, and, in the past, subsistence farming was much more
important than plantation agriculture. Since 1890, lumber has
replaced agriculture as the primary economic resource. With its
comparatively late development, its reliance on commercial fishing
and shipbuilding, and its relatively cosmopolitan population, Gulf
Mississippi provides a third type of social organization, while New
Orleans, a major urban center with a unique cultural history, is
distinct from all of these.

The Sample

The data in this study come from 122 of the 123 LAGS informants in East Louisiana, Gulf Mississippi, and Lower Mississippi.
(An interview with an American Indian whose first language is
Choctaw has been disregarded.) Of the 122 informants, thirty-nine
are black, eighty-three are white, fifty-one are Type I, forty-eight
are Type II, and twenty-three are Type III. Appendix A gives the
residence, sex, social class, race, age, and atlas subtype for each
informant.

Distribution of Invariant Be

Thirty-five of the 122 informants (29%) use some form of invariant be. As table 1 illustrates, however, the form is distributed
unevenly across the population. Four factors restrict its occurrence, with race the most obvious of these. Invariant be is used by
eight of eighty-three white informants (10%) but by twenty-seven
of thirty-nine black informants (69%). However, while invariant be
is far more common among blacks than whites, the form is clearly
not unique to black speech. Furthermore, invariant be is restricted
within both black and white speech. As table 1 shows, in both
races the form is most common among Type I, less common among
Type II, and rare among Type III. Although unconjugated be is
more common in black speech for each atlas type--in fact, it is
more common among black Type II than white Type I--the same
pattern of distribution emerges for each race.

Age is a third factor in the use of invariant be, as tables 2
and 3 illustrate. Only one white under age 65 uses the form--a
57-year-old Type III from Labadieville, Louisiana, the heart of

Table 1
Distribution of Invariant Be by Race, Sector,
and Atlas Type (with the Total Number of Informants
in Each Category in Parentheses)

East Louisiana

Type	Whites	Blacks
I	4 (15)	7 (8)
II	1 (15)	3 (5)
III	1 (7)	0 (1)
	6 (37)	10 (14)

Gulf Mississippi

I	1 (3)	1 (2)
II	0 (8)	0 (1)
III	0 (1)	0 (1)
	1 (12)	1 (4)

Lower Mississippi

I	0 (12)	11 (11)
II	1 (14)	4 (5)
III	0 (8)	1 (5)
	1 (34)	16 (21)

Totals

I	5 (30)	19 (21)
II	2 (37)	7 (11)
III	1 (16)	1 (7)
	8 (83)	27 (39)

Table 2
Distribution of Invariant Be among Whites
by Age and Sector

	65+	40-64	13-39	Totals
East Louisiana	5 (22)	1 (8)	0 (7)	6 (37)
Gulf Mississippi	1 (9)	0 (2)	0 (1)	1 (12)
Lower Mississippi	1 (27)	0 (5)	0 (2)	1 (34)
	7 (58)	1 (15)	0 (10)	8 (83)

Note: 5 of 26 folk speakers use the form.

Table 3
Distribution of Invariant Be among Blacks
by Age and Sector

	65+	40-64	13-39	Totals
East Louisiana	10 (11)	0 (1)	0 (2)	10 (14)
Gulf Mississippi	1 (2)	0 (0)	0 (2)	1 (4)
Lower Mississippi	12 (16)	2 (3)	2 (2)	16 (21)
	23 (29)	2 (4)	2 (6)	27 (39)

Note: 19 of 21 folk speakers use the form.

sugar country. While blacks of all ages, including a 13-year-old from Jackson, Mississippi, use unconjugated be, the form is most common in the speech of older people, with twenty-three of twenty-nine informants over age 65 (79%) using it. Only four of ten (40%) of those under 65 use the form.

Sex is the final factor that governs the distribution of invariant be (see tables 4 and 5). Again, the pattern of distribution

Table 4
Distribution of Invariant Be among Whites, by Sex

	Male	Female
East Louisiana	5 (22)	1 (15)
Gulf Mississippi	1 (9)	0 (3)
Lower Mississippi	1 (16)	0 (18)
	7 (47)	1 (36)

Note: 1 of 13 female folk speakers uses the form; 4 of 13 male
       folk speakers use the form.

Table 5
Distribution of Invariant Be among Blacks, by Sex

	Male	Female
East Louisiana	5 (8)	5 (6)
Gulf Mississippi	1 (2)	0 (2)
Lower Mississippi	11 (13)	5 (8)
	17 (23)	10 (16)

is similar for both races. All but one of the whites who use the
form are male. Although 63% of the black females use unconjugated be, 74% of the black males do.

Invariant be, then, occurs in both black and white speech,
although it is much more common among blacks. Nevertheless, a
similar pattern of distribution emerges for both races, with education, age, and sex all affecting the pattern.[6] The interaction of
these variables is clearest in white speech: six of the eight whites
who use unconjugated be are Type I males over sixty-five. Four of
those six are clear examples of Kurath's "folk speakers"; in fact,
of thirteen male, white folk speakers in the sample, four use some
form of invariant be. Among whites, then, unconjugated be is a
relic form largely restricted to folk speech; among blacks, the
form seems to be gradually becoming restricted in much the same
way.

The most important question about the racial distribution of
invarant be, however, concerns who uses which kind of be. While
most investigators readily acknowledge that whites use invariant
be which results from the deletion of will or would, they have
found little or no use of "distributive be" by whites (see, e.g.,
Wolfram 1974:522). The findings here are somewhat different. As
tables 6 and 7 illustrate, whites do use "distributive be." In fact,
the sources of invariant be in white speech are much the same as
those in black speech, and the pattern of distribution by source is
also quite similar. In black speech, 43% of the instances of invariant be are "distributive"; in white speech, 47% are "distributive."
Of the eight white speakers who use some form of unconjugated
be, only two use forms which are clearly not "distributive." Four
whites, three from East Louisiana and one from Lower Mississippi,
provide incontrovertible instances of "distributive" be. (See informants ED 413.01, examples 7, 8, and 9; EF 423.01, example 10; EF
425.01, example 11; and DV 381.02, examples 40 and 41.)

Table 6
Sources of Invariant Be in White and Black Speech

	Underlying will or or would	No will or would	Ambig- uous	Subjunc- tive	Deleted to	Totals
Whites	5	7	2	1	0	15
Blacks	18	40	32	0	1	91
Totals	23	47	34	1	1	106

Meaning and Functions of Invariant Be

The meaning and functions of invariant be are even more complex than its distribution. For that reason, the entire corpus of 106 examples (in 90 sentences) is given in appendix B. This corpus contains four types of unconjugated be: those resulting from deletion of will or would, those which approximate Fasold's category

---

Table 7

Classification of Instances of Invariant Be by Source

Underlying will or would: 1a, 1b, 2, 6, 12, 29, 31, 34, 37, 38, 39a,
        39b, 39c, 44, 45a, 45b, 47, 59, 61, 72, 74, 81, 82

No underlying will or would: 7, 8, 9, 10, 11, 13, 14, 15, 18, 24, 26,
        28, 32, 35, 36, 40, 41, 42, 43, 46, 49a, 49b, 50, 52,
        53, 54, 55, 56, 57, 63, 64, 65, 68, 69, 70, 71, 73a,
        73b, 73c, 73d, 76, 77, 79, 85, 86, 89, 90

Ambiguous: 3, 5, 16, 17, 19a, 19b, 20a, 20b, 21, 22, 23, 25, 27a,
        27b, 27c, 30, 33, 48a, 48b, 48c, 48d, 51, 60, 62, 66,
        67, 75, 78, 80a, 80b, 83, 84, 87, 88

Subjunctive: 4

Deleted to: 58

"distributive," a single instance of the subjunctive (no. 4 in appendix B), and a single instance resulting from the deletion of an infinitive marker (no. 58). The function and meaning of the last two present no problems, so they are disregarded in the remainder of this discussion. The other two types, however, pose a multitude of problems.

As Fasold (1972:157-58) notes, it is sometimes impossible to determine whether instances of invariant be are "distributive" or result from the deletion of will or would. We have followed Fasold's analysis closely in determining the sources of our examples, classifying them on the basis of overt grammatical and contextual cues. We have labeled "ambiguous" those instances which had no overt cues to their source. Tables 6 and 7 present the results of our analysis. As these tables show, nearly half (44%) of the instances of invariant be clearly have no underlying will or would, while almost a third of the examples (32%) are ambiguous. Deletion of will and would accounts for only 22% of the data. In this corpus, then, invariant be is more frequently a grammatical feature than the result of a phonological process.[7]

The meaning of those instances of invariant be which do not

derive from deletion of <u>will</u> or <u>would</u> is also open to question. Labov, Dunlap, and Brewer all present data which challenge Fasold's contention that in these cases <u>be</u> always indicates a distributive function. Our forty-seven unambiguous examples of <u>be</u> not derived from <u>will</u> or <u>would</u> deletion shed some light on the problem. In order to determine the semantic force of these examples, both authors independently rated them on a three-point scale of time reference (definite, intermittent, and continuous/stative). Tables 8 and 9 present the results of the ratings.

In four cases the authors either disagreed or were uncertain about the semantic force of invariant <u>be</u>; these have been labeled "ambiguous." Of the remaining forty-three examples, twenty-two (51%) refer to continuous actions or to permanent states and conditions. Eighteen instances (40%) refer to actions distributed in time, while four examples (9%) are used for actions which took place at a definite point in time. Clearly, then, as Brewer, Dunlap, and Labov suggest, the invariant <u>be</u> which is not derived from <u>will</u> or <u>would</u> deletion does not always have a distributive function. In fact, in our data the form indicates continuous actions or permanent conditions more frequently than intermittent actions. Further, the uses for actions at a definite point in time cannot be ignored. In this corpus, at least, "distributive <u>be</u>" is used for actions and states across the time spectrum.[8]

Table 8
Time Reference of Instances of Invariant <u>Be</u>
Not Derived from Underlying <u>Will</u> or <u>Would</u>

	Definite	Intermittent	Continuous/Stative	Ambiguous
Whites	1	4	2	0
Blacks	3	13	20	4
Totals	4	17	22	4

Table 9
Classification of Instances of "Distributive <u>Be</u>"
By Time Reference

Definite	Intermittent	Continuous/Stative	Ambiguous
10, 28, 36, 79	8, 9, 13, 24, 32, 40, 41, 43, 46, 50, 52, 57, 65, 76, 77, 85, 90	7, 11, 14, 15, 26, 35, 49a, 49b, 53, 54, 55, 56, 63, 64, 68, 69, 70, 73a, 73b, 73c, 73d, 89	18, 42, 71, 86

Finally, the tense of "distributive be" has posed problems. Fasold 1969, 1972 claims that the form is tenseless, but both Brewer and Dunlap have found instances of be used in past contexts. In the data used here, two examples of "distributive be" clearly refer to past actions. One of them involves the use of did before be:

(46) I never was called a bad man. I never did be out very much in the public. In a crowd, them days you called gamblers.

The other refers to an action that took place the preceding day:

(36) I was telling Mr. _____ yesterday you be here, and he was telling me about he locate some of his people, you know, in the, Virginia. And he said . . . you told him anything about what you used to do in Mr. ____'s yard?

"Distributive be" is clearly used infrequently in past contexts, but these instances cannot be ignored. The occurrence in three independent studies of three different parts of the South suggests that something more than error is involved. Only Rickford 1974 offers an explanation of the use of be in past contexts. He suggests that it is a relic of an earlier stage in the development of black speech from a creole when be signaled "incompleted" actions, whether nonpast or past.[9]

Conclusions

On the basis of the data presented here, a number of our assumptions about invariant be need to be revised. First, invariant be, including "distributive be," is clearly not unique to black speech. In fact, the form has a similar pattern of distribution for both races, with education, age, and sex all influencing the pattern. However, among blacks the form is much more common and is used by a larger segment of the population. Among whites, invariant be is largely restricted to male folk speech, though it occasionally occurs elsewhere.

Second, although both whites and blacks use invariant be resulting from will or would deletion, as well as "distributive be," the latter is apparently more common. Its semantic force, however, is not entirely clear. Unlike Fasold, we have found more examples of be used for continuous actions and permanent conditions than for intermittent actions. In addition, the use of invariant be for actions which occur at a definite point in time cannot be ignored. "Distributive be," then, is actually used to refer to events across the time continuum. While "distributive be" is generally tenseless, the few examples in past contexts deserve further consideration.

The origins of "distributive be" also deserve further consideration. There are four possible explanations for the form, but none of these is without problems. Explanations such as those of Dillard and Stewart, who suggest that "distributive be" is a relexification in black speech in order to match a creole aspectual category, must account for the presence of the form in white speech. While borrowing may be the explanation, creolists need to explain why "distributive be" sometimes occurs in the speech of whites who are not likely to have had extensive contacts with blacks. In addition, creolists must account for the pattern of distribution of invariant be in the speech of those whites.

Likewise, the data presented here pose problems for those who might claim that invariant be derives from British folk speech and was simply borrowed by blacks from whites. This theory must account both for the greater frequency and the less restricted occurrence of the form in black speech. It might be possible, of course, to claim that "distributive be" had different sources in black and white speech, but such a theory would not account for the similar patterns of distribution.

Finally, Jeutonne Brewer 1979 has offered an interesting alternative to all of these theories. On the basis of data in the WPA ex-slave narratives from South Carolina and Texas, Brewer suggests that blacks relexified a form to match with a creole aspectual category. However, that form was am, rather than be; under the influence of Anglo-Irish speech, be later replaced am.

While her theory is tentative, Brewer's historical study is exactly what is needed to resolve questions about the origin of "distributive be." In addition to such historical work, we need more study of Southern white speech. As this paper demonstrates, there can be no accurate account of black-white speech relationships without an accurate description of Southern white speech.

NOTES

[1] For a general overview of black-white speech relationships, see Fasold 1981.

[2] The Linguistic Atlas of the Gulf States is funded by the National Endowment for the Humanities. Because Bailey had resigned from the LAGS Project before the present study was undertaken, we thank the director of LAGS for use of the data in this independent interpretation.

In LAGS, the field records are the tape-recorded interviews; the phonetic transcriptions of these records, which correspond to the work books of other atlases, are called protocols. All of the LAGS protocols, as well as a detailed description of the project and an unabridged table of informants, are available in LAGS: The Basic Materials (Pederson et al. 1980).

[3] Raven I. McDavid, Jr., provided LAGS with a tape-recorded

description of his field methods.

[4]LAGS, Types I, II, and III refer solely to educational level: Type Is have a grade-school education or less, Type IIs have a high-school education, and Type IIIs have at least some college.

[5]For a more detailed description of the LAGS sample, see LAGS: The Basic Materials (Pederson et al. 1981).

[6]Compare these findings with Wolfram 1969, who finds that, among Detroit blacks, social class (determined in part by education) and sex affect the distribution of invariant be, with lower-working-class males using the form most frequently. Differences in the age range of his informants make comparisons along that scale difficult.

[7]Compare this with Sommer's essay in this volume.

[8]Labov (1982:198 fn 27) has suggested that although be "can be used for single events or permanent states when a higher degree of reality is to be signalled," the habitual and iterative meanings form the core of the semantic complex. The data here suggest that extended and permanent references are also a part of the core. The aspectual distinction, then, would be punctual vs. nonpunctual, with invariant be usually signaling the latter.

[9]Bailey and Maynor 1983, a follow-up to this study, based on new fieldwork in Mississippi and Texas, also finds instances of be used in past contexts (e.g., "They didn't be there in the kitchen").

Appendix A
LAGS Informants in East Louisiana, Gulf Mississippi, and Lower Mississippi (Excluding a Single Choctaw Indian Informant)[1]

(S = Sex; C = Class; R = Race; T = Type; Sub = Subtype)

East Louisiana

LAGS Grid	Town	County	S	C	R	Age	T	Sub
EC 407.02	Slidell	St. Tammany	M	L	W	67	1	A
EC 407.03	Slidell	St. Tammany	M	M	W	68	1	A
EC 407.01	Slidell	St. Tammany	M	M	W	62	3	B
EC 408.01	Bogalusa	Washington	M	L	W	79	2	A
EC 408.02	Bogalusa	Washington	M	M	W	60	2	A
EC 409.02	Kentwood	Tangipahoa	F	L	W	78	1	A
EC 409.01	East Fork	Tangipahoa	M	M	W	59	2	A
ED 410.01	Livingston	Livingston	M	L	W	84	1	A
ED 412.02	Clinton	East Feliciana	M	L	B	73	1	A
ED 412.01	Clinton	East Feliciana	M	M	W	73	2	A

ED 413.01	Zachary	East Baton Rouge	M	L	W	81	1	A
ED 413.03	Zachary	East Baton Rouge	M	L	B	67	1	A
ED 413.05	Zachary	East Baton Rouge	M	L	B	46	2	B
ED 413.06	Baton Rouge	East Baton Rouge	M	M	W	70	3	A
ED 413.04	Zachary	East Baton Rouge	F	M	W	39	2	A
ED 413.07	Baton Rouge	East Baton Rouge	M	M.	W	47	3	B
ED 413.02	Baton Rouge	East Baton Rouge	F	M	W	23	3	B
ED 414.01	St. Francisville	West Feliciana	M	M	W	75	1	A
EE 416.01	Boothville	Plaquemines	F	L	B	77	1	A
EE 416.02	Boothville	Plaquemines	F	L	W	46	1	B
EE 416.03	Boothville	Plaquemines	F	M	W	24	2	A
EE 417.08	New Orleans	Orleans	F	M	B	66	2	A
EE 417.10	New Orleans	Orleans	F	M	B	78	2	A
EE 417.01	New Orleans	Orleans	F	L	B	83	2	A
EE 417.09	New Orleans	Orleans	M	L	W	67	1	A
EE 417.02	New Orleans	Orleans	F	L	W	68	2	A
EE 417.06	New Orleans	Orleans	F	L	W	81	2	A
EE 417.05	New Orleans	Orleans	M	L	B	22	2	B
EE 417.07	New Orleans	Orleans	F	M	B	31	3	B
EE 417.03	New Orleans	Orleans	M	M	W	18	2	B
EE 417.04	New Orleans	Orleans	M	U	W	33	3	B
EE 418.01	Grand Isle	Jefferson	F	M	W	66	1	A
EE 418.02	Grand Isle	Jefferson	M	M	W	43	2	B
EF 421.01	Ardoyne	Terrebonne	M	L	B	87	1	A
EF 421.02	Little Bayou Black	Terrebonne	F	M	W	65	1	A
EF 421.03	Schriever	Terrebonne	F	M	W	35	2	B
EF 422.01	Morgan City	St. Mary	M	L	W	86	1	A
EF 423.01	Labadieville	Assumption	M	M	W	57	3	A
EF 425.02	Donaldsonville	Ascension	M	L	B	82	1	A
EF 425.01	Donaldsonville	Ascension	M	M	W	87	1	A
EG 427.01	Olivier	Iberia	M	L	B	80	1	A
EG 427.02	Loreauville	Iberia	F	M	W	69	2	A
EG 428.01	Bayou Chene	St. Martin	F	L	W	67	1	A
EG 429.03	Plaquemine	Iberville	F	L	B	73	1	A
EG 429.04	Grosse Tete	Iberville	F	M	W	87	1	A
EG 429.05	Grosse Tete	Iberville	M	M	W	86	1	A

EG 429.01	Grosse Tete	Iberville	M	M	W	55	2	A
EG 429.06	Grosse Tete	Iberville	F	M	W	75	2	A
EG 429.02	Bayou Sorrel	Iberville	F	M	W	38	2	B
EG 431.01	Mix	Pointe Coupee	M	M	B	85	1	A
EG 431.02	New Roads	Pointe Coupee	M	M	W	68	3	A

Gulf Mississippi

EA 401.04	Ocean Springs	Jackson	M	L	W	85	1	A
EA 401.03	Vancleave	Jackson	M	U	W	75	2	A
EA 401.02	Pascagoula	Jackson	M	L	W	51	2	B
EA 401.01	Moss Point	Jackson	M	A	W	83	2	B
EA 402.02	Biloxi	Harrison	M	L	W	85	1	A
EA 402.04	Biloxi	Harrison	M	M	B	87	1	A
EA 402.03	Biloxi	Harrison	M	L	W	53	2	A
EA 402.06	Gulfport	Harrison	F	M	B	17	2	A
EA 402.01	Saucier	Harrison	F	M	W	66	2	A
EA 402.05	Biloxi	Harrison	M	M	W	72	2	B
EA 404.01	Red Creek	Stone	F	M	B	33	3	B
EB 405.01	Kiln	Hancock	M	L	W	84	2	A
EB 405.02	Kiln	Hancock	M	U	W	70	2	B
EC 406.02	Carriere	Pearl River	M	L	B	79	1	A
EC 406.01	White Chapel	Pearl River	F	L	W	73	1	A
EC 406.03	Picayune	Pearl River	M	M	W	27	3	B

Lower Mississippi

DQ 364.01	Klondike	Kemper	M	M	B	73	2	A
DQ 365.01	Lockhart	Lauderdale	F	M	W	75	1	B
DQ 367.01	Bogue Chitto	Neshoba	M	M	W	44	2	B
DQ 367.02	Philadelphia	Neshoba	F	L	B	24	2	B
DR 371.03	Eden	Yazoo	M	L	B	87	1	B
DR 371.01	Pleasant Hill	Yazoo	F	M	W	63	1	A
DR 371.04	Freerun	Yazoo	F	U	W	80	3	B
DR 371.02	Pleasant Hill	Yazoo	M	U	W	42	1	B
DS 372.02	Vicksburg	Warren	F	M	B	77	1	A
DS 372.03	Redwood	Warren	F	L	W	68	1	A
DS 372.01	Vicksburg	Warren	M	A	W	87	3	B
DS 374.02	Mayersville	Issaquena	M	L	B	78	1	A

DS 374.03	Addie	Issaquena	F	M	W	72	2	A
DS 374.01	Mayersville	Issaquena	F	U	W	77	3	A
DT 375.01	Quitman	Clarke	M	M	W	76	1	A
DT 377.01	Trenton	Smith	M	L	W	77	2	A
DT 377.02	Wicker	Smith	F	M	W	65	3	B
DT 378.01	Pulaski	Scott	M	L	B	52	1	A
DU 379.04	Edwards	Hinds	M	L	B	88	2	A
DU 379.02	Edwards	Hinds	M	M	B	77	1	B
DU 379.05	Raymond	Hinds	M	M	W	78	1	A
DU 379.07	Jackson	Hinds	F	M	B	13	2	A
DU 379.03	Jackson	Hinds	F	M	B	66	3	B
DU 379.06	Jackson	Hinds	M	M	W	19	3	A
DU 379.01	Jackson	Hinds	F	M	W	70	3	B
DV 381.01	Lorman	Jefferson	M	L	B	74	1	A
DV 381.02	Lorman	Jefferson	M	L	W	68	2	A
DV 381.03	Lorman	Jefferson	F	L	W	50	1	A
DV 382.01	Little Springs	Franklin	M	M	B	78	1	B
DW 384.01	Leakesville	Greene	M	M	W	78	2	A
DW 386.01	Hattiesburg	Forrest	F	M	B	81	3	A
DW 386.02	Hattiesburg	Forrest	F	M	W	19	3	A
DW 387.07	Soso	Jones	M	L	W	87	1	A
DW 387.05	Soso	Jones	M	L	B	84	1	A
DW 387.02	Soso	Jones	F	L	W	80	1	B
DW 387.01	Union Line	Jones	M	M	W	85	2	A
DW 387.03	Soso	Jones	F	L	W	69	2	A
DW 387.06	Laurel	Jones	F	M	W	66	2	A
DW 387.04	Soso	Jones	F	L	B	40	3	A
DX 388.01	Baxterville	Lamar	M	I	W	72	1	A
DX 388.02	Lumberton	Lamar	F	M	W	78	2	A
DX 392.01	Weathersby	Simpson	F	M	W	85	1	A
DX 392.02	Mendenhall	Simpson	M	M	W	83	2	B
DY 394.01	Holmesville	Pike	M	M	W	95	1	A
DY 396.02	Bogue Chitto	Lincoln	M	M	W	85	2	B
DY 396.03	Brookhaven	Lincoln	F	M	W	72	2	A
DY 396.01	Brookhaven	Lincoln	F	M	W	79	2	B

DZ 399.02	Lessley	Wilkinson	M	L	B	85	1	A
DZ 399.01	Lake Mary	Wilkinson	M	L	B	66	1	A
DZ 399.03	Woodville	Wilkinson	M	L	B	73	2	A
DZ 399.04	Woodville	Wilkinson	F	U	B	75	3	B
DZ 400.01	Sibley	Adams	F	I	B	70	1	A
DZ 400.02	Natchez	Adams	M	M	W	52	2	B
DZ 400.04	Natchez	Adams	M	M	B	58	3	B
DZ 400.03	Natchez	Adams	F	A	W	79	3	B

Note to Appendix A

[1]This appendix is taken from the LAGS table of informants. For a fuller description of the informants, see LAGS: The Basic Materials (Pederson et al. 1981).

Appendix B
Examples of Invariant Be in the Corpus[1]
(F = Fieldworker; I = Informant)

East Louisiana

Whites

EC 407.02   1. So, we started [planting peppers] out. Some of them be putting on a rows, you know, and the others be putting in the ground with a little trowel.

2. You catch a handful [of hair] on me, you ain't done nothing. I believe you could hang me there. Sometimes some people be combing me, you know, and they taking it light. I'd say, "comb." I'd say, "what y'all doing?" I'd say, "comb me, put down on that comb--y'all ain't hurting my head."

EC 408.01   3. F: Lookout Mountain is in what town?
            I: Tennessee. Tennessee, or it be Georgia.

4. If that be true.

EC 409.02   5. I've heared people say that they [mermaids] get out on chunks and the sun be shining, warm weather and comb their, they have, have long hair, and comb it with their fingers.

6. If we'd get out working and be dirty on that old farm, we'd wash.

ED 413.01   7. [That land] don't be [sandy].

8. See, horses are kind of like people. Like, when people <u>be</u> together, they soon understand one another.

9. Well, I can cook. I can cook as good a corn bread as anybody. Only thing, I can't make good biscuits. My biscuits is hard. They don't <u>be</u> spongy like hers.

EF 423.01   10. [F. apologizes]. I.: I <u>be</u> a-joking with you.

EF 425.01   11. You take it and you put it over the wheel and then you pour water on it right away, you see. And then when it would shrink, well, it'd tighten all that wheel and give it the right cavity that it's supposed to have, you know, so it don't <u>be</u> straight--so it's got a . . .

Blacks

ED 412.02   12. It'd be a one-by-twelve or a one-by-eight or whatever it <u>be</u>.

13. It ain't too much of a river, but it rain like it rain now and water gets up, it <u>bees</u> pretty bad.

14. We don't <u>be</u> bothered with them.

ED 413.03   15. They don't <u>be</u> around here.

16. An armoire is a big-old something. Oh, that thing <u>be</u> tall as--well, the house was twice, the planks'd run sixteen feet. These walls'd be sixteen feet, I believe. And that thing stood about eight to ten foot--well, every bit of eight foot.

17. It had a gallery out there, but it wasn't walled in; just ran planks out there. And these here had planks running like that, and all of them had planks running like that, and you could see the ground any time you look down, and you go out there and get boards out the woods, and, take something and you cut them. It ain't like wood. It's something like, oh, it <u>be</u> about four inches, three to four inches wide.

18. Now, soot <u>bees</u> down here at the bottom. That's what they used to call soot. And this other's up, way up in the chimney, what you sweep out.

EE 416.01   19. I: . . . a stall, a stall what for the horse stayed in. The horse <u>be</u> in the barn to hisself.
        F: Huh?
        I: The horse <u>be</u> in the barn in the stable to hisself and the

corn to itself.

EE 417.08   20. Well, it depends on what it is because it might be something I disagree on. It all depends on what the person be doing or what the person be saying to me because some things I wouldn't agree and some I disagree. It all depends.

21. F: They might holler at you, "hey, will you be ready soon?" And you tell them, "I'll be ready in just a . . ."
    I: Well, it depend on if I <u>be</u> ready at that time.

EE 417.01   22. Weeping willows--they say the trees, they cry.
    F: The trees cry?
    They <u>be</u> falling down like that. That's what they call them--a weeping willow--because they grow and they falls like that.

23. F: Have you ever seen live pigs?
    I: Yeah, I think. When we <u>be</u> going on our little ride, we see things like that--pig and horses and cows and different places when the [unintelligible] take us for a ride.

EE 417.10   24. I don't <u>be</u> around them. [= I don't have occasion to be around them.]

EF 421.01   25. F: What sound does it [a calf] make when it's being weaned?
    I: When he <u>be</u> weaned?

26. I: They had blackland and sandy land and blue land.
    F: Blue?
    I: That's blue, blue, the land <u>be</u> blue, you understand, it don't make . . .

27. You see, squirrels are different colors. Some <u>be</u> brown, some <u>be</u> spotted, and some <u>be</u> white, you understand.

EF 425.02   28. How you <u>be</u> doing?

29. I <u>be</u> just cut the big weeds. [deleted <u>would</u>]

30. I'll cut the flower [s] down. I ain't <u>be</u> bother no flower. I can't eat that.

31. I <u>be</u> out. [= I will be out.]

32. That's why I goes back there and <u>bees</u> with her.

EG 431.01   33. Well. Wait a minute. What you talking about there?

Where your shirt, rubbed? And there be a bump come there? Well, let me see. I call it a black bump.

34. You load it in a way that it swinging, like that. If you put too much in front, it be too heavy on them two mules and you liable to fall--you can break their neck.

35. And they make a little nest up in there. But you got to get that thing away from there. Some of them be bad. Some of them'll bite you.

36. I was telling Mr. _____ yesterday you be here, and he was telling me about he locate some of his people, you know, in the, Virginia. And he said . . . you told him anything about what you used to do in Mr. _____'s yard?

Gulf Mississippi

Whites

EA 402.02   37. I be there. [= I will be there.]

Blacks

EB 406.02   38. F: Did you ever see anybody cook on a fireplace?
            I: Yes, ma'am. They had hangers up in there, and the fire be down here, and they'd put [it] on hangers and cook on it.

39. F: What if you had two horses?
            I: That be the singletree. Both them horses be pulling off the singletree. One be over there, and the other one over there, and the singletree clean across here.

Lower Mississippi

Whites

DV 381.02   40. I be pretty busy. [= I am]

41. When it clabbers, it don't always be sour. The clabber is, the clabber is pretty sweet, you know.

Blacks

DQ 364.01   42. That's made out of flour. And stir him up real good and don't have him thick, you know, too thick or nothing like that. And then have your skillet with your white, with plenty grease in it and it be good and hot and take up a spoon--put him over in that--about two spoonfuls. And that makes you a fritter near about big as your hand.

43. You ain't doing no business if you ain't got them around the water, you know. And sometime you go down there and they be laying up there in mud and stuff, you know. And if they get up to eat, you know, they can't hardly eat for being in the mud.

DQ 367.02   44. Everybody be drinking from the same thing.
[deleted would]

45. F: After they would plow, was there something they could drag, you know, and make the ground . . .
      I: It took a hoe see, everybody be spreaded out like that, you know, there be two or three plowing, and then you came behind them and chop that dirt up.

DR 371:03   46. I never was called a bad man. I never did be out very much in the public. In a crowd, them days you called gamblers.

47. Just like you had two, three, four, five hundred acres out yonder. Well, there was some white babies be done got on your place [hypothetical situation].

DS 372.02   48. Well, there was different kinds of grass--whatever kinds of grasses. Some of it be Bermuda grass, some be crabgrass, and some be cocoa grass--all kinds. And some of them be Johnson grass.

49. F: Talking about the wasp--how many would there be in the nest?
      I: I wouldn't know. I don't know how many would be in there.
      F: You might have about 30 . . .
      I: Might. I don't know. The nest bees full of them, I know. I say it's full of them. I say the nest bees full. I don't know where there would be 30.

DS 374.02   50. [Of tending beans] I used to get mine--that something another catches that trash stuff. On other side of the thing that cuts them. Turn that out on the ground. It don't be as much stuff. See, I don't like--I never had it growed up.

DT 378.01   51. F: What about the wooden thing that the rim fits over?
      I: That be the spokes--spokes.

52. You bees in that beach.

53. I don't be so sure now.

54. Because it bees just like that [of a cotton plant].

55. It bees tttrees all on the other side.

56. It bees, ain't but two. [false start]

DU 379.02   57. F: In this area?
      I: Yes, ma'am.
      F: Really? It gets that cold?
      I: It get cold here, and the ice be on the pond and
don't break. Just ski from one side to the other.

58. F: When it's time for you, now, to gather or harvest something, do you have some help?
      I: Well, sometime I have my grandson be here.
      F: Oh, he was here when I was here before.
      I: That's right. But, like right now, why, I have to do
the best I can.

59. F: Well, if you say that the pond froze over, would this
mean it was thick ice or thin?
      I: Well, depends upon how cold it be. Now, it could be
a thin coat of ice all over the pond.

60. Feed them once a day. Every morning when I get up, they
be coming--to the lot. And I get ready and go out there--everything
there. Whatever I'm going to give them, I give them.

61. [It] be paper. [deleted would]

62. I got a brother that's dead. He have killed them [wild
hogs]. He said some got a hide be a inch thick on them.

63. It don't be like that.

64. Some of them don't be an acre. [of patches]

DU 379.07   65. [Of a haunted house] F: You like to get yourself
scared?
      I: Well, I don't be scared that easy. I like going
through there. It's fun.

66. I usually just buy one [soft drink]. And that's usually
around about 30 minutes or 40 minutes before I go. And I be thirsty
by that time.

67. F: Do you ever see them [pimps] downtown?
          I: No, not really, because I don't go down there at
night. You know, there <u>be</u> some in those cheap hotels, sleeping in
the daytime.

DV 381.01   68. Every month I gets a magazine from Lorman, that
<u>bees</u> on REA.

69. No way to make a living out of farming. Well, lots of
white people turned their places in--put cattle on it, soybeans, such
stuff as that. So that cut the farming out. So there <u>be</u> no farming.

70. It don't <u>be</u> no more of that.

71. [If it wasn't no good from that time] it never <u>bees</u> any
good.

DV 382.01   72. F: What do they call a man who is in charge of a
ship?
          I: Shipmaster, wasn't it?
          F: I'm thinking of something else, a . . .
          I: A captain.
          F: That also would be in the Army?
          I: That's right, that's right. He'd be, that's right, that's
right. He <u>be</u> a captain.

73. F: How big is the onion part?
          I: Well, it don't <u>be</u>--it <u>bees</u> kind of a long onion. It
don't <u>be</u> very big around. It <u>bees</u> long--kind of long roots.

74. My father--they didn't run him out--they told him--he <u>be</u>
quiet, he wouldn't be bothered.

DW 387.05   75. [F asks about mantel over the fireplace]. That's
just, that's just, it <u>be</u> up there, just put that up there; didn't have
to have nothing . . . just put it up there for the looks.

DW 387.04   76. Plenty time it rain, it's just a shower, and it don't
<u>be</u> a cloud, just start raining and that's a shower.

77. F: Is that very heavy rain?
          I: No, not always. Sometime it <u>be</u> and sometime it
don't.

78. F: What was Camp Shelby?
          I: That was an army camp where the soldiers <u>be</u>, and
worked down there.

DZ 399.02   79. I hope it don't be cloudy. [speaking of a particular day]

DZ 399.01   80. Time they go to fall, they'll start to biting. I be down there every day. Fish there at night. Come in with one bunch and carry another bunch out and come back and be dark.

81. They be live. [deleted will or would]

82. Then be dark. [= then it would be dark.]

83. If they be know it [a song], I play it.

DZ 399.03   84. It's not as tall as corn usually be.

DZ 400.00   85. We didn't have no Frigidaires then--just cooked the food and put it up in a safe. If it be sour we throw it out.

86. If two be to the wagon [if two horses are attached].

87. F: Does that keep it from going out and laying?
    I: Keep them from going out laying. See, that egg be in the nest. Just go and gather your eggs where she laid--leave that false egg right in the nest.

88. F: What color is he?
    I: He brown, dark, dark.
    F: He doesn't have a red head like a woodpecker?
    I: No, he don't have . . .
    F: Where do you find him?
    I: He be flying around the elm and the people used to kill them.

89. Put them on top of one another till they get all the way around, far as they want to go. And if they don't be high enough, they come back over and put some more on top.

90. He work every day, but his wife at home. She don't work--she doesn't much of health [sic] for working out. They run a store. But she don't be down there every day. She took sick and she just--like somebody want something, she'll go down there and sell it to them--she come on back to her house.

Note to Appendix B

[1]In most instances we have gone back to the field records to provide the semantic contexts for these examples of invariant be. When clear scribal glosses were given in the protocols, we have sometimes simply reproduced those.

Variation in Southern Urban English

Elisabeth Sommer

This paper reports on three aspects of the verb phrase as it appears in the conversational speech of four groups of black and white school children in Atlanta. It focuses on invariant be, be agreement, and the third person marker in the speech of nine upper-middle white, nine lower white, nine upper-middle black, and nine lower-class black fifth graders. Variation in usage both among the four groups and within each group is presented and analyzed. In the tables, the total number of children within each group of nine who provide examples of a particular structure is listed under "No. Children." Also, heading the lists of sentences taken from the interviews, the number of children providing the examples is given in parentheses. The findings are related to the work of several other researchers: (1) Wolfram 1969, Fasold 1972, and Labov et al. 1968 on the speech of blacks in Northern urban areas; (2) Feagin 1979 on the speech of whites in Alabama; and (3) Wolfram and Christian 1976 on Appalachian English. (The relevance of the last admittedly may be marginal, Atlanta being at the foothills of the Appalachians.)

The Subjects

In 1967, personnel in the Atlanta school system made plans for conducting ninety-six interviews with children in the Atlanta public schools. The interviews were to provide a basis for describing the ethnic and social varieties of speech in the area. With the intention of including a wide range of social classes, the researchers carefully selected six schools, three largely white and three all black, with as nearly socially homogeneous populations within each school as possible. Two schools represented upper-middle-class neighborhoods, two represented lower-middle-class neighborhoods, and two represented lower-class neighborhoods. A description of the schools follows:

> The upper-middle class white school (UMW) [Birney] is located in Atlanta's fashionable northside, about eight miles from the downtown area. Most of the children at this school are highly privileged, living in $75,000-$150,000 homes. One student at this school . . . had spent two summers on safari in Africa. Another of the informants, when asked for his phone number, responded, "Do you want mine or my parents'?" The upper-middle class black school (UMB) [Collier Heights] is located in a fashionable black area about six miles west of downtown Atlanta. The children at this school come from homes mainly in the $50,000-$100,000 range, and are likewise quite privileged. Occupations of their parents include surgeon and bank vice-presidents. The lower-middle class white school (LMW) [Sylvan Hills] is located about four miles south of the downtown area in an older residential area which was beginning to feel the effects of black influx and white departure. The lower-middle class black school (LMB) [M. Agnes Jones] is about two miles southwest of downtown; it has remained fairly stable because it is on the fringe of the fashionable large black area mentioned above and because the nearby Atlanta University complex helps to hold the neighborhood intact. The lower class white school (LW) [Grant Park] is about two miles east of downtown in a textile mill area which is now surrounded by blacks but which has stubbornly resisted their encroachment into the white enclave. The lower class black school (LB) [Bethune] ironically is located on the same thoroughfare as the UMW school, but about seven miles closer to downtown Atlanta in one of the city's most impoverished neighborhoods. A child at this school, when asked what she liked to have for breakfast, answered matter of factly, "It don't be nothing to fix." Another, when asked to describe the longest trip he had ever taken, told about going with his class to see the Atlanta Stadium less than two miles away [Dunlap 1973:14-15, 17].

In each of these schools, sixteen children were identified as potential informants. They were chosen at random from a list made up from permanent record cards of all fifth graders who were born in Atlanta. The children at each school were called together and given general information about the project. They were also told that participation was strictly voluntary and that no one at their schools would ever know the results of each interview. All expressed a desire to participate and were given letters, asking parental permission, to take home and have signed. In the few instances that these letters were not returned, another child was selected at random as a replacement.

Although the students had already been classified into socio-economic classes, in a general way, by the schools they attended, more specific information on each child's socioeconomic standing was sought. The occupation of the head of the household was taken from school records, and the educational level of each parent was established, as well as it could be, by asking the informants. Each of these three factors was assigned a weight in accordance with the scale in table 1 below, a modification of the Hollingshead Two Factor Index of Social Position.

Table 1

Factors 1 and 2: Education of Each Parent

Highest Level Parent Achieved	Weight
College graduate	1
Some college	2
High school graduate	3
Ninth grade	4
Sixth grade	5
Less than sixth grade	6

Factor 3: Occupation of Head of Household

Professional, sales, supervision, business administration	1
Second-level management, public school teaching	3
Skilled industrial or building-trade worker, truck driver or bus driver	5
Unskilled business or industrial worker, day laborer, public sanitation employee	7
Unemployed, relief	9

The four groups of sixteen children from each school were then ranked on the basis of their scores.

This researcher wanted to select from the original group of children the thirty-six children representing the extremes of the upper-middle and lower classes. To this end, the nine whites and nine blacks with the numerically lowest scores (highest socio-economic standing) were chosen from the upper-middle- and lower-middle-class schools; and the nine whites and nine blacks

with the numerically highest scores (lowest socioeconomic standing) were chosen from the lower class schools. Exceptions to this
procedure were made only to balance sex across the groups (the
nature of the original random sample made it feasible to have a
boy to girl ratio of 1 to 2 within each of the four groups), and in
cases in which the acoustical quality of the tape recording made it
impossible to perform a linguistic analysis.

The upper-middle-white group which was selected by this
procedure turned out to consist exclusively of children who
attended the white school originally selected as representing the
highest socioeconomic level in the city. All of them had socioeconomic scores of 3, indicating that both parents were given the
highest score. The upper-middle-black group, on the other hand,
was drawn from both the black school identified as typically
upper-middle class (four children) and the one identified as lower-
middle class (five children). Their socioeconomic scores ranged
from 5 to 9, with a mean of 7. Clearly, their parents did not have
levels of education nor did their heads of household have jobs
equal to the upper-middle white group. However, the positions of
the families of the black children within the black community
probably paralleled the positions of the families of the white
children in the white community.

The selection procedure resulted in lower-class groups, drawn
exclusively from the two lower-class schools, that were more like
one another with respect to socioeconomic scores than were the
upper-middle-class groups. The lower white scores ranged from 13
to 17, the lower black from 13 to 16; the mean score for each
group was 15. For a child to obtain the mean score, both of the
child's parents could not possibly have even some college attend-
ance. To give another example, if the head of the household was
employed as a truck driver or skilled worker, both of the child's
parents could have had a sixth grade education.

The Interview

Each interview was conducted by one of two white Southern
adults, neither of whom any of the children had known previously.
The speech of both interviewers was essentially that of the white
upper-middle-class group of children. The interviews were conducted between 1967 and 1970.

For each interview, the interviewer and the student walked
from the student's classroom to the room where the interview was
to be held--ideally, an empty conference room--where the tape
recorder was waiting. As it was readied, the interviewer made
small talk and again explained what would take place, just as on
the first visit to the school when the child was invited to participate. To "test" the recorder, a minute or so of conversation was
recorded and played back. Then an information sheet was filled

out, giving the child's age, date of birth, home address, and other potentially useful information. Next, a 182-item Linguistic Atlas questionnaire, calling for short-answer responses, was given. This usually took about an hour and helped establish rapport between the interviewer and informant. After the questionnaire, the interviewer conversed with the child. Working with a general set of questions derived partly from the Detroit Dialect Study questionnaire, the interviewer encouraged the child to talk freely about such subjects as after-school activities, pets, favorite TV programs, church, and trips.

Clearly, some aspects of this interview situation tended to make the children speak carefully. They had been singled out to speak with an adult with whom they were not personally acquainted. Moreover, their speech appeared to be a primary object of interest: it was being recorded, presumably for future study, and the interviewer, in giving the questionnaire, went to great lengths to elicit particular words for no apparent reason except to find out if they knew them or how they would say them. In addition, the interviewer was upper-middle class and white, a member of the power elite in the area. Beyond that, the interviewer seemed to have special status in the school system, working outside the daily routines.

In spite of this, for the most part the children were relaxed and often animated, especially in the conversational portion of the interview upon which this study is based. The questionnaire, preceding the interview, served to remove any edge of anxiety. The interviewer was friendly and expressed interest in what the child was saying. Repeatedly, the child was told that if there was anything he or she didn't want to talk about, they would go on to something else. Finally, each child was assured that no one at his or her school would ever hear the tape recording.

The children's conversations were typed, double spaced, on 8 1/2-by-11-inch paper. The first five pages of each interview form the corpus.

Distributive Be

Distributive be has received a great deal of analytical attention. Labov, Wolfram, and Fasold in particular have discussed its use at length. Their important treatments of this unique aspect of black American speech all give attention to identifying distributive be, for in practice it is sometimes difficult to distinguish it from cases of will or would contraction and deletion. The two are phonetically alike, can for the most part appear in the same grammatical environments, and are semantically not sufficiently differentiated to allow for clear-cut separation in all cases on the basis of meaning. Indeed, Fasold feels he cannot classify 10.5 percent (17 of 162) of the examples he drew from a study of the nature of invariant be in black English, because the context does not make sufficiently clear which of the two sources is correct (1972:152-58). And in a publication that appeared two years later, Wolfram writes that "there are admittedly a few cases where the context does not immediately disambiguate the source of be" (1974:520).

In spite of the uncertainties, these researchers have offered guidelines for separating distributive be's from cases of invariant be deriving from will or would deletion. In the application of their guidelines to the Atlanta data, some interesting questions arose regarding the deletion of will or would before be + V + ing--to which both Fasold and Wolfram refer. Fasold writes that "many" cases of invariant be "can be assumed to be cases of will or would deletion, on the basis of general context" (1972:157). Both of the examples of assumed would deletion he gives include be + V + ing:

> When I was supposed to be doing my work, I be talking to girls or talking to somebody.

> They called him. They sent him a letter over this summer and told him that they be writing back to him. (1972:157)

Also, two of his three examples of the false start, which he considers to be "an exceptionally clear indication of deleted will or would" (1972:156), involve be + V + ing:

> On when they had assemblies at school, Miss Rosenzweig, we get ready to go, she be shou--she'd yell at you and make you get on line.

> I be buying--I'd buy a little house and stuff (Fasold 1969:772, 1972:157).

Wolfram follows his statement that "there are admittedly a few cases where the context does not immediately disambiguate the source of be," with four examples, two of which include be + V + ing:

> I be up there playing the piano, practicing, she's up there "bing."

> Daddy's always bringing logs when you be in bed, you know, at night.

> It be running but really it be bucking.

> You have to build you a turkey blind, find you a place where it be hard to see if you move. (1974:520).

He goes on to say that sentences like these "might quite legitimately be interpreted as instances of would or will be," and "there
are several reasons why these potentially ambiguous cases should
be so interpreted" (1974:520).

With their positions in mind, let us turn to the Atlanta data.
The eighteen white children provide no examples, and the eighteen
black children provide seventy-two examples of unconjugated be as
the main verb. All of these are nonstandard (i.e., invariant be)
except one from an LB child, which is a borderline case of a
standard use of unconjugated be and is not tabulated below. Table
2 reports the frequencies.

Table 2
Invariant be: Occurrence in Interviews

Class	No. Children	No. Examples by Group	No. Examples by Race
UMW	0	0	
LW	0	0	0
UMB	7	12	
LB	9	59	71

To suggest the magnitude of invariant be usage that the
seventy-one examples represent, a tabulation of the frequency of
invariant be, relative to occurrences of full and contracted forms
of am, is, and are, and of zero copula, is given in table 3.

Table 3
Occurrences of Invariant be Relative to
Occurrences of am, is, are, and Zero Copula

Class	No. Children	Total Invariant be, am, is, are, and zero copula	% Invariant be by Group	% Invariant be by Race
UMW	9	0/416	0	
LW	9	0/270	0	0
UMB	9	12/287	4.2	
LB	9	59/218	27.1	14

These figures show that, on the average, for every three instances
of am, is, are, or zero copula, the lower-class black children
provide more than one instance of invariant be.

Among the seventy-one examples of invariant be are proportionally many cases of be + V + ing; one third of the UMB and about one-half of the LB children's invariant be's fit this pattern. Some examples follow:

Mama said that sometime she be wanting somebody to hold her.

He take my candy and I be crying.

Well, I be getting out. Then I go home to change my clothes.

The frequencies are reported in table 4.

Table 4
Occurrences of Invariant be + V + ing
Relative to Total Occurrences of Invariant be

Class	No. Children	No. Invariant be + V + ing	Invariant be + V + ing/ Invariant be + anything	
			No.	%
UMB	3	4	4/12	33
LB	8	29	29/59	49

Another example, not tabulated in Table 4 but possibly related, is from an LB child:

Some of them, they be live [lɪv] kind of far.

To what extent are these examples of will or would deletion, and to what extent are they distributive be's? Following the lines of thinking of Fasold and Wolfram, one might conclude that many, or even almost all of them, are cases of will or would deletion. And there is no proof that this is not the case. However, a disturbing asymmetry in the data and some other evidence suggest that casually attributing will and would deletion before be + V + ing to black speakers may be wrong.

Rather than examine the likelihood of deletion by studying phonological patterns, let us focus on syntactic evidence, evidence too often overlooked. To say on phonological grounds that contraction and deletion of will or would before be is common says nothing about the likelihood of there having been anything there to delete in the first place.

If many of the be + V + ing forms that the black children use derive from will or would deletion, one might anticipate finding the full forms in the speech of the white children, or an explanation for their absence. In fact, not a single white child of either class uses will or would + be + V + ing. How does this come about? It is not because the white children do not use the modals will or would. Table 5 shows their frequency before any verb but be to be about the same for the two white as for the two black groups.

Table 5
Occurrence of will or would before any Verb but be

Class	No. Children	No. Occurrences
UMW	9	98
LW	9	124
UMB	9	128
LB	9	90

Nor do the white children avoid the progressive. Table 6 shows the frequency with which the simple present progressive is used by each of the four groups.

Table 6
Occurrence of Simple Present Progressive

Class	No. Children	No. Occurrences
UMW	8	26
LW	7	22
UMB	6	33
LB	5	14

The complete absence of full or potential will or would + be + V + ing in the interviews of the white children is set against the following among the black children: (1) two full forms in the interviews, both from UMB children and given below,

> And if someone, if a player made a home run, you--you would be on first and he would be coming to first and you would go all around the bases and he would be behind you. And then the next player comes up and then the pitcher pitched the ball. And when he pitched the ball and you swing at it . . .

> We'd be playing.

and (2) thirty-three other potential cases of will or would + be + V

+ ing (as shown in table 4), with eight of the nine LB children providing examples.

Thus we have a sharp contrast between the black and white children with respect to full and potential occurrences of will or would + be + V + ing; and we have only two examples (in 90 pages of interviews) of the full form imagined to underlie cases in BEV of NP + be + V + ing.

If Wolfram and Fasold's positions on will and would deletion before be + V + ing are in need of revision and most or all of the thirty-three examples of NP + be + V + ing are distributive, then near symmetry in the data is restored. A case could even be made that the two full forms that do occur in the interviews are the result of special efforts by the UMB children to use standard English that result in structures rarely used in standard English. Thus we can observe that the first example is from a child who uses many features of Black English Vernacular, but--except for the "invisible" existential it--at a very low rate. This child does not (in her simple description of baseball, cited above) maintain parallel or near parallel auxiliaries (tense and modals) or a consistent point of view, creating a jumble that is not characteristic of the rest of her interview and suggesting that a nervous self-consciousness may characterize her speech at that point. This child also says they'll have, they will have in a self-correcting sequence (the only such example in the interviews). This child never contracts would in the nineteen times she uses it, and she ties for the highest frequency of would usage among the UMB children. As further testimony to her efforts at correct English, she provides one of the only three so-called hypercorrect third person markers in the UMB interviews. And the second example, we'd be playing, is from the same boy who may have used would in at least one other place before be to mask an otherwise nonstandard construction. He says:

It'd be my brother's time to wash the dishes, and he says it doesn't.

The presence of doesn't calls for the reading of distributive doesn't be--clearly not parallel to the opening would be. (That we be playing is a likely structure is attested to by the fact that occurrences of it are three of the four UMB invariant be's.)

If, on the other hand, Fasold and Wolfram's positions are essentially correct and will or would are often deleted before V + ing, the sequence would or will + be + V + ing may be more characteristic of black than white American speech. To my knowledge, such an observation has not appeared in the literature to date. If one imagines it to be the case that will or would + be + V + ing is more characteristic of black than white American speech, the next question is: How did this come to be? Perhaps black Americans, while using will or would before anything but be about

as often as whites (as suggested in table 5), use it far more often
before be as a way of legitimizing an otherwise distributive be.
The Atlanta data suggest this may hold true, with blacks using
more than eight times as many will be's or would be's as whites,
and with the supposed tendency toward correction represented by
the use of will or would be stronger among the upper-middle than
the lower-class black children (see table 7).

Table 7
Use of will + be or would + be

Class	No. Children	No. Occurrences
UMW	2	4
LW	0	0
UMB	7	24
LB	5	10

That this may account for a higher use of will or would + be +
V + ing among blacks than whites is admissible. But are we to
imagine that the very construction we are now assuming to be
used eight times as often by blacks, because it promises avoidance
of incorrect structures, is regularly not phonologically realized,
with will or would before be + V + ing being generally contracted
and deleted, leaving us with large numbers of invariant be's
derived from will and would deletion? Consideration of the information presented on the Atlanta interviews and another look at
Fasold's examples of false starts suggests the answer is no--not
without more reservations than other researchers have exhibited.

Among Fasold's three examples of false starts, each of which
he takes to be an exceptionally clear case of will or would deletion, we find that in both cases in which the child begins with an
apparent be + V + ing, "She be shou . . ." and "I be buying," the
correction is not to that rare will or would + be + V + ing, but to
would + V: "She'd yell" and "I'd buy." Thus even when the child
has set the pattern by beginning with a be + V + ing, upon introducing would, the progressive is dropped. The construction would +
be + V + ing is thus not just absent here, as it generally is in the
interviews, but most significantly absent. The children's changes
once again support the point made throughout his discussion that
further examination of distributive be, especially before be + V
-ing, is needed.

Be Agreement

In contrast to the use of invariant be, agreement of be with
the subject has not been the topic of extensive analytical discussion. It has, however, consistently been treated in school grammars, while invariant be has not. The reason for this seems
evident: nonagreement of be is common enough among white
speakers to warrant its being singled out for special explanation
and drilling in the schools. In this section, it will be shown that
for each of the Atlanta groups, nonagreement of be is more
common when dummy there, it, or they precedes be and the
subject follows than when the subject precedes be; and is more
common for was than is. Overall, nonagreement of be is found to
be greater within the lower-class groups, the white lower class in
particular.

Dummy There, It, or They + Was/Were or Is/Are

The context most conducive to be nonagreement, dummy there,
it, or they with a plural subject, shows 91 percent nonagreement
for was/were (10 of 11 cases) and 59 percent for is/are (10 of 17
cases) for all groups combined. By group, nonagreement is UMW 57
percent, LW 86 percent, UMB 25 percent, and LB 90 percent (see
table 8). Nonagreement with a following singular subject does not
occur.

Table 8
Dummy there, it, or they + is/was + NP Plural
(Occurrence in Interviews)

Class	No. Children	was/ Total	%	No. Children	is/ Total	%
UMW	1	1/1	100	2	3/6	50
LW	1	2/2	100	2	4/5	80
UMB	1	1/2	50	0	0/2	0
LB	3	6/6	100	3	3/4	75

Class	No. Children	was & is/Total	%
UMW	3	4/7	57
LW	2	6/7	86
UMB	1	1/4	25
LB	4	9/10	90

While dummy _there_ with nonagreement characterizes both classes and races, as we would expect, dummy _it_ or _they_ with nonagreement is used only by the lower black children, as the ten examples of _was/were_ nonagreement (below) show.

UMW
There _was_ a couple of men.

LW (1)
There _was_ these two boys.
There _was_ fish.

UMB
There _was_ a lot of people coming around.

LB (4)
It _was_ some girls but they were playing like they were boys.
It _was_ two houses.
It _was_ some Indians around there.
It _was_ some horsies over there.
They _was_ them people.
They _was_ some eggs.

The small number of examples of nonagreement--a total of twenty--and the small number of children providing examples--a total of ten--would suggest caution in drawing conclusions regarding ethnic and class patterns. It is noteworthy, certainly, that three of the upper-middle-class whites show this form of nonagreement. The figures on the upper-middle black group, showing they provide proportionally very few examples of nonagreement, suggest they may be more aware of the standard than other groups. The one case of standard English dummy _there_, rather than _it_ or _they_, from LB children is also the only example from this group showing agreement. One is tempted to speculate about the influence of grammar books on the speech of the black children, a group linguistically different and perhaps somewhat insecure, aware of language, and willing to change their speech.

A check of six commonly used school grammars shows all specifically treat dummy _there_, followed by a plural subject; none specifically treats copula deletion, third person present verb markers, invariant _be_, and many other features typical of Black English Vernacular speakers. Perhaps the upper-middle-class black children take what they read in grammars seriously, and perhaps their parents did too and now provide correction and examples at home.

In studying other aspects of the grammars of this group of Atlanta children, evidence of this sort of influence will be sought, but a bit of anecdotal information must suffice for now. During her interview, as she reported what she said to a cashier who attempted to shortchange her, an upper-middle-class girl said: "This kind of fruit cocktail, um these kind of fruit cocktail only cost twenty-five cents a can." No obvious parallel to this evidently grammar-book-based effort at correction exists in the interviews from the other three groups. However, generalizations about such patterns must await further inquiry since the numbers on non-agreement, though suggestive, are admittedly small.

We can compare the figures in table 5 to Feagin's findings on dummy there in Anniston white English. Her teenage upper-class speakers show 32 percent (22/68) nonagreement and the upper-class older people show 17 percent (14/81) nonagreement, both low, in comparison to my overall upper-middle white figure of 57 percent nonagreement. Her working-class white teenagers show 86 percent (71/82) nonagreement--precisely the same as my lower whites--and the older working-class whites show 91 percent (155/171) (Feagin 1979:206).

Subject + Was/Were

Nonagreement for was/were, following a plural subject, is zero (0/32) for UMW, 71 percent (17/24) for LW, 6 percent (2/33) for UMB, and 40 percent (19/47) for LB. See table 9.

Table 9
Plural Subject + was
(Occurrence in Interviews)

| Class | Plural Noun Phrase | | | | we, you, they | |
	No. Children	was/ Total	%	No. Children	was/ Total	%
UMW	0	0/6	0	0	0/26	0
LW	1	1/2	50	7	16/22	73
UWB	0	0/9	0	1	2/23	9
LB	2	2/4	50	2	17/43	40

Total Plural Subjects

Class	No. Children	was/Total	%
UMW	0	0/32	0
LW	7	17/24	71
UMB	1	2/33	6
LB	2	19/47	40

The lower white group has both the highest percent and the largest number of children (seven of the nine) providing examples. Of these seven children, only three also provide correct agreement of was/were with a plural subject. The lower black group members provide examples. Unlike the majority of the LW children, both of these black children vary in their use of was or were, each one providing a number of instances of correct were: ten incorrect was and eight correct were by one, and nine incorrect was and four correct were by the other. For the upper-middle-class groups, was/were nonagreement with plural subjects was almost completely absent, the only two examples out of sixty-five being from one upper-middle-class black child.

As table 9 shows, in almost all the examples of was/were nonagreement with plural subjects, a pronoun is the subject. The only three examples of nonagreement after NP plural subjects include two compound subjects with a singular noun closest to the verb:

LB (2)
The meatballs and spaghetti and stuff was on top.
My mama and my aunty was going with us up there.

The only other case of nonagreement with an NP plural subject is:

LW
All them cars was out of there.

All the remaining instances of nonagreement are of we or they immediately followed by the verb. (You occurs only once in the interviews with the past of be. In the interview situation, the child talks to a stranger whose past he or she doesn't know.) Some examples of nonagreement with the plural pronouns we and they follow:

LW
They was scared.

UMB
And all the while we was looking for the ghost house, we
    were riding in everything on this side.

LB
Last night when we 'uz playing musical chairs, I was
    fixing to win.

The figures for invariable was in table 9 can be compared to those from Feagin's study. The totals are startlingly similar. Feagin's upper-middle Atlanta whites show zero usage, the upper-class teens 1 percent (2/205), and older persons 3.3 percent (15/453); the lower-class Atlanta whites have 71 percent invariant was, the Anniston teens have 57.8 percent, and older persons 76.1 percent, an average of 69.5 percent (Feagin 1979:202). Labov, however, finds a low 12 percent invariable was by eight white working-class New York City boys (the Inwood gang), who did not associate with blacks (Labov et al. 1968:I:247). Wolfram and Christian find 91 percent nonstandard was/were agreement in the speech of West Virginia working-class subjects they studied (1976:112), considerably higher than the 71 percent of the Atlanta lowwer-working-class children.

Nonagreement following a singular subject is so rare that percentages of occurrence are not counted. The only two examples from the interviews follow:

UMW
The judge weren't very good. (The speaker makes repeated reference to one judge.)

LB
And this man mother were already . . .

Subject + Is/Are

In contrast to the thirty-eight examples of was/were non-agreement, is/are nonagreement with plural subjects is restricted to the five examples (see table 10) listed below.

UMB
Well, some of the things we do in music, well, is sit, you know.

LW (4)
No. He won't, he won't. Only things he likes is to be rubbed and to, uh, he'll . . .

Chuck Connors is in Africa, and they fix animals up that's hurt and everything.

See, we've got two couches that's made out into beds.

The cars is real close, and you have to run right out in front of them, and they stop.

The first two examples are similar to each other in having things as the subject, plus a relative clause followed by only the first verb that things promises. The next two examples are like each other too, in that both show nonagreement with the relative

Table 10
Plural Subject + is
(Occurrences in Interviews)

| Class | NP Plural | | | we, you, they | | |
	No. Children	is/ Total	%	No. Children	is/ Total	%
UMW	0	0/12	0	0	0/32	0
LW	4	4/5	80	0	0/20	0
UMB	1	1/7	14	0	0/33	0
LB	0	0/5	0	0	0/7	0

Total Plural Subjects

Class	No. Children	is/ Total	%
UMW	0	0/44	0
LW	4	4/25	16
UMB	1	1/40	2
LB	0	0/12	0

pronoun that, which in each case has a plural noun antecedent. Only the last example does not present these complexities in syntax. The child who says the cars is real close also uses the correct are with plural nouns. Not surprisingly, she is one of the children who has complete nonagreement for was/were, using was six times with a plural subject.

In sum, there is far less is/are than was/were nonagreement; and the few cases of is/are nonagreement are of is for are following only noun phrase plural subjects, not pronouns.

These findings parallel those of Feagin in that she also finds no examples of is/are nonagreement with pronouns among the white teenagers of both classes. In general, figures for nonagreement of is/are with plural nouns are far higher in her study than in mine: 15.1 percent for upper-class teenagers and 32.7 percent for upper-class older persons, compared to zero in mine; 29.4 percent for working-class teenagers and 40.4 percent for working-class older persons, compared to 16 percent in mine. She does not report in detail on the syntax, so it is not possible to determine if the same features of syntax are associated with nonagreement in her study as they are here.

Third Person Marker

This section takes up the deletion of {-s} from finite verbs, and shows that -∅ patterns according to race, except in doesn't, where it patterns by class. Following the discussion of -∅, findings on hyper--s are presented.

{-S} Deletion from all Verbs but Do + Negative

Following a third person singular noun, {-s} is deleted by the UMWs 0 percent (0/189), is deleted by the LWs 1.5 percent (4/260), by the UMBs 5.1 percent (10/197), and by the LBs 76.4 percent (120/157) (see table 11). The figures for do and have are shown separately in table 11, since both have pronunciations that deviate from the patterns for the other verbs and both may serve as auxiliaries, making them potentially different. However, the few cases do not suggest they are used in their nonstandard forms at a different rate than the other verbs.

Table 11
Deletion of {-s} from a Verb Other than do + Negative
(Occurrence in Interviews)

Class	All Verbs but do and have			Do not Followed by Negative		
	No. Children	∅ {s}/ Total	%	No. Children	∅ {s}/ Total	%
UMW	0	0/138	0	0	0/5	0
LW	4	4/212	1.9	0	0/6	0
UMB	4	10/150	6.7	0	0/4	0
LB	9	113/147	76.9	2	3/4	75

Class	have			All Verbs		
	No. Children	∅ {s}/ Total	%	No. Children	∅ {s}/ Total	%
UMW	0	0/46	0	0	0/189	0
LW	0	0/42	0	4	4/260	1.5
UMB	0	0/43	0	4	10/197	5.1
LB	4	4/6	66.7	9	120/157	76.4

A few examples of -∅ in the interviews follow:

LB
My mama <u>wake</u> me up.
They mama <u>make</u> a nest.
He <u>eat</u> dinner with us on Sunday.
That why Daddy <u>wear</u> his boots.

The figures show {-s} deletion to be almost exclusively characteristic of the black speakers, and especially of the lower-class
blacks.
The frequency and salience of -∅ make it a feature of considerable social consequence. To give a more complete picture of its
use, figures for each of the thirty-six children are given in table
12.

Table 12
Deletion of -s from a Verb after the Third Person Singular
Noun or Pronoun (Have and Do Not Included)
in Interview of Each Child

UMW		LW		UMB		LB	
-∅/Total	%	-∅/Total	%	-∅/Total	%	-∅/Total	%
0/8	0	0/14	0	0/21	0	7/19	36.8
0/18	0	0/7	0	0/11	0	9/14	64.3
0/11	0	0/15	0	0/2	0	23/24	95.8
0/21	0	1/12	8.3	0/10	0	7/7	100.0
0/18	0	1/48	2.1	0/22	0	39/40	97.5
0/16	0	0/15	0	4/12	33.3	4/7	57.1
0/13	0	0/35	0	3/36	8.3	9/11	81.8
0/24	0	1/40	2.5	1/14	7.1	1/5	20.0
0/9	0	1/25	4.0	2/22	9.1	14/20	70.0

This table shows speakers with a high proportion of -∅ concentrated in the lower black group. In this group, deletion ranges
from 20 percent to 100 percent, with three of the nine children
ranging above 95 percent deletion. The upper-middle-class black
child with 33 percent deletion is the only child outside the lower
black group whose deletion rate falls into the lower-class black
range.
Comparing the findings to Feagin's on white Southern speech
reveals nearly identical results for -∅ (excluding do and have): the
rate for upper-middle-class whites in this study is zero, while for
the upper-class teens in her study the rate is also zero (0/288),
and for upper class older persons 0.4 percent (1/235). The lower-
class whites in this study show -∅ in 2.4 percent of all contexts,
while the working-class teens in Feagin's study show 2.3 percent

(10/438) and the working-class urban older persons 2.7 percent (23/844) (1979:188). Commenting on the possible significance of the few deletions among the white speakers she interviewed, Feagin writes:

> Each age and category had two or three individuals who displayed this kind of agreement. Wolfram says that he found the same sort of variation in his Mississippi informants [1975:personal communication].

> While several examples do lend themselves to the performance error explanation, it is important not to dismiss the issue entirely, since neither Hackenberg nor the Labov team found any examples among either West Virginia whites or New York City teenage white males of the Inwood area. The Inwood data was based on seven informants with 171 examples, while the Anniston data base was much greater [1979:189].

Comparing my figures on the black children to Labov's findings on black adolescent gang members in New York City, we find a higher rate among the Southern lower-class black children: the lower blacks in this study average 76.9 percent deletion, compared to the 64.2 percent (669/1089) for Harlem gang members and lames (Labov et al. 1968:I:161-67).

The Atlanta findings support the contention that deletion of the third person marker in verbs, other than in do plus a negative, is a defining characteristic of Black English Vernacular. It is interesting to note that not a single example of -∅ is followed by a self-correction toward the standard.

{-S} Deletion in Do + Negative

{-S} in doesn't (does not does not occur in the interviews) is zero for UMW, 83.3 percent for LW, 29.4 percent for UMB, and 84.2 percent for LB (see table 13). Whereas -∅ in other environments is linked to race, in do + negative, it patterns according to social class. The lower-class white children use don't for standard English doesn't about as often as the lower-class black children: 83 and 84 percent of all occurrences. The upper-middle-class black children use it far less, and the upper-middle white not at all. Examples from the data include:

UMB
Barnabas don't want him to kill nobody.

LW
She don't think she'll ever go back again.

Table 13
Deletion of -s in Do + Negative (Occurrence in Interviews)

	No. Children	-∅/Total	%
UMW	0	0/13	0
LW	7	15/18	83.3
UMB	4	5/17	29.4
LB	5	16/19	84.2

LB
He don't go deep down in there.

Comparison of the totals to Feagin's on white Southern speech reveals--just as for general -∅--similar patterns. The upper-middle-class rate in this study is zero and in hers 1.3 percent (1/79) for upper-class teenagers and 4.4 percent (2/45) for upper-class older subjects; the lower-class percentage here is 83.3 percent and in hers 97.7 percent (86/88) for upper-class teenagers, and 83.1 percent (49/59) for upper-class older persons (Feagin 1979:198). Our figures also closely approximate Wolfram and Christian's finding in West Virginia of 85 percent don't among speakers they studied (1976:79). Altogether, only 14 examples of hyper {-s} occur in the interviews. They are listed below:

LW (6)
Water and syrup goes into it.
That's when all the boys and girls gets together.
And every summer me and Connie has a jama party.
These boy that lives upstairs.
They're two teenagers that goes to Roosevelt.
And they got these little animals that looks like
    dinosaurs.
I says "I caught mine."
And I says . . .
Some boys just come up, starts hitting on you and all.
(How many people are in this?) Goes to the club? The
    whole club? Oh, I don't know.

UMB (3)
I get all the papers I can until my father and my mother
    buys me another, you know, science lab.
There're neighbors that has a creek down there.
And some children in our classroom speak--speaks out of
    turn.

LB
It <u>bes</u> bout a boy.

These sentences have a high percentage of certain syntactic patterns. Four have conjoined subjects, three with a similar noun next to the verb; and four have the relative pronoun <u>that</u>, which refers back to a plural noun that serves as the subject. Of the remaining six examples, two are <u>I says</u>, one is <u>it bes</u>, and one clearly involves a self-correction toward the hypercorrect form. The self-correction occurs in a discussion by an upper-middle-class black girl of correctness in spoken language:

> Well, um when we speak, we don't speak correctly. And she [the teacher] make our mistakes correct. And . . . [Interviewer: Can you give me an example?] Well, like some person in our classroom says "ain't" and "not" and all that. And some children in our classroom speak--speaks out of turn. And she says, <u>"Do not speak out of turn. Speaken when you're supposed to</u>--when you are spoken to."

The same child elsewhere calls attention to her awareness and uncertainty regarding verb endings by pronouncing <u>does</u> sometimes [dəz] and at other times [duwz]. She is the only child who uses [duwz], the phonetic form that follows the general morphophonemic rule for the third person marker.

The Atlanta data show hypercorrect <u>-s</u> to be connected to syntax and not characteristic of the lower-class blacks. This finding is in contrast to Labov's discovery of many hypercorrect <u>-s</u> examples by black children in his New York City study.

Conclusion

This paper has examined the use of distributive <u>be</u>, the agreement of <u>be</u>, and the use of the third person marker in the speech of four groups of Atlanta school children. For several structures, definite ethnic and/or class patterns emerge. In addition to providing data on the two races and classes, the discussion has demonstrated the importance of studying conversational black speech in relationship to white speech of the same area. For distributive <u>be</u>, in particular, contrasting the speech of the two races reveals patterns that otherwise would have remained obscure. It is my intent that this article and further research on the Atlanta interviews will provide the basis for a better understanding of the sources and extent of variation in Southern speech.

Some Features of the *Be* Verb in the Speech of Blacks of Pope County, Arkansas

Earl F. Schrock, Jr.

In the last several years, much has been written about the speech of black Americans, how it differs from or resembles the speech of white Americans, whether it is a derivative of Southern American English, or whether it developed from an African-American pidgin. However, much of the study of black speech has been conducted in the large urban areas of the North. Relatively little has been done in the rural areas of the South.

My 1979 study, from which the material for this paper is taken, was prompted by the lack of data on Southern rural black speech. The purpose of the study was to describe the pronunciation and selected morphological and syntactical patterns used by the blacks of Pope County, Arkansas, and to determine some of their attitudes toward their own speech.

According to the 1970 census report, 28,607 people were living in Pope County, of whom only 671 (2.3%) were black. The entire black population lives in Russellville (the county seat) and Atkins, the two largest towns in the county, and in two small rural settlements outside of Atkins: Happy Bend to the north and Gold Hill to the south.

Northwestern Arkansas, in which Pope County is located, has never had as large a black population as southeastern Arkansas. The northern and western sections of Arkansas are not as suitable for plantation-type farming as are the southern and eastern sections. As a result, in 1835, although 58 percent of the white population of the state lived in the north and west, only 34 percent of the slaves lived in these districts. In the same year, according to the territorial census, Pope County had a population of 1,318, of which 146 (or 11%) were slaves (White 1964:185, 186).

Many of the blacks who now live in Pope County descend from the slaves who were brought into the state in the nineteenth century. The informants of this study are descendants of people who came to Arkansas from Virginia, Mississippi, North Carolina,

South Carolina, and Tennessee; 43 percent have grandparents or great-grandparents who came to Arkansas from South Carolina.

The black neighborhoods are clearly defined in Pope County, and very few black families live in white residential sections. In Russellville, most of the blacks live just southeast of the business section, in an area recently renovated by urban renewal. This area is referred to by many of the blacks as "the project" or, since most of the houses are small brick homes, as "brick city." In Atkins, there is one small area in Town Hill, south of the business district, where blacks live, and there are also two rural black communities.

Each decade the percentage of blacks in Pope County declines. Although several blacks are engaged in professions (teaching, nursing, social work, and ministry) and in business, most of the young blacks who obtain college degrees (especially males) move to larger cities. The ones who stay are primarily blue-collar workers.

The fourteen blacks who served as informants for the study are residents of Pope County. The classification of informants into types basically follows Kurath in his Handbook of the Linguistic Geography of New England. Type I informants have not finished high school; Type II informants have graduated from high school; and Type III informants have received college degrees. The four Type III informants include two school librarians, a counselor, and a model. Among the five Type II informants are a beautician, a janitor, two factory workers, and a retired operator of a day-care center. Of the five Type I informants, two are in the nursing home, one is a domestic worker, and two are junior high school students. At the time this study was conducted, I could find no male natives of Pope County, currently residing in the county, who had a college education (see table 1).

Table 1
Informants

Type	I		II		III	
Sex:	Male	Female	Male	Female	Male	Female
Age:	12	41	28	23		21
	13	82	33	69		36
		100	59			42
						51

One of the purposes of this study is to determine which dialect features blacks in a rural Southern area have in common with blacks who live in the large metropolitan areas of the North.

Although my 1979 study attempts to examine phonology, selected morphological and syntactic features, and language attitudes, this paper is limited to some features of the be verb in the speech of blacks in this northwestern Arkansas county. These features are (1) concord between subject and the be verb, (2) deletion of be, (3) deletion of have and will in be verb phrases, and (4) the use of invariant be.

Each interview consisted of eight parts, designed to elicit four language styles: that closest to the vernacular of everyday life (a free conversation at the end of the interview); relatively careful speech (answering specific questions with a single word or phrase); casual reading ("Arthur the Rat"); and the more careful reading of isolated word lists. For this paper, only two sections of the interview have been used: the "free speech" sections and a section dealing exclusively with the be verb (as intransitive verb, auxiliary verb, and copula). In the free speech sections, the informants were asked to talk about their family backgrounds, wedding customs, sayings about the weather, superstitions about birth or babies, a childhood game, a favorite sport or television show, how to make a favorite dish, etc. In the section dealing with the be verb (section VI of the interview), the informants were handed a sheet containing eight sentences with omission of main verb be, omission of auxiliary be, invariant be, and deletion of the future auxiliary before be. They were asked to read the sentences and comment upon them.

From the free-speech section of each interview, a 20-minute portion has been taken, and all of the be verb sentences have been extracted. The fourteen samples yield 529 be verb sentences.

Lack of Concord between Subject and Verb

In the 529 sentences from the free-speech sections of the interviews that contain be verbs, there are 64 occurrences of lack of concord between subject and be verb. Table 2 shows the occurrences of lack of concord by informant type, sex, and age. The highest frequencies are in the speech of the older, less educated informants. (The number for the 82-year-old female informant is a little misleading; the reason for the low frequency in her free-speech section, I am sure, is that she refused to converse with me freely and would answer questions only with fragmentary responses.) Fifty-eight of the 64 occurrences (91%) are found in the speech of informants who are 40 years or older. No occurrences of lack of concord between subject and be verb are found in the free-speech sections of the 20-year-old female Type III informant and the 12-year-old male Type I informant.

In sentences that contain lack of concord, the tendency is to use singular be verbs (both past and present) with plural subjects, rather than plural be verbs with singular subjects. There are 41

Table 2
Lack of Concord between Subject and Be Verb

Type I		Type II		Type III	
IM13	2	IIF23	2	IIIF36	1
IF40	1	IIM28	2	IIIF42	2
IF82	3	IIM33	6	IIIF51	2
IF100	14	IIM59	10		
		IIF69	19		
Total	20		39		5

examples of lack of subject-verb agreement in which the subject (either noun or pronoun) is plural and the form of be is singular. (Sentence examples will be followed by informant type, sex, and age.)

Baptist ways is all that I know. (IIIF51)

Those prayers is a part of our service. (IIM59)

They was from Tennessee. (IIM33)

His folks was in South Carolina. (IF100)

Whatever you is, be that. (IF100)

In 23 sentences, the subject is singular and the be verb is plural:

Their native language from the islands were French. (IIM59)

I learned to say that when I were going to school in Kansas. (IIF69)

I had 'em since I were a woman. (IF82)

Therefore, in sentences containing lack of concord between subject and be verb, singular forms of be occur twice as often as plural forms of be. One of the informants (IIF69) often used the plural form were with the singular subject I. This informant accounts for 19 of the 23 examples of singular subject and plural be verb.

Of the 64 sentences in which there is lack of concord between subject and verb, 15 are sentences beginning with expletives:

They's several of 'em been here. (IF100)

They's some come here from Chicago. (IF100)

There's quite a few. (IIF23)

There is more places that fear a discrimination suit.
(IIIF36)

There is quite a few people there. (IIM28)

There is people that will accept you. (IIM59)

It's plenty of jobs for them. (IIM33)

No, it's not very many. (IIM33)

It's a lot of jobs. (IIM33)

Used to be a lot of black people lived here, but now it's
very few, and that same thing is true of Happy Bend.
(IIIF42)

It's degrees of black speech right here in Atkins. (IIIF42)

There wasn't /wədn/ any cars. (IIM59)

There were people from California; there was people from
all over the country come in. (IIM59)

Ordinarily, from the beginning, there was seven. (IIM59)

There was people from all over. (IIM59)

Eleven of these sentences contain be verbs in the present
tense; four contain be verbs in the past tense. All of the sentences contain plural subjects and singular verbs. Five of them
employ the expletive it, which takes the singular verb regardless
of the number of the subject.

Table 3 shows, by informant type, sex, and age, the distribution of lack of concord between subject and be verb when the
sentence begins with an expletive.

Deletion of Be

In these 529 sentences, the be verb is deleted only 28 times
(5.3%). Only present tense forms (is, are, am) are deleted. Labov
(1972a:52) says that, in his New York study, are is deleted about
twice as often as is.

Table 3
Lack of Concord between Subject and Be Verb in Sentences
Beginning with Expletives

Type I		Type II		Type III	
IF100	2	IIF23	1	IIIF36	1
		IIFM28	1	IIIF42	2
		IIM33	3		
		IIM59	5		
Total	2		10		3

In the 28 deletions in the free-speech sections, deletion of be occurs as follows:

Deletion of is	5
Deletion of are	22
Deletion of am	1
Total	28

The deletion of are is over four times as frequent as the deletion of is.

The sentences are divided into those that contain be as the auxiliary (intentional future with gonna, progressive, and passive) and those that contain be as the main verb (intransitive or linking):

1. Sentence patterns with be as auxiliary verb.

S	be	gonna	(Intentional future)
S	be	-ing	(Progressive)
S	be	Past Participle	(Passive)

2. Sentence patterns with be as main verb.

S	be	Locative (Intransitive verb + Adverb of place)
S	be	Pred. Adjective
S	be	Pred. Nominative

Deletion, according to Labov (1972a:87), occurs in Black Vernacular English least frequently before a noun phrase, more often before predicate adjectives and locatives, still more often before -ing, and most often before the future form gonna. Although the frequency of deletion is much lower in the speech of the blacks in this study than in that of the New York City blacks studied by

Labov, the order of the patterns in which be verbs are deleted is
the same. Table 4 shows this order.

Table 4
Syntactic Constraints on Be Deletion

Sentence Type	Full or Contracted Forms	Deleted Forms	Percentage of Deletion
S be gonna	2	1	33
S be -ing	81	9	10
S be Locative	73	5	6.4
S be Past Participle	50	3	5.7
S be Pred. Adjective	156	9	5.5
S be Pred. Nominative	139	1	0.7

To Labov's list, S-be-past participle (passive voice) was added. Of
the 53 sentences conforming to this pattern, 50 have full or contracted forms and 3 have deleted forms.

Twenty-five of the 28 deletions of the be verb (8.93%) occur
after a pronoun (I, you, he, it, we, they). Instead of deletion of
the be verb, several of the informants in this study use the contracted forms [wiə̯, juə̯, ǯeə̯]. For example:

Know what [juə̯] doing. (IIIF51)

When we get somebody that know what [ǯeə̯] doing . . .
(IIF69)

If [juə̯] educated . . . (IF40)

The contracted forms of is and are + the pronoun yield the
following:

I'm	[aɪm]	he's	[hiz]
you're	[juə̯] ~ [juɚ]	she's	[šiz]
we're	[wiə̯] ~ [wiɚ]	it's	[ɪts] ~ [ɪs]
they're	[ǯeə̯] ~ [ǯeɚ]	that's	[ǯæts] ~ [ǯæs]

In this study, as in that of Dunlap (1974:28), [ɪs] and [ǯæs] are
considered contracted forms of be rather than deleted forms.

In contrast to the 25 deletions of be when the subject is a
pronoun, only three of the deletions occur after noun subjects.
Two occur before the verb supposed.

The white man ____ supposed to have his voice. (IF100)

and the colored man _____ supposed to have his voice.
(IF100)

This deletion is probably a result of the contracted form -s, /z/, being assimilated with the following /s/. The other deletion is found in the sentence:

Another reason I stayed is because my grandmother _____ here. (IIIF36)

In one sentence, am or 'm is deleted after the pronoun I:

I ____ not too much on this car business. (IF100)

Of the 28 deletions of be, two are found in the speech of the Type III informants, 12 in the speech of the Type II informants, and 14 in the speech of the Type I informants. Twenty of the 28 deletions of be (or 71.4%) occur in the speech of informants who are 40 years old or older. Table 5 shows the distribution of be deletion by informant type, sex, and age.

Table 5
Distribution of Be Deletion by Type, Sex, and Age

Type I		Type II		Type III	
IM12	1	IIM28	5	IIIF36	1
IM13	1	IIM59	2	IIIF42	1
IM40	2	IIF69	5		
IF82	1				
IF100	9				
Total	14		12		2

Deletion of Have and Has in the Verb Phrase

Be verb phrases in the present perfect tense sometimes occur without the auxiliary (have or has). In the free-speech section of the interviews, there are 13 such occurrences. Twelve have omission of have, and one has omission of has.

1. You can tell that they ____ been to school. (IF40)

2. They've been different papers ____ ____ been here.
(IF100)

3. I've had so many visitors--well known men, nurses--___
   ___ been to see me and talk with me. (IF100)

4. They's several of 'em ___ ___ been here. (IF100)

5. I ___ been to Kansas. (IF100)

6. I had two brothers younger'n me. They ___ been gone.
   (IF100)

7. They ___ been under the white people. (IF100)

8. They ___ been snaggin' over there at the dam. (IM33)

9. I ___ been teaching in the Atkins school system twenty
   years. (IIIF42)

10. Like now, we got a whole new crew, you might say,
    and we ___ just been on three shift since January
    so we got a lot of new people and we have to get
    everybody trained in on what we doing in order to
    get our product and stuff out. (IIM28)

11. . . . since they ___ been mixin' like they is. (IF100)

12. I ___ been working there ever since. (IM28)

13. She ___ been teachin' there since January. (IIM33)

Sentences 2, 3, and 4 show not only deletion of _have_ but absence
of the relative pronoun as well.

Only one of these 13 sentences occurs in Type III speech, four
are in Type II, and eight are in Type I. Nine of the 13 occur in the
speech of the informants who are 40 years old or older. Table 6
shows the distribution of omission of _have_ and _has._

Table 6
Omission of Have and Has in Be Verb Phrases

Type I		Type II		Type III	
IF 40	1	IIM28	2	IIIF42	1
IF100	7	IIM33	2		
Total	8		4		1

Omission of Will and Would in Be Verb Phrases and Invariant Be

In four sentences, be occurs in its uninflected form:

You don't do that or you be whipped for doing that. (IIM59)

If they not doin' it right, I try to show 'em--you know--
where it be easier or something on 'em. (IIM28)

You know, I be at work. (IF40)

My mind be scatterin' at times. (IF82)

The first two sentences clearly seem to indicate future time; the uninflected be, then, is probably a derivative of the verb phrase will be--the will first having been contracted and then deleted (Labov 1972a:239). The context of the third sentence suggests that the be is derived from the phrase would be. Wolfram (1969:185) says that "in the same sense that be with an underlying will can be viewed as a phonological pattern operating on the contracted form of the auxiliary, it is also possible to view be which is the realization of would be as a phonological pattern operating on the contracted form 'd be." The last sentence, "My mind be scatterin' at times," is the only unambiguous example of invariant be in the corpus used for this study. The adverbial phrase at times indicates the recurrent nature of the state referred to in the verb phrase. These four sentences are from four different informants (two Type II male informants and two Type I female informants). Three of these four informants are 40 years old or older.

The speech which has been thus far described is neither overly formal nor completely casual. It is certainly more relaxed than that observed in the question section and in the reading section of the interview. The informants were, for the most part, talking about subjects they were interested in (e.g., hunting, fishing, cooking, sports, work, local history, television, etc.). They were using the kind of language they use when talking to someone they do not know well.

In order to test their knowledge of the standard English rules governing the use of the be verb, the interviewer asked the informants to read eight sentences employing the following features of Black Vernacular English: omission of intransitive be, omission of copula be, omission of auxiliary be in a progressive verb phrase, invariant be, and deletion of future auxiliary will or 'll. The sentences are as follows:

14. He here now.

15. But everybody not black.

16. You out the game.

17. She looking good.

18. Most of the time he be in the library.

19. He be doing that all the time.

20. They always be messing around.

21. She be coming home tomorrow.

After reading the sentences, informants were asked to tell whether they would use such sentences. If they said they would not, they were asked to change the sentence to make it like one they would use.

In sentence 14, "He here now," all of the informants added is or 's /z/. Likewise, in sentence 15, "But everybody not black," all informants but two added is or 's. One informant (IIM28) said, "But everybody isn't black," and another (IIIF51) said, "Some people are not black." In sentence 16, "You out the game," all of the informants but three added are or 're and of. Two (IIIF42 and IIM28) added are but did not add of. The youngest informant (IM12) added of but did not add a form of be: "You out of the game." In sentence 17, "She looking good," one informant (IIM33) changed looking to looks. All of the others added is or 's.

Although there is only one deletion in these four sentences, it is perhaps significant that it is an omission of are rather than is, thus supporting the four-to-one deletion of are over is in the free-speech section examined earlier. The fact that, with one exception, the informants changed all four of these sentences to conform to standard English rules for use of the be verb before locatives, predicate adjectives, and -ing verbs indicates that they are familiar with the rules and use them, at least in their guarded speech.

Sentences 18 through 20 contain examples of invariant be. Each sentence contains a "frequency of occurrence" adverb which several studies (e.g., Crystal 1966, Dunlap 1974, Wolfram and Fasold 1974) have found to co-occur with invariant be. These adverbs are most of the time (5), all the time (6), and always (7).

In sentence 18, "Most of the time he be in the library," all but three of the informants changed be to is or 's. One informant (IIM28) said will be, and another informant (IIM33) added the third person singular suffix /-z/ to be, producing /biz/. Only one informant (IIM12) left it as it was, with invariant be.

In sentence 19, "He be doing that all the time," there is considerable variation in the changes the informants made:

Type I	Type II	Type III
's been doing (IM13)	's been doing (IIM33) (IIF69)	
is doing (IF40)	's doing (IIF23)	is doing (IIIF42)
	does (IIM59)	does (IIIF20) (IIIF36) (IIIF51)
	will be doing (IIM28)	
No change (IM12)		

In sentence 20, "They always be messing around," all but three changed be to are or 're. One informant (IIM28) said will always be, and two informants (IIM33 and IM12) said they would say the sentence as it is.

In sentence 21, "She be coming home tomorrow," all of the informants but one changed the verb to will be coming, 'll be coming, is coming, or 's coming. One informant (IIM33) said he would make no change.

Of the 96 responses to these eight sentences, only seven instances (7.3%) of nonstandard be occur. All seven of these nonstandard forms are found in the speech of two informants (IM12 and IIM33). The one informant who did not change invariant be in sentences 5 through 7 was the youngest informant (12 years old). The two oldest informants (both Type I, ages 82 and 100) tired before this section of the interview, so there are no responses from them.

The low frequency of occurrence of nonstandard be forms seems to indicate one of two things: Black Vernacular English features found in the Northern metropolitan studies do not often occur in this dialect, or most informants of this study know both the standard English and the Black Vernacular English forms and can switch from one to the other, depending upon the company they are in. From discussions with the informants in the free-speech section of the interviews, I maintain that the latter is true.

Informants' Attitudes about Deletion of Be and Use of Invariant Be

After the sentence exercise was completed, the informants were asked the following questions:

Do you ever use sentences like these?
Where would you say them?

Have you ever heard others use sentences like these?

The responses were fairly uniform. One informant (IIIF42) replied: "Yes. 'He be such and such a place' or 'She be lookin' good.' Yes, of course. And 'You out the game.' Yes. From blacks. These are just everyday sayings. You go to school for six hours a day, and then go back to the family, and you revert to the family. I'm sure I do that."

Another of the Type III informants (IIIF36) and the interviewer had the following exchange:

> Interviewer: About the fourth one down, you began to smile. Why?
> Informant: I was thinking how often I've heard this.
> Interviewer: Where?
> Informant: In the black neighborhood.
> Interviewer: Are these sentences typical of black speech?
> Informant: Yes. And I can do this, too. I can have two sets of English.

One of the Type II informants (IIF69) answered the question, "Do you identify sentences such as these with black English?" in the following way:

> Not altogether. I find that, in the poorer class of whites, it's hardly any difference. It's common among some of the poorer class of whites. It's a matter of economics or family background--not race.

When asked whether he would say, "He be doing that all the time," a Type I informant (IM13) said, "Yes. Sometimes. When I'm around home or around my friends, I'd say it the way it's written down here, and when I'm in class or school, I'd say it different."

It is apparent from the responses to the sentence exercise and from the free-speech section of the interviews that the informants of this study know the standard English rules for the use of be as auxiliary, as intransitive verb, and as copula. Even though some of them delete be, have or has, and will from be verb phrases, or use the invariant form, none do it consistently. And in guarded speech, the frequency of these nonstandard forms is very low.

Summary

The observations about use of the be verb in the speech of the blacks of Pope County, Arkansas, can be summarized in the following way:

1. In sentences containing lack of concord between subject and be verb, those with plural subjects and singular forms of be outnumber those with singular subjects and plural forms of be two to one. In the sentences beginning with expletives, all have plural subjects and singular verbs.

2. Ninety-one percent of the occurrences of lack of concord between subject and be verb are found in the speech of informants who are 40 or older.

3. Deletion of the be verb, at least in guarded speech, occurs with much less frequency than in the speech of Northern urban blacks studied by Labov, Wolfram, and others.

4. Only present tense forms (is, am, are) are deleted.

5. Deletion of are is over four times as frequent as deletion of is.

6. Deletion occurs in the following environments, in order of decreasing frequency: before gonna, before verb -ing, before locatives, before past participles (passive voice), before predicate adjectives, and before predicate nominatives.

7. More deletions occur after pronoun subjects than after noun subjects.

8. More of the deletions occur in the speech of Types I and II informants than in the speech of Type III informants. More occur in the speech of the older informants: 71.4 percent of the deletions are found in the speech of the informants who are 40 or older.

9. Present perfect forms sometimes occur without the auxiliaries have or has, leaving been as the head word in the verb phrase. Of the omissions, 8% are found in the speech of Type III informants, 31% in the speech of Type II informants, and 61% in the speech of Type I informants. Sixty-nine percent of the deletions of have and has occur in sentences of informants who are 40 or older.

10. Uninflected be occurs rarely--only four times in the corpus of this study. Invariant be occurs only once; omission of will or would three times. Three of the four informants who used the uninflected form are over 40.

11. A sentence exercise using be verbs found in Black Vernacular English showed that, even though they sometimes use non-standard forms, the informants know the standard English rules for usage of the be verb.

Competing Norms in the White Speech of Anniston, Alabama

Crawford Feagin

Earlier work in sociolinguistics--for example, Labov 1966 in Lower East Side New York and Trudgill 1974 in Norwich--have shown a clear relationship between variation in the phonology of an urban community and its social classes and ethnic groups.[1] These studies emphasize the existence of a single speech community, based on awareness of and agreement among all the speakers--regardless of class or ethnic group--on a single prestige norm that is demonstrated through style shifting in increasingly formal situations. In Labov's Harlem studies (Labov et al. 1968) and more recently in the Milroys' work in Belfast (Milroy 1980, Milroy and Margrain 1980), more emphasis has been placed on the relationship between small groups or networks and speech, where a second set of norms--this time, nonstandard norms--can be observed under increasingly informal, intimate situations. The extent to which a speaker follows these nonstandard norms reflects the degree of integration into the smaller group to which he or she belongs.

I have been struck with how much these two norms, the local prestige norm and the local vernacular norm, can be observed in the data from my study in Alabama, which is based on the grammar of the verb phrase (Feagin 1979). This paper demonstrates that the entire native white community of Anniston, Alabama, agrees on the existence of two opposing norms and on their social significance. The evidence for these two norms comes from informal tape-recorded conversations with Annistonians of both the upper and working classes, from indirect testing for attitudes toward language, and from observations of speech when informants are not being tape recorded. From these sources of information it is clear that the prestige norm is used to express formality, respect, and social distance, while the vernacular norm expresses informality, intimacy, friendliness, and solidarity.

The location of my research was Anniston, Alabama, a town with a metropolitan population of 60,000, between Birmingham and

Atlanta in the east central section of Alabama. People who live there, however, see themselves as living in north Alabama, as contrasted with Montgomery, Selma, or Mobile in south Alabama. G. Wood 1971 places Anniston in his Gulf Southern dialect area, based on the lexicon, though Foscue 1971, who also studied the lexicon, places it in the Southern Midlands or Midsouthern area.

Using a stratified sample, I interviewed eighty-two people in Anniston (keeping the sexes equal in number) from the urban upper and working classes and from the rural working class. I interviewed at least twelve teenagers and twelve older people from both the urban upper and working classes; I dealt only with older people from the rural working class. The rural working class is of interest here insofar as those data add to the larger picture of change in progress shown on tables 6a and 6b. (See table 1 for a more precise breakdown of the population of the sample.)

Table 1
Population of Primary Sample:
Number of Persons Interviewed by Age, Sex, Social Class,
Place of Origin (Rural/Urban)
(Subset of Sample)

| | Urban | | Rural | Class Total |
	Teenagers	Over 65		
Upper Class				
Female	11 (6)	7 (6)		18 (12)
Male	8 (6)	6 (6)		14 (12)
				32 (24)
Working Class				
Female	7 (7)	8 (6)	8 (8)	23 (21)
Male	8 (7)	7 (6)	7 (7)	22 (20)
				45 (41)
			Total	77 (65)

Miscellaneous
    1 middle-age working-class man
    1 middle-age middle-class man
    1 middle-class teenage girl
    2 middle-age upper-class women

I began each interview by asking about the informant's age, education, work experience (or that of the father for teenagers or the husband for adult women), and other matters which would help place the informant in a social class. Other questions established when informants arrived in Anniston. (All urban informants were born in Anniston or had moved there by age six). To elicit more natural, unself-conscious speech, I designed other questions to distract the informant from the interview through such topics as childhood games and insults, frightening experiences (danger of death), and ghost stories. All the interviews were tape recorded.

Three ancillary sources of data supplement the interviews. First, I was able to make what I call "informal" recordings of some working-class girls during a home economics sewing class (hanging the microphone around one girl's neck and getting out of sight as soon as I could). Second, I did a small amount of direct testing for attitudes toward grammatical forms, as well as questioning my informants about their feeling toward the town. And third, I jotted down sentences from 127 people who were subjects of my "anonymous observations"--that is, notations of speech in a natural situation.

The tape-recorded interviews were searched for the presence of certain grammatical forms, particularly those of the verb phrase, although negation was also treated since it has such an intimate relation to the verb. The resulting data were analyzed both quantitatively and qualitatively, depending on whether or not a variant is always present. (Quantitative data consist of counts of both occurrence and nonoccurrence of forms, providing a percentage of occurrence of a particular form out of all possible places in the data where it could have been found. Qualitative data are simply the enumeration of occurrences of the form.) The data presented here involve eight quantitative and five qualitative items.

The quantitative items are (1) third person singular + don't (He don't); (2) third person plural + was (They was); (3) third person singular + is (They is); (4) third personal plural (except they) + -s (Clyde and Billy goes everywhere together); (5) multiple negation in the clause (Nobody don't like him); (6) ain't (both negative have and be) (I ain't going); (7) nonstandard irregular preterit (She seen him last week); and (8) a nonstandard irregular past participle (Johnny has already went to school).

The qualitative items are (1) perfective done (He's done finished it); (2) liketa (Uncle Wirt liketa died laughin'); (3) prefixed present participle a + verb + ing (She's a-runnin' just as fast as she can); (4) double modals (I might could get there by tomorrow); and (5) negative inversion (Isn't anybody planning to go).

Before discussing the two competing norms, I want to demonstrate the extent of the divergence in the community. Of all the factors considered--age, sex, rural versus urban residence, and social class--it was social class that distinguished speakers most dramatically. Grouping ages and sexes together, tables 2 and 3 contrast the data from the urban upper class with the data of the urban working class for the thirteen variables. The quantitative data are from forty-nine informants (60 hours of tape), the qualitative from sixty-one (72 hours of tape).

Table 2
Quantitative Class Differences:
Percentage of Nonstandard Items out of Total Standard
and Nonstandard Items

	Working Class (N = 25)	Upper Class (N = 24)
Invariable don't	91.4	2.4
Multiple negation	75.8	1.1
Invariable was	70.3	2.5
Ain't (have + be)	43.5	0.3
Invariable is	35.5	5.3
NP plural + s	32.4	0.7
Nonstandard irregular past participle	31.9	0.0
Nonstandard irregular preterit	19.7	0.0

Table 3
Qualitative Class Differences:
Individuals Using Item at Least Once during an Interview

	Working Class	Upper Class
Perfecive done	55% (16/29)	0% (0/32)
Liketa	55% (16/29)	0% (0/32)
A + verb + ing	52% (15/29)	3% (1/32)
Double modal	31% (9/29)	6% (2/32)
Negative inversion	21% (6/29)	3% (1/32)

It is obvious that the difference between the two classes is considerable, which might lead one to suspect that what we are dealing with here is not one but two grammars in the community. However, the evidence points toward a single polylectal grammar with two norms, one a prestige norm, based on standard or cultivated English,[2] the other a solidarity norm, based on local nonstandard forms. Both the upper class and working class know about these opposing norms, and manipulate the variables to reflect this knowledge. Furthermore, these norms are understood and used by the time local residents reach their middle adolescent years.

Prestige Norms

First, let us look at evidence for the prestige norm. It is not surprising that the upwardly mobile and others outside the mainstream of the vernacular culture show a sensitivity to the fact that nonstandard forms are not highly esteemed outside their own networks. At the beginning of an interview with three working-class teenage boys, one of them--clearly upwardly mobile--said to the other two, talking about me:

1. What she's doin' is she's come down here an' she's
    gon' make--she's makin' fun of our language.
    (W 17:47.I.006)[3]

Of course, not everyone is that sensitive, since one of the other boys said right away,

2. I don't see nothin' so funny about the way we talk. I
    mean, I don't know it's nothin' different.
    (W 17:47.I.002)

I mention above that I was able to make some informal recordings of working-class girls in their sewing class. From that source, I obtained some interesting data on how they feel about their speech vis-à-vis local prestige norms. One girl muttered to her partner about me when I was out of hearing:

3. She may be makin' fun of us. (A.8.026)

The same girl, later in the recording, corrected herself and then her friend. In another recording in the same sewing class, a second girl produced a particularly striking monologue, again with me out of sight:

4. You don't need no scissors--any scissors. Use a double
    negative. You don't--You don't--You [giggle]. Try
    again. 'No' and 'not' are negatives, not double
    negatives. (A.6.394)

During the regular interviews, which were with two teenagers at a time, there were other self-corrections, all from working-class informants. Ain't and multiple negation seem to be the most corrected. One girl said:

5. There'll always be a feelin' there, but it ain't--it's
    not love. (Pam F. W 17:10.II.261)

A boy of the same age said:

6. I was little and I didn't think noth--much about it.
    (Jimmy F. W 17:47.II.095)

Aside from such miscellaneous examples of self-correction, I was able to determine three patterns in style shifting among working-class girls, contrasting the findings from the interviews (which were of two girls at once) and the informal recording made in the sewing class of the same girls (with the exception of one who declined to be interviewed, the speaker in example 3): No change--invariable don't and nonstandard irregular preterits and past participles stay at about the same level; moderate change--invariable was and multiple negation increase 15 and 25 percent respectively; and dramatic change--the frequency of ain't actually doubles. (See table 4.)

Table 4
Percentage of Style Shifting among Working-Class Girls
(Same Population as Table 2)

	Interview (N = 7)	Informal Recording (N = 6)
Invariable don't	98	100
Multiple negation	60	80
Invariable was	48	57
Ain't	19	37
Nonstandard irregular past participle	32	29
Nonstandard irregular preterit	12	9

Although the preceding discussion and examples have been concerned with urban working-class teenagers, the older working-class people are not exempt from the pressures of the prestige norm. One older urban woman, for example, corrected herself in the middle of quoting someone:

7. Why, Miss Milly, that don't make no matter--that--it--
    [deep breath] why, it don't matter at all now. (Milly
    B. W 77:36.III.237).

The speech of the upper class is so near the standard that styleshifting toward the standard would hardly be possible to observe in tape-recorded material. Most of the information on nonstandard speech among members of the upper class had to come from anonymous observations. From those data I can say that while upper-class people are able to use nonstandard grammar (as I will demonstrate shortly), they declined to use it in their interviews (tables 2 and 3). On the other hand, I need only point out that natives of Anniston definitely are able to produce the same cultivated grammatical forms found elsewhere in the English-speaking world.[4]

Solidarity Norms

A particularly interesting aspect of language use in Anniston is the way in which nonstandard English is employed there by people as a symbol of intimacy and local loyalty--as well as a gauge of the level of integration into a close-knit network.

Milroy (1980:74) defines a social network as "the informal social relationships contracted by an individual" in which there is a reciprocal exchange of goods and services. These goods and services can range from a cup of sugar to a ride to school, an invitation to a wedding and the present it involves, or a hot tip on the stock market. The individuals concerned can be relatives, neighbors, coworkers, or friends of any sort.

Networks are defined as dense or diffuse, simple or multiplex. Dense networks are those in which all of one's friends know each other, while multiplex networks are those in which members of the network have multiple roles. An example of a dense network is a situation in which a woman lives next door to her parents and works at the same factory as her mother. Another example is that of a man working in his father's law firm, belonging to the same social clubs, and visiting back and forth frequently with his parents. In a diffuse network, which is more characteristic of middle-class people who live in big cities, a person's life is not so circular or self-contained; that person's friends would not be likely to know each other, much less be relatives, neighbors, or coworkers. Moreover, that person's family, friendships, neighborhood, and business relationships would not overlap so much; in simplex relationships, these roles would be compartmentalized.

Whether one participates in a dense and multiplex or a diffuse and simplex network is reflected in language, as well as in other types of behavior. In a dense network, an individual is much more subject to supervision and regimentation according to the values of the network and therefore must observe the rules of solidarity, so to speak. Milroy (1980:28, 61) reports that in Belfast, in a dense, multiplex network, speakers must show linguistic solidarity in front of fellow network members or suffer teasing, despite the presence of a tape recorder. In a diffuse, simplex network, which characterizes those who are more mobile geographically or socially, there is less necessity to observe the local loyalty or solidarity rules and therefore more opportunity to follow the prestige norm if one wants to. So-called "lames" (Labov 1973) would fit into this second category.

This model of networks helps to explain some of the variation I found within the subgroups or cells of my Anniston working-class informants. It also adds to our understanding of why members of the upper class use the vernacular nonstandard grammatical forms in intimate situations.

Most of the evidence for the use of Southern vernacular among the upper class comes from informal observations rather than tape-recorded material. Through these observations, it becomes obvious that members of the local upper class definitely use ain't for negative be and use invariable don't when talking among friends and relatives (i.e., members of their own network), though use of the nonstandard forms is highly variable. One old lawyer, for instance, who had been president of the Alabama Bar, argued jokingly with his wife:

   8. If that ain't a hill, what is it! (Richard K. U 90)

Another example comes from a woman in her thirties whose husband's family used to own one of the local steel mills. (She, incidentally, had been to prep school: Forest Park, in Chicago.) She was talking to an old friend of her brother's and said:

   9. I may be fat, but I ain't that fat! (Margaret W. U 30)

My last example is from a man in his fifties, a corporation executive, who was joking with close friends and exclaimed:

   10. She don't change at all! (Malcolm H. Jr. U 56)

In each case, the addressee was part of the speaker's social network, not a stranger.

Another use of nonstandard forms among the upper class is in downward quotation, either in baby talk, a joking situation, or in a context where one can practically hear the deleted "as the country folks say." During her tape-recorded interview, one elderly lady used a nonstandard past participle:

   11. I went up there to "be bawned." (Harriet H. U
        81:15.I.018)

Although I was not personally intimate with the lady, she was a friend of my grandmother's--a distant relative, I think--and had recently included me in a luncheon for her niece's wedding in Atlanta. Because of these factors, I was given honorary network status. I doubt that she would have used that form in front of someone not in her network.

These forms are consciously used both to symbolize intimacy and for stylistic emphasis. They are not used in formal situations or with outsiders. That is, there is appropriate and inappropriate use of this sort of language, and the pragmatic rules governing such use are learned and shared as part of the linguistic repertoire of the upper class. As one person explained, "You only use it when you're with people who know that you know better." I have evidence that these rules are learned by midadolescence. When I asked some of the upper-class teenage girls and boys to read some sentences with double negatives, invariable <u>don't</u>, and <u>ain't</u>, one girl's immediate reaction was class oriented:

> 12. That sounds like somebody from the other side of the tracks! (Ellen K. U 17.9.III.124)

When pressed, however, she admitted that she would use double negatives if she were "just kiddin' around."

Her companion, Allison B., said the same thing about using a third person singular subject with <u>don't</u>. Moreover, she explained that <u>ain't</u> made it "sound like you were expressing yourself more strongly," and that a double modal (<u>shouldn't otta</u>) "would catch people's attention better."

One of the upper-class boys, after reading the same set of nonstandard sentences, told me:

> 13. We're <u>aware</u> that we're sayin' the wrong thing. That's what I mean when I'm jokin' and I say "ain't." I go out of my way to say "ain't" instead of "isn't." (Kenneth F. U 17.23.III.265)

This boy, incidentally, was the grandson of the elderly lady who talked about being <u>bawned</u>.

How can we talk about networks here? First, it is necessary to observe the potential members of a network, to see who visits whom and so forth, in order to enumerate the members of a network. I was not aware of the need to observe networks in this way while I was doing my fieldwork, but I can point out that, within the upper class, the network is a tightly woven one in which everybody knows everybody else--what Milroy calls a dense network. To illustrate this, I need only say that twelve of the twenty-six upper-class informants were close relatives of each other, that twenty of the twenty-six belonged to the Anniston Country Club, that all the teenagers went to the same private school, that seven of the eight girls were in the same high school sorority, that nearly half of the informants were neighbors of one or two other informants, and that the twenty-six informants belonged to only five different churches; nineteen of them went to either of two churches (out of 92 churches in the Anniston area). In fact, one complaint of the teenagers is the stultifying atmosphere of the town. Most of them couldn't wait to leave and go away to college. One put it:

14. Most people . . . don't really like [living here]. They
say it's boring here, not enough happening. That's
what you hear most of all about Anniston. (22.II.147.)

On the other hand, it is this same dense network that the
older people like. While such a network is undoubtedly censorious
and gossipy--regulating behavior in a serious, unforgiving manner
(familiar to anyone from a small town), it is the source of the
close relationships which "pay off" when people get older, and the
positive, supportive aspects of the network are more apparent.
One older man, who had been to prep school at St. George's in
Rhode Island and had graduated from Princeton, said to me:

15. Well, I'd rather live in Anniston than any place in the
world! . . . I think it's the best place to live of any
place I know . . . Well, I like the people in Anniston, I
like the rather easy life without the rush and the
push--and just a nice, genteel place. I have a high
regard for Anniston. (26.289-90)

While this evidence for style shifting in the upper class is
entirely anecdotal, evidence from the working class is found in the
series of informal recordings of the girls in the sewing class,
which may be compared with the more formal interviews of the
same girls, as discussed earlier. In addition to those data are the
comments of the working-class girls during their readings of the
same set of nonstandard sentences used by the upper-class teens.
When one working-class girl read the sentences, she exclaimed:

16. I talk just like this! (Pam F. W 17:10.III.280)

Her friend added:

17. And we've had college prep English! You wouldn't
believe that! (Sue T. W 17:10.III.300)

So, despite education and other outside social pressures to drop
the vernacular--and the teenage girls exhibited the nearest
approach to standard grammar of all the working-class inform-
ants--they certainly were not rushing to "upgrade" their English.
Tables 5 and 6 show that, of fourteen features, only six can be
said to be decreasing across the generations for the working class,
and even those are far from reaching the vanishing point.
Earlier, in discussing examples 1 to 7, I pointed out that the
working class is definitely aware of the prestige norm. The
working-class teenagers were certainly no less well educated than
those of the upper class, since they were all in the same grades in
school (though in different schools). The number of years of education is clearly not directly related to the use of standard as

opposed to nonstandard grammar. I have data from one older working-class man and one upper-class man of the same age with about the same amount of education. But the upper-class man spoke the local standard, while the working-class man spoke nonstandard. This is shown in table 7.

If the data were based on phonology, we could say with some assurance that whether someone uses the standard or nonstandard forms is below the threshold of awareness and cannot be consciously controlled very easily by the speakers. But since we are dealing with grammar here, that is not necessarily the case, particularly since many of the data are based on relatively formal interviews rather than more natural interaction among friends, such as the informal recordings of the sewing class. The teenagers were all interviewed in pairs of or threesomes; so perhaps they were constrained by network relationships to use the nonstandard. But half of the older working-class informants were alone with me, a total stranger; so they could have switched to standard without censure if either they had wanted to or had been able to. However, that was not the case at all.

Table 5
Language Change in Anniston Area among Working Class
Quantitative Features: Percentage Use of
Nonstandard Features by Group

| | Over 60 | | | | Teenage | |
| | Rural | | Urban | | Urban | |
	Men	Women	Men	Women	Boys	Girls
STABLE						
Invariable don't	100	199	69	91	94	98
Nonstandard irregular past participle	31	37	31	30	34	32
DECREASING						
Invariable was	96	98	74	77	79	48
Multiple negation	88	75	69	84	70	60
Invariable is	70	55	42	38	36	27
NP plural + -s	42	81	38	59	27	10
Nonstandard irregular preterit	34	27	20	23	22	12
ERRATIC						
Ain't	42	50	41	47	61	19

Obviously, then, what we are observing is adherence to solidarity norms enforced by networks, despite the fact that I was not dealing with a single network, as I was with the upper class.

Table 6
Language Change in Anniston Area among Working Class
Qualitative Features:
Percentage of Group Using Item at Least Once

	Over 60				Teenage	
	Rural		Urban		Urban	
	Men	Women	Men	Women	Boys	Girls
STABLE						
Done	28	75	57	85	37	57
Double modals	0	25	28	71	25	0
Liketa	14	37	28	100	25	71
Negative inversion	71	12	0	28	37	14
DECREASING						
A + verb + ing	71	87	71	85	12	42

Table 7
Working-Class Man and Upper-Class Man Compared
Same Education: Both Completed High School
(Working-Class Man, 80; Upper-Class Man, 78)
(Interviewed Same Month)

	Working-Class Men Nonstandard/		Upper-Class Men Nonstandard/	
	Total	%	Total	%
Invariable don't	1/1	100	0/1	0
Multiple negation	15/18	83.3	0/8	0
Invariable was	13/15	86.6	0/10	0
Ain't	1/4	25	0/8	0
Invariable is	13/15	86.6	0/1	0
NP plural + -s	0/4	0	0/0	0
Nonstandard irregular past participle	10/23	43.3	0/4	0
Nonstandard irregular preterit	20/67	29.8	0/11	0

	Examples		Examples	
Perfective done	1		0	
Liketa	0		0	
A + verb + -ing	2		0	
Double modal	1		0	
Negative inversion	0		0	

In contrast to the upper class, only a quarter of the urban working-class people whom I interviewed were relatives of one another. They were from six different neighborhoods, some separated by several miles from each other, and were scattered almost evenly among nine different churches. Consequently, unlike the upper class, they did not all know each other, much less know each other's relatives across several generations. (The working-class teenagers were more cohesive than the older working-class informants, since they all went to the same high school and since I located them through networks.)

Despite this heterogeneity, I found among the working-class informants very strong evidence of feelings of solidarity toward West Side--or their side of town and their kind of people, as they would put it. The most vivid expression of this came from three generations of the same family, the Elliots, who were discussing whether where they live (on the outskirts of Anniston) was in the country or was part of Anniston:

> 18. Father (age 38): I don't want to think of it as part of
> Anniston.
> Grandmother (age 63): We always considered it
> country, kiney, y'know, because we're all--well,
> it's a community more than just the country. We
> have a wonderful community.
> Son (age 17): We consider it separate. We consider--on
> this side of the railroad tracks--we consider that
> we are "us" and this is the country and that all
> those other people on the other side of the
> railroad tracks--they're different. But they're
> okay, but they're on the other side of the fence.
> Father: I think he's speakin' of the people on the East
> Side of Anniston. They're different people from
> us--the way he thinks. Actually, they're not
> but--
> Grandmother: He's just not acquainted with the ones
> up there, y'know, jus-, that's what he means (W
> 43.I.109-20).

When I asked Fred, the teenage son, how he defined "us," he answered, "Everything from the tracks down to the Coosa River is 'us.'" (43.I.122).

The railroad tracks divide the town between upper and middle class on one side and the working class (and most of the blacks) on the other. The Coosa River, 20 miles to the west, is the county line. Fred was absolutely right, if we consider the linguistic evidence on table 2 (all classes together). According to Ferguson and Gumperz:

Any group of speakers of language X which regards itself as a close social unit will tend to express its group solidarity by favoring those linguistic innovations which set it apart from other speakers of X who are not part of the group [1960:9].

That the other side of town--the middle- and upper-class side--is perceived as alien territory by more than that one family can be seen in such comments as this one from an old bricklayer, who moved beyond the city limits forty years before:

19. I liked comin' out West. I was born and raised in West Anniston, and this is west of town, you know. The further out you come, the better I like it. (55.I.173)

One last example comes from a teenage girl who was telling me about the East Side of town, which, according to her, is "the other side of town where everybody's supposed to be so rich." When I asked her if they really were rich, she laughed, "If you seen the houses over there, you'd say, yeah!" (38.I.310).

As Trudgill 1974 has shown, the solidarity norm also serves as a vehicle for expressing masculinity as well as class and neighborhood affiliation. In this light, it is not surprising that, of the working class, the teenage boys use ain't 61 percent of the time, ahead of the older urban and rural men and women, as well as the teenage girls, who use it the least (see table 5). A striking illustration of a teenage boy's having to re-establish his credentials as a member of the network is the following case. I was interviewing a pair of teenagers, Tom and Ronny, at Tom's house. To my dismay, Tom's mother joined us and made comments from time to time. I asked if somebody could be a "brain" and still be part of their crowd.

20. Tom: Ronny's 'bout the smartest one in school.
    Tom's mother: Made better grades than the others.
    Ronny: Don't mean nothin', though. (40.I.149)

Ronny was one of the most standard of the working-class boys, so far as negative concord is concerned, but this discussion of his grades made it necessary for him to come back with an "Aw shucks" double negative, as well as his normal invariable don't. Clearly, he did not want to lose his position as a member of the network.

Network Correlations

So far, I have discussed networks in somewhat general terms, showing how speakers demonstrate their solidarity with their network by using the local vernacular according to the demands of their particular network, whether the speaker is upper class or working class. However, what is especially new and advantageous about using networks as an investigatory concept or tool in linguistic research is that it led to the discovery of the surprising extent of correlation between an individual's degree of integration into a network and his or her use of linguistic variants. Milroy showed that, in Belfast, fully integrated members of working-class networks have significantly higher use of vernacular variants than less fully integrated informants.

In order to discuss individual variation in this way, it is necessary to set up a network strength scale. Milroy establishes five conditions for scoring her informants and then is able to demonstrate, with correlation tests, the unexpected degree of relationship between her informants' close (or loose) ties to their network and their use of nonstandard phonology. These conditions are (1) membership in a high-density, territorially based cluster; (2) having substantial ties of kinship in the neighborhood; (3) working at the same place as two others from the same area; (4) having the same place of work as at least two others of the same sex from the same area; (5) having voluntary association with workmates in leisure hours (only when conditions 3 and 4 are satisfied).

An attempt to use Milroy's conditions to set up a post-facto network strength scale for my Anniston informants was unsuccessful. My fieldwork was not designed to obtain the sort of information needed to establish such a scale, and an after-the-fact examination of field notes and interviews could not fill in the gaps for the core informants. My interviews had concentrated on the past life of my informants in order to be sure that they had arrived in Anniston by the age of six and to place them in a socioeconomic class. Furthermore, Milroy's conditions 4, 5, and 6 depend on the informants' being in the work force. An attempt to treat school as work for the young and to refer to the previous work experience of the old was not successful. For instance, it did not discriminate between teenagers with different aspirations, which were shown in their grammar but not in the network scores, by using Milroy's conditions.

This problem can be seen in a comparison of the linguistic scores of Ronny Flanders (the "brain" of example 20) and Rodney Sampson, the youngster who started the interview (example 1) by telling his buddies I had come down South to make fun of them (see table 8). Their scores contrast with the averages of all six teenage boys. These two, Ronny Flanders and Rodney Sampson, are the most standard of the six, but, despite the small numbers involved, it would surprise no one to discover that, at the time of the interview, the Flanders boy was planning to be a welder while the Sampson boy intended to go to the University of Alabama and then on to law school. (Which he did, I found out later.)

Table 8
Two Working-Class Boys
Differing Networks, Aspirations
Compared to Group Scores of Working-Class Boys

	Ronny Flanders Nonstandard/		Rodney Sampson Nonstandard/		Working-Class
	Total	%	Total	%	Boys
Invariable don't	6/6	100	0/0	–	94%
Multiple negation	13/26	50	0/4	(0)	70%
Invariable was	19/27	70.3	11/19	57.8	79%
Ain't (have + be)	6/22	27.3	0/2	0	61%
Invariable is	2/12	16.7	1/6	16.7	36%
NP plural + -s	0/2	(0)	1/3	(33.3)	27%
Nonstandard irregular past participle	2/10	20	0/4	(0)	34%
Nonstandard irregular preterit	12/68	17.6	4/28	14.1	22%

Moreover, the elder Flanders, Ronny's parents, both worked at a sportswear factory in the working-class section of town, and had been there for eighteen and twenty-two years. The Sampsons did not work in that section of town. Rodney's father worked at the Army depot ten miles west of town, while Mrs. Sampson had progressed from being a bank teller to head of the central bookkeeping office of the largest bank in town, which is in Anniston's most elegant office building (on the East Side, on a beautiful avenue with trees, churches, and other banks). The Flanders boy had six guns and hunted quail and dove; the Sampson boy used his father's .22, but didn't hunt much. Rather, he was president of the student body and the dramatics club. However, according to Milroy's network strength scale, these two boys appear to have the same degree of integration into their network (see table 9). Perhaps for children and teenagers, the network strength scale has to relate simply to the parents, just as social status indices (income, profession, education) have to reflect parents' status rather than the not-yet-existing status of children (see table 10).

One of the advantages of this approach is the correlation of the network strength scale with linguistic scores of individuals, which Milroy amply demonstrates with examples from Belfast phonology.

Table 9
Network Strength Scores for Two Working-Class Boys

	1 High Density Cluster	2 Kinship Ties	3 Work Place	4 Work Place Same Sex	5 Voluntary Association	Score
Flanders	Yes	?	Yes	Yes	Yes	4
Sampson	Yes	?	Yes	Yes	Yes	4

Table 10
Network Strength Scores for Parents
of Two Working-Class Boys

	1	2	3	4	5	Score	
Flanders'	?	?	Yes	Yes	Yes?	4	
Parents	?	?	Yes	Yes	Yes?	4	(= 8)
Sampson's	?	?	Yes	Yes	No?	2	
Parents	?	?	No	No	No?	0	(= 2)

Unfortunately, this does not seem to work out as well in the study of grammatical variation, since there are too few tokens of each variable to have a reliable linguistic score for an individual. For example, Rodney Sampson had no instances of don't or doesn't, only four examples of potential multiple negation, two of negative have or be, and four of irregular past participles (see table 8). Only three of eight grammatical variables have enough tokens to be validly compared for young Flanders and young Sampson: invariable was, invariable is, and nonstandard irregular preterit. Milroy's work is with phonology, which is more likely to produce an adequate number of tokens of the variants from individuals.

Perhaps a different network strength score--or the same one, with an assessment of parents' characteristics--used in conjunction with a study of phonology, would produce a more successful result from my data. Nevertheless, it is clear from a more general use of the concept of network loyalties that the degree of integration into the community is certainly reflected in the grammatical score in a survey of the sort that I undertook.

Conclusion

What I have demonstrated here is the pull of two norms in the white community of a small Southern city. On the one hand is the prestige norm, which receives lip service from every segment of society, as well as life-long service from the local English teachers. However, this norm competes--not very successfully--with a local solidarity norm which also affects the whole society, though to varying degrees. This solidarity norm commands a visceral-level loyalty since it symbolizes a person's degree of integration into local networks, to being part of the local community.

Although I have not investigated it, I am confident that the local black community has similar competing norms. The black solidarity norm would be somewhat different from that of the whites of the community. (See Feagin 1979:245-57 for a comparison of nonstandard white Anniston speech and black English). But the prestige norm is probably the same as that of the whites, so far as grammar is concerned. Nevertheless, depending on whether the blacks have the same prestige grammar or a slightly different one, I would speculate that most communities in the South have a similar three- or four-way system of norms, such as the one I have proposed for Anniston.[5]

I am also convinced that more linguistic evidence of dense/multiplex or diffuse/simplex networks will appear in a close investigation of the phonology of a speech community such as Anniston.[6] Not only will more tokens appear in such a study, but phonology is less under the conscious control of the informants than grammar.

NOTES

[1]I very much appreciate the comments of Charles-James N. Bailey, Dee Ann Holisky, Michael Montgomery, Stephen T. Moskey, and James W. Stone on an earlier draft of this paper.

[2]The term "standard English" opens a complex topic. The term has no generally agreed-upon definition. Here it simply refers to both grammar-book prescriptive English (what is taught in the schools) and cultivated speech. "Cultivated" and "uncultivated" are alternative terms to "standard" and "nonstandard." I use "standard" and "nonstandard" here because these terms are widely accepted. See C.-J. Bailey 1981 and Heath 1980b for further discussion of the issues.

[3]"(W 17:47.I.002)" indicates that the citation comes from a working-class person (W), age 17, interview number 47, reel I, 002 on the tape counter. Sex is indicated by first name. U indicates upper class; R means rural (all rural informants were working class); and A refers to the series of taped conversations in the sewing class. All informant names are pseudonyms.

[4]Indeed, it could be said that Annistonians excel in this

respect, if any weight is given to the evidence of editorials from the Anniston Star, penned by the owner-editor, H. Brandt Ayers (a native of Anniston), and reprinted in the Washington Post on a regular basis during the Carter administration. A young man from Anniston, John Hemphill, was a correspondent for the New York Times (until his early death some years ago) and five novels by two native Anniston writers, who live there permanently, have been published by Scribner, McGraw-Hill, and Holt, Rinehart and Winston.

[5]McDavid has frequently alluded to the opposing norms in white communities of the South in remarks about style shifting, such as the following:

> It is interesting to note that . . . [Southern speech] seems to have greater differences between formal and consultative and casual styles. There may also be a greater tendency of the Southerner to shift into his casual style as he comes to accept someone as an equal, or at least worth talking to. . . . Whatever its origins, its manifestations are clear, in various social clues. In Charleston, particularly, . . . ain't drops into the conversation, signalling that ladies and gentlemen recognizing each other's status can afford to relax. In most communities the copula-auxiliary will disappear, or at least its frequency will be reduced [1970:56].

[6]Perhaps I will find out something along these lines in my current investigation of change in progress in the Anniston vowel system.

The Greatest Blemish: Plurals in *-sp, -st, -sk*

Michael I. Miller

In the Harper Dictionary of Contemporary Usage, William and Mary Morris tell people confused by variant plurals to "consult a recent and reliable dictionary. . . .If no example of the plural is given, you may count on it that the plural is regularly formed by the addition of a terminal 's' or 'es'" (1975:476). Dictionaries themselves repeat this claim. The Merriam-Webster books, for example, say they show plurals when, among other reasons, "the noun has variant plurals, and when it is believed that the dictionary user might have reasonable doubt about the spelling" (Woolf 1981:12a). The Random House Dictionary and its college-market spinoff say "where variant inflected forms occur, all forms are shown, with labels where appropriate" (Stein 1975:xxviii). Norman Hoss, author of the "Guide" to William Morris' own The American Heritage Dictionary says, confusingly, "the regular -s plural is shown when there is a variant plural that is irregular or when any question might arise" (1969:xliii). (Hoss doesn't mean what he says; the AHD shows the irregular form.)

Dictionaries typically describe irregular plurals like oxen, scarves, scissors, government, and data but usually omit the plurals of measure--like two year--that Noah Webster found so interesting in his 1828 dictionary, and dictionaries always omit plurals of words ending in -sp, -st, and -sk. No current dictionary or usage guide considers words ending in -sp, -st, -sk in any way irregular, though all current dictionaries attempt to record both the pronunciations and spellings of other irregular plurals. And no standard grammar hints that the paradigm for these words might include anything but the allomorphs Morris calls -s.

Older grammarians, dialectologists, and experts on black speech typically see this point differently. Both Jespersen 1909-19 and Curme 1935, for example, notice disyllabic plurals like waspes. In the English Dialect Dictionary (1905), Wright lists no fewer than eighteen different plurals of nest, and under post he lists sixteen.

In the English Dialect Grammar (1898-1905), Wright comments that all nouns ending in -st have disyllabic -es plurals (like beastes) below the Humber. Wright even books trisyllabic plurals and a triple plural, nestsezes, from Suffolk. Similarly, Wentworth's American Dialect Dictionary (1944) comments that -es forms the plurals for nouns ending in -sp, -st, and -sk in American folk speech, and Wentworth itemizes twenty-one different examples. Further, Wentworth adds wasses, ghosses, and nesses--with the medial stop lost on the model of words like listen--and a monosyllabic was. Wentworth marks several of these examples "Negro."

Dillard comments on only one such word but implies he is thinking of a class. In Black English, he says that wasp "will have the plural [wɔsˑ] (or [wɔss])" (1972:310). But Burling (1973:51) argues that loss of plural -s in black speech would affect "the meaning of the word and the sentence in a crucial way"; so, unlike Dillard, Burling thinks most black people use disyllabic desses, tesses, and ghosses. In "Some Linguistic Features of Negro Dialect" (1970), Fasold and Wolfram agree that black people use disyllabic desses, ghosses, wasses, and tesses commonly, and some blacks use disyllabic deskes and testes. Fasold and Wolfram add in a footnote that "in standard English these sequences are often pronounced by lengthening the s instead of pronouncing the full sequence (e.g., tess for tests or dess for desks)" (1970:45n), thereby claiming for standard English the monosyllabic pronunciations that Dillard claims for "Black English."

Adding weight to the argument, Labov (1972a:22) agrees with Burling, Wolfram, and Fasold that deses, ghoses, and toses (plural of toast) typify black speech (Labov's spellings). Labov adds that "clusters such as -sps, -sts, and -sks are almost impossible for many black children to articulate" (22-23). Labov says monosyllabic variants like des occur infrequently, and he thinks disyllabic deskes, testes, and waspes characterize "white Appalachian speech rather than southern black speech" (23). Yet, in a well-known study of white Appalachian speech, Wolfram and Christian (1976:39) claim that white Appalachians form -sp, -st, and -sk plurals by lengthening -s, while black speakers typically lengthen -s and eliminate the stop, as Dillard earlier claimed and Wolfram earlier denied.

Wolfram and Christian offer seven examples taken from actual speech--seven more than any previous study--to support their conclusion. But since they conducted 130 interviews, the preponderance of their evidence seems to argue otherwise. Furthermore, they systematically investigated only one such word, ghost, and the form of their question, "Lots of people talk about ghosts. Do you believe they could be real?" (1976:167), would prejudice the response. Given the contradictions, confusions, and paucity of evidence among the "experts" on black speech, it is unclear how seriously anyone should take any of these claims and counterclaims.

My own research in Augusta, Georgia, contributes to the information on Southern speech by reporting the usage of thirty-seven primary informants in the city and in the surrounding semi-industrial, suburban, and rural communities.[1] My sample includes representatives of every social group, both sexes, both racial castes, and both urban and rural residents in an age range from eighteen to eighty-seven. (For my use of the terms caste and racial caste see Myrdal 1944, Park 1950:177-88, Dollard 1957, and Berreman 1960.) Myrdal's term color caste may be more accurate, but common usage sanctions caste and racial caste. For an opposed view, see Cox 1959.) Many of my informants, both black and white, trace their Augusta roots to well before the Civil War. Table 1 lists each informant, classifies each in one of six social groups, and lists other relevant data, like residence, caste, sex, age, linguistic atlas type, and interview date. My dissertation (M. Miller 1978) gives a fuller description of this sample and of the sociohistorical background. Interviews used the "indirect method" elaborated by Jaberg and Jud 1928. I developed specific questionnaire items from Davis, McDavid, and McDavid 1969 and Pederson, McDavid, Foster, and Billiard 1974.

Grammatical items include seven nouns ending in -sp, -st, and -sk: wasp, fist, ghost, nest, post, desk, and tusk. Since my sample consists of thirty-seven primary informants, I could presumably have collected 259 responses, but in fact I got 228, with an effective loss rate of about 17 percent. Table 2 lists every one of the 228 responses for each word and for each informant. Some people gave no or few responses, and others gave multiple responses.

As table 2 shows, I prepared thirty-seven protocols for the forty-one informants listed in Table 1. A protocol outlines the speech of one tape-text (Pederson 1974), which in four cases--6, 7, 27, and 34--includes an auxiliary informant. Each of the auxiliaries was an immediate family member of the primary. I conducted all but two of the interviews myself. Sara Sanders interviewed 7 and 27 for a related project (S. Sanders 1978), but she is not guilty of my transcriptions.

Understanding the morphology of these words for this sample requires close attention to phonemics, phonotactics, and even the raw phonic data. For most of my purposes, however, narrow transcription would be pedantic. So wherever possible I will present the material using a "normalized" spelling (cf. Bloomfield and Bolling 1927). Before generalizing or projecting to the entire community, I will summarize the results for each phonemic group. Statistical considerations, historical characteristics, data from elsewhere, and details of my interview style all bear on the conclusions.

Wasp

I investigated only one -sp plural, of which I found six variants: wasp, wasps, wasses, was, waps, and wast. Disyllabic waspes, an expected form, did not occur, though it may occur in Augusta usage. However, in lower Southern field records of The Linguistic Atlas of the Middle and South Atlantic States (LAMSAS), waspes occurred only twice. The more common disyllabic plural, wastes, occurred nine times in widely scattered communities. But if either waspes or wastes occurs in current black or white Augusta speech, it must be rare.

The plural wast occurred only once, in the free conversation of informant 19, a 45-year-old, white, upper-middle-class male. Forms with an alveolar rather than bilabial stop (wast, wasts, and wastes) occur in about 13 percent (35/261) of the lower Southern LAMSAS field records. In this single Augusta case, wast alternated with wasp.

Waps, without the Middle English metathesis to wasp and without further inflection, occurred twice in the speech of two upper-middle-class black urban males (informants 9 and 12). Both alternated waps with wasp. Informant 9 commented that he heard waps from older people and sometimes used it himself. Informant 12 used waps but then spontaneously corrected to wasp. Both speakers presumably interpret waps as a base, wap-, plus the affix -s, alternating with a second plural wasp. In any case, the pronunciation itself is rare.

After reviewing the English evidence from the Survey of English Dialects and from Lowman's survey of Southern England, Viereck 1975 notes that the high frequency of wapses in English folk speech almost demands similar forms in American English. (The high frequency of waps in English folk speech almost guarantees that the form is not a remetathesis, even in the isolated American examples.) Yet neither waps nor wapses occurs in American linguistic atlas records from New England, the North Central States, or the Upper Midwest. Outside of these two Augusta examples, LAMSAS alone records two American instances of waps, at widely separated locations. These may be the only recorded American examples, but perhaps The Linguistic Atlas of the Gulf States (LAGS) contains others.

Wasses, the form that is supposed to be most characteristic of black speech, also occurred twice, in the usage of two older black males living in rural communities on the periphery of the survey area: Ridge Spring, far to the east, and Thomson, 40 miles west. The difference between my results and the results of the sociolinguists cited above may be due to geography, sample size, elicitation technique, or other factors. Perhaps wasses has spread at the expense of other forms in Northern black ghettoes, where sociolinguists normally conduct their research. But of the 261 lower Southern LAMSAS records, I count only three instances of wasses, all from whites.

The form was, /wɔs/, occurred six times in my sample: twice in upper-class white speech (1 and 5), once in the speech of an 18-year-old lower-middle-class black male (24), once in the speech of a 29-year-old working-class white male (30), once in the speech of a 68-year-old illiterate black male (34), and once in the speech of a 32-year-old rural black male (37). Was thus occurs in black, white, cultivated, middle class, white working-class, and rural black speech. The evidence does not support the view that was characterizes any one social group or racial caste. Furthermore, was occurs infrequently.

Wasp, the presumed "standard" form, also occurred six times (informants 1, 2, 4, 8, 20, and 22), but three of the six also used unmarked forms, either was or wasp. Of the three who carefully pronounced the triple consonant cluster at the end of the word each time they used it, two (2 and 8) are teachers and the third (22) had recently taken night school courses and knew that I was a teacher. Far from being "standard," wasps is merely a spelling pronunciation confined to fastidious speech.

By far the most common plural (21/38; 55%) was the unmarked one, wasp. It occurred at almost every social level, every age level, and in the usage of both sexes, both racial castes, and urban and rural residents. In LAMSAS, wasp occurs in nearly one-third of 261 field records. Yet dictionaries, usage guides, and sociolinguists seem to have missed it entirely. It is almost certainly the most common form in both black and white Southern speech.

So far, this discussion has concentrated on phonemics, with a single digression into phonotactics at waps. I should add one point regarding phonic detail and a related point regarding phonotactics (for my use of the term phonic and a general perspective on phonology, see Kurath 1961, Kurath 1964, and Kurath and McDavid 1961). Few individuals lengthen penultimate s regardless of plurality. In LAMSAS records from the lower South, McDavid transcribed individuals who used a long s for the singular and a shorter s, followed by a bilabial stop, for the plural. But I have found no clear pattern among use of long penultimate s, use or omission of final p, and use or omission of final s. Possibly a following vowel encourages plosion--and thus audible articulation-- of final p, whereas a following labial, alveolar, or dental consonant might reduce the cluster due to assimilation of the already unreleased stop, but I do not have the experimental data readily available to test this view. Furthermore, consistent impressionistic transcription of consonant length seems much more difficult than consistent transcriptions of vowel quality, even for difficult vowels like the low-back group, and even for highly trained phoneticians like Bloch, Lowman, or R. McDavid (cf. Ladefoged 1960). I do not, therefore, fully trust my own transcriptions on this point, though I was trained in the Bloch-Lowman-McDavid tradition. But the question and the tapes are ripe for instrumental analysis.

A note on field technique may also be relevant. I usually elicited wasps by asking for names of insects. This generally produced a list. A narrower frame asked for names of insects that sting, and if that didn't work, the narrowest frame asked for the kind of insect that builds a paper nest on a branch or under the eaves of a house (see Pederson, McDavid, Foster, and Billiard 1974:162). My informants, therefore, usually gave hypostasized words. The effects of connected discourse seldom occur, even though the records contain conversational variants here and there.

I did not investigate any other noun ending in -sp. The words that immediately suggest themselves--clasp, wisp, and cusp--would be difficult to elicit with the indirect method. Perhaps, however, future research will investigate wasps, clasps, wisps, and cusps as part of a reading list. The last three words might be investigated by using the admittedly old-fashioned direct method, as favored by Wolfram and Christian. Properly designed, this experiment might also test my suggestion that wasps is a conscious spelling pronunciation.

Fist, Ghost, Nest, and Post

Words ending in -sts illustrate the scarcity of triple consonant clusters in Augusta speech more clearly. I investigated four: fist, ghost, nest, and post.

As with wasp, my elicitation frames might have some interest. I elicited fist near the end of each interview as part of a general survey of the names of body parts. Usually, I illustrated with first one, then both hands, for the plural. Ghosts usually came conversationally in discussion of holidays, superstitions, or death, and commonly produced the lexical variants haunts or haints. Informants normally used nests also in free conversation, either as part of the discussion that produced wasps or in a discussion of local birds. To get posts, I asked about types of fences and how to put them together. For further details and specific elicitation frames of various fieldworkers, see Pederson, McDavid, Foster, and Billiard (1974:117, 174, 194).

Perhaps the most interesting response on Table 2 is the disyllabic form postes in the usage of informant 37. The other disyllabic plurals include fisses (32), ghosses (33 and 35), nesses (32 and 33), and posses (26, 28, 34, and 35). As with wasses, the disyllabic forms occur only in black speech.

Almost as rare as disyllabic plurals are the twenty-three instances ending in a triple cluster -sts--18 percent of 125 responses. Informant 22 used the triple cluster most consistently. Close behind him are informants 8 and 2, both teachers. In the civilian population, only three people use the triple cluster for as many as half of their responses (4, 9, and 10). Informants 4 and 10 are wealthy whites who travel frequently. Informant 9 is a black minister, educated in the North. The remainder who use triple clusters do so for only one of four words. Most are upper or upper-middle class. But the single and interestingly anomalous exception is informant 37, a black laborer, who has never traveled outside the immediate area and who never finished high school.

People may be less likely to pronounce the -sts cluster for frequently occurring words. Table 3 summarizes the number of -st pronunciations for each word, regardless of age, social group, or caste, then computes the ratio for -st responses compared with total responses, compared with total responses for that word. The third column in Table 3 lists the frequency of each plural in the Brown Corpus (Kučera and Francis 1967). As the Brown Corpus frequencies increase, the Augusta proportions decrease. I have not prepared a scatter diagram or calculated the probability of error because the sources of data are so different that the procedures would be misleading and overprecise. Yet if posts actually occurs in speech more frequently than nests, the frequency of the word may influence its grammatical form.

Table 4 shifts to a larger view. Each row lists the percentage of responses and the total number of responses for each word. I group fis, fist, and so on because even though they differ phonemically, they are monosyllables. I also group posses and postes because both are disyllabic. I separate out fists, posts, etc. because they are the supposed "standard" forms. The most important set of figures is the total frequencies for all four words. Unmarked plurals account for 74 percent of the responses, triple clusters for 18 percent, and disyllables for 8 percent. Since the words are listed in order of frequency of use, and the hierarchy from nest to post may be considered an ordinal scale, I have also calculated the value of gamma, which measures the strength of the relationship between an increase in scale and plural form. (For the statistical procedures used in the paper, see Blalock 1972 or any standard text.) The value of gamma is .79, respectably high.

However, I also tested for sampling error, using chi-square. The chi-square value is 5.8790, too low to reject the null hypothesis for these data. As opposed to the dubious test of reliability in table 3 and the convincing test of association revealed by gamma, this test suggests that the relationships between words and grammatical forms does not determine the configuration of responses. In fact, the probability that this pattern results from chance or sampling error is around 50 percent. Yet this figure implies that further research has about a 50 percent chance of proving that the frequency of a word determines its grammatical form. Further, the table itself reveals an unexpectedly low number of disyllabic responses for fist and ghost, low triple cluster responses for post, and a markedly high number of disyllabic responses for post.

Following the same procedure, Table 5 groups six social levels into three: upper, middle, and lower--and gives the results for both the gamma and chi-square tests. The high value of chi-square suggests that social stratification bears heavily on grammatical form, and the extremely high value of gamma confirms this relationship. Disyllabic plurals occur only in middle and lower social groups. Triple clusters occur hardly at all in the lower groups, regardless of caste, and infrequently in middle and upper groups. The upper groups use monosyllabic plurals without final -s less than the middle and lower groups, but unmarked monosyllabic plurals are nevertheless the most common form even for these highly cultivated and well-placed members of the community. Furthermore, the differences between expected and observed values are high for most cells. The "normal" or chance distribution predicts fewer triple clusters for the upper groups, more triple clusters in lower group usage, more disyllabic plurals in the middle groups, and much lower values for disyllabic plurals in the lower groups.

In a marked contrast to Tables 4 and 5, Table 6 reorganizes the -st data by racial caste to disclose an unmistakable caste distinction. As with wasp, the most common forms for both castes are unmarked. But triple clusters undoubtedly occur more commonly in white than in black usage. And disyllables occur exclusively in black speech. The chi-square test produces a high value, 26.4178, which is significant at the .001 level with two degrees of freedom. That is, the probability that chance would produce this patterning of the data is less than one in a thousand. There can be no doubt that caste relates significantly to plural form in Augusta speech much more significantly, as a main effect, than social class. Yet the data does not support the view that some people use disyllables because they are black, that race determines grammatical form.

Desk and Tusk

The survey also investigated two words ending with -s plus a voiceless velar stop, desk and tusk, though the well-known palatalization of -sk in tusk complicates the data and their interpretation.

Three plurals of desk occur: desk (20/32; 63%), desks (8/32; 25%), and desses (4/32; 13%). Informant 16 gave two responses with no apparent stylistic difference. Unmarked forms predominate, except in the usage of the most highly educated group, where desks occurs frequently. Desks also appears in the speech of informant 24, a younger, middle-class black male who reduced the plural to -s for each of his other responses. Desses occurs primarily in older blacks' speech.

Tusk has six different plurals. As usual, the unmarked form occurs most commonly (16/32; 50%). Tusks occurred six times (19%)

in white upper-class and upper-middle-class usage. The disyllabic form is palatalized to tushes, which also occurred six times. The expected "hypercorrect" forms, tusses and tuskes, do not occur (though Lowman recorded the historically expected tuskes twice to the southeast of London; see Viereck 1975). Instead, exactly parallel to wasses, fisses, ghosses, nesses, and posses, Augustans (like many Southerners) use tushes, the most common LAMSAS form and an obvious descendant of the disyllabic plurals that pervade Middle English and early Modern English speech outside cultivated London circles. Unlike the other disyllabic form, tushes also occurs in white speech, mostly as a conscious archaism.

I recorded, in addition, a single example of tush as plural from informant 25. Two forms not in LAMSAS are tuft (9) and tutch (29 and 34), the former perhaps a nonce form.

Reliability

Before generalizing from these data, let me consider two objections. First, some believe it is impossible for a white fieldworker to elicit true responses from black informants. Second, some might claim that the sample is not representative. But neither objection, even if granted in part, seriously undermines the major conclusions.

The belief that blacks speak "a completely different language" when whites leave the room is mythological. When pressed to give examples, most people, whether white or black, lamely repeat a few obvious terms of endearment or homely words (like hoecake or baits) in the mistaken belief that these are unique to intimate black speech. I have not found a single convincing example of pronunciation, grammar, or vocabulary that would exemplify this supposedly hidden language, nor have I seen a convincing argument that whites cannot successfully interview blacks (M. Miller 1981). Turner's list of Gullah names (1949:43-190), usually invoked in this context, refers to an entirely different social, historical, and geographical setting and has no clear or immediate bearing on this question.

Of course, some interviews produced guarded responses. Six of my black informants (32%) gave guarded interviews, but ten of the whites (45%) also gave guarded interviews. Interviewing more middle-class blacks caused the difference in percentages. Among the blacks, informants 9, 12, 21, 24, 28, and 37 were guarded; among the whites, informants 3, 4, 5, 14, 17, 18, 19, 20, 22, and 31. But the tapes of informants 11, 15, 16, 23, and all the older blacks are full of free, easy, relaxed, and anecdotal conversation. With some older people, I squeezed questions in between long stretches of even intimate conversation. The more self-assured middle-class blacks laughed, joked, and told stories throughout interviews that lasted from two to nine or ten hours.

On the other hand, people of either racial caste who saw themselves as upwardly mobile, the types who strive for correctness even at the expense of communication, were difficult to relax. For example, informant 12, a black male English teacher, told me in so many words that he consciously strives to maintain the highest standards in every aspect of his life. His tape usage, though frequently hypercorrect, is in fact his daily usage, not a performance. Informant 19, a white female, descended from three generations of people who had "worked the floor" in a prominent Augusta cotton mill, that is, three generations of "lintheads" or "rednecks." She was painfully aware of her elevated status, due to a promotion off the floor to the front office, and she gave me the most strained interview of the group. But even the most guarded interviews produced responses like <u>waps</u> from informants 9 and 12 or <u>postes</u> from informant 37, who had gone so far as to call me "cap'n" when we began. I must nevertheless concede that informant 37's <u>fists</u>, informant 24's <u>desks</u>, and even some upper-class triple clusters result from conscious attempts at correctness.

Second, to say this sample is skewed is not a serious objection; every sample is skewed. Even a cursory comparison with 1970 census records shows that this sample overrepresents the highest income groups, professional and technical occupations, and those educated beyond high school. The sample also overrepresents illiterate older blacks. Middle-class speech, particularly at the lower ends, is underrepresented. Middle-age speech is underrepresented. Therefore, to project these results to the community as a whole requires definable corrections. For example, disyllabic plurals probably occur in the total black population somewhat less frequently than in my sample; monosyllabic plurals ending in a triple cluster must occur much less frequently. But the skewing of the sample emphasizes my thesis: plurals of nouns ending in -<u>sp</u>, -<u>st</u>, and -<u>sk</u> are most commonly unmarked, regardless of class or racial caste.

Caste, Phonetic Structure, and Morphological Fusion

This thesis leads to several related conclusions. Obviously, it would be a mistake to think disyllabic plurals characterize black speech. Most blacks in the Augusta area, and probably throughout the lower South (possibly in Northern ghettoes as well), do not use disyllabic forms. Of the nineteen black individuals in my sample, only nine (six of them over 65 years old) use disyllabic plurals. Disyllabic plurals occur rarely in younger or middle-class black speech, not only in Augusta but elsewhere as well. For example, Juanita Williamson (1961:77) finds only six disyllabic plurals of <u>post</u> and two of <u>wasp</u> among twenty-four Memphis blacks chosen from all social levels.

Furthermore, disyllabic plurals occur in older white speech. In

addition to the single example (tushes) in my sample, the lower
Southern LAMSAS records contain twenty instances of postes, five
of posses, five of ghostes, four of fistes, and one of fisss. Of
these thirty-five examples, all but ten--over two-thirds--come from
whites. In some cases, a white uses a disyllabic plural while a
nearby black uses a monosyllable. On top of all this, disyllabic
plurals occur commonly in white English folk speech. The Survey
of English Dialects (Orton et al. 1962-71) shows posses and postes
everywhere below the Humber, just as Wright 1905 predicted
almost eighty years ago. Forty years ago, Lowman found posses,
postes, ghosses, ghostes, fisses, fistes, tuskes, and tushes
everywhere below the Wash (Viereck 1975).

The caste distinction in current Augusta speech (revealed by
table 6) must therefore be new, and it is not hard to trace its
historical development. Plurals that end in a triple cluster do not
occur in Middle English, though disyllabic spellings of deskes,
fistes, ghostes, and nestes are commonplace in the Middle English
Dictionary (Kurath et al. 1952). Disyllabic spellings continue in
OED texts until the late seventeenth century. Eighteenth- and
nineteenth-century comments attest that disyllabic pronunciations
continued long after literary usage changed. For example, in A
Critical Pronouncing Dictionary (1791), published one year before
the introduction of cotton-economy plantation slavery around
Augusta, Walker comments that "the inhabitants of London of the
lower order"--that is, just those Englishmen who peopled upcountry
towns like Augusta--pronounced the plurals of post and fist in two
syllables, and Walker added, "this is to be avoided as the greatest
blemish in speaking; the three last letters in post, fists, mists, etc.
must all be distinctly heard in one syllable" (xii). He recommended
that his readers practice these words daily, and he added that
they would find his riming dictionary "peculiarly useful" for this
purpose. Jespersen (1909-19:V:257) notes a similar comment in an
1833 English grammar, and Sherwood's famous list of Georgia
"Provincialisms" of 1837 (M. Matthews 1931:118-21) attacks the
local use of Baptises for Baptists (presumably Sherwood's New
England pronunciation) and texes for texts. The LAMSAS, SED, and
Lowman records, cited earlier, show that disyllabic plurals
continued in white usage for another century, at least.

Raven and Virginia McDavid have argued that "nothing in the
geographical distribution suggests that the use of these disyllabic
forms is necessarily a mark of 'Negro dialect' (or of any Negro
dialect, for the speech of Negro Americans is not a monolithic
entity); rather they seem to be found in old-fashioned folk speech,
and are preserved by geographical or social isolation or a
combination of the two" (1978:76). Ad hoc pseudopsychological
explanations contribute little to our understanding of these forms
or of black speech. For example, the view that forms like postes
in the usage of informant 37 "result from the failure to eliminate
Negro dialect pluralization after realizing that words like test and

desk are to be pronounced with a cluster" (Fasold and Wolfram 1970:56) is doubtful at best. Informant 37 is just as likely using the plural he has used since childhood and that occurs most commonly in the speech of people he associates with. No "hypercorrection" need be involved. Furthermore, the view that disyllabic plurals result from "a regular pluralization pattern due to the status of final consonant clusters in negro dialect" (Fasold and Wolfram 1970:58) also seems mistaken. Generations of English speakers, regardless of racial caste, have learned disyllabic plurals with and without a medial stop consonant.

Though unmarked plurals are the norm for both racial castes, the difference between black and white usage boils down to a difference between those who use book forms, ending in a triple cluster, and those who (in Walker's phrase) cut the knot with a disyllable. The book forms must result from schooling, or at least from extended exposure to the conventions of writing.

Having thrown some doubt, I hope, on purely psychological explanations (really mentalistic speculations at best) for the causes of disyllabic plurals in current black speech, I would like to suggest two other causes, social and historical.

First, though Augusta blacks have managed to provide exceptionally good schooling for themselves from the earliest times, the official policy until recently has worked to keep as many blacks as possible out of schools or, failing that, at least to keep blacks in poorly staffed and poorly equipped schools. The first publicly supported black high school appeared in Augusta in 1938; the first (reluctant) attempts at adequate schooling in 1972, following a riot. It is unusual for a black person who is now over forty to have finished even the eighth grade. While Augusta's Richmond Academy worked from the earliest settlement of the town to enforce the "correct" forms prescribed in compendia like Walker and Sherwood and to stamp out the oral tradition of disyllabic forms, most older blacks were spared this initiation.

Second, technological developments since World War II, and especially since 1950, have led Augusta away from its traditional cotton economy to an entirely new economic and social organization. As a result, the communication gaps between older blacks, younger whites, and younger blacks, ultimately traceable to the advent of the boll weevil and the Great Migration following World War I, have increasingly widened. Though blacks and whites lived closely intermeshed lives until two generations ago, Augustans now live in segregated neighborhoods (on the Northern model), and it is axiomatic that communication boundaries produce linguistic boundaries (Bohnenberger 1902).

Yet my evidence suggests that substantial differences between black and white Augustans with respect to this set of grammatical features are more apparent than real. Lexicographers mistakenly assume the normalcy of book forms and teach their mistakes to others. Students of "black English" and assorted sociolinguists, on the other hand, mark the disyllabic forms that crop up occasionally and appear so striking in older black speech. Hardly anyone notices the most common forms. But to claim descriptive adequacy, writers of dictionaries, grammars, and textbooks need to add another statement to their generalizations.

For most Augustans, if not most Southerners, a phonemically conditioned and automatic alternant determines the plural forms of words that end in -sp, -st, and -sk. A phonetician might explain the unmarked plurals in words like post as cases of progressive assimilation. But this explanation cannot account for wasp or desk, which seem to force an appeal to "analogy." Calling on assimilation and analogy, however, provides two explanations (or perhaps three) for what seems to be a single, unified process. A similar objection applies to the fiction that plural -s is "deleted" when it follows -sp, -st, and -sk. Historically, there is no evidence that final -s was ever there to delete; so the explanation is superfluous.

A classic structural model (e.g., Bloch 1947) might describe unmarked plurals as zero allomorphs, alternating with the /-s/, /-z/, and /- z/ recognized in most dictionaries and texts. Currently fashionable "process" models, on the other hand, might explain words ending in -sp, -st, and -sk as instances of sandhi (cf. D. H. Matthews 1974:97-115). I would argue that this speech community has probably always used three different morphological patterns for these words: (1) disyllabic forms inherited from English folk speech, including London speech; (2) unmarked forms inherited from the same sources; and (3) marked forms probably introduced as spelling pronunciations in the late eighteenth century. The unmarked forms predominate because the community now stigmatizes the disyllabics by association with uneducated black speech and because the spelling pronunciations do not follow a more general rule of English phonetics, that "the more sonorous consonant adjoins the vowel" (Kurath 1964:30). (Compare Old English acsian, Late Modern English ask, and common phonetic structures like left, elm, barn; abnormal clusters of course occur, especially in nonnative words like lapse.) This phonetic rule produces the morphological fusion and accounts for the facts without resorting to the fictions for "deletion," "Black English Pluralization," or "zero allomorph."

Whatever the theory, reference works should recognize that words that end in -sp, -st, and -sk do not form the plural with the expected -s. Recognizing this fact might have saved the "experts" on black speech some confusion. And in fact, nothing new appears in the proposal here. Poutsma noticed unmarked plurals for -sp, -st, and -sk words as early as 1914. Ekwall, who followed the OED evidence closely, noticed unmarked post and cask in seventeenth century usage (though I believe he explained post incorrectly as a noun of measure). Though the MED has no examples of desks, fists, ghosts, or nests, it dates and cites unmarked plurals of fist, ghost, and nest back to the early fourteenth century. And though Walker accused "the inhabitants of London of the lower order" of pronouncing posts as a disyllable, he makes clear that the "first fault" of the better sort of Londoners is "pronouncing s indistinctly after st." Oddly, no subsequent American dictionary, and few grammarians, have noticed one of the most commonplace facts of American English.

NOTE

[1] I would like to thank Professor Paul Minton, Director of the Institute of Statistics at Virginia Commonwealth University, for help with the statistical analysis in this paper. Errors of concept or application are of course my own. I would also like to thank Raven I. McDavid, Jr., Raymond K. O'Cain, George Dorrill, and Sara Sanders for guidance in use of the Linguistic Atlas collections. Data from the Linguistic Atlas are used with permission of the editors and the American Council of Learned Societies.

Table 1
Augusta Informants
(Educ. = Level of Education)

No.	Residence	Age	Race	Sex	Occupation	Educ.	Type	Date
I.	**Old Family Upper Class**							
1.	Hill	83	w	m	lawyer	6	IIIA	76
2.	Hill	35	w	m	teacher	6	IIB	76
II.	**New Upper Class**							
3.	Beech Island	35	w	f	housewife	5	IIIB	77
4.	Thomson	32	w	m	executive	5	IIB	76
5.	Hill	20	w	m	student	4	IIB	77
III.	**Upper Middle Class**							
6.	Blythe	82	w	f	postmistress	5	IIIA	77
*6.	Blythe	77	w	f	postmistress	5	IIIA	77
7.	Fairfax	68	w	f	housewife	4	IIA	77
*7.	Fairfax	58	w	m	lawyer	6	IIIB	77
8.	Forest Hill	49	w	m	teacher	6	IIB	76
9.	Terri	47	b	m	minister	5	IIB	77
10.	Beech Island	45	w	m	property owner	3	IIB	77
11.	May Park	39	b	m	administrator	6	IIIB	76
12.	Gwinnett St.	26	b	m	teacher	6	IIB	76
IV.	**Lower Middle Class**							
13.	Pinch Gut	73	w	f	nurse	4	IIA	76
14.	Hill	68	w	f	secretary	3	IIA	76
15.	Elizabethtown	49	b	f	teacher	5	IIB	77
16.	Elizabethtown	42	b	m	army	4	IIB	77
17.	Forest Hill	39	w	f	secretary	4	IIB	77
18.	Terri	34	b	f	secretary	4	IIB	76
19.	West End	33	w	f	administrator	3	IIB	76
20.	Beech Island	22	w	m	cotton classer	4	IIB	76
21.	Terri	22	b	f	student	4	IIB	77
22.	Woodlawn	20	w	m	student	4	IIB	76
23.	Terri	18	b	f	student	4	IIB	77
24.	Elizabethtown	18	b	m	student	3	IIB	77
V.	**Working Class**							
25.	West Augusta	71	w	f	seamstress	2	IA	77
26.	West Augusta	41	w	m	mill worker	3	IB	77
27.	Fairfax	36	b	f	domestic worker	2	IB	77

*27.	Fairfax	18	b	m	student	3	IB	77
28.	Terri	32	b	m	roofer	3	IB	77
29.	Tobacco Road	30	w	m	mill worker	2	IB	77
30.	West Augusta	29	w	m	bill collector	4	IB	77
31.	North Augusta	23	w	f	waitress	3	IB	76

VI. Folk

32.	Thomson	87	b	m	farmer	1	IA	77
33.	Ridge Spring	78	b	m	laborer	1	IA	77
34.	Elizabethtown	77	b	m	han dyman	1	IA	77
*34.	Elizabethtown	68	b	f	domestic worker	3	IA	77
35.	Gwinnett St.	76	b	f	domestic worker	1	IA	76
36.	Beech Island	74	b	m	yard man	1	IA	77
37.	Cherokee	32	b	m	laborer	2	IB	76

Column 1: The numbers refer to protocols; that is, transcribed outlines of speech, not informants themselves. Four protocols, each marked with an asterisk, include auxiliary informants (6, 7, 27, and 34).

Column 2: The Hill, Forest Hill, Terri, May Park, Gwinnett Street, Pinch Gut, Elizabethtown, West End, and North Augusta are in the Augusta urbanized area. Beech Island, Blythe, West Augusta, and Tobacco Road are on the periphery of the urbanized area. Thomson, Fairfax, Woodlawn, Ridge Spring, and Cherokee are more than 25 miles from the center of Augusta.

Column 7: (1) 0-5 years of schooling; (2) more than 5 but less than 12 years of schooling; (3) 12 years of schooling; (4) more than 12 years of schooling, including technical training and students currently enrolled in colleges or technical schools; (5) a college degree; (6) university or professional training in addition to baccalaureate.

Column 8: The classification system described in the LANE Handbook (Kurath et al. 1939).

Table 2
Diamorphs of Nouns Ending -sp, -st, -sk

No.	wasp	fist	ghost	nest	post	desk	tusk
1	s, sps	st	st	sts	st	sks	shes, sks
2	sps	sts	sts	sts	st, s	sks	sks
3	sp	st	st	st	st	sks	--
4	sp, sps	s	sts	sts, s	st, sts	sks	sks
5	s	st	sts	st	st	sk	sk
6	sp	st	sts	st	st	sk	sk
7	--	--	--	--	--	--	--
8	sps	sts	sts	sts	st	sks	sks
9	sp, ps	st	st	sts	sts	sk	ft
10	sp, st	sts	st	sts	s	sks	sks
11	sp	st	st	st	st	sk	sk
12	sp, ps	s	st	sts	st	sk	sk
13	sp	st	st	st	--	sks	sks
14	sp	st	st	st	--	sk	sk
15	--	--	--	--	--	--	--
16	sp	s	--	s	ses	sk, ses	sk, shes
17	sp	st	st	st	st	sk	sk
18	sp	st	st	st	--	sk	--
19	sp	sts	st	st	st	sk	sk
20	sps	sts	sts	sts	st, sts	sk	sk
21	sp	st	st	st	st	sk	sk
22	sp, sps	st	st	st	st	sk	sk
23	sp	st	st	st	st	sk	sk
24	s	s	s	s	s	sks	--
25	sp	st	st	st	st	sk	sh
26	sp	s	st	s	st	sk	sk
27	sp	--	--	--	--	--	--
28	--	--	--	--	ses	--	sk
29	sp	st	st	st	st	sk	tch
30	s	st	st	st	st	--	sk
31	sp	st	st	st	st	sk	sk
32	ses	ses	--	ses	--	ses	shes
33	ses	st	ses	ses	--	sk	shes
34	s	st	s	--	ses	sk	tch
35	--	--	ses	--	ses	--	--
36	--	st	--	s	s	ses	shes
37	s	sts	--	st	stes	ses	shes

Table 3
Augusta -sts Plurals and Brown Corpus Frequencies

	Augusta		Brown Corpus
	n/N	%	Frequency
nests	8/30	27	3
ghosts	6/29	21	5
fists	6/32	19	14
posts	4/33	12	22

Table 4
Plurals of four -sts Words (P = .50)

	-s/-st		-sts		-ses/-stes		Total
	n	%	n	%	n	%	
fist	25	78	6	19	1	3	32
	23.5532		5.8800		2.5800		
	.0890		.0021		.9676		1.0587
ghost	21	72	6	21	2	2	29
	21.3440		5.3380		2.3200		
	.0052		.0820		.0441		.1313
nest	22	69	8	27	2	6	32
	23.5520		5.8800		2.5800		
	.1022		.7515		.1304		.9901
post	24	75	3	9	5	16	32
	23.5520		5.8800		2.5800		
	.0085		1.4165		2.2699		3.6949
Total	92	74	23	18	10	8	125
							5.8790

Table 5
-st Plurals and Social Group (P = .001)

	-s/-st		-sts		-ses/-stes		Total
	n	%	n	%	n	%	
1 & 2	15	65	8	35	0	0	23
	16.9280		4.2320		1.8400		
	.1033		3.3549		1.8400		5.2982
3 & 4	50	77	14	22	1	2	65
	47.8400		11.9600		5.2000		
	.0975		.3480		3.3923		3.3878
5 & 6	27	73	1	3	9	24	37
	27.2320		6.8080		2.9600		
	.0020		4.9549		12.3249		17.2818
Total	92	74	23	18	10	8	125
							26.4178

Table 6
-st Plurals and Racial Caste (P = .001)

	-s/-st		-sts		-ses/-stes		Total
	n	%	n	%	n	%	
Black	33	70	44	9	10	21	47
	34.5920		8.64803		.7600		
	.0733		2.4981		10.3557		12.9271
White	59	76	19	24	0	0	78
	57.4080		14.3520		6.2400		
	.0441		1.9958		6.2400		8.2799
Total	92		23		10		125
							21.2070

The English of Blacks in Wilmington, North Carolina

Ronald R. Butters and Ruth A. Nix

This report is part of a much larger study of linguistic variation in North Carolina among black and white speakers.[1] Our research began with the collection of data in 1973 and 1974 in Wilmington and in 1974 in Asheville. The study involves the application, to the analysis of North Carolina English, of research methods developed in the urban North during the past fifteen years by Fasold, Shuy, Wolfram, and others, and especially in the landmark work of Labov (who shares, with Chomsky, the distinction of having produced the most important work in American linguistics since the Second World War).

It is of course well known that the counties of North Carolina (as well as South Carolina and Virginia) were surveyed in the 1930s and 1940s by the dialect geographers McDavid and Lowman as part of the Linguistic Atlas of the United States and Canada project (Kurath and McDavid 1961). Our study can thus be seen, in some part, as a natural extension of their work for a population some forty to a hundred years younger. Moreover, other scholars of North Carolina English have produced significant work, against which we are measuring our results, such as Howren, Colemen, Eliason, Morgan, Nicholas, Anshen, and Levine and Crockett.

Methodology

Informants for this study of language variation were selected in four categories, according to age, race, and sex: young black males, ages 16-18; young white males, ages 16-18; elderly black females, over 50 years old; and elderly white females, over 50 years old. Adolescent males were chosen in order to replicate the studies done in the urban North. The elderly females were chosen with the idea of comparing their speech patterns to those of the younger-generation males in order to investigate linguistic change.

The black informants were further grouped by social class, according to the social class index developed by Warner et al. 1960. The young black males were representative of three social classes: lower middle (LMC), upper working (UWC), and lower working (LWC). The elderly black females were all working-class informants.

All subjects were interviewed for at least one hour by the principal investigator or his research assistant. With most of the young males, group interviews were also conducted which generally lasted up to one additional hour. During the second part of the interview, the two informants and the two interviewers gathered in one room for informal conversation. The elderly females were interviewed only by the principal investigator. Group interviews with them were not held.

A questionnaire was used to elicit conversation from the informants which is quite similar to the ones used in the Northern urban studies (e.g., Wolfram 1973:226-32). Topics of special interest to the informants were included when these topics became apparent (e.g., racial riots in the schools and the growing of tobacco).

Purposes

1. We wished to compare our results with those of the dialect geographers to gain insight into linguistic change in North Carolina in the twentieth century.

2. We have looked at large amounts of data from two (and perhaps eventually three) localities with the hope of better understanding the sociolinguistic structure of expanding urban communities in the South, communities in which long-standing patterns of racial segregation have been disrupted (e.g., by school integration) and migrational changes have been large scale.

3. We were interested in how Southern blacks compare with each other and, especially, how their speech compares with that of blacks in urban areas of the North, as described in the works of Fasold, Wolfram, Shuy, Labov, and others.

4. In general, we were interested in the theoretical implications, especially for variation theory, of our data and our observational and descriptive findings.

Findings

The results are a long way from final. Some have been reported in reviews (Butters 1979, 1981b), some in journal articles (Butters 1977, 1980a, 1980b, 1981b), and some in conference papers (Butters 1974, 1981c). The Wilmington data were the basis for Nix's 1980 Duke University dissertation, which forms a portion of our larger study (Butters and Nix, Linguistic Variation in Wilmington, North Carolina, in preparation). What follows is an outline of our findings to date.

Embedded Questions

With respect to the English of blacks in Wilmington, we have reported thus far (Butters 1980a) that the supposedly "standard" noninverted forms for embedded questions (e.g., John wonders whether/if there is water on the moon) predominate in the speech of lower-class elderly black female speakers. This in turn strongly suggests that Northern urban black adolescents, whom Labov 1972a concludes do not have whether/if in their productive grammars, are manifesting age-grading and not a feature that is somehow fundamental to the English of blacks in the United States. This is supported further by Nix 1980, who shows the variable presence of whether/if for Wilmington adolescent black males, with only mild correlation with social class (see table 1) and with a trend toward considerable individual variation (see table 2).

Likewise, reanalysis of the data in Labov et al. 1968, McKay 1970, and Mitchell 1970 reveals that their claims for the categorical nature of inversion for this rule are unwarranted (Nix 1980: 166-81, 185-92). For example, Labov et al.'s claim is based upon a deletion rate of 34/59, or 57.6 percent among their black adolescent subjects (1968:I:198). Finally, in Butters 1977 we discuss the high degree of inversion in "standard" middle-class white speech.

All of these factors point toward stylistic factors and age-grading as the appropriate explanations. Some of our adolescent black males have simply not yet learned all there is to know about English indirect question rules, or are still in the process of learning the subtleties.[2]

Table 1
Inversion in Positive Main Clause Yes/No Embedded Questions
(Wilmington)

Informants	Standard	Nonstandard	% Standard
Black Adolescent Males			
LMC	36	5	87.8
UWC	28	8	77.8
LWC	8	6	57.1

Table 2
Individual Variation in Embedded Questions (Wilmington)

Informants by Social Class	% Nonstandard Forms
Black Adolescent Males	
UW, UW, UW, LW, LW	100.0
LW	66.6
LM, LM	33.3
LM, LM, UW, UW, UW	0.0

Agreement

Nix reports similar results for black adolescent male Wilming-ton subjects in their use of the present tense verbal agreement morpheme. These speakers are, again, not so different in their speech from standard English as their Northern urban counterparts have been reported to be, and the degree of intragroup variability is far greater than has generally been noted for the Northern urban studies. Labov et al. (1968:I:164) actually claim that "there is no underlying third person singular -s" in vernacular black English; and though individual peer groups vary from 53.7 percent to 89.7 percent deletion, the compilers of the New York City study place little emphasis on the intragroup variability.

Wolfram (1969:150) reaches the same conclusion, with Detroit black upper-working-class (UWC) deletion rates of 56.4 percent and lower-working-class (LWC) rates of 76.5 percent--almost iden-tical to Fasold's 57.3 percent and 73.4 percent for Washington, D.C. (1972:208-11). Nix's analysis of the Wilmington data, however, shows a trend toward considerable variation from peer group to peer group: 45.1 percent deletion for "hang-out" group I, 15.3 percent for group II, and 36.3 percent for group III. Nix also ana-lyzes by social class, to make her data comparable to Wolfram's for Detroit and Fasold's for Washington, and she finds a much flatter curve than either of theirs: 51.6 percent LWC, 33.9 per-cent UWC, and 10.8 percent LMC (compared to less than 2% for LMC blacks in Detroit).[3] In short, the English of blacks in Wilming-ton is apparently not so unlike the standard as the English of blacks in the urban North with respect to the third person singular agreement morpheme.

Furthermore, Nix finds a high degree of individual variation with respect to this feature, ranging from 4.3 to 75 percent dele-tion for the sixteen adolescent black males (LMC: 7.1%, 35.9%, 4.3%, 28.9%, and 14.3%; UWC: 21.1%, 48.1%, 9.4%, 31.3%, 43.4%, and 68.6%; and LWC: 12.1%, 73.3%, 55.3%, 75%, and 50%). This might suggest age-grading, except that an even wider distribution is found (1980:155) for our eight Wilmington elderly black LWC females (16.7%, 35.7%, 38.9%, 48.3%, 50%, 63%, 77.5%, and 92.9%). Of course, we might defend the notion that {Z_3} is not really an "agreement" morpheme if /s/ endings were found in "hypercorrect" environments with a percentage approaching that for third singular--I comes, you comes, they comes, etc.[4] In fact, there are some of these forms, but they are rare (Nix 1980:146-47), and they show little significant correlation with the rate of {Z_3} absence or presence in third singular environments.

The surprisingly high individual variation from the group norm, as well as the comparatively "mainstream" quality of black speech in Wilmington, needs some discussion. One explanation may be the integrated character of this community, compared with Northern urban ghettos. High school integration in Wilmington by the early 1970s was an established fact; furthermore, even our elderly black female informants had had considerable exposure to whites, through their lengthy work experiences as domestics.

A second possibility is that our "free conversation" interviews were more formal than those of previous studies, eliciting more "mainstream" English. However, since hypercorrection is apparently of minimal importance, it seems clear that we have been uncovering the actual linguistic knowledge of our subjects, not their guesswork. On the contrary, one might well question how much linguistic competence might be obscured by performance factors in more informal situations.

Finally, the nature of our informant selection process may have turned up more upwardly mobile, middle-class-oriented black male adolescents; perhaps there were in Wilmington in 1973 and 1974 LWC and UWC black males who spoke a dialect closer to that of urban blacks of the earlier studies. However, our informant selection techniques did not differ substantially from those of Fasold 1972 (see Nix 1980:227). And again, we made use of identical analytic procedures in classifying our informants according to social class.

Phonological Variables: /θ/, Final Consonant Clusters

The validity of our data as representative of black speech is further confirmed by our analysis of two phonological variables. Here, though to some extent we still find a continuation of the patterns for our syntactic and morphological variables, there are two important differences. First, the amount of intragroup variability is somewhat smaller. Second, one of the variables, final consonant cluster simplification, shows a pattern of social class distribution which comes closer to duplicating the pattern of the Northern ghetto studies.

Consider, first of all, Nix's discussion (1980:71) of nonstandard realizations of noninitial /θ/. For our black male adolescents, she finds the percentages of the nonstandard variants [f], zero, and [t] (shown in table 3). The best comparison is with Wolfram's Detroit data, where he finds the following total nonstandard deletion rates: LMC, 7 percent; UWC, 66 percent; LWC, 82.4 percent.[5] It seems particularly significant that the LMC Wilmington rate is three times the Detroit rate (and this despite the fact that half of Wolfram's informants are female and he shows that sex is a significant standardizing influence for this variable). But as Nix (1980:73) points out, Wolfram's informants are in the age range 14-17 while the Wilmington informants were 16-18, thus tending to counterbalance slightly the sexual bias by skewing the Wilmington data back in the direction of the standard.

Again, however, the Wilmington curve is flatter than that of the urban Northern ghetto. And again, the flatness may be explained in part in terms of the social structure of Wilmington: the Wilmington black working class is not so isolated from middle-class blacks and from the white population as are the working-class adolescents of urban street gangs. Moreover, it is certainly the case that this phonological feature is not so stigmatized in the South as in the North; the pronunciation of birthday as birfday, for example, is quite common among the white population of Wilmington. Being less stigmatized, the feature does not exhibit quite the strong break between LMC and UWC that is usually found to be characteristic of strongly stigmatized features.

Table 3
Percentage of Nonstandard Realizations of /θ/ by Social Class

Social Class	[f]	[θ]	[t̯]	Other	Total
LMC	13.2	1.8	7.9		22.8
UWC	26.3	3.2	13.7	1.1	44.2
LWC	41.3	2.4	11.1		54.7

Still, this is not the whole story, as a look at the individual data makes clear (see table 4). Only three of our middle-class speakers behave in a middle-class way, with percentages fairly close to those of the Detroit study. The other two--JN and GE--showed deviant /θ/ rates which are among the highest of all our subjects.

Table 4
Individual Variation for Noninitial /θ/

LMC (Informant)		UWC (Informant)		LWC (Informant)	
83.3%	(JN)	75.7%	(JW)	82.3%	(MJ)
72.2%	(GE)	41.6%	(MG)	69.2%	(ML)
10.5%	(DM)	31.5%	(WG)	64.4%	(KJ)
10.3%	(DK)	29.6%	(TW)	45.4%	(RB)
8.3%	(MS)	23.5%	(BC)	26.3%	(RJ)

The patterning for final consonant cluster simplification, moreover, is different. Again, our methods of analysis essentially replicate those of earlier Northern studies. Only monomorphemic, like-voiced clusters are analyzed, for example, wasp, most, mask, left, project, box, stand, old. Ignored are bimorphemic clusters (e.g., laughed) and also such clusters as generally do not participate in simplification, including "clusters" in /rC/ (e.g., help, pint, bird). Also ignored are clusters in environments where it is impossible to tell, because of an immediately following homorganic stop (e.g., most toys, most things, old days, wasp poison, mask carriers, etc.), whether a final consonant is present or not. (In practice, it is probably the case that simplification in these environments is categorical for most speakers in all but the most formal styles).

Instances of and and just are tabulated separately, and then only the first twenty occurrences for each informant are counted (in some cases, there are not quite twenty examples of just). As indicated below, simplification of and and just is generally higher than for other words--virtually categorical, in fact, in free conversation for all social classes.

Again, it is not so easy as might be imagined to find Northern data which are legitimately comparable to ours. Table 5 makes such a comparison with Wolfram's results, but again one must keep in mind the sex and age differences, as well as the fact that Wolfram includes up to three instances of and and just in his sample for each speaker, whereas we exclude these words.

Although the figures are close, there is a statistically significant difference between the LMC and the combined UWC/LWC data for both Wolfram's study (significant at the .0005 level) and the Wilmington study (significant at the .005 level).

Table 5
Percentage of Final Consonant Cluster Simplification

Social Class	Wilmington Black Adolescent Males	Detroit Black Adolescents (Wolfram)	New York Oscar Brothers (Labov et al.)	Florida/ Georgia Black Adolescent Males (Summerlin)
UMC	—	--	--	76.0
LMC	86.1	79.2	--	
UWC	89.6	79.2	--	89.7
	91.4			
LWC	93.4	84.2	90.3	

As before, the Wilmington curve is flatter than the Northern one. However, in this case the results for the LWC are almost identical to those for the New York Oscar Brothers, and almost the same as Summerlin's results for a northern Florida/southern Georgia population of senior high school black males. (Summerlin's data, however, combine some "free" interview material with elicited data.) The Southern middle-class speakers, however, are rather more deviant from standard English than are Wolfram's Detroit middle-class black adolescents.

This time, moreover, the individual data show a generally consistent pattern. The LMC speakers are like each other (84.3, 86.2, 84.1, 88 and 90.4% deletion). The LWC speakers are like each other (88.1, 98.2, 98.2, 92.4, and 81.0% deletion).[6] A similar, though less cohesive, bunching was observed for the UWC (ranging from 97.8 to 78.8%).

Thus the data for consonant cluster simplification seem to validate our social class analysis and to connect black speech in Wilmington, North Carolina, with that in other areas of the country. Why this should be so for this variable and not the others is not at all clear, however. We hope that our projected comparison with the behavior of the Wilmington white community will shed some light on this mystery.

In the meantime, several things are clear: (1) black speech in Wilmington, North Carolina, is generally not so extreme as that reported for Northern urban ghettos; (2) LMC black speech in Wilmington is often more extreme than that reported for Northern urban ghettos; and (3) a look beyond the statistically idealized speaker-hearer is often necessary in order to get the full story of linguistic variation.

Conclusion

Perhaps the most prominent conclusion from our examination of these linguistic variables is that the speech of blacks in Wilmington is by no means as extreme a variation from standard American English as the variation found among blacks in Northern urban ghettos in the 1960s and 1970s. In part, this may reflect the relatively greater degree of integration of the races in the American South, particularly in such small, growing, urban communities as Wilmington.

But we feel that we have also clarified some larger methodological and theoretical issues. For the most part, the Northern studies deemphasize the significance of individual variation. Moreover, they focus, with what we believe was excessive emphasis, on the speech of male adolescents from the most impoverished and isolated segments of the communities they examine. Thus time after time they have identified features as somehow basic to the English of black Americans which are really less central for the majority of black Americans and which seem to represent merely age-grading. Recent interest in individual variation (e.g., Labov 1980, Milroy 1980) offers what we feel is a step in the right direction (for further discussion, see Butters 1981c).

In terms of our study, a great deal remains to be done. The Asheville, North Carolina, tapes have yet to be analyzed, and so our geographical comparison of coastal and mountain urban communities is yet to be made. In the future, it will be very useful to do follow-up interviews with our younger Wilmington informants to determine what linguistic changes they have undergone as they move as individuals from adolescence to adulthood. The immediate task, though, is completion of the analysis of our Wilmington tapes (already collected) and final preparation of our Linguistic Variation in Wilmington, North Carolina.

Notes

[1] This research was sponsored by Duke University and the National Endowment for the Humanities (Grant Number RO-8949-73-405).

[2] Indeed, some may never learn these rules completely. Even so, we find no compelling reason for defining vernacular black English (VBE) as the speech of such least-knowledgeable speakers. Of course, defining the dialect of black Americans as the dialect which shows greatest deviation from standard English tends to eliminate the possibility that the most deviant lects will be considered "substandard" or "linguistically deprived." However, though the political motivation may be impeccable and the social goals

worthy, such a definition of VBE seems to obscure the linguistic facts and to exclude age-grading from the role in theory that it deserves.

[3] The informants are analyzed according to social class, using the methodology of Warner et al. 1960 as outlined in Nix (1980: 32-39). Five are classified as Lower Middle Class (MS, GE, DM, JN, and DK). Six subjects are classified as Upper Working Class (MG, TW, WG, RG, BC, and JW). Five are classified as Lower Working Class (RB, MJ, KJ, RJ, and ML), though one of them (RJ) demonstrates essentially Lower Middle Class speech norms.

[4] The term "hypercorrection" is probably a misnomer for many speakers, who may associate with this nonstandard use of the {Z} marker an intensive or durative force (see Brewer's essay in this volume). Also, it is important to note that the term itself is ambiguous. Sometimes it is used to refer to misapplication of a linguistic rule, as when case marking is incorrectly assigned to a relative clause marker because the speaker incorrectly identifies the marker as an object (e.g., Give it to whomever wants it). Other times, the rule has been reconstituted in the speaker's mind, as when the nominative case is used immediately after the conjunction and (e.g., They have been very kind to my wife and I).

[5] A comparison with the New York City data is not very helpful because Labov et al. 1968 omit from their /θ/ analysis the Oscar Brothers (the group most analogous to our subjects in age and "hang out" group status). Likewise, a comparison with Anshen's dissertation is not too meaningful because he interviews only adults. However, he finds a nonstandard rate among his adult black females of 32.4% (ages 19-55+), which roughly can be compared to our eight elderly black females' rate of 59.1% (Nix 1980:60).

[6] Again, RJ is in speech much more like his LMC counterparts than like his LWC socioeconomic peers. A close look at RJ's personality explains this, for he is anomalous in several ways: he is rather religious; he expresses a great deal of interest in journalism and has worked on the student newspaper as sportswriter and editor; and he is the only child of rather doting parents. Still, RJ "hung out" with other LWC black adolescent males (KJ is his best friend), and he expresses no interest in going to college.

Kentucky Verb Forms

Raven I. McDavid, Jr., and Virginia McDavid

Among the Southern states, Kentucky has particular linguistic interest. Because of its geography and history, it has ties with such Southern states as Virginia and North Carolina and also with states we think of as Midwestern, such as Illinois and Indiana. It is thus worthwhile to see what linguistic features in Kentucky reflect its geographical and historical position. To what extent do regional differences along the Eastern Seaboard persist as one moves inland into an area of secondary settlement such as Kentucky?

Before we turn to linguistic matters, it may be useful to say a word about Kentucky's geography and history. The state extends more than 500 miles from east to west, from the Appalachians to the Mississippi. It is only about a third as wide. It touches seven states, and all its boundaries except with Tennessee are natural ones. It had, in the Cumberland Gap, an important route from the East into the Ohio River Valley.

Daniel Boone began exploration in Kentucky before the Revolution, opening a route to central Kentucky. Settlement started in the 1770s. In 1776 the Virginia legislature created Kentucky County, which was later subdivided. In 1792 Kentucky became a state. The settlers were principally from Virginia and North Carolina. In the nineteenth century there were German settlers.

Kentucky then became the springboard for expansion into southern Ohio, much of Indiana, and southern Illinois. Ties with Kentucky in these states may be found in their place names. Industrialization and urbanization also affected Kentucky, as did the spread of public education, though the effect of education has not been so strong as north of the Ohio.

One source of evidence for Kentucky speech and for answering the questions just raised about regional and social patterns there is the linguistic atlas records for the North-Central States and the related records for the Eastern Seaboard and the Upper

Midwest.[1] The materials for the North-Central atlas comprise 564 records from Wisconsin, Michigan, Illinois, Indiana, Ohio, Kentucky, and some from southern Ontario. Ninety-six of these (17%) are from Kentucky, and fifty-four (56%) of these Kentucky records are from Type I informants, the oldest and least educated. Thirty (31%) are from Type II informants, generally middle-aged and having a high school education. Twelve (13%) are from Type III informants--those with a college education. The records were largely compiled between 1952 and 1956. Some of them were originally taped and have been retranscribed within the last six years, with consequent addition of many grammatical forms. The entire body of 564 records is available on microfilm (R. McDavid et al. 1976-79).

The plan for a study of speech in this North-Central area really began in the 1920s, when Kurath laid plans for a linguistic atlas of the United States. As a result of his travels in the eastern United States, he singled out Kentucky as being of special interest because of its linguistic complexity.

Fieldwork for the Linguistic Atlas of New England was completed in the early 1930s, with results from 413 records published in Kurath et al. 1939-43. In the same decade, fieldwork proceeded in the Middle and South Atlantic States, from New York into eastern Georgia and Florida. These 1,216 records were completed by the late 1940s. From what this material along the Eastern Seaboard revealed, it was thought desirable to make a pilot study in the North-Central states, an area of early secondary settlement. Such a study was made in the late 1930s, principally by Frederic G. Cassidy and Harold B. Allen. Their records are now part of the larger collection.

The diversity shown by these records led to plans for a complete survey, directed by Albert H. Marckwardt. The 51 records for Wisconsin were completed by Cassidy in 1940; the work for the entire area was largely finished by 1960. Marckwardt had first planned to include only river communities in Kentucky (Maysville, Louisville, Ashland, and Paducah). Later, all of Kentucky was included, with the result that we now have materials for a key state, tying the Eastern Seaboard to areas farther west.

The basis and methods for collecting these materials have often been described: a balanced selection of communities, informants who are native to the county or community where they live, and recording of the data in phonetic transcription. The questionnaire for the North-Central atlas is similar to that of other surveys of this kind. There are items that deal with vocabulary, pronunciation, and grammar. Some of them involve noun plurals; others deal with personal, demonstrative, and relative pronouns, with adjectives and adverbs, and with prepositions; and there are items on verb forms (about 55) that include forms of the present indicative revealing agreement (like we was or we were) and negative forms (like ain't and hain't). Among the verbs, the most common are the preterit and past tense forms of irregular verbs.

It is often said that, in the United States, grammatical differences tell more about social origins and education than about the region the speaker comes from. So it is with <u>did</u> and <u>done</u> as preterits, and with <u>saw</u> and <u>seen</u>. But there are exceptions, and some grammatical forms are more common in one region than in another. E. Bagby Atwood notes many of these in his Verb Forms in the Eastern United States (1953). He notes as typically Northern the preterits <u>dove</u> and <u>et</u>; as Midland, <u>boilt</u> and the compound <u>dogbit</u>; as Midland and Southern, the preterits <u>eat</u> and <u>sweated</u>; and as Southern, the past participle <u>heern</u>.

The 38 verbs that are dealt with here confirm the generalization that grammatical forms reveal both social and regional differences. The use of standard forms is higher among better-educated informants, as might be expected, and such use becomes more common as one moves from east to west across the state. The regional patterns in the Eastern states, specifically in Virginia and North Carolina, persist (though weakened) in Kentucky and, to a lesser extent, the South Midland area of Ohio, Indiana, and Illinois. These regional forms appear only occasionally in the Upper Midwest. (See figures 1-10.)

The discussion of each verb begins with a summary of the distribution of its forms in the Eastern states (ES), drawn largely from Atwood's Verb Forms. This area includes New England, New York, New Jersey, Pennsylvania, Delaware, Maryland, Virginia, West Virginia, North Carolina, South Carolina, and parts of Georgia and Florida. It is the area of the Linguistic Atlas of New England and the Linguistic Atlas of the Middle and South Atlantic States. The discussion concentrates on forms in the Midland and South because these are the areas that formed Kentucky speech.

Next are the forms in the North-Central States (NCS): Wisconsin, Michigan, southern Ontario (omitted in this study), Illinois, Indiana, Ohio, and Kentucky. The Linguistic Atlas of the North-Central States is the source of this material.

Finally, there is a brief discussion of these verb forms in the Upper Midwest (UM): Minnesota, Iowa, North Dakota, South Dakota, and Nebraska. The material here is summarized from Harold B. Allen's Linguistic Atlas of the Upper Midwest, Volume 2 (1975).

NOTES

[1]Linguistic Atlas of the North Central States: Basic Materials, edited by Raven I. McDavid, Jr. et al., Chicago Manuscripts on Cultural Anthropology Series XXXVIII, 200-208, 1976-79; Linguistic Atlas of the Upper Midwest, edited by Harold B. Allen, 3 vols. (Minneapolis: University of Minnesota Press, 1973-76).

[2]The material for this study is drawn from The Grammar of the North-Central States by Virginia McDavid and Lawrence Davis

(forthcoming). For a statistical analysis of some of these data, see
V. McDavid 1977.

Abbreviations

c.	central
e.	eastern
ES	Eastern States
GA	Georgia
IL	Illinois
IN	Indiana
IO	Iowa
KY	Kentucky
MAS	Middle Atlantic States
MD	Maryland
MI	Michigan
MSAS	Middle and South Atlantic States
n.	north
NC	North Carolina
NCS	North Central States
NE	New England
NJ	New Jersey
NY	New York
OH	Ohio
PA	Pennsylvania
s.	south
SAS	South Atlantic States
SC	South Carolina
SD	South Dakota
UM	Upper Midwest
VA	Virginia
WI	Wisconsin
WV	West Virginia

Begin; Preterit Began, Begin, Begun

ES Because so many informants use commenced or started as
    a response, it is difficult to state the relative frequency
    of began, begin, begun. Begin is rare in NE and the MAS.
    It becomes more common in the SAS and is used more
    frequently than begun in e.VA. Begun is used by nearly
    half of the Type I and II informants in the entire area.

NCS Begin is used by nearly one-third of the informants. It is
    most common in KY; and in the rest of the NCS, except
    MI, it is more common than begun. Begun is used by
    fewer than one-fifth of the informants. In KY, 57 per-
    cent of the informants use begin, 25 percent began, and
    17 percent begun.

UM   Among the informants who choose this lexical item, rather than <u>commenced</u> or <u>started</u>, more than three-fourths use <u>began</u>. <u>Begin</u> and <u>begun</u>, where they <u>do</u> occur, are most common among Type I informants.

Bite; Past Participle <u>Bit</u>, <u>Bitten</u>

ES   In NE, <u>bit</u> is used by over one-fourth of the Type I and II informants. In the MSAS, <u>bit</u> predominates among these informants.

NCS   <u>Bit</u> is used by three-fifths of the informants, with Type <u>III</u> informants preferring <u>bitten</u>, but not heavily. In KY, <u>bit</u> predominates over <u>bitten</u> two to one.

UM   <u>Bit</u> is chosen by slightly over half of the Type I informants, and by about one-third of the other two types.

Blow; Preterit <u>Blew</u>, <u>Blowed</u>

ES   <u>Blew</u> predominates among all informants throughout s.NE and the MAS. <u>Blowed</u> predominates in n.NE; south of PA, it becomes increasingly common. In the SAS, <u>blowed</u> is almost universal in Type I informants and is used by more than half the Type II informants.

NCS   <u>Blew</u> occurs in the speech of 60 percent of the informants. <u>Blowed</u> is used by about 30 percent, and in KY by more than half. The same social pattern found in the Eastern states prevails, with <u>blowed</u> used by 40 percent of the Type I informants, 25 percent of the Type II informants, and only 5 percent of the Type IIIs.

UM   <u>Blowed</u> occurs in the speech of four-fifths of the Type I informants, but in less than one-tenth of the Type IIs.

Boil; Preterit <u>Boiled</u>, <u>Boilt</u>

ES   <u>Boiled</u> is nearly universal as far south as central PA and among Type II informants elsewhere. <u>Boilt</u> appears in the Midland and is most common in s.PA and in WV, where it is used by more than half of all informants. It is less common in the rest of the Midland and South.

NCS   Ten percent of the informants use <u>boilt</u>, mainly in IN, OH, and KY. Two-thirds of these occurrences are from Type I informants.

UM   Only three examples of <u>boilt</u> occur, all from Type I speakers.

Bring; Past Participle <u>Brought</u>, <u>Brung</u>

ES   <u>Brought</u> is almost the only form among all social classes and in all areas. Only fifty-one informants use <u>brung</u>.

NCS   Brought is dominant in all areas and among all types of informants. Seventeen examples of brung appear: eight in KY, the rest scattered, but largely in IL, IN, and OH. Eighty-two percent of those who use brung are Type I informants.

UM   Only four informants use brung.

Buy; Attributive Past Participle Bought, Boughten

ES   In NE, there are fifty-seven occurrences of boughten, largely in e.NE, but only two of bought in this adjectival use. In the MSAS the proportion changes, and bought becomes progressively more common toward the south, until in SC and GA there are seventy-one occurrences of bought and only two of boughten.

NCS   Boughten occurs in the speech of 19 percent of the informants, bought in the speech of 8 percent. In all states except KY, boughten outnumbers bought substantially. In KY, thirty-three informants use bought, only three boughten.

UM   Boughten is used by one-fourth of the informants, bought by only three. As elsewhere, the pattern is regional rather than social.

Catch; Preterit Caught, Catched

ES   In all areas caught is the most common form and, with some limitations, among Type I informants, among all classes. The main nonstandard variant is catched, usually pronounced /kɛčt/, which is recorded for about 15 percent of the informants. It occurs in about half the communities in WV and NC.

NCS   Catched is used by about 12 percent of the informants. It is a heavily Type I form, being the choice of 19 percent of the Type I speakers. In KY, 25 percent of the informants use it.

UM   There are only six examples, all from Type I speakers.

Climb; Preterit Clim, Climbed, Clum

ES   Climbed is the choice of cultivated speakers in all areas. Among other types of informants, the strong preterits, principally clim and clum, predominate, and are used by one-half to nine-tenths of the informants. In NE, clim is the most common strong form; elsewhere it is clum, though clim appears in NC along with clum.

NCS   Climbed is used by slightly over half the informants. It is least common among the Type I informants and most common among the Type IIIs, for whom clim and clum are rare. The regional pattern found in the East continues, with clim most common in WI and MI, and in e.KY. Clum is scattered throughout the area. (See figure 1.)

UM   Here, climbed is used by 81 percent of all informants. Clum is the choice of 13 percent, scattered throughout the area. Clim is used by 5 percent in the Northern speech area of the UM.

Come; Preterit Came, Come

ES   Came is the dominant form everywhere among Type III informants. Among the less educated, come is much more common.

NCS   Come is favored heavily by the Type I informants, but nearly half of these also use came. Came heavily predominates among the Type III informants, but nearly one-fifth also use come. No regional pattern emerges.

UM   Again, the pattern is social rather than regional, with the less educated informants using come.

Dive; Preterit Div, Dived, Dove

ES   Dived is uncommon in NE, where dove is the usual form. In c.PA and along the Ohio, both dived and dove occur. In the rest of the MAS and in the SAS, dived heavily predominates on all social levels. Div is typically archaic, appearing in NE and coastal and mountain areas in the MSAS.

NCS   Dove is common in WI, MI, n.IL, and OH, less so in IN. There are only seven examples of dove in KY. Div is restricted to e.KY and is commoner than dove in KY. Of the four examples of div outside KY, all are in s.IL, s.IN, and s.OH. (See figure 2.)

UM   Among all types of informants, about two-thirds have dove and one-third dived. There is only one example of div, from a South Midland Type I speaker in NE.

Do; Preterit Did, Done

ES   Not recorded.

NCS   Done predominates, except among Type III informants. In KY four-fifths of the Type I informants use done, as do nearly half of the Type IIs.

UM   Done is used by a slight majority of the least educated informants and by about one-fourth of the Type IIs. Almost all Type III informants choose did. As in the ES, the pattern is social, not regional.

Dream; Preterit <u>Dreamed</u>, <u>Dreamt</u> (/drɛmpt, drɛmt, drɛmp, drɪm, drɪmp/)

ES   <u>Dreamt</u> predominates over <u>dreamed</u>, in a ratio of two to one, in all the eastern area. In the northern area, <u>dreamt</u> is holding its own; in PA and WV, it is favored by Type III informants. In the SAS, <u>dreamt</u> is receding, with Type III usage about equally divided. <u>Dreamt</u> usually has the intrusive /p/ sound, and often, especially in the MSAS, loss of the final /t/. In NC, four-fifths of those who use <u>dreamt</u> drop the final /t/. Some fifteen informants, all in NC or SC, have /drɪm/ or /drɪmp/, probably the result of /ɛ/ and /ɪ/ falling together before nasals.

NCS   <u>Dreamed</u> and <u>dreamt</u> are used about equally by all types of informants in all areas, except in KY, where 45 percent of the informants use <u>dreamed</u>, 45 percent use /drɛmpt/, and 21 percent use /drɪmp/. (See figure 3.)

UM   <u>Dreamt</u> is used by nearly three-fourths of all informants, <u>dreamed</u> by one-third. There is no difference among types. Pronunciations with /ɪ/ do not occur.

Drink; Preterit <u>Drank</u>, <u>Drinked</u>, <u>Drunk</u>

ES   Except in areas where limited by <u>drinked</u> and <u>drunk</u>, <u>drank</u> is the most common preterit form, and the only one used by Type III informants. The form <u>drunk</u> is rare in the Northern and Southern areas. It is more common in the Midland, especially in w.VA, w.NC, and w.SC. The form <u>drinked</u> is scattered throughout the East, and is almost the only form used by Type I informants in NC.

NCS   <u>Drank</u> is the most common preterit in all areas and among all social types. In the area as a whole, it is used by 86 percent of all informants; in KY by 57 percent of all informants. Among the Type I informants in KY, <u>drank</u> is the choice of 39 percent, <u>drunk</u> of 33 percent, and <u>drink(ed)</u> of 54 percent. <u>Drunk</u> is strongly a Midland form in the area. <u>Drink(ed)</u> is restricted almost entirely to KY.

UM   <u>Drank</u> is almost unanimous in the UM. The only exceptions are two informants who use <u>drunk</u> and two who use <u>drinked</u>. (See figure 4.)

Drive; Preterit and Past Participle <u>Driv</u>, <u>Driven</u>, <u>Drove</u>

ES   <u>Drove</u>, as preterit, predominates in all areas and among all classes. <u>Driv</u> is most common in the coastal and mountain areas of the South Midland and South, especially in NC. It is generally a Type I form.

       As past participle, <u>driven</u> is the most common in NE and around New York City. Elsewhere, most Type I inform-

ants use the leveled pair drove-drove, as do one-third of
the Type II informants. Most informants who use driv as
the preterit use it also as the past participle. Drived is
rare.

NCS   As the preterit, drove is overwhelmingly the most
common form. Only in KY is there much evidence of
competing forms. Here 74 percent of the Type I informants have drove, 11 percent druv, 9 percent drived, and
11 percent driv.
In the area as a whole, 53 percent of all informants use
driven as past participle, and 34 percent use drove. Two
percent have driv and 2 percent druv; almost all examples of these two forms occur in KY.

UM   Almost all informants use drove as the preterit; druv
occurs twice, driv twice, and droved once. Driven occurs
as past participle in the speech of 78 percent of the
informants, drove in the speech of 26 percent. No other
forms occur as past participles. (See figure 5.)

Drown; Past Participle Drowned, Drownded

ES   In the speech of Type III informants, drowned is almost
universal. Drownded is used by about one-fourth of the
Type I and II informants in NE. In the rest of the ES, it
is most common among Type I informants; in NC it is
almost the only form among this group.

NCS   Among the Type I informants, 47 percent use drowned
and the same percent drownded. A much smaller number
of the Type II and III informants use drownded. In KY,
nearly three-fourths of the Type I informants have
drownded.

UM   Among the Type I informants, about one-third use
drownded. Drowned is heavily preferred by the Type II
and III informants.

Eat; Preterit Ate, Eat, Et

ES   The standard preterit, ate, is most common among the
Type III informants in all areas, and fairly common among
the Type II informants. From NE south through PA, about
one-half the informants use eat or et. South of PA, from
one-half to three-fourths of the informants use one of
these variants. Both variant forms are characteristic of
the older informants and both are receding, eat somewhat
more than et. Et is more characteristic of the Northern
area, eat of the Midland and South. In NC, nearly all the
Type I informants use eat.

NCS   Ate is used by 56 percent of all informants, and four-
fifths of the Type IIIs. The most common nonstandard

variant is eat, used by 35 percent of all informants, then et, used by 14 percent. In KY, ate is the choice of less than half of all informants, and eat of two-thirds. For the Type I informants in KY, 20 percent use ate, 80 percent eat, and 13 percent et.

UM   Here too, ate is the most common form. One-fifth of the Type I informants use eat; et is rare.

Fight; Preterit Fit, Fought, Fout

ES   The preterit of fight was not recorded in NE. Fit is most common in Type I speech south of PA. Fout is common among Type I and II informants in e.VA and all of NC. Both fit and fout are typically old-fashioned, rustic forms, with fought dominant in Type III speech everywhere.

NCS   Fought predominates everywhere. Only in KY are there any significant numbers of fit. Here, fought occurs in the speech of 46 percent of the Type I informants, fit in that of 31 percent, and fout in that of only 4 percent. Clearly, fit has come to dominate over fout in this area of secondary settlement.

UM   Fought is almost universal. There are three examples of fit, none of fout. (See figure 6.)

Fit; Preterit Fit, Fitted

ES   In NE, the inflected form fitted is chosen by three-fourths of all informants of all types. In NY and southward, fitted predominates only in e.NC. Everywhere else, fit is almost universal.

NCS   Nearly four-fifths of all informants use the uninflected fit. Fitted is somewhat more common in WI and MI, as might be predicted from their settlement. The percentages for KY are like those for the area as a whole.

UM   The percentages for fit and fitted are almost exactly the same in the UM as in the NCS: about four-fifths of the informants choose fit.

Freeze; Preterit Freezed, Froze, Frozed

ES   Froze is almost the only form used in NE and the MAS. The variants are most common in the coastal areas of the SAS. Freezed occurs in the speech of about one-tenth of the informants in VA and NC. Frozed is about as common as freezed, and occurs in the same area.

NCS   Froze is almost universal. KY has two examples of frozed and one of freezed.

UM   Froze is universal, except for one example of friz.

Give; Preterit <u>Gave</u>, <u>Give</u>

ES   <u>Gave</u> is almost universal in Type III speech in all areas, and predominates in Type II speech. <u>Give</u> is used by two-thirds of the Type I informants and one-third of the Type IIs.

NCS   Again, <u>gave</u> is most common in Type III speech, being used by four-fifths of the informants. Among the least educated, 44 percent use <u>gave</u> and 62 percent <u>give</u>. The average for all types is almost equally divided between the two forms. In KY, only 7 percent of the Type I informants use <u>gave</u>, and 83 percent <u>give</u>. <u>Give</u> is used by about two-thirds of all KY informants.

UM   In the UM, more than three-fourths of all informants use <u>gave</u>--a considerable change from the percentages for the <u>NCS</u>. Among the Type I informants, over half use <u>give</u>. More than 90 percent of the most cultivated informants choose <u>gave</u>.

Grow; Preterit <u>Grew</u>, <u>Growed</u>

ES   <u>Grew</u> as a preterit is universal in Type III speech; it prevails in Type II speech. <u>Growed</u> is used by roughly one-third of the Type I and II informants in NE. It occurs with increasing frequency to the south, and is used by nine-tenths of the Type I informants in NC and by half of the Type IIs there.

NCS   The standard <u>grew</u> is used by about four-fifths of the Type III informants. Type I informants are equally divided between <u>grew</u> and <u>growed</u>. For all informants in the area, two-thirds use <u>grew</u> and one-third <u>growed</u>. In KY, about three-fourths of the Type I informants choose <u>growed</u>, and for the state as a whole, half the informants use <u>growed</u>.

UM   <u>Grew</u> is more common among the Type I informants in the UM, where nearly three-fourths use it, than in the NCS. Among the Type III informants it is universal.

Hear; Preterit <u>Heard</u>, <u>Heared</u>, <u>Heern</u>

ES   <u>Heard</u> predominates in NE and among cultivated informants throughout the entire area. <u>Heared</u> or <u>heern</u> is used by almost all Type I informants in the South Midland and South, with <u>heern</u> being a typically Southern form.

NCS   <u>Heard</u> is almost universal. There are infrequent instances of <u>heared</u> in the area, three of them in KY. There are seven examples of <u>heern</u> in KY, one in s.IL.

UM   <u>Heard</u> is universal except for three examples of <u>heared</u>. <u>Heern</u> does not occur.

Kneel; Preterit Kneeled, Knelt

ES   Knelt is the dominant form in all areas and among all types of informants. Kneeled is used by about one-fourth of the Type I and II informants, and much less commonly by the most cultivated group.

NCS   Knelt is used by about three-fifths of all informants, kneeled by one-fourth. The figures for the Type III informants are not different from those for the entire group. KY conforms to the same pattern.

UM   Knelt is the choice of about four-fifths of the informants and about 90 percent of the Type III informants.

Lie; Infinitive Lay, Lie

ES   Lie predominates in all areas, being used by about three-fifths of all informants. About half the Type I informants use lay, but very few of the Type IIIs.

NCS   Lie and lay are used by almost exactly the same number of informants. Among the most cultivated, four-fifths use lie, and about one-fourth lay. In KY, lay is used by two-thirds of the informants; three-fourths of the Type III informants use lie.

UM   Lie is used by about two-thirds of the informants. Among the Type III informants, the proportions are the same as in the NCS, with four-fifths using lie.

Lie; Preterit Laid, Lay

ES   Laid is the most common preterit form except in some areas of NC and SC, where lay also occurs. Thus in the ES, both combinations, lie-laid and lay-laid, are found. The combination lie-lay is more frequently used by the cultivated speakers than by others, but is not always the most common combination for them.

NCS   Lay is the preterit used by about 44 percent of all informants of all types. Laid is used by 60 percent of the entire group, but by 36 percent of the Type III inform-ants. In KY, about two-thirds of the entire group of informants choose laid, and 58 percent of the Type IIIs.

UM   Lay is used by 23 percent of all informants and laid by 71 percent. The Type III informants are almost equally divided. For all three areas studied here, laid is the most common preterit, whether the infinitive is lie or lay.

Ride, Past Participle Rid, Ridden, Rode

ES   Ridden is the only form in cultivated speech and is common in Type II speech in NE. Rode predominates in

Type I speech in the MAS and SAS and is used by at least half the Type II informants. Rid is scattered and rare, except in the coastal and mountain areas of the South. In NC, it is used by one-third of the Type I informants.

NCS Ridden and rode are used by almost exactly equal numbers of all informants in the NCS. Among the cultivated informants, 80 percent choose ridden and 14 percent rode. In KY, 54 percent of the entire group use rode and 30 percent ridden. The percentages for the Type III informants are like those for the entire area. There are nine examples of rid, six in KY. (See figure 7.)

UM Sixty-five percent of all informants use ridden and 39 percent rode. The percent of the Type IIIs who use ridden is eighty-one--almost exactly the same as in the NCS.

Rise; Preterit Raised, Riz, Rised, Rose

ES The frequency of the various forms cannot be determined because many informants choose a lexical alternative, like come up. Rose prevails in NE and south to the PA-MD border, and among younger informants, in all areas. Riz is scatterd in NE and the MAS. In the SAS, it is the dominant form in Type I informants. Raised, the preterit of raise, is rare in NE and the SAS but scattered throughout the MAS. It is most common in WV.

NCS Rose is the most commonly used form. Raised is scattered throughout KY and s.OH and s.IN. Rised occurs mainly in e.KY, where there are six examples. Riz is also confined to KY, with sixteen occurrences.

UM Of those responding with a form of rise, 90 percent used rose. Raised and rised occur rarely. (See figure 8.)

Run; Preterit Ran, Run

ES In NE, ran occurs in cultivated speech; run is very common elsewhere. Ran generally does not occur except in the speech of Type III informants south of the Potomac or in n.e.NE. About one-fourth of the cultivated informants in NE use run, but almost none of those in the MSAS.

NCS Sixty-one percent of all informants use run as preterit and 44 percent ran. Among the Type III informants, 91 percent use ran and 18 percent run. In KY, run is almost universal among the least educated, and three-fourths of the Type III informants use it.

UM Forty-nine percent of all informants choose run, and 77 percent ran--a considerable difference from the figures for the NCS. Among the Type III informants, <u>ran</u> is universal, and 19 percent use <u>run</u> as well.

See; Preterit <u>Saw</u>, <u>See</u>, <u>Seed</u>, <u>Seen</u>

ES <u>Saw</u> is almost the only form in cultivated speech. <u>See</u> is the most common nonstandard variant in NE and the Northern area, as well as parts of VA and e.NC. <u>Seen</u> is uncommon in the Northern area but predominates in the Midland, where it is often used by both Type I and Type II informants. <u>Seed</u> occurs only once north of the PA-MD boundary. To the south, it becomes common, and in NC is the main variant of <u>saw</u>.

NCS <u>Saw</u> is used by 60 percent of the informants, <u>seen</u> by 49 percent, <u>see</u> by 11 percent, and <u>seen</u> by 7 percent. <u>See</u> and <u>seed</u> are concentrated in KY, as might be expected. <u>Saw</u> is used by 87 percent of the cultivated informants.

UM <u>Saw</u> is the choice of 78 percent of all informants, <u>see</u> of 8 percent, and <u>seen</u> of 35 percent. (See figure 9.) <u>Seed</u> occurs only twice. Among the Type III informants, <u>saw</u> is used by 87 percent.

Sit; Present Imperative <u>Sit</u>, <u>Set</u>

ES The records for NE are incomplete. <u>Sit</u> predominates in the area around New York City, the Hudson Valley, and e.PA. South of PA, <u>sit</u> is uncommon except in cultivated speech.

NCS <u>Sit</u> is used by 68 percent of all informants and <u>set</u> by 28 percent. Among the cultivated informants, 80 percent use <u>sit</u> and 9 percent <u>set</u>. <u>Sit</u> is relatively uncommon in n. and c.IL. In KY, the number of informants using the two forms is about equal, with slightly more favoring <u>sit</u>. Only in KY do more than half the Type I informants use <u>set</u> (65 percent).

UM <u>Sit</u> occurs with 58 percent of all informants and <u>set</u> with 12 percent. No Type III speakers use <u>set</u>.

Sit; Preterit <u>Sat</u>, <u>Set</u>, <u>Sot</u>

ES For the informants who use the present tense <u>sit</u>, the usual preterit is <u>sat</u>. Among those who use <u>set</u>, the most common preterit in the MSAS is the leveled <u>set</u>, although <u>sot</u> occurs among older informants in all areas, including nearly all of NC. <u>Sit</u> is found in PA and WV, but is not so common where <u>sot</u> prevails.

NCS Among all informants, <u>sat</u> occurs with 42 percent, <u>set</u> with 39, <u>sit</u> with 15, and <u>sot</u> with 1. For the Type III informants, <u>sat</u> is the most common, used by 65 percent.

Set is used by 16 and sit by 5 percent. In KY, set is the choice of over half of all informants and sit of 32 percent. As might be expected, all examples of sot occur here.

UM   Sat predominates in the entire region, where it is used by 74 percent of the speakers, with most of the other 26 percent who use set being Type I. Sit occurs with 5 percent of the informants. Here the contrast with the NCS is sharp. There are no examples of sot. Ninety-three percent of the cultivated speakers choose sat.

Sweat; Preterit Sweat, Sweated

ES   Sweat is almost universal in the Northern area; sweated becomes increasingly common from c.PA southward. In VA and SC, the two forms are about equally common. In NC it is used by four-fifths of the informants. The usage of the cultivated informants is like that of the other speakers in their area.

NCS   Sweat is predominant everywhere except in KY, where, as might be expected, sweated is used over sweat in a ratio of two to one.

UM   Sweat heavily predominates, with scattered instances of sweated in all states.

Swim; Preterit Swam, Swim, Swimmed, Swum

ES   Swam is most common in cultivated speech everywhere and in much of Type II speech. Swum predominates in older speech in parts of NE and in the MSAS, especially in NC. There are scattered examples of swim and swimmed in the MSAS, especially in NC and SC.

NCS   Swam is used by 61 percent of all informants and swum by 23 percent. There are nineteen examples of swim, ten in KY; and eight of swimmed, six in KY. Among the cultivated informants, 78 percent choose swam and 7 percent swum. None used swim or swimmed.

UM   Ninety-one percent of all informants use swam and 11 percent swum. Most of those using swum are Type I informants.

Take; Preterit Taken, Took, Tuck

ES   Took is almost universal among all informants from NE as far south as the PA-MD boundary. South of this border, tuck becomes more and more common and is used by half the Type I informants in NC. It is primarily a Type I form. Taken is also a South Midland and Southern form. It occurs among both Type I and Type II informants and is a newer form than <u>tuck</u>.

NCS   Although the form was not always recorded, <u>took</u> is the most common variant. In KY alone are there many other forms. Here 75 percent of all informants use <u>took</u>; 29 percent have <u>tuck</u>, 35 percent have <u>taken</u>; and there are occasional examples of <u>taked</u>, <u>tucked</u>, and <u>take</u>. <u>Took</u> is universal among Type III informants.

UM   <u>Took</u> is almost universal. <u>Tuck</u> occurs three times, and <u>taken</u> six. (See figure 10.)

<u>Take</u>; Past Participle <u>Taken</u>, <u>Took</u>, <u>Tuck</u>

ES   <u>Taken</u> is by far the most common participial form, and the usual one chosen by informants who use <u>took</u> as the preterit. Those who use the preterit <u>taken</u> usually have <u>taken</u> as the participle as well. Of those who use the preterit <u>tuck</u>, about half use <u>tuck</u> as the participle and half use <u>taken</u>.

NCS   <u>Taken</u> is by far the most common participle, used by three-fourths of the informants. <u>Took</u> is used by 18 percent. <u>Tuck</u> is used by twenty-seven informants, twenty-two of them in KY. <u>Taken</u> is the choice of 87 percent of the Type III informants; only two use <u>took</u>. KY exhibits the greatest diversity of forms of any state in the area, with 55 percent using <u>taken</u>, 32 percent <u>took</u>, 23 percent <u>tuck</u>, and there are scattered examples of <u>take</u>, <u>taked</u>, and <u>takened</u>.

UM   <u>Taken</u> is universal as the participle, with only two informants using <u>took</u>.

<u>Tear</u>; Past Participle <u>Tore</u>, <u>Torn</u>

ES   <u>Torn</u> is almost the only form in cultivated speech in all areas. In NE, <u>tore</u> predominates among the other types. In the SAS, <u>tore</u> is almost universal in Type I speech, and dominates in Type II as well. In PA and southward, <u>tore</u> predominates among Type I informants and is used by about half of the Type IIs.

NCS   <u>Torn</u> is used by half of all informants and <u>tore</u> by 37 percent. Among the Type III informants, nearly three-fourths choose <u>torn</u>; only six use <u>tore</u>. Only in KY do more than half the informants use <u>tore</u> as participle (fifty-one percent); forty percent prefer <u>torn</u>.

UM   <u>Torn</u> is used by 70 percent of all speakers, and <u>tore</u> by 32 percent. Ninety-three percent of the Type III speakers choose <u>torn</u>.

Throw; Preterit Threw, Throwed, Thrown

ES   In NE, threw occurs in all areas, as does throwed, which
          is less common. In e.NY, threw predominates. To the
          south, throwed (often pronounced /θod/ in the SAS and
          KY) predominates among Type I speakers. Throwed is
          never dominant among Type II informants, being used by
          about one-fifth to one-third of the speakers.
NCS   Threw is used by about two-thirds of all informants and
          throwed by 39 percent. Only five informants use thrown.
          Seventy-one percent of the Type III informants (thirty-
          nine) choose threw; only one uses throwed. Only in KY
          do more than half the informants (59 percent) use
          throwed.
UM   Eighty-six percent of the informants use threw and 19
          percent throwed, a form more common in IO and SD. All
          Type III informants use threw.

Wear; Past Participle Wore, Worn

ES   Worn predominates among all informants in s.NE, NY, and
          northern New Jersey. Wore is used by more than half of
          the other informants in NE. Elsewhere in the MSAS, wore
          predominates among the noncultured informants.
NCS   The item was not always obtained in this area. Among
          those who responded, 45 percent used the standard form,
          worn, and 33 percent wore. Seventy-five percent of the
          Type III informants choose worn. In IN and KY, approxi-
          mately equal numbers use wear and worn. In the other
          states, worn predominates.
UM   Worn occurs in the speech of 93 percent of the Type III
          informants. In the area, about two-thirds of all inform-
          ants use worn and one-third wore.

Write; Past Participle Writ, Written, Wrote

ES   The standard form written predominates in cultivated
          speech in all areas. In NE, wrote is used by about half of
          the Type I informants and one-fourth of the Type IIs.
          Elsewhere wrote predominates, most heavily among Type
          I speakers. Writ occurs rarely.
NCS   Written, the most common form among all informants, is
          used by 62 percent; wrote is used by 27 percent. Writ is
          used by only seven informants, four of them in KY.
          Eighty percent of the Type III speakers use written and
          only 7 percent wrote. Only in KY do more informants say
          wrote than written.
UM   Here written is used by 86 percent of the informants and
          wrote by 15. All Type III informants use written. No

examples of any other variant occur.

Both regional and social differences appear in the study of these verb forms. These differences are summarized in Tables 1 and 2 and in Figures 1 through 10. Kentucky reveals its early connections with Virginia and especially with North Carolina, in the presence of South Midland variants like div, fit (preterit of fight), rid, and seed--variants carried from the East. Most of these minor forms appear but weakly in the rest of the area of South Midland settlement. Kentucky, and especially eastern Kentucky, is their stronghold (see Figures 1-10). All are limited to the speech of the Type I and II informants, as they were in the East.

In all geographical regions, the Type III informants use the standard forms. Among the Type I and II informants, the nonstandard variants appear--for example, come as a preterit and wrote as a participle. With these nonstandard forms, differences appear between Kentucky and the North-Central states as a whole and between the North Central states and the Upper Midwest (see Table 2). The percentage of informants who use the standard form is lower, often considerably lower (as with ate and written) in Kentucky. Even more striking is the difference between the North-Central states and the Upper Midwest, as with did and grew.

Such a study as this raises as many questions as it answers. Do grammatical features, other than verb forms, exhibit similar regional and social patterns? What are the roles of age, sex, and cultural forces in causing such differences? The increasing amount of comparable data we now have available and more sophisticated techniques of analyzing the data are making the answers to these questions an expectation rather than a hope.

Table 1

Verb Forms Largely Restricted to Kentucky and Adjacent South Midland Areas

boil, pret.	boilt
climb, pret.	clim (in WI and MI, of Northern origin)
dive, pret.	div
dream, pret.	/drɪm, drɪmp/
drink, pret.	drinked, drunk
drive, pret., ppl.	driv, drived, druv
fight, pret.	fit
fit, pret.	fit
freeze, pret.	freezed, frozed
hear, ppl.	heern
ride, ppl.	rid

rise, pret.	rised, riz
see, pret.	see, seed
sit, pret.	sot
sweat, pret.	sweated
take, pret., ppl.	taken, tuck

Verb Forms with a Largely Social Distribution in the North-Central Area and Upper Midwest

begin, pret.	begin, begun
bite, ppl.	bit
blow, pret.	blowed
bring, ppl.	brung
catch, pret.	catched
climb, pret.	clum
come, pret.	come
drown, ppl.	drownded
eat, pret.	eat, et
give, pret.	give
grow, pret., ppl.	growed
lie, inf., pret.	lay, laid
ride, ppl.	rode
run, pret.	run
see, pret.	seen
sit, inf., pret.	set, sit
swim, pret.	swum
tear, ppl.	tore
throw, pret.	throwed
wear, ppl.	wore
write, ppl.	wrote

Dream and kneel both seem to have two standard preterits: dreamed and dreamt for the first, and kneeled and knelt for the second.

Table 2
Percentages of Informants Using Standard Forms

	NCS	KY	UM
bitten	34	23	62
climbed, pret.	55	45	81
came	57	41	78
did	43	35	70
dreamt*	49	25	72
drowned	58	38	80
ate	56	42	86

gave	52	26	80
grew	66	41	83
knelt*	60	54	79
lie, infin.	50	35	66
lay, pret.	44	22	23
ridden	43	30	65
ran	44	35	77
saw	60	58	78
sit, imp.	68	55	58
sat	42	22	74
swam	61	41	91
torn	50	40	70
threw	66	54	86
written	62	39	86

*These two forms should perhaps be omitted, since their status as the only standard forms is far from clear.

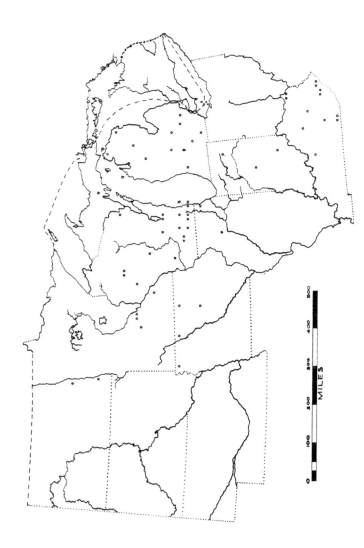

Figure 1 Distribution of <u>Climb</u>, Preterit /klɪm/

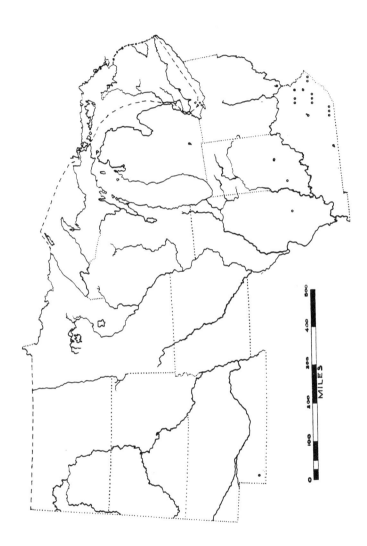

Figure 2 Distribution of Dive, Preterit /dɪv/

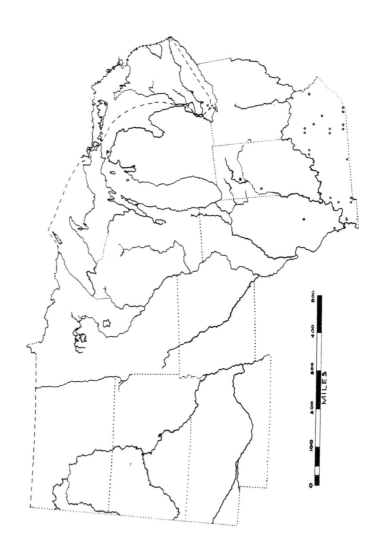

Figure 3 Distribution of <u>Dream</u>, Preterit /drɪmp(t)/

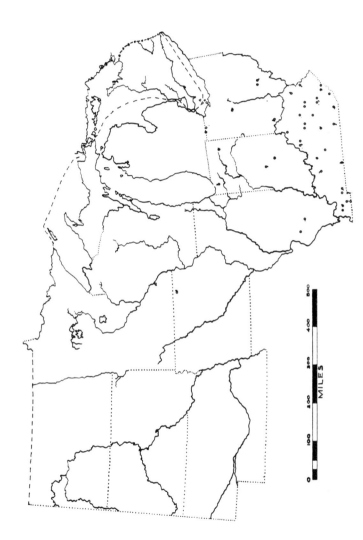

Figure 4 Distribution of Drink, Preterit /drɪŋk(t)/

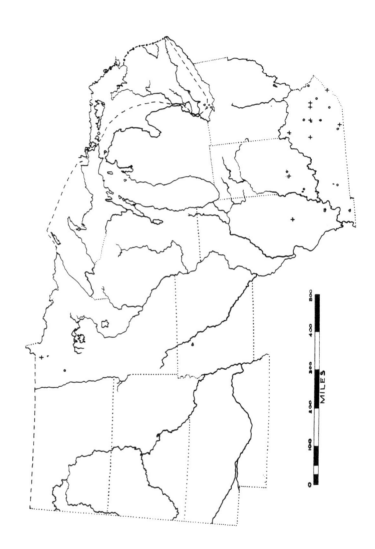
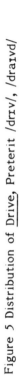

Figure 5 Distribution of Drive, Preterit /drɪv/, /draɪvd/

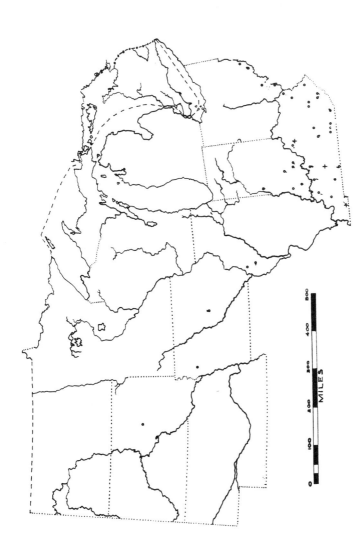

Figure 6 Distribution of Fight, Preterit /fɪt/, /faʊt/

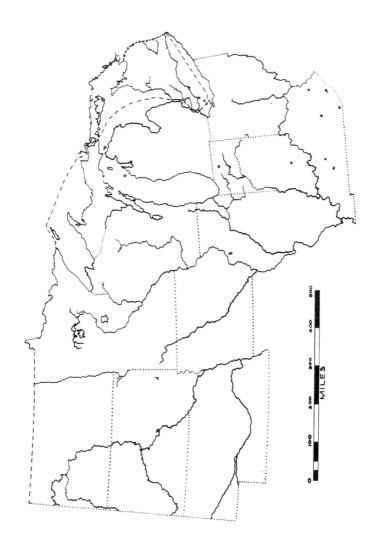

Figure 7 Distribution of <u>Ride</u>, Past Participle /rɪd/

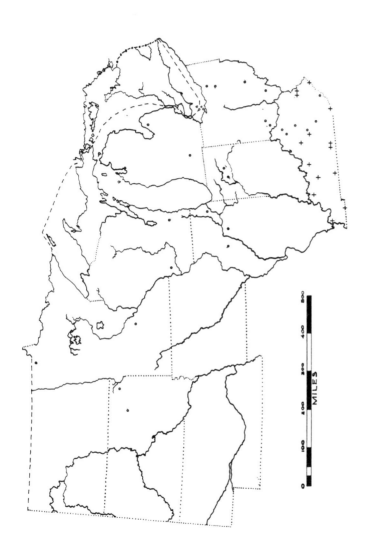

Figure 8 Distribution of <u>Rise</u>, Preterit /raɪzd/, /rɪz/

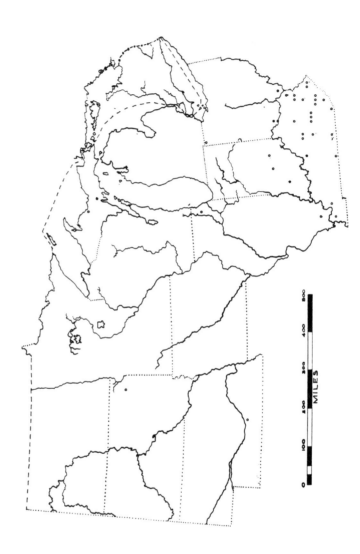

Figure 9 Distribution of See, Preterit /sid/

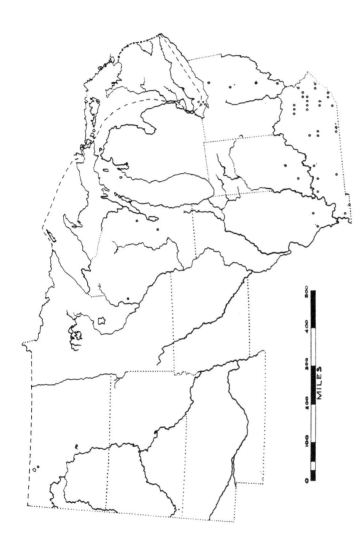

Figure 10 Distribution of Take, Preterit /tʌk/

Constituent Structure of
Double Modals

Harmon S. Boertien

While explicit syntactic analyses of double modals have been presented in the literature (Whitley 1975, Coleman 1975, Boertien 1979), all fail in one important respect: they fail to account for the behavior of certain modal pairs such as <u>might could</u> or <u>might should</u> which, in certain constructions, behave like single verbs. Moreover, while these analyses are to a greater or lesser degree compatible with the behavior of other modal pairs, such as <u>should ought</u> or <u>might ought</u>, which manifest properties of a head verb-complement verb construction, they are unnecessarily abstract.

In the following discussion, I shall motivate two different constituent structures for double modals and, in so doing, present a considerable body of evidence that the initial modal in these constructions, contrary to the suggestions of some researchers, is a true auxiliary verb. I shall also present a body of evidence for the distribution of the tense morpheme in double-modal constructions and argue that this distribution provides a partial explanation for some of the syntactic properties of the verbs that participate in these constructions. Finally, I shall sketch some structural relations between the single-modal and double-modal varieties of English.

The primary evidence supporting the conclusions that follow was developed in interviews with five native Texans, selected for convenience, who have used double modals colloquially since childhood. (A brief informant profile is provided in appendix A.) Data were elicited in two ways: by asking the informants to produce sentences that illustrate uses of double modals or sentences of certain kinds (e.g., negations of sentences that had already been volunteered) and by asking the informants to judge the acceptability of a sentence furnished by the interviewer. Although the shortcomings of data elicited in this way are recognized, it is nevertheless necessary to rely on at least some data developed in this way because of the extreme rarity in spontaneous speech of a number of constructions that have a crucial bearing on the descriptive questions addressed here. At appropriate points in the following discussion, the data from the interviews are compared with data developed by other researchers in Texas and elsewhere in the American South--as well as with data gathered in anonymous observations of spontaneous speech. As will be apparent, there is considerable agreement among the bodies of data from these different sources, and this agreement contributes to the validity of our evidence.

The modal combinations used by one or more informants are listed in table 1, and grouped for convenient reference.

Table 1   Modal Combinations

1	2	3	4
might ought	must can	may can	should ought
might could	must ought	may could	
might should	must would		
might would			
might can			

5

might should ought
might had ought

The behavior of these combinations was observed with respect to six rules that apply in the context of or affect elements of the auxiliary system: Negative Placement, Contraction, NP Aux Inversion, Tag Question Formation, Quantifier Floating, and Niching. The results for each rule are summarized in the tables in appendix B. The tables for the first four rules contain information that was originally reported in Boertien 1979, although the criteria for counting applications of Negative Placement have been modified (as explained in the next section). A few errors in the earlier summaries have been silently corrected here. Because the progress of the interviews was only imperfectly systematic, gaps appear here and there in the summaries.

There are two basic structural configurations in which double modals occur, and these are illustrated in figures 1 and 2 on the next page.

Following Ross 1969, Pullum and Wilson 1977, and others, I shall represent all verbs--auxiliaries and nonauxiliaries alike--as dominated by V. I shall also, following these authors, represent all auxiliary verbs as head verbs of their own VPs, except where syntactic evidence to the contrary appears (as is the case with modal pairs assigned the structure in figure 1). I do not, however, follow these authors in making each auxiliary verb the main verb of its own clause.

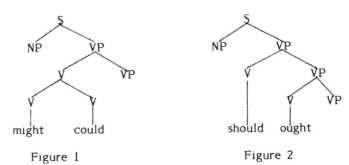

Figure 1   Figure 2

The V node over each modal is motivated by the applicability patterns of the rules of Negative Placement, Negative Contraction, NP Aux Inversion, and Tag Question Formation, all of which are generally assumed to apply directly to, or in the environment of, auxiliary verbs.

The first and largest body of evidence for the verbal status of the modals is provided by the behavior of Negative Placement. In general, the rule of Negative Placement positions not immediately after an auxiliary verb: if an adverb immediately precedes not in the surface structure of a simple sentence, an auxiliary verb must precede the adverb. Thus English permits such strings as they may possibly not want it but disallows strings like they possibly not want it. The somewhat greater number of possibilities for the distribution of not in complex sentences is irrelevant here since all of the examples of negated double modals are simple sentences in form. In the classical transformational analysis, the occurrence of contracted not is evidence that Negative Placement has applied, but here I shall count only occurrences of uncontracted not as applications of that rule, leaving the details of the operation of Negative Contraction an open question (but see Pullum and Wilson 1977, and Gazdar, Pullum, and Sag 1982 and references there, for a nontransformational analysis).

As exemplified below, not may be placed after either modal of a double-modal pair (informant designation is in parentheses):

I may not can. (A)

I may cannot. (A)

I might not oughta do that. (B)

We should oughta not do that. (D)

Although not every speaker was able to place <u>not</u> after each modal, most modals could be so negated by at least one, and often several, speakers. The exceptions are the second modals of <u>might could</u>, <u>might can</u>, <u>must can</u>, <u>must ought</u>, <u>must would</u>, and <u>might should ought</u>; the first modal of <u>should ought</u>; and both modals of <u>may could</u>. Only two speakers admitted using <u>may could</u>, and judgments were obtained from only one speaker who rejected all negative forms of the double modal. Feagin (1979:336), however, reports an instance of <u>may not could</u> in Alabama speech.

A second source of evidence for the verbal status of the individual modals comes from their behavior with respect to Negative Contraction. Applicability of this rule is largely restricted to second-position modals. All second-position modals, except <u>could</u> of <u>may could</u> and <u>ought</u> of <u>should ought</u>, participate in Negative Contraction for one or more speakers, while, of the initial modals, only those of <u>might ought</u>, <u>should ought</u>, and <u>might should ought</u> can participate. Third-position <u>ought</u> cannot form negative contractions. Examples of contractions in these two positions are given below.

I shouldn't oughta do that. (A)

I mightn't oughta do that. (B)

You might couldn't do that. (B)

I might shouldn't oughta. (A)

Although not attested in Texas speech, the form <u>may couldn't</u> is reported for Mississippi speech in Labov et al. (1968:1:261). The observed distribution of negative contractions is very strong evidence that some initial and virtually all second modals are auxiliary verbs.

Additional evidence for the verbal status of the individual modals is provided by the facts of NP Aux Inversion. Applicability of the rule is far from uniform, but at least two initial modals and nearly half of the second-position modals can be inverted to form yes-no questions by one or another speaker. Examples of these question forms appear below:

Shouldn't you oughta do that? (C) (From: "You shouldn't oughta do that.")

Could you may go? (A)   (From: "You may could go.")

Could you might go? (A)   (From: "You might could
                                     go.")

Mightn't we oughta do that? (D)   (From: "We mightn't
                                     oughta do that.")

Inversion of the initial modal is very restricted--only should
and might, when preceding ought, being free to invert alone. A
greater proportion of the second modals can invert, but most
appear unable to do so, there being no examples of simple inversion of the second modals of might ought, might should, might
would, must can, must ought, must would, may can, should ought,
or might had ought. Again, third-position ought is entirely outside
the operation of the rule. Pampell (1975:121), however, reports the
inversion of would (of might would) by a Texas speaker, as does
DiPaolo 1980b. A fourth source of evidence for the verbal status
of the individual modals comes from tag questions based on double-
modal sentences. Some examples of these tag questions are given
below:

I shouldn't oughta do that, should I? (A)

He must wouldn't steal, would he? (B)

I might could do that, couldn't I? (A)

Only three initial modals can be copied in a tag: those of
might ought, might could, and should ought--a pattern only slightly
less restrictive than that for Inversion and Contraction. All second
modals, except those of might would, must can, and must ought,
can be copied in tags, although the tag based on ought (of should
ought) is only marginally acceptable. Third position ought is not
copied in tags. Since there are many gaps in the data, it is possible that tags can be based on a wider range of modals than is
observed here.
The evidence of the applicability of these four rules permits a
reasonably confident conclusion that each modal in the double and
triple modal combinations is a verb, and not some other part of
speech. Evidence from Texas English is available for every modal
except may of may could. However, since no data on the application of Negative Placement to this modal pair were gathered from
one of the two speakers who used it, and since applicability of
this rule to double modals is not uniform from speaker to speaker,
there is no basis for concluding that may is not an auxiliary verb
here, just as it demonstrably is in may can. Furthermore, the
evidence from Negative Placement in Alabama English shows that
it is indeed an auxiliary verb for speakers there. It therefore
seems reasonable to treat may could as a construction made up of
two auxiliary verbs, like all of the other modal pairs studied here.

The conclusion that the initial as well as the second modal in these constructions is a verb runs counter to the opinion of a number of researchers who, following Labov (1972a:59), have cautiously suggested that it has adverbial rather than verbal status. However, the evidence of the inverted, and especially the negative, structures seems to me decisive. Whatever adverbial qualities the initial modal may have semantically, it is clearly a verb syntactically. Coleman (1975:64n8) and Pampell (1975:115) have other, distributional arguments for the same conclusion. What has apparently led some researchers to suggest that initial modals are adverbs is their resistance to inversion and contraction. However, I shall suggest (below) that a possible explanation for this is that the resistant verbs are not marked for tense.

The choice of a common V node for most modal pairs (as in figure 1) versus the separate VP nodes for each modal (as in figure 2) is motivated primarily by the distribution of different modal pairs in yes-no questions.

For a number of modal pairs, inversion of the pair as a unit is possible, as illustrated below:

Might ought you to've done that? (B)

Might can you do this later? (B)

Inversion of these and other pairs is reported in other studies of Southern English as well: Pampell 1975 reports the inversion of might could, might should, and might would; Coleman (1975:205) reports the inversion of might could, might couldn't, and might shouldn't; and DiPaolo 1980b reports that might should is inverted. In fact, DiPaolo 1980b reports that 29 percent of the eighty-four Texas speakers to whom she posed a repetition task involving questions produced questions with an inverted pair. All modal pairs that begin with might can be inverted as a unit by at least one speaker; to this extent, the pair acts like a single verb and is therefore assigned the structure in figure 1. It is important to bear in mind that the modals in these pairs have not lost their verbal status for the speakers who invert them. For all of my and Pampell's informants who invert pairs, Negative Placement applies after all initial modals in these pairs, except might of might would, and Tag Question Formation applies to either modal of might ought and can of might can.

The rather different inversion behavior of should ought motivates the structure in figure 2: it is always the first modal that inverts, never the second, and the pair never inverts as a unit. Two other properties distinguish this double modal from those in column 1: first, it is the first modal, and never the second, that forms a negative contraction; and second, except for the tag question marginally accepted by D, it is always the first modal that is copied in the tag.

These characteristics of should ought have already been illustrated among the example sentences with Negative Contraction, NP Aux Inversion, and Tag Question Formation. Because should shows characteristics normally expected of the first auxiliary verb in a tensed clause, and ought almost none of them, this particular pair is naturally assigned the structure of a standard English auxiliary verb sequence, where each auxiliary is treated as the head verb of its own VP.[1]

Although I have assigned the structure in figure 1 to might ought, it appears to be structurally ambiguous in that might in this pair also shares the characteristics manifested by should (above). Thus it can invert as a single modal, can be copied in tags, and can form negative contractions. The following sentences illustrate.

Mightn't we oughta do that? (D)

You might ought to have done that, mightn't you? (B)

It appears, therefore, that might ought may have the structure in either figure 1 or figure 2.

This analysis makes the syntax of ought different from that of other modals, and this could be viewed as a reason to seek a more uniform treatment. However, the syntax of ought is unique among modals in a number of different dialects of English, and its behavior in the double modal constructon of Southern American English is in fact in agreement in many important respects with its behavior elsewhere, two examples of which I shall briefly describe.

First, there is the behavior of ought in the Northern and Midwestern form had ought, which is that of a nonfinite complement of a tensed auxiliary. The following sentences are cited in Bryant 1952:

He hadn't ought to go getting drunk. (Sinclair Lewis)

I had ought to have met you. (Ohio speaker)

Because it forms a negative contraction, had must be a tensed auxiliary in the first sentence. It also appears to be a modal morphologically and syntactically.

Although the time reference of the first sentence is present, as the context of the novel from which it was taken makes clear (Lewis 1952:174), the form of the auxiliary is past, a characteristic of a number of modals which are past in form. Moreover, like many of these modals, it appears impossible for it to have past time reference. When a past time is referred to, as in the second sentence, perfect have appears (in the complement) to move the reference back in time. Furthermore, there are no examples or reports of had, in this usage, preceded by other auxiliaries or occurring in nonfinite clauses. If <u>had</u> is a tensed modal, <u>ought</u> in this construction is an infinitive.

Second, there is the behavior of <u>ought</u> in the British form <u>did ought</u>, which is illustrated in Pullum and Wilson (1977:757) with the following example sentences:

You didn't ought to do that.

Did he ought to do that?

You ought to leave, didn't you?

Because it inverts and forms negative contractions, <u>did</u> is clearly a tensed auxiliary in these sentences, but its syntactic class is not so clear. Its distributional properties suggest that it is a form of supportive <u>do</u>, as Pullum and Wilson claim, but its invariant preterit form suggests it may be a modal. Either way, where <u>ought</u> follows <u>did</u>, <u>ought</u> is again an infinitive.

The behavior of <u>ought</u> in these constructions is almost exactly parallel to its behavior in <u>might ought</u> and <u>should ought</u>. Moreover, the analysis of <u>ought</u> as an infinitival complement is entirely compatible with the constituent analysis represented in figure 2. This analysis, then, receives additional support in that it correctly assigns to <u>ought</u> what is in fact a widespread syntactic role.

Since the structure in figure 2 seems to be associated with pairs that have <u>ought</u> as the second modal, it might be expected that <u>must ought</u> would also have this structure. However, <u>must</u> does not form negative contractions, invert, or permit copying in tags for the only speaker (B) who uses this pair, and it therefore does not appear to have that structure. In fact, there is no reason to expect it to, given the normal assumption that verbs are subcategorized for their complements. On that assumption, it is strictly an idiosyncratic property of <u>might</u> and <u>should</u> that each is subcategorized for infinitival <u>ought</u>, a property not necessarily shared by other modals.

Given the two structures in figures 1 and 2 and the subcategorization of <u>should</u> for an infinitival <u>ought</u> complement, the possibility of a third structure is predicted, resulting from the substitution of the $[_V VV]$ structure in figure 1 for the highest V node in figure 2. This structure, illustrated in figure 3, in fact exists and is that of the triple modal <u>might should ought</u>--a combination that is used by three of the speakers reported on here. This triple appears to have the properties that would be predicted for this structure by analogy with the simpler structures that constitute it: all modals can be followed by <u>not</u>, but only <u>should</u> can form negative contractions, be inverted, or be copied in a tag. Example sentences, illustrating two of the predicted properties for <u>should</u>, appear below:

I might should oughta go, shouldn't I? (A)

I might shouldn't oughta. (A)

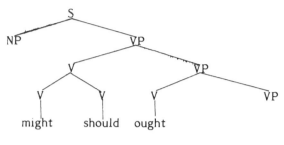

Figure 3

One more predicted property, the inversion of might should as a unit, does not seem to occur for Texas speakers, but is attested for North Carolina speakers by Coleman (1975:205) in the following sentence:

Might shouldn't he ought to go?

A second triple modal, used by two of my informants, might had ought, also appears to have the structure in figure 3. Although data are sketchy, had in this triple can form negative contractions and be copied in tags for informant A. The following sentence illustrates.[2]

I might had oughta, hadn't I? (A)

A third triple is reported in North Carolina speech by Coleman (1975:106ff): may should ought.

So far, structures have been motivated for the modal combinations in columns 1, 4, and 5; structures have not yet been assigned to the pairs in 2 and 3. These pairs do not appear to invert as units, nor do the initial modals ever invert independently; thus they lack the primary distinguishing properties of the structures in figure 1 and figure 2. However, they should probably be assigned the structure in figure 1 because of other distinctive properties they possess in common with the pairs that have that structure-- namely, the ability of the second modal to participate in negative contraction, inversion, and tag questions. These pairs will there- fore be assigned the structure in figure 1.

An interesting and unsettled question in the syntax of double modals is the distribution of tense. Labov et al. (1968:I:260ff) argue that, in the speech of New York City blacks, only the second modal is marked for tense. I have argued that, with the exception of second-position <u>ought</u>, this is also true for Texas English (Boertien 1979, Boertien and Said 1980). However, DiPaolo 1980a argues that both modals are specified for tense. In the following paragraphs, I shall advance three independent arguments for one possible distribution of tense; I shall also consider a possible counteranalysis.

The first argument is based on the distribution of double modal forms in past time contexts that require, in standard English, the verb to be in past tense form. Such a context is exemplified by the following sentences, where <u>him</u> and <u>he</u> are understood to be coreferential:

It scared him that he $\begin{Bmatrix} *\text{is} \\ \text{was} \end{Bmatrix}$ almost killed yesterday.

It scared him that he $\begin{Bmatrix} *\text{can} \\ \text{could} \end{Bmatrix}$ have been killed yesterday.

Note that past tense <u>was</u> and <u>could</u>, but not present tense <u>is</u> and <u>can</u>, are acceptable here.

The same acceptability pattern holds for second-position <u>can</u> and <u>could</u> for all four informants who use both <u>might can</u> and <u>might could</u>:

It scared him that he might $\begin{Bmatrix} *\text{can've} \\ \text{could've} \end{Bmatrix}$ been killed yesterday. (A)

That I might $\begin{Bmatrix} *\text{can've} \\ \text{could've} \end{Bmatrix}$ done it yesterday excited me. (B)

In the past, an ocean voyage might $\begin{Bmatrix} *\text{can} \\ \text{could} \end{Bmatrix}$ be very dangerous. (C)

That I might $\begin{Bmatrix} *\text{can} \\ \text{could} \end{Bmatrix}$ have done that yesterday surprised me. (E)

This is strong evidence that the second modal is subject to the same constraints on form to which the tensed verb is generally subject and, therefore, that the second modal is marked for tense. However, a similar demonstration for second modals, other than <u>can</u> and <u>could</u>, is impossible since the requisite occurrence in second position of both present and past tense forms is nonexistent.

The second argument is based on the distribution of negative contractions in double-modal constructions. I take it as obvious that only tensed auxiliaries form negative contractions in standard English. I assume that the same condition on negative contraction holds for double modal constructions as well. As detailed above, it is almost always the case that the second modal forms negations.

This is very good evidence that all second-position modals, except _should ought_, are tensed. Of the first-position modals, only those of _should ought_ and _might ought_ are regularly contracted, so that they too appear to be tensed.

In addition, _might_ (of _might should ought_) can be contracted by one speaker (D), but only if _should_ is simultaneously contracted. Also, since _shouldn't_ cannot occur in declarative sentences without _mightn't_, it appears that, for this speaker, _mightn't shouldn't_ is the preferred negative form of the affirmative verb _might should_. This would be a natural development in a grammar where _might should_ is a phrasal verb and, thus, a single lexical entry, and where negative contractions are not transformationally derived but are listed in the lexicon, along the lines proposed by Pullum and Wilson 1977 and others. The single contracted form, _shouldn't_, would of course be available for use in negative questions.

The patterns of negative contraction reported by other researchers are consistent with the pattern reported here. Labov et al. (1968:I:261) report that in Mississippi the second modal of all eight pairs they mention as current there can form negative contractions. Pampell 1975 states that all second modals of the combinations he reports can be contracted, except _ought_ of _should ought_ and _should_ of _might should ought_, but he doesn't find any instances of _mightn't ought_. Coleman (1975:201-05) records _might couldn't_, _might shouldn't_, _mightn't ought_, and _might shouldn't ought_. He also reports instances of _mightn't could not_, which he says has a low level of acceptability. He also reports that some speakers accept _might should oughtn't_, but says this is a "highly questionable" construction which should be considered "ungrammatical." Feagin (1979:339) reports an instance of _shouldn't ought_. DiPaolo 1980b reports _might couldn't_ and _might can't_.

Their argument is based on the possibility of inversion of individual modals. Again, I take it as given that only tensed auxiliaries may be inverted in yes-no questions. Again (as detailed earlier), it is only second-position modals that may be individually inverted, except for _might_ and _should_ preceding _ought_. All these modals must therefore be tensed. Where modal pairs are inverted, it is not necessarily the case that both modals are individually tensed; what _is_ necessary is that the phrasal verb constituted by the pair be marked as tensed. Since, with the exception of _might_ of _might ought_, there is no good, independent evidence that the initial modals of the inverted pairs are tensed, and there is considerable independent evidence that the second modals are, it appears that, for the phrasal verb to be tensed, it is sufficient that just one constituent of it be tensed.

The results of other investigations are consistent with those reported here. Coleman 1975 reports that the second modals of _might could_ and _might shouldn't ought_ and the initial modal of _mightn't ought_ invert in questions. Pampell 1975 reports the inversion of the second modals of _might could_, _might should_, _might_

would, and might should ought, and the inversion of the initial
modals of might ought and should ought. Pampell also reports that
the initial modals of might should and might would can be very
marginally inverted by a single informant each. DiPaolo 1980b
reports that the second modal of might ought inverts.

Since there is skepticism in the literature regarding the existence of double-modal yes-no questions, it is worth pointing out
that they have also been observed in spontaneous speech. Feagin
(1979:162) gives the following example (furnished by Frank
Anshen):

> Could you might tell me where the administration building
> is? (Black man on campus of SUNY, Stony Brook)

The following two examples, furnished by Jerry Edmondson and
Marshall Smith respectively, are from Texas speakers:

> Could you might come over here for a minute?
> (White female secretary, about 25, College Station,
> Texas)

> Would you might want to let your sister-in-law do that?
> (White male undertaker, about 25, Houston, Texas)

These examples, too, show the very common pattern of second
modal inversion.

There is a nice agreement among the three kinds of evidence
showing that most second-position modals are tensed and between
the evidence of contraction and inversion showing that at least
two initial modals are also tensed. Of the second-position modals,
only ought of should ought lacks direct evidence of any kind that
it is tensed. Of the initial modals, there is very strong direct
evidence that might and should before ought are tensed. There is
no evidence that third-position ought is tensed. Thus the following
distribution of tense has been strongly motivated: all pairs with
the structure in figure 1 have the tensed modal in second position,
and all pairs with the structure in figure 2 have the tensed modal
in initial position; triples with the structure in figure 3 have the
tensed modal in second position. Since might ought is structurally
ambiguous between the structures in figures 1 and 2, either
member of that pair may be tensed. This, of course, is exactly
what our evidence shows.

Whether modals in other positions are also tensed is an open
question; the available evidence is not decisive. One piece of
evidence suggesting that some initial modals are not tensed is the
following sentence, which contains a present tense initial modal in
a context that ordinarily requires a past tense form verb:

It scared him that he may could've been killed yesterday. (A)

Evidently the first modal is not subject to the same constraints on formal tense as the second modal, and we may therefore cautiously conclude that the first modal here is untensed.
Whether this conclusion may be generalized to all initial modals of
phrasal verb structure is not clear. Informant C rejects may in a
similar context, and DiPaolo 1980a, b reports similar mixed results.
Of course, might may be selected over may for reasons that have
nothing to do with tense. A preference for the more tentative
over the less tentative modal in these contexts may be involved,
for example.

Evidence that modals in other positions may be tensed is
provided by inversion and contraction, as in the following sentence:

Might you oughtn't to have done that? (B)

Here, both modals simultaneously manifest independent signs of
tense. Furthermore, as already mentioned, Pampell reports the
marginal inversion of the initial modal of might should and might
would, and Coleman reports the marginal contraction of the third-
position ought and the might of might could.

Nevertheless, despite these suggestive cases, there is a widespread and striking absence of evidence for the tensing of modals
in any positions other than those described above. This can be
readily explained on the plausible assumption that, in English, no
more than one verb is tensed per simple clause. Thus the marginal
status of the inversions and contractions just mentioned is explainable as the result of applying processes to untensed verbs that
normally are restricted to tensed verbs. Still, the acceptability of
B's sentence (above) remains exceptional.

An alternative explanation for the distribution of inverted and
contracted forms ought to be considered, an explanation that does
not take account of tense. It is apparent that, of the initial
modals, should inverts and contracts most consistently (six out of
six possible applications of the rules), might less consistently (five
of thirty-eight possible applications), and must and may not at all.
Intuitively, we may say, this approximates the consistency of
contraction and inversion of these modals in similar single-modal
constructions, in which they are all (presumably) tensed. We might
expect, therefore, that whatever accounts for the greater flexibility of single-modal should, the lesser flexibility of single-modal
epistemic might and must, and the considerable inflexibility of
single-modal epistemic may, will also account for their behavior in
double-modal constructions. This view has merit and has been
proposed as an at least partial explanation by a number of writers
(Pampell 1975:115, Feagin 1979:162-63, Boertien 1979:21-22, and

DiPaolo 1980a).

On this view, all double modals would presumably have the phrasal verb structure, the phrasal verb would be tensed as a unit, and principles independent of tense or internal structure would determine which of the two modals would be selected for inversion or contraction. DiPaolo 1980b proposes an analysis something like this, claiming all double modals are two-word verbs. Attractive as this approach is, however, there appear to be at least two difficulties with this view as the sole explanation for the syntactic behavior that has been documented here.

First, against the view that some principle independent of tense distribution is the sole determiner of the modal that is affected by the rule in question, it is the case that epistemic must is somewhat more susceptible to inversion and contraction than the double-modal data would indicate. Palmer (1979:54-56) provides the following examples of constructions that contain epistemic must-- the first two of his own construction, the last two taken from the Survey of English Usage records at University College, London:

He mustn't be there after all.

Must they be on holiday?

. . . think there must be, mustn't there?

. . . and mustn't there be endless stories about this mansion?

Quirk and Greenbaum (1973:56) provide this example:

Mustn't there be another reason for his behavior?

Although not terribly common, epistemic must is apparently at least as acceptable in contraction and interrogation as epistemic might, and the inversion and contraction of must of must ought should be at least as acceptable as that of might of might ought. Yet, for the one informant who uses both pairs, inversion and contraction of might is fully acceptable while that of must is judged ungrammatical. Nor is there mention elsewhere in the literature of these processes applying to double-modal must.

Second, against the view that all modal pairs have the same internal structure, it is the case that a number of optional constituents may be more freely inserted between modals that are claimed to have the structure in figure 2 than between other pairs of modals. Specifically, the quantifier all is more readily insertable there by Quantifier Floating and parenthetical expressions like I think or I guess by Niching. In addition, an optional auxiliary, have, may occur there for some speakers. As Zwicky 1978 points out, higher-level constituents, such as NP and VP, tend to be more loosely bound together than lower-level ones, such as Det, Adj, and N, and therefore tend to be more easily interruptible by parenthetical material of various kinds. The VP-level break of the structure in figure 2 would seem to be intermediate between an NP-VP constituent break at the S level and a Det-N constituent break at the NP level, but it is certainly at a much higher level than the one in figure 1, which is entirely within a V. We would therefore expect that the constituent break before <u>ought</u>, in <u>might ought</u>, should ought, <u>might had ought</u>, and <u>might should ought</u>, would be more likely to accept parenthetical and other optional material than would the breaks between other modals if the structures are as have been proposed. This expectation is in fact realized.

Quantifier Floating takes a quantifier, such as <u>all</u>, and positions it immediately before an auxiliary or main verb. It is the rule that positions <u>all</u> in the following sentences:

They all might oughta do that. (B)

They might all oughta do that. (B)

Pledges might oughta all carry their pledge book with them at all times. (D)

Of the nine instances of contexts that are claimed to have the structure in figure 2 where there are relevant data, an application of Quantifier Floating is permitted in six of them. By contrast, the rule applies in only six out of twenty-two instances of the other context.

Niching is the rule that optionally inserts parenthetical material, such as <u>I think</u> or <u>I guess</u>, into any number of positions in a sentence. The following are examples of the application of this rule:

John, I guess, may could do that. (A)

?John might, I guess, oughta do that. (A)

John might, I think, could do that. (B)

John might could, I think, do that. (B)

Niching applies in three of the ten contexts that are claimed to have the structure in figure 2 where there are relevant data. Of the twenty contexts claimed to have the structure in figure 1, Niching applies in four.

While all five informants permit auxiliary <u>have</u> to follow most modal combinations, as illustrated in a number of example sentences already given. Two of them permit an additional <u>have</u> to occur before <u>ought</u>. It need not occur at all, of course, but when it does, it may occur either as the only auxiliary have in a clause (as in the first two sentences below) or as one of two have's (as illustrated in the second two):

There might've oughta been a better way. (D)

John might, I think, have oughta. (B)

I think that we should have ought've done that yesterday. (D)

There might've ought've been somebody up there. (B)

While intermodal have may occur before should, could, and would for some speakers elsewhere (Coleman 1975:86-87), that is not the case for the speakers reported on here. For the two speakers who permit it, intermodal have occurs in three of the five contexts claimed to have the structure in figure 2 where there are relevant data, and it occurs in none of the eleven contexts claimed to have the structure in figure 1. Table 2 summarizes the figures.

Table 2
Interruptibility of Double Modals in Two Contexts

Context	Quantifier Floating		Niching		Intermodal Have		Combined Total	
	N	% Apply	N	% Apply	N	% Apply	N	% Apply
V__VP (fig. 1)	9	66.7	10	30.0	5	60.00	24	50.00
V__V (fig. 2)	22	27.3	20	20.0	11	5.00	53	18.9

For all three types of insertions, there is a clear tendency to prefer the contexts claimed to have the structure in figure 2. (For the combined totals, the difference between the two contexts is statistically significant at the .025 level, where x^2 (corrected) = 6.39.) This tendency may be explainable on grounds other than structure--for example, on the grounds of semantic relations within different modal pairs--but in the absence of any other explanation, it must be considered support for the structural difference proposed in this paper and evidence against the view that all double modals have the same internal structure.

Partly on the basis of the foregoing analysis, it is possible to suggest a few things about the syntactic relation of double- and single-modal varieties of English. First of all, it should be appar-

ent that the phrase structure component of the varieties is the
same. For example, the tree diagram in figure 4 represents (in
outline) the phrase structure of each of the four sentences beneath it:

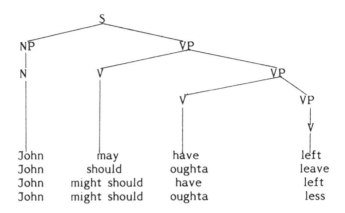

John	may	have	left
John	should	oughta	leave
John	might should	have	left
John	might should	oughta	less

Figure 4

The highest V node would dominate the single-modal may in
the first sentence; it would dominate the initial modal of should
ought in the second sentence, as detailed in figure 2; it would
dominate the phrasal verb might should in the third and fourth
sentences, as detailed in figures 1 and 3.

The differences show up primarily in the lexicon. Users of
double modals will have both additional lexical entries, to accommodate the phrasal verbs, and additional information in some
single-modal entries, to accommodate the modal complement ought
(for example). To illustrate these differences, a very tentative,
very incomplete representation of two lexical entries is sketched
below:

< _Vshould + _____ [_{VP} [_Vought] VP], . . .>

< [_V [_Vmight] [_Vshould]] , . . .>

The label of the outermost square brackets is the "category
label" of the lexical item--in effect specifying the node of the
tree that dominates this lexical item. Both items (above) are
subcategorized for an ought complement, but only the entry for
should makes this explicit. I assume that it holds for might should
as well, by virtue of the fact that should is part of the entry, but
I have no mechanism for guaranteeing this to propose here. The
entry for might should specifies the internal structure of the

double modal, just as I assume the entry would do for verb-particle constructions such as turn on or throw out, or for VP idioms such as kick the bucket or let the cat out of the bag. This kind of lexical information makes sense if one assumes that most double modals are learned as idioms, which seems plausible. In the lexicon of a single-modal variety of English, of course, there would not be either subcategorization for ought or an entry for might should.

Tense assignment, however effected, would apply in single- and double-modal varieties of English in the same way; in all cases, the highest V would dominate the tensed verb. However, tense assignment within the phrasal verb is an unsettled matter; perhaps the second modal--if only the second modal is involved-- would be marked for tense as part of the lexical representation of the phrasal verb, but I have no explicit proposal to make.

Finally, there are transformational rules--a matter far too complex to address in any detail here. I shall therefore give just the barest sketch of an analysis. I know no reason why essentially the same rules of Negative Placement, Contraction, NP Aux Inversion, and so on cannot be shared by both single- and double-modal varieties of English. While not may occur after either the first or second modal, it may occur also after any auxiliary verb in single-modal varieties, as in John may not have paid the rent or John may have not paid it out of spite. The tendency to place not after the first auxiliary may be captured by making Negative Placement a variable rule--that is, a rule whose likelihood of application is affected by enhancing or inhibiting features of the context. In this case, application is enhanced when the auxiliary is in initial position. Tag Question Formation, which introduces an auxiliary copy into a tag, is enhanced when the copied auxiliary is tensed and when the copy is exact, rather than just semantically similar. Quantifier Floating positions a quantifier before a V and is enhanced when the constituent break is at the VP or S level. Boertien and Said 1980 argue that a number of these rules are in fact variable rules, shared by both single- and double-modal varieties of English.

Clearly, more has been left vague than has been made precise, but as the analysis and description of double-modal and other regional and stylistic varieties of English approach the breadth of coverage and the explicitness already achieved for large fragments of standard English, it will become increasingly possible to identify and characterize, with testable precision, the kinds of relations that hold among these varieties. Proceeding in this way, we may ultimately give a principled account of the limits on the kind and extent of variation permitted across a language.

NOTES

[1]Ought may well show none of the first auxiliary characteristics. Although I have described the tag as formed on the basis of ought of main clause should ought, it may instead, especially in view of its marginal status, be formed on the basis of semantically similar should. Tags that are formed on the basis of semantic rather than lexical identity are well attested: Bryant 1952, citing Krapp's Comprehensive Guide to Good English, reports I oughtn't to have done that, had I? and McDavid 1953 reports I ought to do it, hadn't I? Moreover, Pampell 1975 reports that four of his informants use shouldn't in a tag based on main clause might ought, and Langendoen (1970:15-16) reports numerous examples of this sort, including I may see you tomorrow, won't I/mayn't I/ mightn't I/can't I? and You ought to smoke, oughtn't you/ shouldn't you/hadn't you?

[2]Had is considered a modal in this construction on the basis of its parallel behavior with should of might should ought and in the apparently related had ought (already discussed). It is not a perfect auxiliary, as I mistakenly claimed in Boertien 1979.

Appendix A

Informant Profile

A   White female, about 21, University of Texas senior, raised in Beaumont, Texas.

B   White male, about 20, University of Texas sophomore, raised in San Antonio, Texas.

C   White female, 32, University of Houston senior, raised in Matagorda City, Texas.

D   White female, about 19, University of Houston sophomore, raised in Dickenson, Texas.

E   White female, about 30, University of Houston graduate student, raised in Beaumont, Texas.

Appendix B

Data Summaries

Key:
x = result of applying rule is acceptable.
? = result of applying rule is marginally acceptable.
* = result of applying rule is unacceptable.
- = modal combination is absent from informant's lect.
No symbol = no relevant data.

Negative Placement (Uncontracted not)

Informants	1st Modal					2nd/3rd Modal				
	A	B	C	D	E	A	B	C	D	E
might ought	x	x	x	x	-	x	x	*	x	-
might could		x	x	x	*	*	*	*	*	*
might should	x	x	x	x	-	x	*	?	x	-
might would	x	-	-	-	-	x	-	-	-	-
might can		x	x	-	*		*	*	-	*
must can	-	x	-	-	-	-		-	-	-
must ought	-	x	-	-	-	-		-	-	-
must would	-	x	-	-	-	-		-	-	-
may can	x	x	?	-	*	x	*	*	-	*
may could		-	*	-	-		-	*	-	-
should ought		-	*		-		-	*	x	-
might should ought	*	-	*	x	-	*/*	-	*/*	*/x	-
might had ought	x		-	-	-	x/x		-	-	-

Negative Contraction

Informants	1st Modal					2nd/3rd Modal				
	A	B	C	D	E	A	B	C	D	E
might ought	*	x	x	x	-	*	x	*	*	-
might could	*	*	*	*	*	x	x	*	*	*
might should	*	*	*	*	-	x	x	?	?	-
might would	*	-	-	-	-	x	-	-	-	-
might can	*	*	*	-	*		x	*	-	*
must can	-	*	-	-	-	-	x	-	-	-
must ought	-	*	-	-	-	-	x	-	-	-
must would	-	*	-	-	-	-	x	-	-	-
may can	*	*	*	-	*	x	x	*	-	*
may could	*	-	*	-	-		-	*	-	-
should ought	x	-	x	x	-	*	-	*	*	-
might should ought	*	-	*	x(f)	-	x/*	-	*/*	x(p)/	-
might had ought		-	-	-		x/	-	-	-	-

f = following modal must simultaneously undergo rule.
p = preceding modal must simultaneously undergo rule (in declarative sentence only).

NP Aux Inversion

Informants	1st Modal					2nd/3rd Modal				
	A	B	C	D	E	A	B	C	D	E
might ought	*	x(a)	*	x(nu)	-	*	x(p,nu)	*		-
might could		*	*	*	*	x	*	*	*	*
might should	*	*			-	*	*			-
might would	*	-	-	-	-	*	-	-	-	-
might can		x(f,a)	*	-	*	x(a)	x(p)	*	-	*
must can	-	*	-	-	-	-	*	-	-	-
must ought	-	*	-	-	-	-	*	-	-	-
must would	-	*	-	-	-	-	*	-	-	-
may can	*	*	*	-	*	*	*	*	-	*
may could	*	-	*	-	-	x(a)	-	*	-	-
should ought	x	-	x	x	-	-				-
might should ought	*	-	*		-	*/*	-	*/*	x(i,au)/	-
might had ought	*		-	-	-	*/*		-	-	-

f = following modal must simultaneously undergo rule.
p = preceding modal must simultaneously undergo rule.
a = affirmative form is only form attested here.
au = affirmative form is unacceptable here.
n = negative contraction is only form attested here.
nu = negative contraction is unacceptable here.
i = postsubject NP <u>might</u> and <u>ought</u> obligatorily invert order here.

Tag Question Formation

Informants	1st Modal					2nd/3rd Modal				
	A	B	C	D	E	A	B	C	D	E
might ought	*	x(n)	*	x(n)	–	*	x	?(n,s)		–
might could		*	?(n)	x(n)	*	x	x	x(n)	x(n)	*
might should		*			–	x	x			–
might would	*	–	–	–	–	*	–	–	–	–
might can	*			–	*	*	x	x(n,c)	–	*
must can	–		–	–	–	–		–	–	–
must ought	–		–	–	–	–		–	–	–
must would	–		–	–	–	–	x(a)	–	–	–
may can	*			–	*	x(a)	x(n)	*(c)	–	*
may could	*	–		–	–	*	–	x(n)	–	–
should ought	x(a)	–	x(n)	x(au)	–			–	*	?(au)	–
might should ought		–	*		–	x(n)/	–	x(n)/*	x(n)/–	
might had ought	*		–	–	–	x(n)/		–	–	

a = affirmative form is only form acceptable here.
au = affirmative form is unacceptable here.
n = negative contraction is only form attested here.
nu = negative contraction is unacceptable here.
s = shouldn't is fully acceptable here.
c = couldn't is preferable/fully acceptable here.

Quantifier Floating

Informants	Before 1st Modal					Before 2nd Modal					Before 3rd Modal				
	A	B	C	D	E	A	B	C	D	E	A	B	C	D	E
might ought	x	x	?	x(hu)	–	?	x	*	x	–	x	*	x	x	–
might could	x	x	x	x	*	*	x	*	x	*	x	x	x	x	x
might should	x	?	x	–	–	*	x	*		–	x	x	x		–
might would	x	–	–	–	–	*	–	–	–	–	x	–	–	–	–
might can	x	x	*	–	*	*	x	*	–	*	x	x	x	–	x
must can	–		–	–	–	–		–	–	–	–		–	–	–
must ought	–		–	–	–	–		–	–	–	–		–	–	–
must would	–		–	–	–	–		–	–	–	–		–	–	–
may can	x	x	x	–	*	*	x	*	–	*	x	x	x	–	x
may could	x	–	*	*	–	*	–	*		–	x	–	x		–
should ought		–	*	*	–		–	*	?(hu)	–		–	x	x(hu)	–
might should															
ought	x	–	x	*	–	*		–	x	–	*/x	–	x/*	x/x	–
might had ought		–	–	–	–		–	–	–	–		–	–	–	–

hu = intermodal <u>have</u> unacceptable here.

Niching

Informants	Before 1st Modal					Before 2nd Modal					After 2nd/3rd Modal				
	A	B	C	D	E	A	B	C	D	E	A	B	C	D	E
might ought	?	x	x		–	?	x	*	*	–		x	x	*	–
might could		x	x		x	*	x	*	*	*		x	x	*	*
might should		–	x	–	–	*	–	*	*	–			x	*	–
might would		x	x	–	x	*	x	–	–	*		?	–	–	*
might can	–		–	–	–	–		?	–	–	–		x	–	–
must can	–		–	–	–	–		–	–	–	–		–	–	–
must ought	–		–	–	–	–		–	–	–	–		–	–	–
must would	x	x	x	–	x	*	x	*	–	*	*	?(m)?	x	–	*
may can	x	–	x	–	–	*	–	*	*	–	*	–	x	–	–
may could	*	–	x	–	–	*	–	*	*	–	*	–	x	*	–
should ought						*	–	*	*	–	*	–	x	–	–
might should			x	–	–	*	–	*	*	–	*	–	x	*	–
ought		–	–	–			–	–	–		*	–	x	x/x	–
might had ought														–	–

hu = intermodal have
m = may can pronounced [mey kæn] here.

Black Speech: Lexical Evidence from *DARE*

Joan Hall

A major temptation in any investigation is to concentrate on the exotic or the unusual and in celebrating colorful finds to suppress, ignore, or even forget findings that are equally important but relatively mundane. In the study of the vocabulary of American blacks, this temptation has been fatal to a number of investigators and we have as a result glossaries of student jargon, drug use, religion, jazz, sex, crime, and the whole "street hustle," purporting to represent the speech of black America.[1] While the words in such lists are undoubtedly used by some--or even many--blacks, to imply that they form the nucleus of a black lexicon, or even that they are not used by whites engaged in the same activities (a possibility not considered by these investigators), is to capitalize on the sensational and ignore the fundamental.

A different tack, taken by some investigators, has been to comb through slave narratives and folk tales for "black" words and phrases.[2] While such works are indeed rich sources of language data and deserve to be studied carefully, the appearance of a word in such a place does not render it "black." Many of the words cited by such investigators are provably part of the normal vocabulary of white speakers in the same region. To be carried away by one's enthusiasm, then, before searching the basic reference sources, is to fail to do one's homework.

Homework, or fieldwork, is what it's all about. Before an adequate lexicon of black American English can even be attempted, comprehensive and comparable data for black and white speakers throughout the country need to be available. In addition, criteria as to what constitute "black" terms need to be established. When the Questionnaire for the <u>Dictionary of American Regional English</u> (DARE) was prepared, one of its goals was to provide this kind of broad-based data. The idea was to make the worksheets as comprehensive as possible, covering the topics of everyday living.

The questions asked by DARE fieldworkers did not address such "colorful" areas as gambling or drug use; instead, they dealt with those mundane subjects of daily life that all of us know. The 1,847 questions covered such topics as eating, working, playing, going to school, the weather, time, money, nature, friendship, courtship, and other relations among people. The informants came from 1,002 communities across the country; and the responses number approximately 2.5 million. From these responses, conclusions can be drawn not only about geographic distribution of words but also about their use by different social groups. These include distinctions among speakers of different ages, sexes, educational backgrounds, and community types, as well as different races.

In the DARE sample nationwide, 7 percent of the informants were black. Because we sought to reflect population distributions of regions, however, the percentage of black informants is greater in areas with large black populations. Therefore in Mississippi we interviewed 27 percent black informants, in Georgia 20 percent, in New York City, 28 percent. Thus the DARE materials provide comparable data from which we can begin to make generalizations about differences in black and white usage.

But how should such distinctions be made? And what words can legitimately be considered more characteristic of black speakers than white? The criteria used by DARE editors can be generalized as follows: A dictionary entry may be labeled with respect to race if it falls into one of three classes: (1) words or phrases which are used both by blacks and by whites, but demonstrably more frequently by blacks than would be expected by their proportions in the sample; 2) items used, so far as we know, only by black speakers; and (3) items that are provably or probably of African origin, whether they are now used chiefly by blacks or have been widely adopted by whites as well.

Within each of these categories, labels will be applied as they describe the data. For instance, for words for which we have much documentation, all of it from black speakers or writers, we will not hesitate to use the label among Blacks in the dictionary entry; when appropriate, we will use the label Gullah; when the evidence is preponderantly but not solely from blacks, labels such as chiefly among Blacks or especially frequent among Blacks can be applied. Other options include originally among Blacks, now more widespread, and formerly Southern, now also among Blacks in the North. For each entry, the label is tailored to fit the evidence.

For some words, DARE's evidence corroborates the work of other investigators, or simply documents what Americans as speakers and listeners know intuitively. For instance, words like dig, hip, rap, and jive are in countless glossaries as words used by blacks, and when whites use them, they do so knowing they have borrowed the terms. Other words, such as fox (an attractive woman), sharp (well dressed), boss (good, terrific), and right on (as a call of encouragement or enthusiasm), are frequently associated with black speakers, though until recently they were not regularly anthologized. All of these terms (and others) are shown by the DARE Questionnaire data to have been used, between 1965 and 1970, solely or almost solely by black informants. With the rapid spread of these words to the wider community, it is especially interesting to have stopped time (as it were) in this five-year span and to demonstrate the limited use by blacks before the dissemination. In this sense, DARE can function as a diachronic tool much sooner than was expected.

But most of the words found in DARE to be especially frequent among blacks are not of the hip, dig, and jive type. Most have not been listed in glossaries of "black" speech, and they cannot easily be categorized as to subject, for they touch almost every topic. Figures 2 through 7 give a few examples. (DARE's computer-drawn maps have been distorted to reflect the country's population density, but the general shapes of the states have been retained. Figure 1 provides orientation.) In figures 2 to 5 are examples of the first class of words mentioned earlier: terms used by blacks and whites alike, but more frequently by blacks than would have been expected. Figure 2 shows the phrase calling the hogs and a few variants: calling hogs from the bottom, calling pigs, calling (the) cows, and calling the dogs. These responses all came in answer to "What joking expressions do you have around here for snoring?" The phrase calling the hogs is fairly widespread geographically, but the proportions of black and white informants are not what would have been expected. Of the informants who responded to this question, 6 percent were black, but of the informants who used this response, 61 percent were black. In the dictionary, then, this entry can safely be labeled chiefly among Blacks.

Figure 3 illustrates the distribution of hickey. There is much documentation for this word, in DARE and elsewhere, in the sense of a pimple, and there were 234 DARE informants who used the word as a term for "a mark on the skin where somebody has sucked it hard and brought the blood to the surface." For both of these senses, the word hickey was especially frequent among young informants. But the distribution on the map is for still another sense: "a lump that comes up on your head when you get a sharp blow or knock." In this meaning, it is still especially common among young speakers, but is also disproportionately frequent among blacks. Forty-nine percent of the forty-one informants are black, against 7 percent in the survey for this question.

The topic of children's games proved fruitful, and numerous maps in the dictionary will show regional and social variants in names of games. Figure 4 shows the informants who gave the name Little Sally Walker in response to the question about games in which children form a ring and either sing or recite a rhyme. This map too shows significant racial distribution, with 58 percent of the thirty-one informants being black, which compares to 6 percent for blacks who answered the question. A second map, showing geographic distribution, will probably also go in the dictionary, since the name Little Sally Water (rather than Walker) is chiefly an eastern term, especially common in Pennsylvania.

Figure 5 shows an expression which is still something of an etymological puzzle. The phrases dead cat on the line and dead cat on the line behind me came in response to "When you suspect that somebody is trying to deceive you, or that something is going on behind your back, you say, 'There's _____.'" Common responses were: There's something rotten in Denmark (or in the state of Denmark), There's a nigger in the woodpile, or There's something fishy going on. But twenty-one informants, fourteen of them black, responded There's a dead cat on the line. None of the DARE staff had heard this expression, and all were puzzled as to what kind of cat might be involved and what sort of line. A fishing line, or telephone line? Did cat mean a feline? a catfish? a person?

In an attempt to find out, we put a query in the October 1977 issue of the Newsletter of the American Dialect Society, and a number of people responded. The "cat," one person said, is someone who listens in on a telephone party line, and the phrase is intended to warn callers to be circumspect in what they say. But on questioning the individual further, we found that he did not know the expression and that his "explanation" was pure speculation. Another fanciful suggestion was that the "line" is a Congo line, while the "dead cat" is a dancer who doesn't know the right steps. A more convincing explanation came from a Louisiana fisherman, who said the "cat" is a catfish and the "line" a trot line. If a person noticed dead fish on a neighbor's lines, he knew something had prevented the neighbor from tending to his business, and someone ought to see if he needed help. So far, that's our best guess. Alternative explanations from those familiar with the phrase are still welcome, however.

The second category of words--those attested only in the speech of blacks--is illustrated by figures 6 and 7. Figure 6 shows one response to the question "If you meet somebody who used to be a friend, and he pretends not to know you [you might say]: 'When I met him on the street he _____.'" Sixteen informants, all of them black, said "When I met him on the street he igged me." Presumably from ignore, the word was attested as early as 1946 in Mezz Mezzrow's Really The Blues and has been included in a number of fairly recent books on black speech, including Smitherman's Talkin and Testifyin. That the word is productive in terms of English use is demonstrated by its shift from verb to noun. In the DARE materials, we have an informant who says of a woman who refuses a proposal, "She gave him the igg"; and Smitherman includes the phrase "Put the ig on," meaning to ignore someone.

Figure 7 represents informants who gave the responses riding a pony, riding ponies or pony-riding to the words for cheating in school examinations. While the term pony for a crib sheet has been used in this country at least since 1832, the phrase riding a pony is used, so far as our materials show, only by black speakers.[3]

Although maps such as figures 6 and 7 are striking illustrations, DARE will not include maps for most of the terms used solely by blacks, for the numbers of informants are small enough to be itemized in the entry. But small numbers do not diminish the importance of such entries. When only 7 percent of the informants in the sample as a whole are black and all who use the term are black (whether 15, 10, or 5), the implication that race is a determining factor cannot be ignored. Therefore, items such as in the streets (gadding around), with fourteen black informants; looking clean (attractive), with eight; blood (wine), with seven; chicken eater (preacher), with five; and hard liver (a result of excessive drinking), with four, will all be entered in the dictionary with the social label among Blacks. Where we have only two or three informants, the usual practice is not to apply the label unless there are corroborating sources; rather, we add a bracketed statement in the entry, saying that both or all the informants are black. In that way, where evidence is sketchy, readers can draw their own conclusions.

The third category, words that have African sources, includes both widely used examples, and, at the other extreme, the well known words which are rather tentatively grouped here and require more investigation. At the sure end of the scale we have, of course, words like buckra, cooter, goober, juke, pinder, and hoodoo, which have been adopted by the general population in the South and are recognized (if not used) by Americans in other regions. Less widely used, but well documented, are such words as badmouth, bloodynoun, cush, dayclean, det rain (folk-etymologized as "death rain"), jigger, pinto, table-tapper, and yard-ax. DARE's contribution is perhaps most important where little other evidence has been gathered, but use by our informants illustrates currency of a term.

In some cases, exact etymologies have not been determined, but the probability of African sources must be pursued. For instance, crack one's side (or sides), meaning "to laugh hard," is given by twenty informants, twelve of them black. (We have two other citations, both in the work of J. Mason Brewer, that represent the speech of blacks.) It is not only the predominant use by blacks, however, but also the parallelism with African-based phrases--such as crack one's breath (to speak) and suck one's teeth (as an indication of scorn)--which suggests the need to check African sources further. Another phrase with the same structure, break one's leg (or toe), meaning "to become pregnant," is given by six black and four white informants. It also occurs in a wordlist for east Alabama and west Georgia in 1908 and has a parallel in Jamaican English, where broke-foot means the first pregnancy of

an unwed young woman. A final idiom of similar form is to have
one's nose open, meaning to be in love or sexually desirous. It is
used by five black DARE informants, has been noted in McDavid's
version of Mencken's American Language (in a section on jive
talk), and is in several recent collections of black speech.

A word for which we have found a highly probable African
source is ninnies, which also occurs in the compound ninnie jugs,
meaning a woman's breasts. Of our thirteen informants, seven are
black or say that the word is used by blacks. The likely source is
the Mende word [ɲinɪ], "female breast, udder." A final example
which seems to be of African origin, but whose precise source or
sources haven't been found, is kittledee, which came in response
to the question about "creatures that make a clicking or shrilling
or chirping kind of sound." Seven black informants in coastal
states from Mississippi to Virginia gave the term. The similarity to
katydid is striking--but why, if kittledee is simply a phonological
variant of katydid, should all informants be black? Etymological
suggestions for any of these words are welcomed.

Earlier I mentioned that the words we have found at DARE to
be especially frequent among blacks are difficult to categorize
because they are so diverse. In spite of that, I should like to categorize some of them, to illustrate their number and variety. I will
start with clothing. We had brads (metal tips on shoes), bully
woolies (underwear), gall shirt (an undergarment for women), your
garage door is open and your ice-box is open (to warn a man that
his fly is not closed), hip-slip (a woman's half-slip), keen(-toed)
shoes (pointed-toe shoes), and vines for clothing in general. In
appearance, someone might be buck-eyed or parrot-toed, have a
keen nose, broken veins, nature bumps, or a blue eye. On the other
hand, if a man is attractive or well dressed, he is said to be
lookin' clean. To describe people or characterize their attitudes,
we have Mr. It (someone who thinks highly of himself), a peace-
breaker (a feisty person), cheese-eater (an apple-polisher), crumb-
crusher (a child), and clock-head (for one who seems a bit
"cuckoo"). An easygoing person is don't-care-ish, a go-getter is
smart, one who is particular is ticky, and a deadbeat is a beater
or someone you wouldn't trust behind a dime or behind a broom-
straw.

The names of dances which were mentioned only or almost
solely by black informants include ball and jack, cold duck,
football, funky Broadway, funky chicken, James Brown, moonwalk,
popcorn, and sissy or sophisticated sissy. Contrary to my expectation, I did not find that a core group of young black informants
was giving all the dance names; the informants were scattered
geographically and all age groups were represented. The same was
true for names of card games, which include bid whist, dirty
hearts, pitty-pat, po-ke-no (perhaps a trade name, though descriptions of the game varied), skin, and straight whist.

Finally, as examples of terms for objects around the house, we have company room (living room or family room), crabapple switch (pocketknife), plantation matches (the kind you can strike anywhere), struggle-buggy (a jalopy), swish broom (a whisk broom), night-pot (a chamber pot), lookers (for glasses), and, for false teeth, dead man teeth or dead man choppers, I-bought-you teeth, and S.I.B. or S.S.B. for (you guessed it) "some I bought" or "some she bought."

From this sampling of DARE data, it is evident that the kinds of words that are characteristic of "black" speech encompass every aspect of daily living in America. The exotic glossaries and the wordlists of underground or seamy activities do a disservice to black people when impressionable or naive readers fail to see beyond the contents of such a book. While the materials gathered for DARE cannot be said to be exhaustive, they come closer to providing a comprehensive collection than any other study that has yet been undertaken. If they in turn serve as an impetus to further systematic and careful investigation, the work of the "harmless drudges" at DARE will have been doubly rewarding.

NOTES

[1] See, for example, Clarence Major, Dictionary of Afro-American Slang (New York: International Publishers, 1970); Hermese E. Roberts, The Third Ear: A Black Glossary (Chicago: English-Language Institute of America, 1971); David Claerbaut, Black Jargon in White America (Grand Rapids, Mich.: William B. Eerdmans Publishing Co., 1972); J.L. Dillard, Lexicon of Black English (New York: Seabury Press, 1977).

[2] See the works of J. Mason Brewer, such as The Word on the Brazos (Austin: University of Texas Press, 1953) and Dog Ghosts, and other Texas Negro Folk Tales (Austin: University of Texas Press, 1958), and Martha Emmons, Deep Like the Rivers (Austin, Tex.: Encino Press, 1969).

[3] A participant in the Columbia conference reported the use of the phrase among whites in Cleveland in the 1960s.

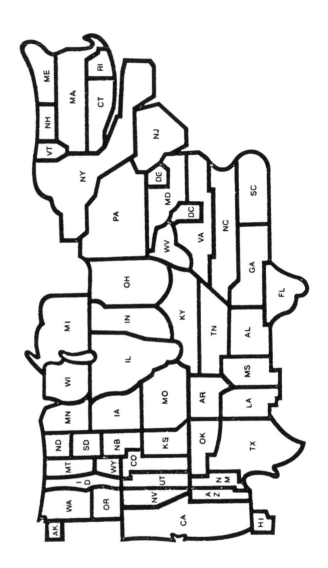

Figure 1 Key to DARE Maps

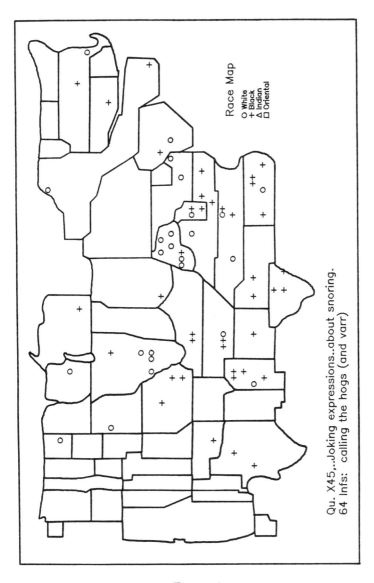

Figure 2
Distribution of <u>Calling</u> <u>the</u> <u>Hogs</u> and Its Variants

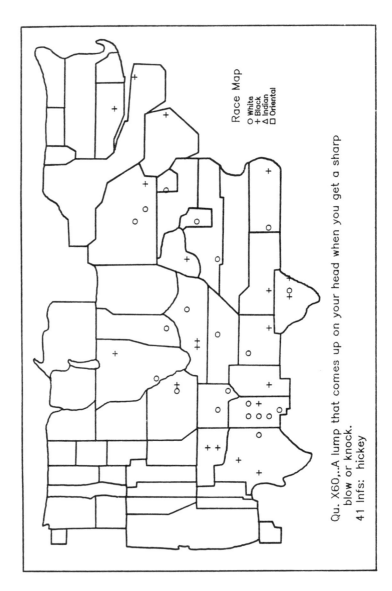

Figure 3
Distribution of Hickey

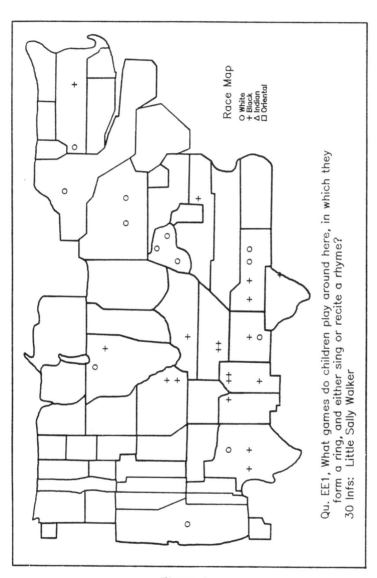

Figure 4
Distribution of <u>Little</u> <u>Sally</u> <u>Walker</u>

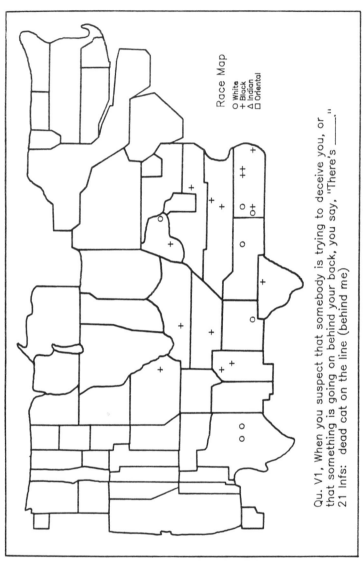

Figure 5
Distribution of Dead Cat on the Line

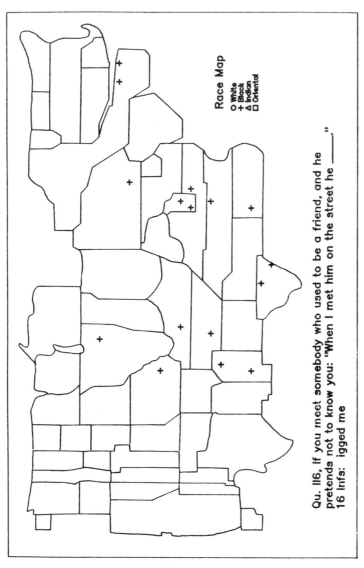

Figure 6
Distribution of <u>Igged</u> <u>Me</u>

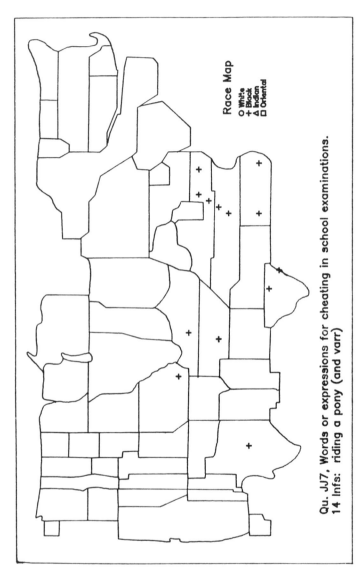

Figure 7
Distribution of Riding a Pony and Its Variants

Mixed Dialects in the Composition Classroom

Jerrie Scott

Discussions of mixed dialects or dialect variation in the composition classroom usually focus on the mixing of two social dialects. Corder 1974 makes a distinction between social dialects, which represent shared language rules of a social group, and idiosyncratic dialects, which represent rules particular to an individual, especially in a language learning situation. Such rules are distinct from the idiolect, for the idiolect still represents shared rules of social dialects. In this paper, I intend to show that patterns found in the oral and written compositions of a group of black college freshmen represent not just a mixture of two social dialects but a mixture of social and idiosyncratic dialects. Although contrastive patterns of two social dialects, black English (BE) and standard English (SE), will be discussed, attention is given primarily to those patterns that represent the idiosyncratic component of dialect mixture. The term intralectal patterns (IL) will refer to patterns that reflect the formation of idiosyncratic rules, in other words--patterns that cannot be accounted for on the basis of rules posited for either of the social dialects.

This paper presents a

1. Rationale for examining intralectal patterns in studies of dialect mixture,

2. Description of intralectal patterns that occurred in data from a study that investigated relationships between spoken and written language,

3. Summary of research findings relevant to the possible sources of intralectal patterns, and

4. Discussion of implications of research findings for the dialect-interference theory and for the contrastive analysis approach to language instruction.

Rationale for Examining Intralectal Patterns

There are at least three important reasons for examining intralectal patterns in studies of dialect variation. First, there is evidence that such patterns have been found in studies of the language of black students. For example, in Sternglass's description of features in the written language of black and white students, she lists hypercorrect articles as well as two other patterns of article use, article absence, and nonstandard a/an (Sternglass 1974). She also lists hypercorrect prepositions, preposition absence, and nonstandard prepositions.

"Hypercorrect" has also been used by others to refer to these nonnative/nontarget lect patterns. Fasold and Wolfram 1970 use "hypercorrect" to describe the use of verb -s with subjects other than third person (e.g., I walks, you walks, they walks) and with nonfinite verbs (e.g., They want to goes). Although the hypercorrect designation for verb -s with all persons has been questioned (Rickford 1974, Scott 1973, Brewer, this volume), the designation itself provides evidence that other investigators have noted the occurrence of features that cannot easily be classified as BE, SE, or any other variety of American English.

The second reason for examining intralectal patterns has to do with findings in research on second-language learning. Sentences such as Did he comed? and I can to speak French represent a class of errors that can be linked to rules in neither the learner's mother tongue nor the target language (Richards 1974). Richards calls such errors "intralingual errors"; they are frequently produced by students who are learning English, regardless of their language background. Richards notes further that "intralingual and developmental errors reflect the learner's competence at a particular stage and illustrate some of the general characteristics of language acquisition" (1974:173). Intralingual errors provide information not only about language-learning processes but also about language instruction. In fact, Richards has proposed that more attention be given to instructional interference. Thus a more thorough investigation of the intralectal patterns produced by black students could lead to a better understanding of the processes involved in learning to speak or write a second dialect and of the procedures needed to improve language instruction for student writers who are speakers of nonmainstream dialects.

Finally, analyses of intralectal patterns may lead to useful information about transitional stages in the language-learning process. It is important to consider the possible stages in shifting from BE to SE because we tend to assume that the movement toward "bidialectalism" represents a simple switch from one social dialect to another. However, from studies of both first- and second-language acquisition we find convincing evidence that language learning takes place in stages. One assumes that the move toward bidialectalism also occurs in stages. When we add the very complicated dimension of learning-to-write, we expect to find even more evidence of stages in the development of language competence. Intralectal patterns may provide specific information about stages in the development of oral and written language competence, particularly for learners who speak nonmainstream dialects of English.

Description of Intralectal Patterns

Given these three reasons for examining intralectal patterns in studies of dialect variation, the next important question is "What, if anything, can these intralectal patterns tell us about language learning?" I suggest that intralectal patterns can be used to identify rules of standard English that students do not fully understand. My argument is based on data from a group of forty black college freshmen, all first-term college students, who had been designated for remedial writing instruction. Thirty-nine of the forty students had attended high school in Florida, and thirty-six had attended both elementary and secondary school in Florida. These three characteristics of the subjects--that is, the fact that they were black, unskilled writers who grew up in the South--are certain to have influenced the kinds of patterns in my data. Since the students who produced the patterns were black, the variety of English associated with their ethnic group, black English, serves as the basis for the discussion of rule formation processes. The kinds of language samples elicited could also have influenced the patterns that students produced. Students were asked to read a selection, "Roots" (a narrative account of Alex Haley's experience writing the book Roots), to summarize the selection orally, and to summarize the selection in writing. Thus the study was designed to control for speech style and discourse mode, a control that has generally not been used in other studies.

Five patterns that could be placed in the intralectal category were found:

A. Modals	Mod-past + Ved	"Then he would returned to the states to make information lucid."
B. Modals	Mod-pres + Ved	"There Alex Haley asked many questions to the senior natives and his interpretors will interpreted what they answered."

C. Infinitives   To + Ved   "The only thing he cared about was his ambition to trac<u>ed</u> his family as far back as possible."

D. Plural Nouns   N-pl + /N-pl + s   "The actual characters did a very fairly well job touching many peopl<u>es</u> and reaching them."

E. Subject-Verb   Subj-sg + were   "The book, <u>Roots</u>, wasn't an
   Agreement   easy book to write because there <u>were</u> so many <u>informa-</u>
<u>tion</u> to be obtained."

"Like many other Africans, <u>Kunta were</u> taken to Amer-ica, the U.S., where . . ."

The overinflected verb forms in samples A, B, and C suggest that the students were confused about the constraints on rules that govern the presence and absence of the -<u>ed</u> suffix and, more specifically, how to construct verb phrases that contain modal auxiliaries and verbal phrases that contain infinitive forms. Discussions of modal auxiliaries in nonmainstream dialects have focused primarily on double modal constructions (e.g., <u>might could go</u>). Obviously the double modal is not the problem here. In fact, there are no double modals in the language samples, suggesting that double modals are not part of the students' formal language system. The variable occurrence of -<u>ed</u> suffixes in BE, a feature that might have some bearing on the problem, has been discussed by others. Fasold and Wolfram (1970:44) describe one of the favored environments for -<u>ed</u> absence as follows:

> In Negro dialect, when the addition of the -<u>ed</u> suffix results in either a voiced or voiceless cluster, the cluster may be reduced by removing the final member of the cluster. This affects -ed when it functions as a past tense marker . . . , a participle . . . , or an adjective . . . , although its association with the past tense is the most frequent.

What is most interesting about samples A, B, and C is that the overinflected -<u>ed</u> suffixes could have been deleted or reduced, according to the phonological rules posited to account for black speakers' use of -<u>ed</u> suffixes. In sample A, <u>returned</u> ends with two voiced consonants, /nd/, and in sample C, <u>traced</u> ends with two voiceless consonants, /st/; the cluster in both could have been reduced, leaving no marker for the -<u>ed</u> suffix. In B, the bisyllabic

/ɨd/ could have been deleted, especially since it occurs before a consonant (Fasold 1972). The correct standard English form would have been generated, if not by the correct rules. We suspect, then, that the students were not simply attempting to produce SE forms but much more likely were attempting to form SE rules.

The overinflected noun form in sample D suggests that students were confused about the constraints that govern the presence and absence of -s plural forms in SE. Concerning the inflection of irregular nouns or the use of "double plurals," Fasold and Wolfram (1970:78-79) explain that

> Where standard English forms plurals irregularly, Negro dialect may add the -s suffix to the irregular plural (peoples, childrens). A possible historical reason relates to an earlier stage of Negro dialect in which the plural category was not part of the grammar. In learning standard English, speakers of the dialect tended to add the -s suffix to words which were already pluralized in an irregular way. These doubly pluralized words became fossilized and are preserved to the present.

This explanation supports the IL classification assigned to the overinflected nouns, for as Fasold and Wolfram suggest, such patterns are best explained in relation to language-learning processes and fossilized structures.

The concept of fossilization, as explained by Selinker, is also quite useful here. In his discussion of interlanguage structures and psycholinguistic processes in second-language learning, Selinker (1972:215) describes fossilized structures as:

> linguistic items, rules as subsystems which speakers of a particular NL [native language] will tend to keep in their IL [interlanguage] relative to a particular TL [target language] no matter what the age of the learner or amount of explanation he receives in the TL.

This does not mean that the learner cannot understand the rules of the target language; it means that even after the rule is understood, "fossilizable structures tend to remain as potential performance" (p. 215). They are most likely to emerge, Selinker notes, when the learner's attention is "focused upon new and difficult intellectual subject matter or when he is in a state of anxiety or other excitement, and sometimes when he is in a state of relaxation" (p. 215). Selinker is careful to explain that this type of "backsliding" is not toward the speaker's native language but toward an IL or an idiosyncratic norm. Certainly the conditions under which language samples were elicited in this study were conducive to the production of fossilized structures. Moreover, sociolinguistic evidence suggests that blacks who use these overinflected plural forms are not backsliding toward normative BE patterns. The overinflected noun forms are generally considered ungrammatical by black people and are associated with "talking proper," which refers to unnecessarily hypercorrect, pretentious uses of language.

Beyond these theoretical and sociolinguistic explanations of the noun-plural pattern, we might look at the noun plural pattern in relation to another posited rule for accounting for noun pluralization in BE. In noun-phrase constructions, quantifiers can mark plurality, making it unnecessary to inflect the noun, and this rule would account for structures such as many year and six year old. Similar constructions were found frequently in the language samples. Funkhouser 1973 reports that over half of the uninflected nouns that occurred in the written samples of the black students in his study consisted of a plural quantifier or numeral followed by a noun. Although some have claimed that the quantifier is the main conditioning factor in the presence or absence of -s plural suffixes, Fasold and Wolfram (1970:78) question the claim:

> For some speakers of Southern Negro dialect, particularly young children, the plural suffix is almost always absent and may well not be part of the grammar of their dialect at all. The occasional claim that the plural suffix may only be absent when the plural noun is preceded by a quantifier (two, several, etc.), and not otherwise, is invalid.

Again, though, if BE rules had been used to generate the structures, the correct SE noun plural patterns would have been generated, if not by the correct SE rules.

One other potential problem with noun-phrase constructions is found in sample E: many information. This construction suggests that students may not fully understand the selection restraints for combining determiners with noncount nouns. That is, the quantifier many cannot be followed by a noncount noun such as information. We would need to choose a different determiner (e.g., much = much information) or a different noun (e.g., kinds of information = many kinds of information). This inappropriate combination may have influenced the application of the subject-verb agreement rule, which is the focal point of pattern E. In pattern E the verb agrees with plurality, as signaled by the quantifier many, but the verb does not agree with the headword information.

The overinflected verb forms in sample E suggest confusion in the application of SE rules for subject-verb agreement. For subject-verb agreement patterns in BE, Fasold and Wolfram (1970:69) offer the following:

> Some speakers show no person-number agreement when full forms of to be are used. The past tense form is was

regardless of the subject, giving sentences like <u>They was</u> <u>there</u>, <u>You was there</u>, etc.

The use of <u>were</u> with singular subjects has been noted for black speakers. For example, Schrock (this volume) found many uses of <u>were</u> with <u>I</u>. We might have another example of a fossilized structure, for again the use of <u>I were</u>, like the use of <u>many peoples</u>, is generally associated with the "trying to talk proper" by blacks. The structure is both nonnormative according to BE usage and incorrect according to SE usage. The SE subject-verb agreement rules are complicated by the various syntactic positions of the subject and by the variant forms of irregular verbs. Nevertheless, this analysis illustrates that we can gain more specific information about the aspects of SE rules that students do not understand by examining the IL patterns.

Two important points need to be considered in relation to the IL patterns. First, they suggest aspects of SE rules that are not fully understood by students. Although this study focused on language use by black students, it is quite possible that any group of learners develops idiosyncratic rules and produces patterns that cannot be accounted for within the rule system of a social dialect. Second, the IL patterns produced by these black students suggest that the use of patterns from two different social dialects does not represent a simple feature-matching process. Rather, the IL patterns suggest that students were attempting to form rules, and possibly even abandoning rules, that might have yielded a target structure.

The contrast between the formation of rules and the matching of features raises an interesting empirical question: "Can different rules yield the same form?" If so, how do learners discover the differences and adjust the rules of their language system to accommodate the differences? This contrast between feature matching and rule formations also raises an interesting pedagogical question: "How well can structure-oriented instruction accommodate the needs of a rule-oriented language-learning system?"

Source of Intralectal Patterns

The dialect-interference theory, which has served as the basis of most of the research on dialect and learning, identifies spoken language as the main source of the non-SE patterns produced by speakers of nonmainstream dialects and describes such patterns as playing an intrusive role in the learner's development of competence in the second dialect. As explained by Hartwell,

The term "dialect interference" in writing, as conventionally used, would seem to have the following meaning: the surface features of the spoken dialects of some native speakers of English interfere with, or inhibit, the production, in writing, of the correct forms of the accepted orthography (Edited American English or EAE) [1980:101].

This overly simplified, conventional interpretation of the term "dialect interference" has created more problems than it has solved (Scott 1981). Nevertheless, Hartwell's definition makes clear the need to consider whether intralectal patterns that occur in writing can be attributed to spoken language. Since the intralectal patterns are by definition nonnormative, one might expect them to be less susceptible to influence from speech than either BE or SE patterns.

Questions about the influence of spoken language on written language patterns are deceptively complex. Clearly, some of the same non-SE patterns occur in the writing of students from different social or ethnic groups. Sternglass 1974 finds, for example, that black and white students produce the same type of non-SE patterns in their writing, but that black students produce more error patterns than white students. In other words, responses by the two groups are quantitatively different but not qualitatively different.

Does the absence of qualitative differences suggest that the source of the non-SE patterns is the same for both groups? Although Sternglass does not directly address this question, she questions the need for special or separate language instruction for the two groups. From the work of variation theorists (Labov 1972a, Fasold 1972), we now know that quantitative differences can be quite important in differentiating social dialects. The quantitative-qualitative distinction does not completely differentiate social dialects, and we might assume that the distinction is incapable of differentiating sources of non-SE patterns in writing.

Whiteman 1981 offers a possible solution to this problem. In her study of relationships between black and white students' use of oral and written language, Whiteman considers quantitative differences in her analysis of data. She reasons that if percentages of usage in speech are equal to or greater than percentages in writing, the written pattern can be attributed to influence from speech. For example:

Verbal -s was absent (e.g., He go- to the pool every day in the summer) 30.8% of the time in the writing of the white students, but only 14.5% of the time in their speech. [1981:159]

Whiteman concludes that the occurrence of this feature in white students' writing "cannot be attributed solely to dialect influence" (p. 159). In other words, the feature is not simply transferred from speech to writing. One can readily see that equal usage in speech and writing provides evidence of transfer: the learner simply produces the pattern with the same frequency in both speech and writing. However, the rationale for higher percentages of use in speech than in writing, as evidence of transfer, is not so readily apparent. Although not discussed by Whiteman, a possible and quite plausible explanation has to do with modality and style. In general, we would expect to find fewer non-SE features in writing than in speech, and we would expect the differences to be even greater when the style used in speech differs from the style used in writing. In Whiteman's study, informal language was elicited for speech samples and formal language was elicited for the writing samples. Unlike Whiteman's study, formal language was elicited for both speech and writing for this study; Whiteman's guidelines for interpreting the data were therefore modified.

Similar, rather than identical, percentages of use in speech and writing were taken as evidence that the written pattern was influenced by speech. "Similar" was operationally defined in terms of levels of usage: levels of 50 percent or more were characterized as [+dominant], and levels less than 50 percent were characterized as [-dominant]. Patterns that shared dominance features in speech and writing were classed as transfer--that is, the pattern in writing could be attributed to speech; patterns that did not share dominance features in speech and writing were classed as nontransfer--that is, the pattern in writing could not be attributed to speech.

Before we discuss the results of these analyses of intralectal patterns, two other methodological procedures should be mentioned. In quantifying the data, it was important to use responses of only those subjects who produced intralectal patterns. The use of total group data for this analysis would have resulted in an aggregation of responses that could obscure information about the source of IL patterns. Only sixteen of the forty subjects produced IL patterns; their responses were extracted from the data for the total group and quantified. Second, the standard linguistic procedure for arriving at usage levels was used: the number of occurrences of a given pattern was divided by the number of possible occurrences of the pattern. In counting the possible occurrences, it was necessary to combine IL representations of a pattern with the corresponding BE and SE representations of the same pattern. Table 1 shows the usage levels for four constructions: (1) modal-auxiliary, with SE and IL variants; (2) verbal-infinitive, with SE and IL variants; (3) noun-plural, with SE, IL, and BE variants; and (4) subject-verb agreement (plural subjects with past tense forms of be), with SE, IL, and BE variants.

Focusing on whether IL patterns in writing can be attributed to speech, we can make two important observations. First, the IL variants are no more susceptible to influence from speech than the other two variants. While the IL variants of the modal-auxiliary and verbal-infinitive patterns cannot be attributed to speech, the IL variants of the noun-plural and subject-verb agreement patterns can be attributed to influence from speech (compare Ib and IIb to IIIb and IVb). Notice that the IL variants of the modal-auxiliary and verbal-infinitive patterns are classed as nontransfer (NT), whereas the IL variants of the noun-plural and subject-verb agreement patterns are classed as transfer (T). Like the IL variants, the BE and SE variants are sometimes attributable to speech, but other times are not.

The second observation is that IL patterns vary either with SE, as in the modal-auxiliary and verbal infinitive patterns, or with BE and SE, as in the noun-plural and subject-verb agreement patterns, but not with BE. The IL patterns could very well signal that rules are undergoing change and that the change is toward SE norms. As a signal of rule change, the IL variants may be unique, but our results do not support a unique source for the IL patterns. If all non-SE patterns in writing are not attributable to speech, how are they to be accounted for?

With this question in mind, it is useful to examine the data in table 1 more carefully. These data show that students' production of the modal-auxiliary and verbal-infinitive patterns was quite similar: all three variants were classed as nontransfer. Although the SE variable, which we assume to be the target structure, had +dominant usage in speech, it was not transferred to writing. Had the rules that govern the use of modal-auxiliaries and verbal-infinitives been stable, students would not have experienced difficulty generating the correct target structure. These results suggest that students inspect SE forms and consciously attempt to form rules for generating the correct SE forms. This process I will call "monitoring," for the SE forms must continue to be inspected and the rules in the language system must continue to be adjusted until the learner is able to generate the appropriate target structure. Since the IL variants have [+dominant] usage in writing, we can assume that more attention is given to rule adjustments when students are writing than when they are reading.

In the noun-plural pattern, all three variants were classed as transfer. The SE variant, with its [+dominant] usage in speech and writing, indicates that the SE rules dominate students' production of noun-plural patterns. However, since all three variants are transferred from speech to writing, there is reason to believe that their occurrence in writing is not consciously controlled by the students. There is also reason to believe that the SE rules are not consciously formed or learned; rather, the SE rules are acquired by the students.

These results suggest that the students have acquired rules for constructing noun-plural patterns which they unconsciously use in both their speech and writing. This process, which I will call "transferring," is explained quite well by the dialect-interference theory, but it is important to note that transfer is linked here to unconscious language learning, or acquisition, rather than to conscious language learning.

Moving to the subject-verb agreement pattern, we note that all variants are classed in the same way: the IL and BE variants are classed as transfer, but the SE variant is classed as nontransfer. Interestingly, the SE variant has [+dominant] usage in writing but [-dominant] usage in speech, indicating that the SE rules are more often applied correctly when students are writing than when they are speaking. Apparently, students are consciously aware of some of the SE rules for subject-verb agreement and are able to apply these rules correctly, if given enough time.

This process--the conscious application of learned rules--I will refer to as "editing." Notice, however, that the non-SE variants are being transferred from speech to writing, suggesting that students have not learned all the SE rules that govern subject-verb agreement constructions. While the classification of IL and BE patterns in the subject-verb agreement constructions supports the dialect-interference theory, without giving attention to the usage of SE patterns, it is not possible to explain the differential responses to noun-plural and subject-verb agreement patterns. That is, the implication of my explanations is that the noun-plural rules are acquired whereas the subject-verb agreement rules are learned.

I have suggested that some non-SE patterns that occur in writing can be attributed to speech--specifically the non-SE variants for noun-plural and subject-verb agreement patterns. But other non-SE variants in writing cannot be attributed to speech--specifically the non-SE variants for modal auxiliary and verbal-infinitive patterns. While the IL patterns seem to be unique in that they signal rule changes in the learners' language system, the IL patterns are not unique with respect to their source. In other words, IL patterns provide no new information about sources other than speech that influence patterns produced in writing. Rather, when the three variant representations of a pattern are considered in relation to each other, we can see that, in considering speech as a source of non-SE patterns in writing, we might consider the transfer process as only one factor that influences the use of patterns in speech and in writing.

For patterns that are not attributable to speech, the nontransfer patterns, we need to consider at least two other processes that influence language use: monitoring and editing. Both processes require conscious involvement in the production of language patterns. Monitoring, as defined here, involves conscious rule-formation processes; editing involves conscious rule applications.

In contrast, transferring involves unconscious rule formations and applications, and only transferring is accounted for by the dialect-interference theory.

Implications

Because this study was designed to be exploratory and descriptive, the findings and conclusions are tentative. One of the
greatest benefits of the study is that it yields conclusions that
have specific implications for further research. The method that
was used to distinguish between transfer and nontransfer patterns
needs to be applied to other data. We have made no attempt to
generalize the findings to other populations, but we need to know
if the non-SE variants for the modal-auxiliary and verbal infinitive
patterns will emerge as nontransfer patterns for other groups or if
the non-SE variants for the noun-plural and subject-verb agreement patterns will emerge as transfer patterns for other groups. In
essence, further research should make it possible to find out
whether certain structural patterns are more susceptible to influence from speech than others. The three language-production
processes--transferring, monitoring, and editing--need to be
examined further, for these processes may represent stages in
language learning which are comparable to stages in learning a
second dialect or developing writing competence. Concerning the
latter, Kroll 1981 identifies four phases in the development of
writing competence: (1) preparation; (2) consolidation, when writing relies heavily on spoken language; (3) differentiation, when
spoken and written language are distinguished; and (4) integration,
the selective use of spoken language patterns in writing.

The implication for theory that emerges directly from this
study is that the dialect-interference theory needs to be reexam-
ined, particularly with respect to claims about interference phenomena in writing. I have suggested that the dialect-interference
theory correctly predicts transfer from speech to writing for some
patterns, but fails to account for other factors that influence the
use of non-SE patterns in writing.

Theoretical formulations about dialect interference in writing
are complicated by three other problems. First, we do not have a
theory of second-dialect learning. Second, only recently have we
had theories that account for how writers, whether speakers of
mainstream or nonmainstream dialects, use speech when they
perform writing tasks (de Beaugrande 1980, Daiute 1981). Third,
questions are raised about whether non-SE patterns can be best
explained on the basis of relationships between speech differences
and writing or between reading deficiencies and writing.

Hartwell, who offers the print-code hypothesis which focuses
on relationships between reading and writing, argues that "all
apparent dialect interference in writing is reading-related, reflecting partial mastery of the print code" (1980:113). The findings of
this study suggest that not all non-SE patterns can be attributed
to speech, but some can. The print-code hypothesis may represent
an overly simplified explanation of non-SE patterns in writing, for
speech is certain to have some influence on patterns produced in

writing. Hartwell goes on, however, to use the print-code hypothesis to support his argument that pedagogies for teaching writing skills to native speakers of English that assume such interference are theoretically wrong, pedagogically unsound, and socially unwise (1980:101).

To some extent, our findings support Hartwell's claim about pedagogies. Rather than suggesting that the pedagogies are completely wrong, the data suggest that the pedagogical guidelines are too narrow in their focus. Following the guidelines established in the contrastive analysis approach to second-language teaching, instructional guidelines for teaching nonmainstream dialect speakers have been based on contrastive analysis of two social dialects. Assuming, as did Lado, that "those elements that are similar to his [the learner's] native language will be simple for him, and those elements that are different will be difficult" (1957:2), proponents of the contrastive approach to second-language teaching believed that contrastive patterns in the two language systems could be used to identify patterns that would be difficult to learn. In these guidelines for instruction, there is obviously no place for the idiosyncratic patterns that are produced by the learner. Our findings suggest that the idiosyncratic patterns provide specific information about rules in the target dialect that are not understood by the learner; consequently, failure to consider intralectal patterns in establishing guidelines for language instruction limits the instruction to a focus on contrast between two social dialects.

A second limitation of the contrastive approach is implied by findings of this study. The IL patterns provide evidence that the learner attempts to form rules about patterns in the target dialect. However, the contrastive analysis approach has encouraged the use of structure-oriented, rather than rule-oriented, language instruction. The IL patterns in this study imply that more attention needs to be given to the kinds of patterns that receive attention in the classroom. For example, the modal auxiliary patterns that occurred as nontarget dialect patterns did not indicate the need for instruction based on the use of double modals--a construction that receives a good deal of attention whether one uses traditional language instruction for writers or attempts to use a contrastive approach. Rather, the modal-auxiliary patterns in the data indicate that the students were confused about constraints that govern the use of -ed suffixes.

In addition, more attention needs to be given to the manner in which rules are explained to nonnative speakers of the target dialect. For example, the familiar rule, "a singular subject takes a plural verb" (i.e., a subject without an -s ending requires a verb that has an -s ending), is difficult to apply since it erroneously implies that the -s morpheme marks plurality for both nouns and verbs. One could argue that the rule sounds more like a subject-verb disagreement rule than a subject-verb agreement rule. Unless the learner knows the rule implicitly, as one expects of speakers of mainstream dialects, the rule, as expressed above, is difficult to learn and even more difficult to apply. It has been suggested that the distinction between implicit and explicit access to rules be taken into consideration in planning language instruction. Since it has also been suggested that the way in which rules are taught influences the formulation of idiosyncratic rules by learners (Richards 1974), and since the intralectal patterns are viewed here as idiosyncratic, there is clearly a need for instructional guidelines that consider the possible influence of language instruction in general and of explanations of rules in particular on the formation of idiosyncratic rules.

Thus the contrastive approach to language instruction is limited in three ways. First, intralectal patterns are not included among the patterns that are used to predict difficulties of learners. Second, the approach encourages the use of language instruction that emphasizes the matching of surface features, rather than the learning of rules, and that treats language learning as an imitative rather than a generative process. Third, the contrastive approach is limited in that it fails to offer a different approach to teaching.

The new pedagogical guidelines have yielded a pedagogy that is quantitatively, but not qualitatively, different from the old. One would hope for more. We hope the research discussed here will lead to new questions about the whole notion of bidialectalism, but this time with a focus on helping students control the rules of two social dialects, with the recognition that "error," as exemplified by non-SE patterns in this work, may play a facilitative rather than an intrusive role in the development of a bidialectal language system.

Table 1
Variable Usage of Patterns by IL Group

I. Modal Auxiliary

	Speech	Writing	Speech	Writing	
SE	83%	0%	+	0	NT
IL	17%	100%	-	+	NT
BE	0%	0%	0	0	NT

II. Verbal-Infinitive

	Speech	Writing	Speech	Writing	
SE	80%	0%	+	0	NT
IL	20%	100%	-	+	NT
BE	0%	0%	0	0	NT

III. Noun-Plural

	Speech	Writing	Speech	Writing	
SE	87%	59%	+	+	T
IL	6%	11%	-	-	T
BE	7%	30%	-	-	T

IV. Subject-Verb Agreement

	Speech	Writing	Speech	Writing	
SE	30%	74%	-	+	NT
IL	40%	13%	-	-	T
BE	30%	13%	-	-	T

SE = Standard English	NT = Nontransfer	+ = Used more than 50% of time
IL = Intralectal	T = Transfer	- = Used between 0% and 50% of time
BE = Black English		

"I Ain't Got None/You Don't Have Any": Noticing and Correcting Variation in the Classroom

Ceil Lucas

Since the mid-1960s, a great deal of attention has been given to the issues and implications of dialect diversity in school settings. Research on the educational concerns of children and adolescents who speak nonmainstream varieties of English has included examinations of sociolinguistic bias in testing (Wolfram 1976, Vaughn-Cooke 1979), explorations of the concept of dialect interference in the learning of reading and writing (Piestrup 1973, Melmed 1973, W. Hall 1980, Whiteman 1981), and discussions of the role of teacher-student interaction and of the need for teacher awareness of dialect diversity (Piestrup 1973, W. Hall 1980, Lewis 1980).

The goal of the present study is to shed light on another aspect of dialect diversity in educational settings: how dialect features are dealt with in the classroom. The study compares occurrences of dialect features which are noticed and corrected by the teacher with "potentially correctables"--occurrences that are heard by the teacher but not corrected. Three questions will be addressed:

1. Which features seem to merit correction and which do not--is there a discernible pattern?

2. Which features do speakers refer to as "correctable" or "corrected"?

3. What are the strategies of correction--are there principles that unite correction events?

Examples of dialect features are taken from videotapes made in a Washington, D.C. sixth grade classroom over four days in May and June 1981. These videotapes are part of a larger project, funded by the National Institute of Education, concerning functional language in classrooms where dialect diversity may be a factor. The project also includes data from a kindergarten and fourth grade class. All activities within the sixth grade classroom between the opening of school (9 a.m.) and lunch (12 noon) on three days, and between 11 a.m. and the closing of school (3 p.m.) on one day, were videotaped. Videotaped activities can be classified as:

1. Whole-group lessons with the teacher;
2. Small-group lessons, with or without the teacher;
3. Teacher in a one-on-one situation with a student;
4. Free conversation among students, usually at transitional points between academic events;
5. Special events, including the presentation of compositions to the whole group, the acting out of scenes that served as a basis for discussion, and a whole-group spelling bee.

An example of a dialect feature, noticed and corrected by the teacher, is documented in the following segment of a whole-group discussion concerning the upcoming class trip to Jamestown and how much money should be taken for souvenirs and lunch:

Teacher: What do you get for an allowance each week, L?
Student 1: I don't get no allowance.
Teacher: I don't get any allowance.
Student 2: (Laughter.)
Teacher: What was that?
Student 1: I don't get . . . I don't get any allowance.
Teacher: You don't get any allowance?
Student 1: Nope. My grandmother get my money.

This is in contrast to an occurrence of dialect features that was clearly heard by the teacher but not corrected--as is the case in a rather heated discussion about whether one should keep or return the belongings of others that one has found:

Student 1: Billy do, too.
Student 2: You do, too.
Teacher: You know, what does the word too mean?
Student 3: Willy do.
Teacher: What does the word too mean? When he said "You do, too," aren't you admitting you do it yourself? When you s . . .
Student 1: No.
Teacher [and Others]: Yeah.
Teacher: Yeah! So that means I did it and so did you.
Student 1: I don't . . .
Teacher: So you just gave a confession. I did too.
Student 1: He do. I don't.
Teacher: I do too.
Student: Uh uh!

The present study is based on forty-five such examples, extracted from the videotapes: five examples of corrected phonological features, eleven examples of uncorrected phonological features, eight examples of corrected syntactic features, and twenty-one examples of uncorrected syntactic features.

This brings us to the first question: Which features seem to merit correction and which do not? Let us turn to the phonological features. As we see from figure 3, attention is given to unstressed syllable reduction (as in the pronunciation of a student's name, Karen [kʌRn] - [kɛRɪn]); to [t] deletion (at school close); to the variant pronunciation of the indefinite articles (a athlete), and, in one sentence, to consonant cluster simplification (penhouse for penthouse). (See figure 1.)

Corrected	Number of Instances	Uncorrected	Number of Instances
[kʌRnt] vs. [kʌRɛnt]	1	Vocalized [l]	1
[kʌRn] vs. [kɛRɪn]	1	"I 'on know"	1
[t] deletion	1	[θ] --> [f]; [θ] --> [∅]	1 each
a/an	1	[t] deletion	1
Consonant cluster simplification	1	Consonant cluster simplification	6

Figure 1 Corrected vs. Uncorrected Phonological Features

There are many more uncorrected occurrences of consonant cluster simplification, as well as deletion of intervocalic [t], (Saturday); [θ] --> [f], (fifteenth); [θ] --> [∅], (sixth); vocalized [l], (April); and the almost formulaic "I 'on know," involving initial [d] and final [t] deletion.

In figure 2, which shows the breakdown of corrected and uncorrected syntactic items, we see that correction is concentrated on negative concord or multiple negation, on ain't as an auxiliary in place of didn't, and on irregular past tense forms. It is perhaps striking to notice how many different dialect features (as illustrated below) occur without correction.

1. We ain't goin' to P.E.? (ain't as an auxiliary for aren't).
2. A person who come from Vietnam . . . (3rd person singular present -s absence)
3. In the year 2000, if I be livin' . . . (iterative be)
4. They ___ a nuisance. (copula deletion)
5. Both partner benefit. (-s plural absence)
6. It was $10 in it . . . (locative/existential it's construction)

This breakdown leads to another question: Is the same feature sometimes corrected and sometimes not corrected? In this regard, the only area of overlap between corrected and uncorrected phonological features is consonant cluster reduction: the single

Corrected	Number of Instances	Uncorrected	Number of Instances
no/any, anything/ nothing	4	anything/nothing	2
Irregular past tense	2	Irregular past tense	1
ain't/didn't	3	ain't/didn't	1
		3rd person sing. -s	7
		iterative be	3
		copula deletion	2
		locative/existential it	3
		ain't as auxiliary (for haven't, isn't, aren't)	1
		plural -s	1

Figure 2 Corrected vs. Uncorrected Syntactic Features

corrected penthouse, for example, in contrast to uncorrected pronunciations of finished and kept (without the final [t]). There is more of this overlap with the syntactic features, where ain't (for didn't), negative concord with the indefinite nothing, and irregular verb forms occur both with and without correction. After the simple classification and description of the phonological and syntactic features that do or do not receive correction, the next step is to explain why certain features receive attention and others do not, and to account for the overlap areas.

We have said that the videotaped activities could be divided into different kinds of events, and figure 3 shows the breakdown of corrected and uncorrected features by type of event.

Thus, we see that most correction is in whole-group lessons, and that relatively little correction takes place in small group or one-on-one situations. Furthermore, while an almost equal number of uncorrected and corrected features occur in whole groups, the largest number of uncorrected features occurs in "special events": the reading of compositions, the acting out of scenes, a spelling bee, and so forth.

Figure 3 leads us to wonder what the uncorrected features in special events are and whether they differ noticeably from uncorrected features in whole-group lessons. For this we turn to figure 4, where we find that whole groups and special events seem to differ in the occurrence of uncorrected syntactic features, the only overlap being ain't as an auxiliary and third person singular present -s absence. This difference in the occurrence of uncor-

rected syntactic features between whole group lessons and special
events can be accounted for fairly easily: the small range of
features in both events is no doubt caused by the small corpus,
and a larger sample would probably show the occurrence of all

Syntactic

	Corrected	Uncorrected
Whole-group lessons	4	10
Small groups	1	-
One-on-one situations	3	2
Special events	-	10

Phonological

	Corrected	Uncorrected
Whole-group lessons	3	1
Small groups	-	-
One-on-one situations	-	-
Special events	2	10

Syntactic and Phonological

	Corrected	Uncorrected
Whole-group lessons	7	11
Small groups	1	-
One-on-one situations	3	2
Special events	2	20

Figure 3 Corrected and Uncorrected Features
By Type of Event

features in both types of events. However, the high rate of non-
correction in special events can probably be accounted for by the
nature of the events. In comparison to whole-group lessons, special
events are relatively formal functions that include a presentation
of some kind, a performance, or a reading. Special events have
invisible boundaries that the teacher seems reluctant to cross to
effect a correction: once a child's performance or presentation is
under way, the teacher will not interrupt it for the purpose of
correcting the child's speech. Furthermore, there appears to be
general awareness in the participants of the special nature of
these events, since there is no overlap of features between

"uncorrected special event" and "corrected whole group." We suggest that there is a style shifting in special events, defined in part by an avoidance of features that are regularly corrected in other settings, such as negative concord with indefinites, irregular verbs, and the use of ain't for didn't.

Uncorrected Syntactic Features	Uncorrected Phonological Features	Corrected Syntactic Features	Corrected Phonological Features

Whole-Group Lessons

ain't/didn't	"I 'on know"	no/any, any-	[KʌRN]-[KɛRIN]
ain't as		thing/nothing	[KəRɛNT]-[KʌRNT]
auxiliary		ain't/didn't	t deletion
copula deletion		done/did	
3rd person sing. -s			
It's . . .			
anything/nothing			

Special Events

iterative be	consonant cluster		a/an
3rd person	reduction		consonant cluster
sing. -s	[t] deletion		reduction
ain't as	[θ] => [f]; [θ] --> ∅		
auxiliary	vocalized [l]		
plural -s			
irregular past			
tense			

Figure 4 Corrected and Uncorrected Features in Whole Groups and Special Events

There may indeed be style shifting between different types of events, but we must still account for the small overlap within events. How do we account for the fact that only a handful of features, both syntactic and phonological, are corrected whereas many others are not corrected? Furthermore, how do we account for the fact that the same feature is sometimes corrected and sometimes is not? For answers to these questions, we turn to two sources, one of which is Wolfram and Fasold on the stigmatization of dialect features: "nonstandard grammar is more likely than nonstandard pronunciation to arrest attention of speakers of the standard dialects and thus lead to negative reactions on their part" (1974:149).

This observation, that syntactic features are more highly stigmatized than phonological features, has been made by other socio-linguists (e.g., Shuy 1972). It is supported by the reflections of the teacher and the students in this study on language usage in general and on correction in particular. (It will be recalled that the second research question in this study is "which features do speakers refer to as being 'correctable' or 'corrected'?") As part of the data collection, the sixth graders were interviewed in self-selected groups of three or four and were asked (among other things) about the nature of language correction in the classroom. Six items were mentioned as targets for correction (see figure 5): ain't as an auxiliary (e.g., I ain't got no more) and negative concord with indefinites head the list, followed by correction of a politenesss marker, then specific lexical items, such as what not, used as a lexical item (as in "I went to the store for milk and eggs and what not"), and pardon me (which cannot be said to be dialect related). This frequency corresponds to the frequency of correction observed in the classroom. Furthermore, no mention is made of phonological features by the students. In her interview, the teacher used "verb forms and endings" as targets for correction.

Feature	No. of Times Mentioned
ain't as auxiliary (haven't, isn't/aren't)	6
Indefinites (negative concord)	5
huh vs. pardon me	2
what not	1
"Bad words"	1

Figure 5
Frequency of Mention of Dialect Features in Interviews

It would appear, then, that while there is a wide range of phonological and syntactic dialect features, only certain ones are candidates for correction. This does not necessarily mean that other, uncorrected dialect features are not noticed by the teacher, who remarked that there are features one can't correct because they are "reinforced in speech at home." There may be another principle at work here as well, concerning the linguistic nature of the corrected features, as opposed to the uncorrected ones. Recall that the uncorrected features include third person singular present -s, iterative be, copula deletion, plural -s, ain't as an auxiliary, and locative/existential it's--all of which we might want to call "active" features, in that they are general features that can apply to a very wide range of items. The -s plural can be variably deleted from any noun that takes an -s plural; it can be used as an existential in an enormously wide range of linguistic environments.

Similarly, third person singular present -s can be variably deleted in a very large number of present tense verbs. All these features are united in that they are rules that apply to large classes of items--items to which such rules are not easily applicable precisely because of the broad or general nature of the rules. This is in contrast to features that <u>are</u> corrected, such as <u>ain't</u>/<u>didn't</u> substitution or negative concord with indefinites, where the class of items to which the rules apply is much smaller and may be limited (as in <u>ain't</u>/<u>didn't</u>) to one item. It is easy to single an item out, so that the item itself seems to take on the characteristic of a fixed lexical item, as opposed to the object of a general syntactic rule. Indeed, the isolability and singularity of the corrected features may be useful in understanding how certain features became socially stigmatized in the first place.

Also emerging from this discussion is teachers' awareness of the nature of dialect diversity. The question is not whether a teacher should or should not correct dialect; the question is whether a teacher is aware of, and can articulate, general rules for using such features as third person singular -s, -s plural, iterative <u>be</u>, and so forth. Another question is the effect of that awareness on the correction of dialect features.

We have asked why a feature is sometimes corrected and sometimes is not. For example, we have a contrast between examples 8A and 8B:

8A. Teacher: How old's your sister?
    Student: I ain't [unintelligible].
    Teacher: Somebody signed your name.
    Student: I know I ain't sign.
    Teacher: I didn't, I didn't, I didn't.

8B. Student: I ain't get no reward. I be finding money.
    Teacher: Yeah, but you kept the money. Why should
        you get the reward?

One explanation may simply be the dynamics of the classroom and the teacher's necessarily divided attention. An irregular verb, produced orally, was corrected (e.g., <u>buyed-bought</u>) while another verb, written on the board and noticed by the teacher, was not (The man has <u>ran</u> out the door). Another possible explanation (which at this point can only be speculative, given the limited size of the corpus) concerns the teacher's perception and expectations of a child's language usage and language ability and whether it is "worth it" to attempt correction. We should stress that the number of examples is limited, but it is interesting to note that the uncorrected instances of <u>ain't</u> as an auxiliary and negative concord with indefinites are produced by the same child. Similarly, two of four examples of corrected negative concord are from one child. Furthermore, as observed from the group interviews and in-class language usage, the child who is corrected displays sharp awareness of the implications of dialect usage, particularly in later, adult life. Closer analysis of this child's speech would probably reveal her as more a "mixed-code speaker" than a child whose speech is uncorrected and reveals a higher frequency of dialect features.

Although it is speculative, a useful hypothesis for further research might be that more correction is given to children who are perceived to be in the "standard" portion of a dialect-diversity continuum and that a teacher's decision whether or not to correct may be partly based on her perception of a child's language ability and what we might call "standard language potential."[1] This hypothesis is supported by the teacher's comments about home-language usage (mentioned earlier). Note that there are four children whose dialect features are both corrected and uncorrected, and the presence or absence of correction of dialect features may have to do with the linguistic nature of the features in question, with stigmatization, and with tangible instances of language usage. However, it may have as much to do with the less tangible, more elusive, and complex nature of social interaction in the classroom and with the intricate dynamic between individual teachers and individual students.

Finally, a word about correction strategies. Four separate strategies seem to be in use in this classroom, as follows:

1. Question incorporating the dialect feature:
   "He buyed a car?"
2. Question incorporating the correction:
   "You didn't write anything?"
   "You don't have any paper?"
3. Modeling:
   "I didn't, I didn't, I didn't."
   "He did it."
4. Overt comment or question:
   "And don't let me hear 'I didn't write nothing.'"
   "What is it supposed to be?"

As listed, the strategies seem to be ordered by level of indirectness. In strategy 1, by repeating a child's utterance, the teacher's question doubles as a request for clarification or elaboration. It is up to the child to single out which function is intended and to amend the utterance as necessary. Strategy 2 is clearly more direct than 1, since the teacher provides the standard version of the dialect feature. Still embedded in a question, however, the strategy provides indirectness and the benefit of the doubt. Strategy 3 is more direct, as the teacher singles out the item and repeats the standard form, and strategy 4 combines an exact repetition of the dialect feature and a direct, overt comment on what is seen as appropriate. Interestingly, the most common strategies are those that provide the standard form, that is, strategies 2 and 3. It may be that strategy 1 runs the risk of being misunderstood as only a request for clarification or elaboration and that the correcting function may be lost. Similarly, strategies 2 and 3 accomplish the correcting and modeling function by avoiding the explicitness of strategy 4. The correcting function is served while a degree of conversational distance and decorum is maintained.

This preliminary investigation of how dialect features are dealt with in a classroom setting has implications both for sociolinguistics and education. For sociolinguistics, it provides insight into speakers' perceptions of appropriate language usage and the status of features that we, as researchers, isolate and label as dialect or nonstandard features. For education, the importance lies in taking a look at what actually goes on in the classroom, at what teachers actually do about the occurrence of dialect features.

As researchers, we must reexamine the nature of dialect diversity in the school setting, providing an ethnographic reexamination based on actual classroom living. All too often, conclusions about the nature of dialect diversity in educational settings have been based on speculation, superficial observation, or intuitions-- intuitions that often are attractive but have been proved to have little foundation. Specific conclusions that come to mind concern the interference of the phonology of black speakers in the process of learning to read or in participation in classroom acivities.

The overall goal of the project of which these data are part is a description of functional language usage by teachers and students in classrooms where dialect diversity may be a factor.[2] This descriptive process will necessarily entail reexamination of hypotheses about the role of dialect diversity in classrooms and, hence, some redefinition of the issues.

NOTES

I gratefully acknowledge Walt Wolfram's very valuable and insightful comments which contributed significantly to the preparation of this paper.

[1]In an experiment that focuses on teachers' and black students' language attitudes (Politzer and Hoover 1976), teachers and pupils were asked to listen to a variety of speech samples and to assess the achievement, social acceptability, and educational levels of the speakers. Describing the results of the experiment, Lewis states that "although there was wide variation in response to most of the scales, there was general agreement across sites and between pupils and teachers that the standard English speakers were the most likely to achieve in school. This finding showed teachers that language attitudes may be an important factor in school performance and that many bidialectal pupils already see

The Talking World Map: Eliciting Southern Adolescent Language

Boyd H. Davis

We have more than one way to dispossess people in this country; one is by age. Early adolescents--ask any junior high teacher or principal--are isolated into the most neglected and underdeveloped area of American educational research and policy development; they may be orphans within the linguistic establishment as well. The child may well be father of the man; that is, an early adolescent will have internalized the basics of phonology, morphology, and syntax for the first or primary idiolect well before reaching this age, as Loban 1976, for example, substantiates. People have competence in more than one "lect," however, as even the most cursory glance at studies of bilingualism, registers, repertories, or networks will remind us. Pragmatics studies assume such competence; ethnographic analyses try to delineate the variation in language performances and to identify the underlying competencies at work. Working with my Sunbelt adolescents in a study only partly completed, I often wonder whether our definitions may have been more narrow than the range of ability they--and we--display. I seek amplification to theories of language acquisition and language change, especially those portions which relate to norms viewed over the total life span of the speaker.

My current study already suggests that we look more closely at the language development and self-conscious awareness of the developing fluency of a group that is both self-assessing and voluble about that self-assessment. I mean, of course, the early adolescent, and I am particularly interested in those from the emerging urban centers of what is popularly called the Sunbelt. For here we have a test case. With the mobility and urbanization enjoined by economic factors within this country, with factories and corporations relocating and rural migration patterns changing, the Sunbelt cities offer us a chance to study the new immigrants, the new multilinguals, and to observe language change in a new setting.

In 1980-81 I began a study with 315 colleagues: fifteen from each of the twenty-one junior high/middle schools in the Charlotte-Mecklenburg (North Carolina) system. The administrators at each school selected the students: five each from grades seven, eight, and nine, with attention paid to sex, ethnic origin, and literacy attainment as measured by scores on national and state tests. A single sample would not, I felt, serve my purposes: Charlotte employs crosstown busing to maintain racial balance. Neighborhood and other demographic factors could be assessed only by ensuring that each school in the city-county system was represented. My original purpose was to try to develop, with my colleagues, a way to assess definitions of community and perceptions of community expectations for literacy attainment. As with any study that employs ethnographic techniques, new questions have been added and new insights gained. Once general patterns could be discerned, small groups, or individual students, could be studied in depth. There are few maps handy for those who would enter the world of the American adolescent.

It is the process of mapping which has thus far been the most profitable means of working with these students. They are natural ethnographers; their survival is at stake. They must map out what they see as their community, their world, and find their place in it. At their age, they are wary of tests, suspicious of adult-administered surveys. Approached obliquely, given a chance to assume some of the responsibility for the investigation, and presented an opportunity for interaction as equals, they become fairly skilled investigators who can discern what influences them and give it a name.

Together, we began to discern adolescent perceptions of New South expectations for literacy attainment; we have moved to include an assessment of how adolescents use language to define their New South community and their roles within it. This essay discusses one way the students and I have devised that enables me to tap those perceptions and definitions, the Talking World Map. The strategy is an adaptation of rhetorical principles laid down by early writers on oratory. The world of the writer-participant in classical rhetoric is a world not unlike that of the adolescents in my study. The two worlds include the illiterate, the marginally literate, and those who have success in both the literate and predominantly oral spheres. A primary clue for me has been the connection established by classical rhetoricians on how to move the audience from place to place, from idea to idea: to map, in other words, the emergence of a concept in the minds of the audience and its mode of transfer to another concept, with a way of reporting on that transfer. Early rhetoricians were skilled fieldworkers, able to invent precise taxonomies and more interested in what lay beneath their classifications. Their discussions deserve our attention.

A map is something my students can draw, "read," talk about, write from, and explain both to themselves and to others. It is an overt way of reporting where they go and with whom they are in contact; it inadvertently reveals their emerging sense of community and the roles language and register can play. Ours would be called by the geographer a "distorted" map: it has no compass. It does, however, show direction. There is a tie between the places where people go to talk and their sense of community, their perception of community expectations for their acquisition of literacy skills. The Talking World Map (as one of the students named it, because she liked the double meaning of "talking") asks the colleague to freeze spatially the processes of interaction in which language plays the crucial role. Placing themselves at the center of an 8 1/2 by 11-sheet of blank paper, usually in a circle or square, the students rapidly draw circles or squares (or any shapes desired) which represent places they go that are seen as important because those are places where they talk to other people who are important to them. Space, place, and language are crystallized: perceptions of community and of the languages used within that community can be captured and analyzed.

Notions of community and of language usage are not easily tapped in Sunbelt students by traditional means. It is natural to expect early adolescents to be unable to label their speech communities and roles in the ways a linguist commands--Bloomfield's comments on the secondary and tertiary aspects of language are as true as when he first wrote them. What I am finding, however, is that a good bit more is going on at early adolescence than I might have thought, particularly in terms of conscious awareness of language pragmatics. Adolescents are painfully aware of language differences and cue their behaviors to them, though they may not be aware, in scientific terminology, of why they do so. They have, however, their own taxonomy, which is, not unexpectedly, uniform. As Verenne 1982 suggests, labeling behavior is one index not only to people's language behavior, but to their perceptions of their own behavior. This labeling behavior is interesting in the context of the developments in the New South: notions of community are currently in flux in many of the rapidly urbanizing centers in the Sunbelt, and Charlotte can serve as a prototype.

Charlotte is one of the centers in the Piedmont Strip of the Sunbelt Corridor that runs from Washington, D.C. to Atlanta. Rapid expansion and urban development have effected changes that are only now beginning to be considered. Old concepts of neighborhood are changing. Except for a few enclaves which remain and efforts by professionals and preservationists to maintain or develop them, neighborhoods are being replaced by strings of shopping centers and subdivisions, scattered housing sites, and annexed rural clumpings. Geographers have noted that this could be termed a heavily populated urban sprawl; they suggest that this could be the way Sunbelt centers will continue to develop.

With new industry, we find new inmigration. In the fifteen
years since I came to Charlotte, it has become a city containing
nearly sixty languages and has both an international airport and
the status of an international port. Until the last quarter-century,
Charlotte drew its newcomers from the rural Piedmont regions of
the two Carolinas, with some inmigration from the Appalachians.
Population mixtures now include a heady and cosmopolitan brew.

No longer is the concept of community focused exclusively on
the neighborhood school, the community church, the local park or
vacant lot. In many instances, condominiums and office buildings
have sprung up on that lot; the church has relocated to serve its
newly dispersed clientele; students are bused crosstown, and here,
at least, with good results. Nostalgia can play no part in analyzing
the response of adolescents who live in this situation: their nostalgia will take different forms. One place that the Talking World
Maps reveal is important to the Sunbelt adolescent is the convenience store, a relatively recent phenomenon in American culture.
Recent it may be; so are the students. The convenience store
appears on every Talking World Map drawn by the pilot group on
whom I first tried the approaches used in this study. This store
also appears on nearly every map drawn since.

Language socialization is keyed in many cases to the role the
convenience stores can play, according to the reports of the
students with whom I work. Students can walk to them; they are
not dependent on adults for transportation, once those adults have
given them the freedom to go there alone. At first, one goes to a
convenience store with a parent and is carried in or accompanied,
while the adult chooses the items to be bought. Next, the child is
left alone in the car--if a car is part of the context. The child
next visits the convenience store with other (older) children, one
of whom is the "caretaker." Finally, the child can visit the store
alone. The child runs errands, buys a loaf of bread or a candy bar,
socializes, compares prices, and reads comics, magazines, posters,
signs, religious tracts, labels, advertisements, and community
notices. And if the convenience store is well managed and well
guarded, the child plays electronic games with others. Depending
on its location, if it is near a laundromat or garage, the convenience store may be serving the older function of soda shop for
adolescents in America. To go to a convenience store alone is a
signal of maturity; to arrive with your money intact can be a test
of wits. To complete a transaction and "hang around," talking,
reading, noticing, and being noticed, serves as an informal rite of
passage for early adolescents of the New South.

Future linguistic fieldworkers may need to add the convenience store to their repertory; it is apparently a crucial part of
language and literacy acquisition processes for adolescents. We
have learned to expect variation in speech; we should look to
experience variation scales for literacy contexts as well.

In 1980, with students in a reading laboratory at Charlotte's

J. Mason Smith Junior High, I developed the Talking World Map. Talking about their maps enabled the students to discuss the kinds of material they read at convenience stores (and elsewhere) and led to our joint development of a Reading Survey which could elicit reading activities practiced outside of school. Our survey is informal in that its questions do not demand precise calibration from respondents; it is administered by students (who are part of the study) to classes they select under conditions they choose and direct, and they take complete charge of the process. The questions are keyed to what one reads before and after school, broken down into rough time periods (before breakfast, on the school bus, etc.).

An informal reading of the hundreds of surveys returned confirms (unofficially) the results of the surveys conducted by the pilot group. Respondents meet over half the criteria listed by Negin and Krugler 1980 for essential adult literacy skills. All handle food-preparation directions, instructions for housecleaning and home-improvement products, street/traffic signs, medicinal directions and health/safety pamphlets, and information about size, weight, and price on merchandise and advertisements. Some respondents are familiar with job applications. None yet deals with bills, taxes, or bank statement forms, insurance policies, or loan applications.

The Negin-Krugler study shows some correlation with the types of uses of literacy listed in Heath 1980. Of the seven types Heath lists, Milwaukee adults and Charlotte junior high students show comparable levels of mastery. Heath describes the types of literacy functions she discerns as instrumental, social-interactional, news related, memory supportive, a substitute for oral message, provision of permanent records, and confirmation of attitude or idea. The Milwaukee survey of adults revealed that categories 1, 2, and 4 predominate; the Reading Surveys and discussions of them by the pilot group omitted only types 6 and 7 (which does not cast aspersion on the Negin-Krugler sample, since different techniques were used).

Of more interest to the 200-plus students who remain in this study (for many have been transferred, with their parents, to other Sunbelt cities) is the kind of language variation that early adolescents not only develop but show consciousness of having developed. They are well aware that different language styles are demanded by differing social contexts. Excited about their discoveries, they listen earnestly to the tapes of interviews they conduct to try to spot the key that tipped them off to the new situation, the new language role demanded of them. The Talking World Maps they have drawn (and are drawing) over the three years I've been allowed school time for access to them, already spotlight some differences.

Seventh graders often go exclusively to the homes of relatives. Others begin to branch out, visiting the homes of friends or institutionally sponsored areas, such as recreation centers or branch libraries, churches or school-planned events. Then they shift to consumer-oriented places. Shopping centers are added to convenience stores, and ninth graders flood the fast-food outlets. As they draw their maps, they map their concept of where they think they belong, what their community is, and how to speak in their world. They talk a lot; so that one might think they aren't listening. Not so.

Midway through a study of adolescent language, I have learned one thing at least: adolescents' ears are better than mine, and they reflect constantly on what they hear, internalize, and choose to share. Also, they are good teachers and linguists. I am learning to listen to them. They are the New South.

Correlates among Social Dialects, Language Development, and Reading Achievement of Urban Children

Charles E. Billiard

This report is based upon language data elicited during the spring quarters of 1979, 1980, and 1981 from a group of randomly selected urban children as part of a five-year longitudinal study of pupil achievement in the Atlanta public schools. Particularly of concern in the present phase of the longitudinal study is the examination of relationships, where they appear to exist, between social dialects, language development, and reading achievement of these children as they have progressed from the second through the fourth grade. Although the correlations discovered in the analyses of these data cannot be interpreted as cause-and-effect relationships, this paper will consider implications of these correlations for curriculum development and instruction in reading and language arts. (For a discussion of the design and conceptual background of this study, see Billiard, Crosthwait, and Diehl 1981.)

Speech samples of these children include informal conversations, story retelling, and formal sentence repetition. The informal conversation, conducted by interviewers carefully trained to put the children at their ease and to encourage fluent expression, preceded the sentence repetition task. The story retelling samples were obtained by asking the pupils to retell stories they had read orally for the Reading Miscue Inventory.

The language assessment instruments in this study are the Sentence Repetition Task, the California Achievement Test, and the Reading Miscue Inventory.

Developed by Anastasiow and Hanes 1976, the Sentence Repetition Task (SRT) is a useful instrument for probing the extent of relationships between social dialects, language development, and reading achievement. The SRT is based on the assumptions that children acquire the same linguistic structures at about the same age and that, in order to hear and repeat a sentence, they must have acquired the particular forms in the language and be able to understand them. Thus, children will leave out that portion of a sentence that is beyond their language maturity and, in so doing, provide a basis for assessing their language acquisition, irrespective of dialect. Furthermore, the SRT gives a measure of social dialect usage. Children who speak nonstandard English generally reconstruct portions of sentences, given in standard English, with an equivalent form in their own dialects. These reconstructions can be interpreted as evidence of normal cognitive functioning, as well as an approximate limitation of the students' ability to reproduce standard English.

The twenty-eight sentences in the SRT include function words such as although, because, and if, and morphological forms which have nonstandard variants. Anastasiow and Hanes have empirically established the reliability and validity of the SRT. On a test-retest procedure, they established the reliability of the SRT as .74. In a pilot study of inner-city black, poverty children, based on random samples drawn from each grade level (kindergarten through grade 6), they found that developmental changes in function word usage are a valid measure of general language development.

The Reading Miscue Inventory (RMI), developed by Goodman and Burke 1973, is an evaluation procedure based on the notion that reading is a psycholinguistic guessing game. Deviations or miscues made by students as they read a passage orally give insights into the students' use of grammatical, semantic, and phonological cues in the reading process. The students' immediate retellings of the stories are then used as measures of their comprehension.

Although the RMI gives insights into children's abilities to bring intuitive knowledge of language to bear on the reading task, it does not provide grade-equivalent scores for objectively measuring their progress. In this study, the California Achievement Test was used for this purpose.

The overall results of three years of data collection using the SRT show children in the Atlanta school system making normal progress in language acquisition as indicated by the function-word scores. The correct function-word responses increase gradually, from 32.5 for these children as second graders to 35.6 when they are fourth graders (table 1).

Likewise, the function-word omission scores gradually decline from 4.9 to 2.3, also indicating steady language development.

Table 1
Mean Function-Word Scores

Grade	N	Correct Responses	Omissions
2	194	32.5	4.9
3	162	34.4	4.0
4	84	35.6	2.3

The data for reconstruction words (table 2) indicate steady performance for these children across grades two and three (i.e., the second graders reconstructed in their own dialect a mean of 15.0 words and a year later, as third graders, they reconstructed a mean of 15.7 words). However, a sharp change occurs between the end of the third grade and the fourth grade, as shown by the decrease in the mean of reconstructed words from 15.7 to 8.1. Anastasiow has observed a similar marked decrease in the number of reconstructions for black students in the fourth grade in a Midwest inner-city school system. He suggests "a relationship between when a child begins to move from Piaget's concrete operations stage to abstract reasoning and his ability to reconstruct in oral language; and that this relationship can be observed by the child's repeating more of the standard forms" (Anastasiow and Hanes 1976:76).

On the other hand, comparison of the function-word data for these black children with comparative data gathered by Anastasiow for white poverty children living in isolated rural areas suggests the strong influence of environment on language development. The mean function-word omissions for rural white informants in grades 2 and 3 were, respectively, 7.6 and 5.9--compared with 4.9 and 4.0 for inner-city children in this present study. One might speculate that opportunities for language interchange in the inner city are greater than in isolated rural areas.

Table 2
Mean Reconstruction Word Scores

Grade	N	Correct	Reconstruction	Error and Omission
2	194	32.0	15.0	3.0
3	162	33.5	15.7	1.8
4	84	42.2	8.1	0.7

To analyze the factors that affect language growth, particularly reading achievement, this investigator examined data for students whose growth over the period of a year, as indicated on SRT function-word and standard English usage scores, was beyond the upper and lower limits of the first standard deviations. It should be emphasized that these data are growth or change scores, i.e., the amount of change in scores (positive or negative) that pupils made on the SRT and the California Reading Test from spring 1980 to spring 1981. In effect, this procedure yielded four groups of pupils who had unusual language growth (or lack of growth) during their fourth year in school (spring 1980 to spring 1981): group A, in the highest 16% of growth scores on the Function Word Test; group B, in the lowest 16% of growth scores on the FWT; group C, in the highest 16% of growth scores on the Reconstruction Word Test (i.e., standard English usage score); and group D, in the lowest 16% of growth scores on the RWT. It was reasoned that if significant correlations could be found among the factors under consideration in this study, with students showing extraordinary growth (or lack of it), then a critical study of these unusual cases might be helpful in understanding factors that influence achievement in reading and other language arts. Such a procedure, however, may produce a small error in the correlation coefficient. By excluding a large number of students' scores in the first standard deviations, the distribution has been rendered discontinuous and, under these circumstances, will yield a slightly higher correlation coefficient (Minium 1970).

The Spearman rank-order correlation coefficient method was used to examine possible relationships between students' growth on reading achievement scores, based on the California Achievement Test and students' growth on SRT scores.

As mentioned, the SRT also yields a function-word score, a measure of how many abstract function words a child is able to repeat. Inasmuch as children tend to omit function words which are beyond their level of development, function-word use is considered one appropriate measure of language development. Such a view is consistent with Piaget's theory of language acquisition and thought development, which perceives children as moving through stages of more and more mature thinking. As children master more mature modes of thought, they are able to use more abstract forms of language. For example, forms such as if-then and either-or reflect cognitive abilities that are not mastered by most children until they are ten to twelve years of age (Anastasiow and Hanes 1976).

Table 3 shows the correlation between growth scores on the function-word test of the SRT and growth scores on the California Reading Test for students in the highest 16% on the function word task:

Table 3

Group A: Highest 16% on Function-Word Test	r_s	p
	87	<.05

For students who show greatest gains in function-word use, correlation between growth scores on the function-word test and growth scores on the California Reading Test

---

This strong positive correlation supports the widely held view of the close relationship between language development and reading comprehension. Since function words are one means by which English signals meaning, it follows that comprehension of written language should depend at least partially upon the reader's understanding the relationships expressed by these words.

The strong correlation between slow growth in reading achievement (0.3 year mean gain) and minimal growth in function-word use for group B suggests the importance of general language development as a basis for promoting growth in reading (table 4). This idea is further supported by examination of the frequency and the kinds of certain function words omitted or used erroneously by groups A and B in the third and fourth grades (table 5).

Table 4

Group B: Lowest 16% on Function-Word Test $\dfrac{r_s \quad\ p}{.74 \quad <.05}$

For students who show least gains in function-word use, correlation between growth scores on the function-word test and growth scores on the California Reading Test

---

Table 5
Change in Function-Word Omissions and Errors,
Grade 3 to Grade 4,
for Groups A (N = 13) and B (N = 13)

Function Word	Frequency of Occurrences in SRT	Number of Omissions or Errors			
		April 1980		April 1980	
		Group A	Group B	Group A	Group B
where	1	0	1	0	0
what	1	1	2	0	2
when	3	2	5	1	6
either/or	1	5	12	4	9
if/then	1	7	13	7	11
which	1	6	10	4	7
because	6	4	9	3	7
Totals	14	25	52	19	42

For both groups, there is a tendency for the children to make a greater number of errors or omissions on words that represent more abstract aspects of thought, for example, the disjunctive notion in either/or and the causal relation in if/then.

After more than a decade of research on dialect interferences as a cause of reading problems, the evidence remains inconclusive (Weaver and Shonkoff 1978). Positive evidence of nonstandard

(Weaver and Shonkoff 1978). Positive evidence of nonstandard dialect difference as a cause of reading problems has been found by Rosenthal and Jacobson 1968, Stewart 1969, Baratz 1969, Bartel and Axelrod 1973, Gantt et al. 1974-75, and Jaggar and Cullinan 1975. On the other hand, Ames, Rosen, and Olson 1971, Goodman and Buck 1973, Mathewson 1974, and Cagney 1977 have found no significant evidence of dialect interference in reading comprehension. Group C, the children in the upper 16 percent of growth in standard English, as measured by the formal sentence repetition task, showed above-average growth in reading. A moderately positive correlation coefficient of .52 was found between growth in standard English scores and reading comprehension growth scores (1.6 years of mean gain in reading), as indicated in table 6.

Table 6

Group D: Highest 16% on Reconstruction Word Test	r_s	p
	.52	<.05

For students who show greatest gains in use of standard English, correlation between growth scores on the reconstruction word test and growth scores on the California Reading Test

---

This moderately positive correlation between strong growth in acquiring standard English usage and reading comprehension growth scores tends to support the notion that children who use standard English tend to have fewer reading problems than children who use nonstandard English. This view is strengthened by the data for the group in the lower 16 percent of growth on the reconstruction word test, as shown in table 7.

Table 7

Group D: Lowest 16% on Reconstruction Word Test	r_s	p
	.57	<.05

For students who show least gains in use of standard English, correlation between growth scores on the reconstruction word task and growth scores on The California Reading Test

---

This table shows a moderately positive correlation between slow growth in acquiring standard English usage and minimal growth in reading achievement (.2 year mean gain in reading) for this group.

These correlations do not, of course, establish a case for dialect interference in the reading process. As a matter of fact, there have been almost no reported replications of the "Lenora effect," i.e., the case of the young black girl, Lenora, who stopped by William Stewart's home on Christmas Eve, tried--with difficulty--to read a standard English version of "A Visit from St. Nicholas," and read with ease and fluency a black dialect version of the verse which Stewart had composed (Stewart 1969).

Other data from the longitudinal study, gathered in the homes of students, bear on the issue of dialect interference and language development in relation to reading achievement. Among many factors in the home environment related to reading achievement, Crosthwait (another principal investigator in this longitudinal study) has analyzed the language interaction in twenty-eight of these children's homes. He has classified a situation as "high language interaction" when such evidence as the following is reported: one child reads to another, a parent reads to a child or a child reads to a parent and they discuss the text, parent(s) and child discuss TV programs, parent(s) work crossword puzzles with child, and other similar language interaction situations.

By establishing two categories of language interaction for these homes, one of high language interaction and the other of little or virtually no verbal interaction between parents and the child, we were able to use a chi-square test to determine whether the function-word scores for children from linguistically different environments differed significantly. These differences were not significant at the .05 level; however, there was a definite trend (more function words repeated on the SRT) by the children from homes in which oral interaction was observed as high. Also, there appears to be a trend toward more frequent use of function words that represent higher levels of abstraction in these children. The more frequent occurrence of such function words as because, if, then, and either/or, suggests talk in the home that allows for question asking and probing for reasons for events. On the other hand, the reconstruction word scores of these children varied only slightly, and the speech of all parents or guardians of these children was a nonstandard variety with frequent occurrence of many of the social markers on McDavid's "Checklist of Significant Features for Discriminating Social Dialects" (1973a). Thus there appears to be a stonger link between language development and reading achievement than between dialect use and reading achievement.

Correlations, as mentioned at the outset, do not establish cause-and-effect relationships; nevertheless, they invite reasoned speculation. Given the strong positive correlations between function-word scores (language development) and reading achievement, and only moderate correlations between standard English usage and reading achievement, the content of language (the levels of abstraction used) appears more important than the form (the social status of the language) for developing reading comprehension. Educational implications for this position are (1) acceptance of and respect by the teacher for the child's language, (2) much oral language interaction in the home and school, in which probing and questioning are invited, (3) a language-experience approach in the teaching of reading, in which the language of children and their experiences are central, and (4) a plague on the "purple blizzard": the dittoed drill sheets, workbooks, and programmed instruction that isolate children from interaction with their classmates and teacher.

Black-White Dimensions in Sociolinguistic Text Bias

Walt Wolfram

The issue of sociolinguistic bias in testing is no longer confined to the hallowed discussions of speculating sociolinguists at academic conferences. Over the past decade, it clearly has worked its way into the marketplace of American life. We know its day has come when we turn on a popular television comedy to find the episode focused on two black adolescents who have been denied admission to an elite white prep school on the basis of a "honkey" language and culture test. But our heroes in this case, Arnold and Willis Drummond of Diff'rent Strokes, turn their rejection into a platform for cultural relativity as they demonstrate that the prep-school headmaster would be classified as incompetent on the Drummonds' version of a Harlem language and culture test. Sociolinguistically oriented viewers may feel a bit smug at the portrayal of an issue some have confronted for well over a decade. Unfortunately, there is little reason to be smug, for we are left with a number of nagging questions about the role of testing and the consequences of sociolinguistic difference in the testing process. As we shall see, there is still considerably more speculation than empirical data for many of our objections to standardized testing, as reasoned as some of the criticisms may be.

The following discussion attempts to bring together two concerns of applied sociolinguistics that have taken a somewhat independent course in previous explorations. One of the themes we have explored previously is the identification of levels on which sociolinguistic differences may be reflected in testing (Labov 1976, Wolfram 1976). In our studies, we have often illustrated instances of sociolinguistic test bias from different nonmainstream varieties, including Vernacular Black English (Wolfram 1976) and Appalachian English (Wolfram and Christian 1980). However, these explorations were focused on the levels of sociolinguistic bias, rather than on the relationships of the dialects used for illustrative purposes.

At the same time, previous studies have considered the extent to which issues related to dialect diversity and educational equity may apply across different dialects. Most recently, this issue was raised with reference to the landmark Ann Arbor Decision, in which it was determined that a group of Vernacular Black English-speaking children was denied equal access to educational opportunity because their dialect was not taken into account in the educational process. The federal court opinion and order in this civil action suit determined that appropriate steps had to be implemented which recognized "Black English" in the educational process. One question that arose from this decision was the extent to which the conclusions might be applicable to other dialect situations, including Vernacular Black English in other settings and nonmainstream white varieties (Wolfram 1980a). Might such a ruling pertain to Southern white nonmainstream varieties in a way parallel to its application regarding Vernacular Black English in Ann Arbor, Michigan?

It now seems appropriate to bring the issue of sociolinguistic test bias and black-white speech relations into clearer focus. Put simply, we want to see how black and white speakers of nonmainstream varieties in communities in the South may fare with respect to sociolinguistic bias. As we shall see, some dimensions of this question may be easier to answer than others, given our current state of knowledge. Thus our purpose will not be to give a definitive answer, but to direct the focus of discussion on the relevant dimensions of the comparison.

Levels of Bias and Black-White Speech Relations

In previous sociolinguistic explorations of tests, we have identified three levels on which bias might operate: 1) differences in language forms per se; 2) differences in how language is used to tap information, or what has been called "task orientation"; and 3) differences in the social occasions that relate to language use in testing. For convenience, we shall discuss the issue of black-white speech relations in terms of these levels. The potential importance of the distinct levels on the examination of tests cannot be minimized, although considerably more data are relevant to some levels than to others. As we shall see, the issue of black-white speech relations in testing is considerably more complex than we imagined initially, and we are still a long way from its ultimate resolution. Nonetheless, it is important to assess the current state of knowledge and the hypotheses that may emerge from an investigation of the issue.

Differences in Linguistic Form

Some fields of education have a vested interest in assessing language forms per se, so that it is relatively easy to find standardized tests that purport to measure some aspects of language structure. Thus, tests of "language development" or "language usage" often focus on particular structural details of English. In these tests, structural variation among dialects of English often becomes an important variable and, in some instances, is the practical focus of the test, despite theoretical claims to the contrary. In such instances, it is necessary to understand the ways in which the rules of particular nonmainstream varieties systematically depart from the norms that have been established on the basis of surveys or (more frequently) presumptions about standard English. These points of potential conflict are, of course, analogous to points of conflict that arise whenever we compare the rules of two languages or dialects side by side.

The model applied by sociolinguists generally follows that of contrastive linguistics. Sociolinguists predict where speakers of nonmainstream varieties may be expected to depart from the norms of the standard variety, defined as the "correct" response in their test, based on differences in rules of the respective varieties. A classic case of this conflict is illustrated in the Grammatical Closure subtest of the Illinois Test of Psycholinguistic Abilities. In table 1, taken from our previous studies (Wolfram 1980a), we illustrate the differences between the "correct" response in the test manual and the systematically different responses that we might expect from speakers of a Southern white variety (as described in works such as Feagin 1979, Wolfram and Christian 1976) or Vernacular Black English (as described in works such as Labov et al. 1968, and Fasold and Wolfram 1970).

The comparison we are focusing on here is between the Standard English "correct" response, according to the instructions in the test manual, and the alternative forms for speakers from Vernacular Black English and a Southern white rural variety. Alternative forms are defined as "incorrect" responses, predictable on the basis of the rules of the nonmainstream variety. While our illustrated varieties may be somewhat idealized, given regional variation among Southern white varieties and Vernacular Black English, each structure is fully documented in empirically based descriptive analysis. In this regard, the comparative analysis that leads to predictions of alternative forms is in compliance with the guidelines of traditional contrastive analysis.

There are several points of interest in the test illustrated in table 1. With respect to black-white speech relationships, the alternative responses indicate that the nonmainstream black and white versions tend to be similar to each other, rather than different, while in both instances rather drastic differences can be predicted on the basis of structural details of the varieties vis-à-vis the standard English variety. On the basis of such predictions, this test would appear to be biased significantly against some Southern white or black speakers. Superficially, there appears to be no reason for saying that the structural details of Vernacular

Table 1
ITPA Grammatical Closure Subtest with Comparison of "Correct"
Responses and Appalachian and Vernacular Black English
Alternative Forms

Stimulus with "Correct" Item, according to ITPA Test Manual	Southern White English Alternative	Vernacular Black English Alternative
1. Here is a dog. Here are two dogs/doggies.*		dog
2. This cat is under the chair. Where is the cat? She is on/ (any preposition-- other than under--indicating location).		
3. Each child has a ball. This is hers; and this is his.	his'n	
4. This dog likes to bark. Here he is barking.		
5. Here is a dress. Here are two dresses.		dress
6. The boy is opening the gate. Here the gate has been opened.		open
7. There is milk in this glass. It is a glass of/with/for/o'/ lots of milk.		
8. This bicycle belongs to John. Whose bicycle is it? It is John's.		John
9. This boy is writing something. This is what he wrote/has written/did write.	writed/writ has wrote	writed/wrote
10. This is the man's home, and this is where he works. Here he is going to work, and here he is going home/back home/ to his home.	at home	
11. Here it is night, and here it is morning. He goes to work first thing in the morning, and he goes home first thing at night.	of the night	
12. This man is painting. He is a painter/fence painter.	a-paintin'	

13. The boy is going to eat all
    the cookies. Now all the
    cookies have been <u>eaten.</u>   eat/ate/eated/et   <u>ate</u>
14. He wanted another cookie;
    but there weren't <u>any/any-</u>   <u>none/no more</u>   <u>none/no more</u>
    <u>more.</u>
15. This horse is not big. This
    horse is big. This horse is   <u>more bigger</u>   <u>more bigger</u>
    even <u>bigger.</u>
16. And this horse is the very   <u>most biggest</u>   <u>most biggest</u>
    <u>biggest.</u>
17. Here is a man. Here are two   <u>mans/mens</u>   <u>mans/mens</u>
    <u>men/gentlemen.</u>
18. This man is planting a tree.
    Here the tree has been <u>planted.</u>
19. This is soap and these are
    <u>soap/bars of soap/more soap.</u>   <u>soaps</u>   <u>soaps</u>
20. This child has lots of blocks.
    This child has even <u>more.</u>

21. And this child has the <u>most.</u>   <u>mostest</u>   <u>mostest</u>
22. Here is a foot. Here are two   <u>foots/feets</u>   <u>foots/feets</u>
    <u>feet.</u>
23. Here is a sheep. Here are   <u>sheeps</u>   <u>sheeps</u>
    lots of <u>sheep.</u>
24. This cookie is not very good.
    This cookie is good. This
    cookie is even <u>better.</u>   <u>gooder</u>   <u>gooder</u>
25. And this cookie is the very
    <u>best.</u>   <u>bestest</u>

26. This man is hanging the pic-
    ture. Here the picture has
    been <u>hung.</u>   <u>hanged</u>   <u>hanged</u>
27. The thief is stealing the   <u>stoled/</u>   <u>stoled/</u>
    jewels. These are jewels that   <u>stealed</u>   <u>stealed</u>
    he <u>stole.</u>
28. Here is a woman. Here are two   <u>womans/</u>   <u>woman/</u>
    <u>women.</u>   <u>womens</u>   <u>womens</u>
29. The boy had two bananas. He
    gave one away and he kept
    one for <u>himself.</u>   <u>hisself</u>   <u>hisself</u>

30. Here is a leaf. Here are two
    <u>leaves.</u>   <u>leafs</u>   <u>leafs</u>
31. Here is a child. Here are three
    <u>children.</u>   <u>childrens</u>   <u>childrens</u>
32. Here is a mouse. Here are
    two <u>mice.</u>   <u>mouses</u>   <u>mouses</u>

33. These children all fell down.   theirself/
    He hurt himself; and she   theirselves/   theirselves/
    hurt herself. They all hurt   theirself   theyselves/
    themselves.   theyself

*Underlined items are considered correct, according to the scoring instructions in the test manual.

Black English will impose a greater obstacle than the details of the Southern white variety profiled here. In both cases, the "penalty" for speaking a nonmainstream variety is drastic.

To say that black and white varieties exhibit many similarities in the predicted dialect interference should not be taken to mean that we conclude that these varieties are identical in all structural details, in keeping with our conclusions about the varieties based on the careful descriptive examination of the relationships between them (Wolfram 1974, Fasold 1981). We thus would expect to see some of the differences reflected in the alternative responses given by test-takers, who represent the respective varieties.

While we can set up such a comparison on the basis of predictions from contrastive analysis of features of different varieties, we must be careful to be realistic in interpreting the results of this analysis. Limited empirical studies (King 1972) document the incidence of many of the predicted forms from nonmainstream dialect speakers, but we are still in need of studies that examine, in close detail, the relations between predicted and observed alternative forms. On a theoretical level, we must realize that adoption of the predictive contrastive base in test examination is subject to the same limitations that have been suggested for the predictive hypothesis in the field of contrastive language studies (Wardhaugh 1970, Corder 1967, Richards 1971).

There are several important reasons why we would not expect all the predictions to be realized by speakers of the specified varieties. For one, many of the structures predicted as alternative forms are inherently variable (cf. Labov 1969), rather than categorical, in their incidence of occurrence. In the ideal predictions, however, alternative forms may have been set forth as though they were categorical. For example, our predictions for plural absence in Vernacular Black English specify plural absence for regular plural markers (e.g., items 1, 5), but plural absence of -Z is a variable feature, and its incidence for speakers of the dialect is not typically higher than 10-20 percent in all potential cases in which it might be absent. Predictions for test bias as currently specified have not taken this inherent variability into account, but any realistic predictive base would have to recognize it, just as it has been recognized in our descriptive studies (e.g., Labov 1969, Wolfram 1969, Fasold 1972).

Another reason why predicted items might not be realized in an actual testing situation relates to the speech style determined to be appropriate for the testing situation. In virtually all situations of direct elicitation, the speech style is geared toward the more formal styles or registers available to the subject. In this context, forms which might be constrained stylistically would not realistically constitute alternative forms. For example, our contrastive analysis in table 1 predicts a-prefixing as a legitimate alternative test response (cf. item 12). There is reason to doubt that it would actually be produced by speakers of the dialect in question in such a situation, however, even though it is certainly an intrinsic structural unit in the variety, since a-prefixing seems to be stylistically excluded from the more formal styles of language usage in the variety (see Feagin 1979:114-15 and Wolfram 1980b for a discussion of this dimension).

Finally, the formal elicitation style used in many tests of language structures may result in the occurrence of "hyperform," which may differ from the forms indicated by contrastive analyses. These hypercorrect forms, which extend the structural limit of forms under the influence of social factors, are well documented in the sociolinguistic literature (cf. DeCamp 1972, Wolfram and Fasold 1974:88), but they are not necessarily predictable on the basis of a simple comparison of rule differences. Nonetheless, a realistic model of interference in testing should be able to account for these hyperforms, even though they are not completely predictable.

Given the necessary qualifications we must make with respect to the predictive base of alternative forms, it becomes imperative to establish the empirical foundation of black-white speech differences in the structural details of test performance. Such a base not only will serve as the descriptive justification for establishing black-white differences, suggested in our comparison above, it will also serve as an appropriate contrastive model for sociolinguistic examination of structural forms in testing.

Task Characteristics

Aspects of test bias may relate to the operations involved in the actual conduct of a test, rather than diagnostic test forms. Naturally, the range of this level of potential bias extends considerably beyond tests that focus on language forms per se. In fact, virtually every test that uses language to tap information can be subject to bias at the level of task orientation. Considerations on this level typically involve strategies for giving directions, as well as the operations involved in tapping information. Such considerations affect practically all tests that use language for establishing the experimental frame of a test.

Directions call for establishment of a frame of reference, so that a common baseline can be assumed for all test-takers. Obviously, the goal of directions is clarity for the test-taker, so that directions can be eliminated as a variable that affects success. Unfortunately, the negotiated meaning of the directions cannot be assumed, despite traditional methods for their standardization, and even the most apparently "simple" and "obvious" directions may be laden with potential for misreading. This potential may involve a particular item or discourse structure of the directions.

I have pointed out elsewhere (Wolfram 1976) that the simple reading of an instruction to "repeat" as paraphrase repetition rather than as verbatim repetition may have had a significant impact on the scores of working-class black children who were administered a "simple" repetition task. In other instances, problematic directions do not lie in the reading of a word or phrase, but in the interpretation of directions as a type of discourse that governs the act of test-taking. From this perspective, we have found many instances of instructions which rely on implied discourse information which we cannot assume is common to the entire population of test-takers. Thus, our examination (Griffin, Wolfram, and Taylor 1974) of a standardized aptitude test, the Armed Services Vocational Aptitude Battery, revealed that the first subsection contained a direct imperative to work quickly and accurately--even giving a time limit for completion. In the following subtest, however, a time limit was not mentioned. Given the imperative in the directions for the first subsection, a test-taker might decide that working fast was no longer relevant. Such a test-taker would of course be wrong, and would be penalized for making a reasonable inference about the lack of information. Although there are strict procedures for standardizing directions, so that all test-takers may receive equivalent exposure to them, there is no guarantee that the negotiated understanding of the directions is identical for different populations.

Typically, there are many ways of getting at particular bits of information in a test. Some tests use a specialized method which seems to be distinct from how information is approached in everyday uses of language. For example, consider what "knowing a word" means in the real world. Aspects of word knowledge include at least: 1) syntactic constraints, or knowing appropriate sentence structures for the word; 2) semantic constraints, or knowing appropriate ideas for its use; 3) stylistic constraints, or knowing appropriate settings and styles of speaking for its use; 4) morphological information, or knowing what words it is related to and how it "attaches" to other items; 5) pragmatic constraints, or knowing what it entails, presupposes, and implies; and 6) phonological information, or knowing how it is produced.

Now consider how the notion of "word knowledge" is tapped in many standardized aptitude, achievement, and intelligence tests. In the tasks set up, synonymy, antonymy, or "dictionary-like" definitions are often employed as the way to tap such information. Obviously, specialized tasks have been conventionalized for testing purposes, tasks which contrast with real-world information and knowledge. Given such particularized tasks, extracted from real life, we must be assured that the task is not an uncontrolled variable that contributes to success or failure. The fact that some people demonstrate different skill levels in task-type tests (multiple choice versus true-false) ought to be a substantial hint that all ways of tapping information cannot be presumed to be equal.

The close examination of language structure in testing tasks suggests that tests have established their own style or register, if not dialect. Certain conventions found in test tasks cannot be explained simply in terms of a continuum of formality in which testing language falls toward the more standard, formal written end of the continuum (although it may do that, in addition to other stylistic traits). For example, the notion of a question as an incomplete declarative (e.g., When measuring an unknown voltage with a voltmeter, the proper precaution is to start with the___) is considerably different from many everyday requests for information. Or the relationship between a question and an answer may be interactive in the sense that the notion of "correct" responses can be determined only by examining both the explicit question and the range of possible answers. This, of course, is a popular strategy, used in multiple-choice questions. Other stylistic devices may conventionalize a particular option in everyday speech, such as exclusive use of direct imperatives in "directive" speech acts (e.g., Choose the answer most appropriate). Examples of conventionalized styles in test tasks can accumulate rapidly when we survey language usage in tests and in the guides which are used by those who prepare the test items. The upshot is that there is a specialized language style for tapping information in testing tasks--which differs in a number of important respects from language use in everyday situations.

With this understanding of language use as a task-characteristic orientation, we can now turn to the issue of black-white speech relationships. Essential to our discussion here is the observation that language use in the testing task apparently involves a style different from ordinary conversation for ALL speakers, regardless of class or ethnicity. The language of tests is not simple, formal, mainstream standard English; so there is a degree of discontinuity for all test-takers. On a continuum of divergence from everyday language, it may be closer to a formal standard English variety than an informal nonmainstream variety; but it is a matter of degree rather than kind. The real advantage in being oriented to the demands of the task is gained by speakers who have been socialized and have become familiar with the peculiar language conventions in testing tasks. For fairly obvious reasons, given the structure of our society, these test-takers come from the middle classes rather than the working classes, but it seems more a function of class socialization than language difference per

se. Studies which may be interpreted as dealing with a task orientation (cf. Bernstein 1981) suggest that the most essential variable
is class difference, not ethnicity. Dialect differences seem relevant only to the extent that it is reasonable to hypothesize that
the more distant an individual's everyday speaking style is from
the style of testing tasks, the greater the potential for task interference. From this perspective, black-white language differences
seem relatively insignificant, compared to other sociological
factors. Practically speaking, it becomes difficult to interpret
black-white differences along any qualitative dimension, as we
might do for a limited set of linguistic forms. Any group that is
not acclimated to the peculiar language task orientation is at a
disadvantage, whether white or black. In this regard, items which
pose a problem for middle-class speakers because of their specialized task conventions will be even more difficult for black and
white working-class speakers.

Testing as a Social Occasion

Finally, we should say something about the social occasion of
testing and how language use may be affected by social context.
Tests do not take place in a neutral social setting with a noncon-
textual orientation, although many tests make this assumption or,
at least, assume that it is possible to control the occasion so
tightly that unwanted factors do not influence performance in a
significant way. However, these assumptions can be challenged by
probing the underlying orientations that motivate test-takers to
respond in the way they do. Ethnomethodological investigations
that examine the rationale that leads test-takers to "correct" and
"incorrect" answers have provided evidence for recognizing the
social occasion that surrounds testing (Cicourel et al. 1974).

Testing involves a specialized "division of labor," in that it
sets up a particular kind of experimental frame. It calls for the
test-taker to enter the frame created by the test constructor and
administrator, and if the test-taker is unable or unwilling to "play
the game," the resulting measurements will not be accurate. With
respect to language, there are occasions where the test-taker must
enter this frame not only by adapting to the language style of the
test (as discussed above) but also by suspending everyday functions
of language, including aspects of its literal content, presupposi-
tions, and implicatures. In this context, an appeal to generally
accepted uses of language outside the test could actually have a
negative effect in terms of the test-taker's responding with an
answer that will be scored as "correct." For example, tests that
call for rote repetition (e.g., "Repeat the sentence 'Is the car in
the garage?'") or for generally presupposed or implied background
detail, not made explicit in everyday conversation (e.g., "Describe
everything going on in this picture") would be instances where

suspension of everyday language use is at a premium. On the other hand, there are situations where success in test-taking may be found in extended inferencing, even to the point of "reasonable guessing." In these cases, background information is at a premium. Reading comprehension tests, given their current focus on inferencing, often exemplify this extreme. The important point is that orientations with respect to knowledge outside the test situation are called for as a function of defining the experimental frame of testing.

Evidence has been emerging for some time that different groups display different uses of their background experience in entering an experimental frame. In the parlance of current educational psychologists, some groups in particular experimental settings reveal "relatively context independent text, in the sense that the text was not imbedded in a local context/practice," whereas other groups show "relatively context dependent text in that it was more imbedded in a local context/practice and assumed the knowledge of the context/practice" (Bernstein 1981:361). While the reasons for observed differences, and the significance of the differences, certainly may be disputed (see Dittmar 1976 for a critique of such studies), the realization of language use differences in particular experimental frames seems quite real.

To the extent that data are available, differences related to language use within and outside the experimental frame are class dominated, rather than ethnicity dominated. Thus Bernstein's studies, which we interpret as "occasion-oriented" (Bernstein 1981:360-62), show clear-cut class stratification. Investigations which apply an earlier version of Bernstein's "elaborated" and "restricted" code distinction to class and ethnic differences in the United States also show class-dominated, rather than ethnicity-dominated, differences (e.g., Hess and Shipman 1965, 1967). While it is possible that black working-class cultural experiences may lead to orientations different from their white counterparts, which would ultimately effect differences in approaching the experimental frame of testing, empirical evidence at this point does not warrant this conclusion. Obviously, there is a need for detailed ethnographic studies which influence situations within and outside the testing occasion as a comparative base.

Included in the background information that helps determine the social occasion are language-use values. For example, socialized values may govern the amount or kind of language appropriate in the experimental frame (cf. Labov 1976). Among other things, these values may be guided by status relationships between test administrators and test-takers. One ethnographic study of a rural black Southern community concludes that "experience in interacting with adults has taught him [the child] the values of silence and with-drawal" (Ward 1971:88). Status relationships may thus support a common working-class dictum that "children should be seen, not heard" as the appropriate orientation for entering the adult-dominated social situation of testing.

Our own ethnographic observations suggest that this prescription for language behavior is found in both white and black working-class communities to some extent, although there may be different applications in terms of the specific sociolinguistic interactions governed by this value (Ward 1971, Heath 1983). It is not difficult to envision working-class contexts in which a middle-class child's verbosity could be interpreted as rude behavior. Similarly, a working-class child's language deference may be interpreted as uncooperativeness, or even lack of intelligence, in a middle-class context.

Language-use background values are not easy to suspend or reorient upon entering the experimental frame of testing. While these value orientations may not be readily objectifiable in the documentation of sociolinguistic bias, their potential significance is not lessened by their quantitative unwieldiness. And ethnographic evidence is emerging that ethnic as well as class difference eventually will have to be considered (Ward 1971, Smitherman 1977, Heath 1983).

Conclusion

Given the amount of discussion concerning sociolinguistic bias over the past decade, it is somewhat surprising that we are left with so much speculation. Apparently, it has become easy for sociolinguists to pontificate about this matter without the solid empirical base that has been demanded for other dimensions of the black-white speech issue. Ultimately, the same attention that we have given to other details of black-white speech relationships (e.g., Wolfram 1974, Fasold 1981) must be applied to a comparison in testing.

First of all, we need to collect data from actual performance--in particular, the details of responses to test questions among Southern whites and blacks of comparable socioeconomic class. This performance must be compared, in close detail, with the sociolinguistic rules of the respective varieties to determine the role of dialect differences in alternative responses. The predictive contrastive hypothesis we have been using is undoubtedly too strong, but without an adequate data base we cannot employ a more appropriate model. We may expect some structural details of alternative responses to differ for whites and blacks, but without data, we can hardly make strong claims.

Secondly, we need detailed comparative ethnographic descriptions and ethnomethodological analyses of the testing situation. Ethnographic studies of language use outside the testing situation must be coordinated with an understanding of behavior within the experimental frame so that we can see how particular values and orientations about language actually serve as a point of entry into the testing situation (cf. Heath 1983). Then maybe we can be a bit more definitive about our conclusions. At this point, we have some reasonable hypotheses, but they will remain just that until empirical data catch up with, or redirect, our sociolinguistic criticisms of tests. Personal and political convictions about the sociolinguistic bias of tests may seem appropriate, given our impressions about the misuse of tests in our society, but in the long run are no more convincing than a sociopolitical or impressionistic base for determining black-white speech relationships outside of testing.

Bibliography

Agheyisi, Rebecca. 1971. West African Pidgin English: simplification and simplicity. Stanford, CA: Stanford University dissertation.

Allen, Harold B., ed. 1973-1976. The linguistic atlas of the upper midwest. 3 vols. Minneapolis: University of Minnesota Press.

Alleyne, Mervyn. 1980. Comparative Afro-American. Ann Arbor, MI: Karoma.

Ames, W. S., et al. 1971. The effects of nonstandard dialect on the oral reading behavior of fourth grade black children. Language, reading, and the communicative process, edited by C. Braun, 63-70. Newark, DE: International Reading Association.

Anastasiow, N. J., and Michael Hanes. 1976. Language patterns of poverty children. Springfield, IL: Charles E. Thomas.

Anonymous. 1978a. Turkey Tayac, 83, past chief of Piscataway tribe dies. Washington Star. Dec. 10, 6.

Anonymous. 1978b. Chief's son seeks tribal burial for father. Washington Post. Dec. 21, MD7.

Anshen, Frank. 1969. Speech variation among Negroes in a small Southern community. New York: New York University dissertation.

Atwood, E. Bagby. 1953. A survey of verb forms in the eastern United States. Studies in American English 2. Ann Arbor: University of Michigan Press

Atwood, E. Bagby. 1963. The methods of American dialectology. Zeitschrift für Mundartforschung 30.1-29.

Bailey, Beryl Loftman. 1962. Language guide to Jamaica. New York: Research Institute for the Study of Man.

Bailey, Beryl Loftman. 1965. Toward a new perspective in Negro American dialectology. American Speech 40.171-77.

Bailey, Beryl Loftman. 1966. Jamaican creole syntax. New York: Cambridge University Press.

Bailey, Charles-James N. 1981. Standard nonsense. Scottish Literary Journal, Supplement 14.63-66.

Bailey, Charles-James N. 1985. Preface; appendix C: standards. English phonetic transcription. Dallas, TX: Summer Institute of Linguistics.

Bailey, Guy, and Natalie Maynor. 1983. The present tense of be in southern black folk speech. Paper presented to the South Atlantic American Dialect Society, Atlanta.

Baratz, Joan C. 1969. Teaching reading in an urban Negro school system. Teaching black children to read, edited by J. Baratz and R. Shuy, 92-116. Washington: Center for Applied Linguistics.

Bartel, N., and J. Axelrod. 1973. Nonstandard English usage in black junior high students. Exceptional Children 39.653-55.

Baugh, John. 1979. Linguistic style-shifting in black English. Philadelphia: University of Pennsylvania dissertation.

Beale, Calvin L. 1956. American triracial isolates. Eugenics Quarterly 4.187-96.

Berkeley Charleston Dorchester Council of Governments. 1979. Regional housing market analysis.

Berkeley Charleston Dorchester Council of Governments. 1980. Report on economically less developed areas in the Berkeley Charleston Dorchester region.

Bernstein, Basil. 1981. Codes, modalities, and the process of cultural reproduction: a model. Language in Society 10.327-63.

Bernstein, Carl. 1970a. Clan scorned by black, white. Washington Post. Nov. 29, D1, D3.

Bernstein, Carl. 1970b. Wesorts: triracial, scorned by all. Miami Herald. Dec. 21, 7.

Berreman, Gerald. 1960. Caste in India and in the United States. American Journal of Sociology 66.120-27.

Berry, Brewton. 1963. Almost white. New York: Macmillan.

Bickerton, Derek. 1971. Inherent variability and variable rules. Foundations of Language 7.457-92.

Bickerton, Derek. 1972. Guyanese speech. Georgetown, Guyana. [Mimeographed]

Bickerton, Derek. 1973. On the nature of a creole continuum. Language 49.649-69.

Bickerton, Derek. 1975. Dynamics of a creole system. New York: Cambridge University Press.

Bickerton, Derek. 1981. Roots of language. Ann Arbor, MI: Karoma.

Bilby, Kenneth. 1983. How the 'older heads' talk: a Jamaican Maroon spirit possession language and its relationship to the creoles of Suriname and Sierra Leone. Nieuw West-Indische Gide.

Billiard, Charles E., Charles Crosthwait, and John Diehl. 1981. Correlates of social dialects with language development and reading achievement of urban children in the second grade.

SECOL Bulletin 5.11-21.

Blalock, Hubert M., Jr. 1972. Social statistics. New York: McGraw-Hill.

Bloch, Bernard. 1947. English verb inflection. Language 23. 399-418.

Bloomfield, Leonard. 1944. Secondary and tertiary responses to language. Language 20.45-55.

Bloomfield, Leonard, and George Bolling. 1927. What symbols shall we use? Language 3.123-29.

Blu, Karen I. 1980. The Lumbee problem: the making of an American Indian people. New York: Cambridge University Press.

Boertien, Harmon S. 1979. The double modal construction in Texas. Texas Linguistic Forum 13, ed. by Carlota S. Smith and Susan F. Schmerling, 14-33. Austin: University of Texas.

Boertien, Harmon S., and Sally Said. 1980. Syntactic variation in double modal dialects. Journal of the Linguistic Association of the Southwest 3.210-22.

Bohnenberger, Karl. 1902. Sprachgeschichte and politische Geschichte. Zeitschrift für hochdeutsch Mundarte.

Bond, Z. S. 1971. Units in speech perception. Working Papers in Linguistics 9.viii-112.

Boxer, C. R. 1969. The Portuguese seaborne empire 1600-1800. London: Hutchinson.

Brewer, J. Mason. 1953. The word on the Brazos. Austin: University of Texas Press.

Brewer, J. Mason. 1958. Dog ghosts, and other Texas Negro folk tales. Austin: University of Texas Press.

Brewer, Jeutonne P. 1973. Subject concord of be in early black English. American Speech 48.5-21.

Brewer, Jeutonne P. 1974. The verb be in early black English: a study on the WPA ex-slave narratives. Chapel Hill: University of North Carolina dissertation.

Brewer, Jeutonne P. 1979. Nonagreeing am and invariant be in early black English. SECOL Bulletin 3.81-100.

Brewer, Jeutonne P. 1980. The WPA slave narratives as linguistic data. Orbis 29.30-54.

Brewer, Jeutonne P., and R. W. Reising. 1982. Tokens in the Pocosin. American Speech 57.108-20.

Bryant, Margaret M. 1952. Had ought. College English 13.398-99.

Burling, Robbins. 1973. English in black and white. New York: Holt, Rinehart and Winston.

Burrowes, A. E. 1980. Prolegomena for the history of Barbadian English. Paper presented at the Third Biennial Conference of the Society for Caribbean Linguistics, Aruba.

Butters, Ronald R. 1973. Acceptability judgements for double modals in Southern dialects. New ways of analyzing variation in English, ed. by Charles-James N. Bailey and Roger W. Shuy, 276-86. Washington: Georgetown University Press.

Butters, Ronald R. 1974. Linguistic variation in Wilmington, N. C. Paper presented to the Southern Anthropological Society, Blacksburg, Virginia.

Butters, Ronald R. 1977. Variability in indirect questions. American Speech 49.230-34.

Butters, Ronald R. 1979. Review of Appalachian speech, by Walt Wolfram and Donna Christian. Language 55.460-63.

Butters, Ronald R. 1980a. More on indirect questions. American Speech 5.57-62.

Butters, Ronald R. 1980b. Narrative go 'say'. American Speech 55. 304-07.

Butters, Ronald R. 1981a. Review of Variation and change in Alabama English, by Crawford Feagin. Language 57.735-38.

Butters, Ronald R. 1981b. Unstressed vowels in Appalachian English. American Speech 45.104-10.

Butters, Ronald R. 1981c. When is English 'black English vernacular'? Paper presented at NWAVE X, Philadelphia.

Cagney, M. A. 1977. Children's ability to understand standard English and black dialect. Reading Teacher 30.607-10.

Cassidy, Frederic G. 1975. The position of Gullah alongside Caribbean (especially Jamaican) creoles. Paper presented at the Hawaii Conference on Pidgins and Creoles, Honolulu.

Cassidy, Frederic G. 1980a. The place of Gullah. American Speech 55.3-16.

Cassidy, Frederic G. 1980b. Sources of the African element in Gullah. Paper presented at the Third Biennial Conference of the Society for Caribbean Linguistics, Aruba.

Cassidy, Frederic G. 1982. Barbadian Creole: possibility and probability. Paper presented at the Fourth Biennial Conference of the Society for Caribbean Linguistics, Paramaribo.

Cassidy, Frederic G., and Robert B. Le Page. 1967. Dictionary of Jamaican English. New York: Cambridge University Press.

Cedergren, Henrietta, and David Sankoff. 1974. Variable rules: performance as a statistical reflection of competence. Language 50.333-55.

Chen, M. 1972. The time dimension: contribution toward a theory of sound change. Foundations of Language 8.457-98.

Chen, M., and W. S.-Y. Wang. 1975. Sound change: actuation and implementation. Language 51.255-81.

Cheng, C. C., and W. S.-Y. Wang. 1977. Tone change in Chao-zhou Chinese: a study in lexical diffusion. The lexicon in phonological change, edited by W. S.-Y. Wang, 86-100. The Hague: Mouton.

Christophersen, Merrill G. 1976. Biography of an island: General C. Pinckney's Sea Island plantation. Fennimore, WI: Westburg.

Cicourel, Aaron V., et al. 1974. Language use and school performance. New York: Academic Press.

Claerbaut, David. 1972. Black jargon in white America. Grand Rapids, MI: Eerdmans.

Clark, Wayne E. 1980. The origins of the Piscataway and related Indian cultures. Maryland Historical Magazine 75.1.8-22.

Coleman, William L. 1975. Multiple modals in southern states English. Bloomington: Indiana University dissertation.

Cooper, Vincent O'M. 1979. Basilectal creole, decreolization and autonomous language change in St. Kitts-Nevis. Princeton, NJ: Princeton University dissertation.

Corder, S. Pit. 1967. The significance of learners' errors. IRAL 4.161-67.

Corder, S. Pit. 1971. Idiosyncratic dialects and error analysis. International Review of Applied Linguistics 9.147-59.

Cox, Oliver Cromwell. 1959. Caste, class, and race. New York: Monthly Review Press.

Crystal, David. 1966. Specification and English tenses. Journal of Linguistics 2.1-34.

Cunningham, Irma. 1970. A syntactic analysis of Sea Island Creole. Ann Arbor: University of Michigan dissertation.

Curme, George O. 1935. A grammar of the English language. 2 vols. New York: Heath.

Daiute, C. A. 1981. Psycholinguistic foundations of the writing process. Research in the Teaching of English 1.5-22.

Dalby, David. 1972. The African element in black American English. Rappin' and stylin' out: communication in urban black America, ed. by Thomas Kochman, 170-85. Urbana: University of Illinois Press.

Davis, Alva L., Virginia G. McDavid, and Raven I. McDavid, Jr. 1969. A compilation of the work sheets of the linguistic atlas of the United States and Canada and associated projects. Chicago: University of Chicago Press.

Davis, Lawrence M. 1969. Dialect research: mythology vs. reality. Orbis 18.332-37.

Davis, Lawrence M. 1970a. Social dialectology in America: a critical survey. Journal of English Linguistics 4.46-56.

Davis, Lawrence M. 1970b. Some aspects of the speech of bluegrass Kentucky. Orbis 19.336-41.

Day, Charles. 1852. Five years' residence in the West Indies. London.

Deagan, Kathleen A. 1983. Spanish St. Augustine. New York: Academic Press.

de Beaugrande, Robert. 1980. Text, discourse and process: toward a multi-disciplinary science of texts. Norwood, NJ: Ablex.

DeCamp, David. 1971. Introduction: the study of pidgin and creole languages. Pidginization and creolization of languages, ed. by Dell Hymes, 13-39. New York: Cambridge University Press.

DeCamp, David. 1972. Hypercorrection and rule generalization. Language in Society 1.87-90.

Dennis, James, and Jerrie Scott. 1975. Creole formation and reorganization. Paper presented at the Hawaii Conference on Pidgins and Creoles, Honolulu.

Desmond, Ellen Mary. 1962. Mortality in the Brandywine population of Southern Maryland. Catholic University of America Studies in Sociology 47. Washington: Catholic University of America.

Dickson, R. J. 1966. Ulster emigration to colonial America 1718-1775. London: Routledge and Kegan Paul.

Dijkhoff, Martha B. 1982. The process of pluralization in Papiamentu. Amsterdam Creole Studies IV, ed. by Norval Smith, 48-61. Amsterdam.

Dillard, J. L. 1964. The writings of Herskovits and the study of new world Negro language. Caribbean Studies 4.35-43.

Dillard, J. L. 1967. Negro children's dialect in the inner city. Florida FL Reporter 5.7-8,10.

Dillard, J. L. 1968. Non-standard Negro dialects--convergence or divergence? Florida FL Reporter 6.9-10,12.

Dillard, J. L. 1971. Black English in New York. English Record 21.114-20.

Dillard, J. L. 1972. Black English: its history and usage in the United States. New York: Random House.

Dillard, J. L. 1973. The historian's history and the reconstructionist's history in the tracing of linguistic variants. Florida FL Reporter 11.1-2,10-11,41.

Dillard, J. L. 1975. All-American English. New York: Random House.

Dillard, J. L. 1977. Lexicon of black English. New York: Seabury.

Dillard, J. L., James Sledd, Eric P. Hamp, and Archibald A. Hill. 1979. Joinder and rejoinder. American Speech 54.113-19.

DiPaolo, Marianna. 1980a. Double modals and past tense specification. Paper presented to the Southeastern Conference on Linguistics, Memphis.

DiPaolo, Marianna. 1980b. The standard auxiliary system and double modals. Paper presented at the Linguistic Society of America, San Antonio.

Dittmar, Norbert. 1976. A critical survey of sociolinguistics: theory and application. New York: St. Martin's.

Dollard, John. 1957. Caste and class in a southern town. New York: Doubleday.

Dorrill, George T. 1975. A comparison of Negro and white speech in central South Carolina. Columbia: University of South Carolina thesis.

Dorrill, George T. 1982. Black and white speech in the South: evidence from the Linguistic Atlas of the Middle and South Atlantic States. Columbia: University of South Carolina dissertation.

Dunlap, Howard G. 1973. Social aspects of a verb form: native Atlanta fifth-grade speech--the present tense of be. Atlanta: Emory University dissertation.

Dunlap, Howard G. 1974. Social aspects of a verb form: native Atlanta fifth-grade speech--the present tense of be. Publication of the American Dialect Society 61-62.

Dunn, Ernest F. 1976. The black-southern white dialect contro-
versy: who did what to whom? Black English: a seminar, ed. by
Deborah S. Harrison and Tom Trabasso, 105-22. Hillsdale, NJ:
Erlbaum.

Dyson, Hazel R., et al. 1958. Genetics and dentistry. Eugenics
Quarterly 5.22-28.

Ekwall, Eilert. 1912. On the origin and history of the unchanged
plural in English. Lund: C. W. K. Glerrup.

Elgin, Suzette H. 1981. A primer of transformational grammar.
Language: introductory readings, edited by Virginia P. Clark
et al., 350-76. New York: St. Martin's.

Eliason, Norman. 1956. Tarheel talk. Chapel Hill: University of
North Carolina Press.

Emmons, Martha. 1969. Deep like the rivers. Austin, TX: Encino.

Fasold, Ralph W. 1969. Tense and the form be in black English.
Language 45.765-76.

Fasold, Ralph W. 1972. Tense marking in black English: a linguistic
and social analysis. Arlington: Center for Applied Linguistics.

Fasold, Ralph W. 1975a. The Bailey wave model: a dynamic quanti-
tative paradigm. Analyzing variation in language, ed. by Ralph
W. Fasold and Roger W. Shuy, 27-58. Washington: Georgetown
University Press.

Fasold, Ralph W. 1975b. Review of Black English, by J. L. Dillard.
Language in Society 4.198-221.

Fasold, Ralph W. 1976. One hundred years from syntax to phonol-
ogy. Papers from the parasession on diachronic syntax, ed. by
Stanford B. Steever et al., 79-87. Chicago: Chicago Linguistic
Society.

Fasold, Ralph W. 1981. The relationship between black and white
speech in the South. American Speech 56.163-89.

Fasold, Ralph W., and Walt Wolfram. 1970. Some linguistic features of Negro dialect. Teaching standard English in the inner
city, ed. by Ralph W. Fasold and Roger W. Shuy, 41-86. Washington: Center for Applied Linguistics.

Feagin, Crawford. 1979. Variation and change in Alabama English:
a sociolinguistic study of the white community. Washington:
Georgetown University Press.

Ferguson, Charles, and C. Farwell. 1975. Words and sounds in
early language acquisition. Language 51.419-39.

Ferguson, Charles, and John J. Gumperz. 1960. Introduction to
Linguistic diversity in South Asia. International Journal of
American Linguistics 26.3.1-8.

Fetscher, Margaret Elisabeth. 1971. The speech of Atlanta school
children: a phonological study. Athens: University of Georgia
dissertation.

Fickett, Joan. 1970. Aspects of morphemics, syntax, and semology
of an inner-city dialect (Merican). Buffalo: State University of
New York dissertation.

Fickett, Joan. 1972. Tense and aspect in black English. Journal of English Linguistics 6.17-19.

Fletcher, Paul. 1972. The clatter of clogs: life in Lancashire during the twenties as seen through the eyes of a boy. Manchester, Eng.: H. Duffy.

Funkhouser, J. L. 1973. A various standard. College English 34.806-27.

Gantt, W. N., et al. 1974-1975. An initial investigation of the relationship between syntactical divergency and the listening comprehension of black children. Reading Research Quarterly 10.193-211.

Gastil, Raymond D. 1975. Cultural regions of the United States. Seattle: University of Washington Press.

Gazdar, Gerald, Geoffrey K. Pullum, and Ivan A. Sag. 1982. Auxiliaries and related phenomena in a restrictive theory of grammar. Language 58.591-638.

Gilbert, Glenn G. 1982. Final consonant clusters in Jamaican creole: implications for the teaching and learning of English in Jamaica. Paper presented to the Society for Caribbean Linguistics, Paramaribo.

Gilbert, William Harlen, Jr. 1945. The Wesorts of southern Maryland: an out-casted group. Journal of the Washington Academy of Sciences 35.237-46.

Gilbert, William Harlen, Jr. 1946. Memorandum concerning the characteristics of the larger mixed blood racial islands of the eastern United States. Social Forces 24.338-447.

Gilliéron, J., and E. Edmont. 1902-1910. Atlas linguistique de la France. Paris.

Gilman, Charles. 1978. A comparison of Jamaican creole and Cameroonian pidgin English. English Studies 59.57-65.

Goggin, John. 1946. The Seminole Negroes of Andros Island, Bahamas. Florida Historical Quarterly 24.201-06.

Gonzales, Ambrose E. 1922. The black border: Gullah stories of the Carolina coast. Columbia, SC: The State Company.

Goodman, K. S., and C. Buck. 1973. Dialect barriers to reading comprehension revised. Reading Teacher 27.6-12.

Goodman, K. S., and C. L. Burke. 1973. Theoretically biased studies of patterns of miscues in oral reading performance. Washington: Office of Education final report, BR-9-0375.

Gove, Philip, ed. 1961. Webster's third new international dictionary. Springfield, MA: Merriam-Webster.

Graves, Richard Layton. 1967. Language differences among upper- and lower-class negro and white eighth graders in east central Alabama. Tallahassee: Florida State University dissertation.

Greibesland, Solveig C. 1970. A comparison of uncultivated black and white speech in the Upper South. Chicago: University of Chicago thesis.

Griffin, Peg, Walt Wolfram, and Orlando Taylor. 1974. A sociolinguistic analysis of the armed services vocational aptitude

battery. Final report, Department of Defense Project No.
HAHC 15 73C 0364. Washington.

Gumperz, John J. 1967. On the linguistic markers of bilingual communication. Journal of Social Issues 23.2.48-57.

Guy, Gregory. 1975. The Cedergren-Sankoff variable rule program.
Analyzing variation in language, ed. by Ralph W. Fasold and
Roger W. Shuy, 59-69. Washington: Georgetown University
Press.

Hall, Joan H. 1976. Rural southeast Georgia speech: a phonological
analysis. Atlanta: Emory University dissertation.

Hall, Robert A., Jr. 1950. African substratum in Negro English.
American Speech 25.51-54.

Hall, Robert A., Jr. 1966. Pidgin and creole languages. Ithaca:
Cornell University Press.

Hall, William. 1980. Projecting the issue into time: what do we
know and where do we go from here? Reactions to Ann Arbor:
vernacular black English, ed. by Marcia Farr Whiteman, 93-98.
Washington: Center for Applied Linguistics.

Hamp, Eric P. 1975. Further on buckra blarney. American Speech
50.325.

Hancock, Ian F. 1969. A provisional comparison of the English
derived Atlantic creoles. African Language Review 8.7-72.

Hancock, Ian F. 1972. A domestic origin for the English-derived
Atlantic creoles. Florida FL Reporter 10.1-2,7-8,52.

Hancock, Ian F. 1975. Lexical expansion within a closed system.
Socio-cultural dimensions of language change, ed. by Ben
Blount and Mary Sanches, 161-71. New York: Academic Press.

Hancock, Ian F. 1976. Nautical sources of Krio vocabulary. Sociohistorical factors in the formation of the creoles, ed. by J. L.
Dillard, 23-36. The Hague: Mouton.

Hancock, Ian F. 1980a. Texan Gullah: the creole English of the
Bracketville Afro-Seminoles. Perspectives in American English,
ed. by J. L. Dillard, 305-33. The Hague: Mouton.

Hancock, Ian F. 1980b. Gullah and Barbadian: origins and relationships. American Speech 55.17-35.

Hancock, Ian F. 1980c. The Texas Seminoles and their language.
African and Afro-American Studies Research Center Papers,
series 2, no. 1. Austin: University of Texas.

Hancock, Ian F. 1982. A preliminary classification of the anglophone atlantic creoles. Paper presented at the Fourth Biennial
Conference of the Society for Caribbean Linguistics, Paramaribo.

Hancock, Ian F. Forthcoming. Varieties of English around the
world: Gullah. Heidelberg: Julius Groos Verlag.

Harrison, James A. 1884. Negro English. Anglia 7.232-79.

Harte, Thomas J. 1959a. Trends in mate selection in a tri-racial
isolate. Social Forces 37.215-21.

Harte, Thomas J. 1959b. Explorations into the origins of Brandywine population in Maryland. [Manuscript]

Hartwell, Patrick. 1980. Dialect interference in writing: a critical view. Research in the Teaching of English 14.101-18.

Hawkins, Opal. 1978. Overseers' influence on American English. Paper presented to the Linguistic Society of America, Boston.

Hawkins, Opal. 1982. Southern linguistic variation as revealed through overseers' letters, 1829-1858. Chapel Hill: University of North Carolina dissertation.

Heath, Shirley Brice. 1980a. The functions and uses of literacy. Journal of Communications 30.123-33.

Heath, Shirley Brice. 1980b. Standard English: biography of a symbol. Standards and dialects in English, ed. by Timothy Shopen and Joseph M. Williams, 3-32. Cambridge, MA: Winthrop.

Heath, Shirley Brice. 1983. Ways with words: language, life, and work in communities and classrooms. New York: Cambridge University Press.

Heavrin, Nancy Walker. 1982. Final consonant cluster simplification in southern Maryland: two contrasting approaches to data analysis. Department of Linguistics, Southern Illinois University at Carbondale. [Manuscript]

Herskovits, Melville. 1936. Suriname folklore. New York: AMS Press.

Herskovits, Melville. 1941. The myth of the Negro past. New York: Harper and Row.

Hess, Robert D., and Vivian C. Shipman. 1965. Early experience and the socialization of cognitive modes in children. Child Development 36.869-86.

Hess, Robert D., and Vivian C. Shipman. 1967. Cognitive elements in maternal behavior. Minnesota symposia on child psychology, ed. by J. P. Hill, 57-81. Minneapolis.

Hill, Archibald A. 1975. The habituative aspect of verbs in black English, Irish English, and standard English. American Speech 50.323-34.

Hollingshead, August, and F. C. Redlich. 1958. Social class and mental illness. New York: John Wiley.

Holm, John. 1982. The place of Gullah: its lexical affinities with Bahamian. Paper presented to the Society for Caribbean Linguistics Meeting, Paramaribo.

Holm, John, and Alison Watt Shilling. 1982. Dictionary of Bahamian English. Cold Spring, NY: Lexik House.

Hopkins, John. 1975. The white middle class speech of Savannah, Georgia: a phonological analysis. Columbia: University of South Carolina dissertation.

Hopkins, Tometro. 1982. Observations of syntactic change in Sea Island Creole. Bloomington: Indiana University dissertation.

Horn, Roger. 1980. What happened to the Piscataway Indians? Living in Southern Maryland 1.2.30-33.

Houston, Susan. 1969. A sociolinguistic consideration of the black English of children in northern Florida. Language 45.599-607.

Houston, Susan. 1970. Competence and performance in child black English. Language Sciences 12.9-14.

Houston, Susan. 1972. Child black English: the school register. Linguistics 90.20-34.

Howren, Robert S. 1958. The speech of Louisville, Kentucky. Bloomington: Indiana University dissertation.

Howren, Robert S. 1962. The speech of Ocracoke, North Carolina. American Speech 37.161-75.

Hsieh, H.-I. 1972. Lexical diffusion: evidence from child language acquisition. Glossa 6.89-104.

Hurse, Rudoph J., et al. 1956. Dentinogenesis imperfecta in a racial isolate with multiple hereditary defects. Oral Surgery, Oral Medicine, and Oral Pathology 9.641-58.

Jaberg, Karl, and Jakob Jud. 1928. Der sprachatlas als forschungsinstrument. Halle: Max Niemeyer Verlag.

Jacobs, Roderick A., and Peter S. Rosenbaum. 1968. English transformational grammar. Waltham, MA: Blaisdell.

Jaggar, A. M., and B. E. Cullinan. 1975. A study of young black children's receptive and productive language and reading competence in standard English grammatical forms. ERIC document 109 611.

Jameson, Anne Skone. 1973. An analysis of self-esteem and academic achievement of tri-racial isolate, Negro, and Caucasian elementary and middle school boys and girls. College Park: University of Maryland dissertation.

Jeremiah, Milford A. 1977. The linguistic relatedness of black English and Antiguan creole: evidence from the eighteenth and nineteenth centuries. Providence, RI: Brown University dissertation.

Jesperson, Otto. 1909-1919. A modern English grammar on historical principles. 7 vols. Heidelberg: C. Winter.

Johnson, Charles, Jr. 1980. Black seminoles: their history and their quest for land. Journal of the Afro-American Historical and Genealogical Society 1.2.47-58.

Johnson, Guy B. 1930. Folk culture on St. Helena Island, South Carolina. Chapel Hill: University of North Carolina Press.

Joiner, Charles W. 1979. Martin Luther King Junior elementary school children et al. vs. Ann Arbor school district board: memorandum opinion and order. Detroit.

Jones-Jackson, Patricia A. 1978a. The status of Gullah: an investigation of convergent processes. Ann Arbor: University of Michigan dissertation.

Jones-Jackson, Patricia A. 1978b. Gullah: on the question of Afro-American language. Anthropological Linguistics 20.422-28.

Jones-Jackson, Patricia A. 1983. Some persistent linguistic features of contemporary Gullah. Journal of Black Studies 13. 289-303.

Joyner, Charles W. 1971. Folk song in South Carolina. Columbia: University of South Carolina Press.

Joyner, Charles W. 1984. Down by the riverside: a South Carolina slave community. Urbana: University of Illinois Press.

King, Pamela. 1972. An analysis of the northwestern syntax screening test for lower class black children in Prince George's county. Washington: Howard University thesis.

Kloe, Donald. 1974. Buddy Quow: an anonymous poem in Gullah-Jamaican dialect written circa 1800. Southern Folklore Quarterly 38.81-90.

Koiter, Judy. 1978. Wesorts talk different: a linguistic study of an American triracial isolate. Department of Linguistics, Southern Illinois University at Carbondale. [Manuscript]

Kroll, B. M. 1981. Developmental relationships between speaking and writing. Exploring speaking-writing relationships: connections and contrasts, ed. by Barry M. Kroll, 32-54. Urbana, IL: National Council of Teachers of English.

Kučera, Henry, and W. Nelson Francis. 1967. Computational analysis of present-day American English. Providence: Brown University Press.

Kurath, Hans. 1928. The origin of dialectal differences in spoken American English. Modern Philology 25.385-95.

Kurath, Hans. 1939 [1972]. Handbook of the linguistic geography of New England. Providence, RI: Brown University Press.

Kurath, Hans. 1949. Word geography of the eastern United States. Ann Arbor: University of Michigan Press.

Kurath, Hans. 1961. Phonemics and phonics in historical phonology. American Speech 36.93-100.

Kurath, Hans. 1964. A phonology and prosody of modern English. Ann Arbor: University of Michigan Press.

Kurath, Hans, et al., eds. 1939-1943. The linguistic atlas of New England. 3 vols. Providence, RI: Brown University Press.

Kurath, Hans, and Sherman Kuhn, eds. 1952- . Middle English dictionary. Ann Arbor: University of Michigan Press.

Kurath, Hans, and Raven I. McDavid, Jr. 1961. The pronunciation of English in the Atlantic states. Ann Arbor: University of Michigan Press.

Labov, William. 1963. The social motivation of a sound change. Word 19.273-309.

Labov, William. 1966 [1982]. The social stratification of English in New York City. Washington: Center for Applied Linguistics.

Labov, William. 1967. Some sources of reading problems for Negro speakers of non-standard English. New directions in elementary English, ed. by Alexander Frazier, 140-67. Urbana: National Council of Teachers of English.

Labov, William. 1969. Contraction, deletion, and inherent variability in the English copula. Language 45.715-62.

Labov, William. 1971. The notion of 'system' in creole studies. Pidginization and creolization of languages, ed. by Dell Hymes, 447-72. New York: Cambridge University Press.

Labov, William. 1972a. Language in the inner city: studies in the black English vernacular. Philadelphia: University of Pennsylvania Press.

Labov, William. 1972b. Sociolinguistic patterns. Philadelphia: University of Pennsylvania Press.

Labov, William. 1972c. Methodology. A survey of linguistic science, ed. by William Dingwall, 412-91. College Park: University of Maryland Press.

Labov, William. 1973. The linguistic consequences of being a lame. Language in Society 2.81-116.

Labov, William. 1976. Systematically misleading data from test questions. Urban Review 9.146-69.

Labov, William. 1980a. Is there a creole speech community? Theoretical orientations in creole studies, ed. by Albert Valdman and Arnold Highfield, 369-88. New York: Academic Press.

Labov, William. 1980b. The social origins of sound change. Locating language in time and space, ed. by William Labov, 251-65. New York: Academic Press.

Labov, William. 1982. Objectivity and commitment in linguistic science: the case of the black English trial in Ann Arbor. Language in Society 11.165-201.

Labov, William, et al. 1968. A study of the non-standard English of Negro and Puerto Rican speakers in New York City. Final research report. Cooperative Research Project 3288. 2 vols. Philadelphia: U. S. Regional Survey.

Labov, William, et al. 1972. A quantitative study of sound change in progress. Philadelphia: U. S. Regional Survey.

Ladefoged, Peter. 1960. The value of phonetic statements. Language 36.387-96.

Lado, Robert. 1957. Linguistics across cultures. Ann Arbor: University of Michigan Press.

Langendoen, D. Terence. 1970. Essentials of English grammar. New York: Holt.

Lee, Mary Hope. 1972. On the origins of Gullah. Department of Linguistics, University of California at Berkeley. Manuscript.

Legum, Stanley E., et al. 1971. The speech of young black children in Los Angeles. Inglewood, CA: Southwest Regional Laboratory.

Lehiste, Ilse. 1972. Units of speech perception. Speech and cortical functioning, ed. by J. H. Gilbert, 187-230. New York: Academic Press.

Le Page, Robert B., and Andree Tabouret-Keller. 1985. Acts of identity. New York: Cambridge University Press.

Levine, Lewis, and Harry J. Crockett, Jr. 1966. Speech variation in a piedmont community. Sociological Inquiry 36.204-26.

Lewis, Shirley A. R. 1980. Teacher attitude change: does informing make a difference? Reactions to Ann Arbor: vernacular black English and education, ed. by Marcia Farr Whiteman, 85-92. Washington: Center for Applied Linguistics.

Lewis, Sinclair. 1952. Arrowsmith. New York: Harcourt Brace Jovanovich.

Littlefield, Daniel C. 1981. Rice and slaves: ethnicity and the slave trade in colonial South Carolina. Baton Rouge: Louisiana State University Press.

Littlefield, Daniel F. 1977. Africans and seminoles, from removal to emancipation. Westport, CT: Greenwood.

Loban, Walter. 1976. Language development: kindergarten through grade twelve. Research Report 18. Urbana: National Council of Teachers of English.

Loflin, Marvin D. 1967. A note on the deep structure of nonstandard English in Washington, DC. Glossa 1.26-32.

Loflin, Marvin D. 1969. Negro non-standard and standard English: same or different structure? Orbis 18.74-91.

Loflin, Marvin D. 1970. On the structure of the verb in a dialect of American Negro English. Linguistics 59.14-28.

Loflin, Marvin D., Nicholas Sobin, and J. L. Dillard. 1974. Auxiliary structures and time adverbs in American black English. American Speech 48.22-28.

Luelsdorff, Philip A. 1975. A segmental phonology of black English. The Hague: Mouton.

McCright, Grady E. 1981. John Bullis: chief scout. True West 28.12-19.

McDavid, Raven I., Jr. 1953. Oughtn't and hadn't ought. College English 14.472-73.

McDavid, Raven I., Jr. 1965a. American social dialects. College English 26.254-60.

McDavid, Raven I., Jr. 1965b. Social dialects: cause or sympton of social maladjustment. Social dialects and language learning: proceedings of the Bloomington, Indiana, conference; ed. by Roger W. Shuy, 3-7. Champaign: National Council of Teachers of English.

McDavid, Raven I., Jr. 1966a. Sense and nonsense about American dialects. PMLA 81.2.7-17.

McDavid, Raven I., Jr. 1966b. Dialect differences and social differences in an urban society. Sociolinguistics, ed. by William Bright, 72-83. The Hague: Mouton.

McDavid, Raven I., Jr. 1967a. Historical, regional, and social variation. Journal of English Linguistics 1.25-40.

McDavid, Raven I., Jr. 1967b. Dialect differences and the teaching of English. Louisiana English Journal 7.10-12.

McDavid, Raven I., Jr. 1967c. Needed research in Southern dialects. Perspectives on the South: agenda for research, ed. by Edgar T. Thompson, 113-24. Durham, NC: Duke University Press.

McDavid, Raven I., Jr. 1968. Dialectology and the integration of the schools. Zeitschrift für Mundartforschung. Beihefte, NF 4.543-50.

McDavid, Raven I., Jr. 1970. A theory of dialect. Linguistics and

the teaching of standard English to speakers of other languages or dialects, ed. by James E. Alatis, 45-62. Washington:
Georgetown University Press.

McDavid, Raven I., Jr. 1973a. A checklist of significant features
for discriminating social dialects. Culture, class, and language
variety, ed. by Alva L. Davis, 133-39. Urbana, IL: National
Council of Teachers of English.

McDavid, Raven I., Jr. 1973b. Go slow in ethnic attributions: geographic mobility and dialect prejudices. Varieties of present-
day English, ed. by Richard W. Bailey and Jay L. Robinson,
259-70. New York: Macmillan.

McDavid, Raven I., Jr. 1979. Review of Language in the inner city
and Sociolinguistic patterns, by William Labov. American
Speech 54.290-304.

McDavid, Raven I., Jr., and William M. Austin. 1966. Communication barriers to the culturally deprived. Washington: Department of Health, Education, and Welfare. Office of Education
Cooperative Research Project 2107.

McDavid, Raven I., Jr., et al., eds. 1976-1979. Linguistic atlas of
the north-central states: basic materials. Chicago manuscripts
on cultural anthropology series XXXVIII, 200-208. Chicago:
University of Chicago.

McDavid, Raven I., Jr., and Lawrence M. Davis. 1972. The dialects
of Negro Americans. Studies in linguistics in honor of George
L. Trager, ed. by M. Estelle Smith, 303-12. The Hague:
Mouton.

McDavid, Raven I., Jr., and Virginia G. McDavid. 1951. The relationship of the speech of American Negroes to the speech of
whites. American Speech 26.3-27.

McDavid, Raven I., Jr., and Virginia G. McDavid. 1978. Intuitive
rules and factual evidence: /-sp, -st, -sk/ plus [-z]. Linguistic
and literary studies in honor of Archibald A. Hill, ed. by J. A.
Jazayery et al., 2.73-90. The Hague: Mouton.

McDavid, Raven I., Jr., Raymond K. O'Cain, and George T. Dorrill,
eds. 1980-   . Linguistic Atlas of the middle and south
atlantic states. Chicago: University of Chicago Press.

McDavid, Virginia G. 1963. To as a preposition of location in linguistic atlas materials. Publication of the American Dialect
Society 40.12-19.

McDavid, Virginia G. 1977. The social distribution of selected verb
forms in the linguistic atlas of the north central states. James
B. McMillan: essays in linguistics by his friends and colleagues, ed. by James Raymond and I. Willis Russell, 41-52.
University: University of Alabama Press.

McDavid, Virginia G., and Lawrence Davis. Forthcoming. The grammar of the north-central states.

McKay, June. 1970. A partial analysis of a variety of nonstandard
Negro English. Berkeley: University of California dissertation.

McMillan, James B. 1971. Annotated bibliography of southern

American English. Miami, FL: University of Miami Press.

Magens, Jochum M. 1770. Grammatica over det creolske sprog. Copenhagen: G. G. Salikath.

Major, Clarence. 1970. Dictionary of Afro-American slang. New York: International.

Maryland Indian Heritage Society. 1981. Disposition of income . . . current programs . . . objectives. [Pamphlet distributed on Indian Day, 11 July 1981, Prince George's County, Md.]

Mathews, Mitford M. 1981. The beginnings of American English. Chicago: University of Chicago Press.

Mathewson, G. C. 1974. Relationship between ethnic group attitudes toward dialect and comprehension of dialect folktales. Journal of Educational Research 68.15-18,35.

Matthews, P. H. 1974. Morphology: an introduction to the theory of word structure. New York: Cambridge University Press.

Matthews, W. 1935. Sailors' pronunciation in the second half of the seventeenth century. Anglia 59.192-251.

Melmed, Paul Jay. 1973. Black English phonology: the question of reading interference. Language differences: do they interfere? ed. by James L. Laffey and Roger Shuy, 70-85. Newark, DE: International Reading Association.

Miller, Joy L. 1972. Be, finite and absence: features of speech--black and white. Orbis 21.22-27.

Miller, Michael I. 1978. Inflectional morphology in Augusta, Georgia: a socio-linguistic description. Chicago: University of Chicago dissertation.

Miller, Michael I. 1981. Review of Variation and change in Alabama English, by Crawford Feagin. American Speech 67.288-95.

Milroy, Lesley. 1980. Language and social networks. London: Basil Blackwell.

Milroy, Lesley, and Sue Margrain. 1980. Vernacular language loyalty and social network. Language in Society 9.43-70.

Minium, E. W. 1970. Statistical reasoning in psychology and education. New York: John Wiley.

Mitchell-Kernan, Claudia L. 1970. Language behavior in a black urban community. Berkeley: University of California dissertation.

Mooney, James. 1907. The Powhatan confederacy, past and present. American Anthropologist. n.s. 9.144-45.

Morgan, Lucia. 1969. North Carolina accents. Southern Speech Journal 34.223-29.

Morris, William, ed. 1969. American Heritage dictionary. Boston: Houghton Mifflin.

Morris, William, and Mary Morris. 1975. The Harper dictionary of contemporary usage. New York: Harper and Row.

Murray, James A. J., et al., eds. 1933. The Oxford English dictionary. Oxford: Oxford University Press.

Myrdal, Gunnar. 1944. An American dilemma. New York: Harper and Brothers.

Negin, Gary, and Dee Krugler. 1980. Essential literacy skills for functioning in an urban community. Journal of Reading 24.109-26.

Nicholas, J. Karl. 1977. Study of a sound change in progress. Cullowhee: Western Carolina University. [Mimeograph]

Nichols, Patricia C. 1976. Linguistic change in Gullah: sex, age, and mobility. Stanford, CA: Stanford University dissertation.

Nichols, Patricia C. 1981a. Creoles in the USA. Language in the USA, ed. by Charles A. Ferguson and Shirley Brice Heath, 69-91. New York: Cambridge University Press.

Nichols, Patricia C. 1981b. Verbal patterns of black and white speakers in coastal South Carolina. Paper presented at the Symposium on Language and Culture in South Carolina, Columbia.

Nichols, Patricia C. 1981c. Black and white speaking in the rural South: differences in the pronominal system. Paper presented to the Southeastern Conference on Linguistics, Richmond.

Niles, Norma A. 1982. Provincial English dialects and Barbadian English. Ann Arbor: University of Michigan dissertation.

Nix, Ruth A. 1980. Linguistic variation in the speech of Wilmington, North Carolina. Durham: Duke University dissertation.

Nolasco da Silva, Maria de Graça Carcía. 1972. Subsidios para o estudo dos lançados na Guiné. Boletim Cultural da Guiné Portuguesa 105.

O'Cain, Raymond K. 1972. A social dialect survey of Charleston, South Carolina. Chicago: University of Chicago dissertation.

Orton, Harold, et al., eds. 1962-1971. Survey of English dialects: introduction and basic materials. 13 volumes. Leeds, UK: E. J. Arnold and Sons.

Palmer, Frank. 1971. Grammar. Harmondsworth, UK: Penguin.

Palmer, F. R. 1979. Modality and the English modals. New York: Longman.

Pampell, John R. 1975. More on double modals. Texas Linguistic Forum 2, ed. by Susan F. Schmerling and Robert D. King, 110-21. Austin: University of Texas.

Park, Robert E. 1950. Race and culture. Glencoe, IL: Free Press.

Pash, Barbara. 1981. The lost faces of Maryland Indians. Sun (magazine). Baltimore. November 15.15-52.

Pederson, Lee. 1969. The linguistic atlas of Gulf states: an interim report. American Speech 44.279-86.

Pederson, Lee. 1972. Black speech, white speech, and the Al Smith syndrome. Studies in linguistics in honor of Raven I. McDavid, Jr., ed. by L. M. Davis, 124-34. University: University of Alabama Press.

Pederson, Lee. 1973. Dialect patterns in rural northern Georgia. Lexicography and dialect geography: festgabe fur Hans Kurath, ed. by H. Scholler and J. Reidy, 195-207. Wiesbaden: Franz

Steiner.

Pederson, Lee. 1974. Tape/text and analogues. American Speech 49.5-23.

Pederson, Lee. 1975. The plan for a dialect survey of rural Georgia. Orbis 24.38-44.

Pederson, Lee. 1977. Grassroots grammar in the Gulf states. James B. McMillan: essays in linguistics by his friends and colleagues, ed. by James C. Raymond and I. Willis Russell, 91-112. University: University of Alabama Press.

Pederson, Lee et al., eds. 1974. A manual for dialect research in the southern states. 2nd edition. University: University of Alabama Press.

Pederson, Lee et al., eds. 1981. LAGS: the basic materials. Ann Arbor: University Microfilms International.

Pederson, Lee, Grace S. Rueter, and Joan H. Hall. 1974. Biracial dialectology: six years into the Georgia survey. Journal of English Linguistics 9.18-25.

Pederson, Lee, Howard G. Dunlap, and Grace S. Rueter. 1975. Questionnaire for a dialect survey of rural Georgia. Orbis 24.45-71.

Piestrup, Ann M. 1973. Black dialect interference and accommodation of reading instruction in first grade. Monographs of Language-Behavior Research Laboratory No. 4. Berkeley: University of California.

Politzer, Robert L., and Mary R. Hoover. 1976. Teachers' and pupils' attitudes toward black English speech varieties and black pupils' achievement. R & D Memorandum 145. Stanford: Stanford Center for Research and Development in Teaching.

Porter, Frank W. 1945. Notes on the Seminole Negroes in the Bahamas. Florida Historical Quarterly 24.56-60.

Porter, Frank W., III. 1979. Indians in Maryland and Delaware: a critical bibliography. Bloomington: Indiana University Press.

Porter, Frank W., III. 1980. Behind the frontier: Indian survivals in Maryland. Maryland Historical Magazine 75.42-54.

Porter, Kenneth W. 1971. The Negro on the American frontier. New York: Arno.

Poutsma, H. 1914-1928. A grammar of late modern English. 2nd ed. 3 vols. Groningen: P. Nordhoff.

Pullum, G., and D. Wilson. 1977. Autonomous syntax and the analysis of auxiliaries. Language 53.741-88.

Putnam, George N., and Edna M. O'Hern. 1955. The status significance of an isolated urban dialect. Language dissertation no. 53. Language 31.4.2.

Quattlebaum, Laura Janette. 1954. History of Horry county. Conway, SC: Horry County Memorial Library. [Manuscript]

Quirk, Randolph, and Sidney Greenbaum. 1973. A concise grammar of contemporary English. New York: Harcourt Brace Jovanovich.

Rawick, George, ed. 1972. The American slave: a composite auto-

biography. 19 vols. 1978. Supplemental series 1. 12 vols. 1979.
Supplemental series 2. 10 vols. Westport, CT: Greenwood.

Read, Allen Walker. 1933. British recognition of American speech
in the eighteenth century. Dialect Notes 6.313-34.

Read, Allen Walker. 1939. The speech of Negroes in colonial
America. Journal of Negro History 24.247-58.

Reeves, Dick. n.d. Carolina lowcountry patois: Gullah in story and
rhyme. Longplaying record. Charleston: Lenwal Enterprises.

Reinecke, John E. 1938. Trade jargons and creole dialects as marginal languages. Social Forces 17.107-18.

Richards, Jack C. 1971. Error analysis and second language strategies. Language Sciences 17.12-22.

Richards, Jack C. 1974. A non-contrastive approach to error
analysis. Error analysis: perspectives on second language
acquisition, ed. by Jack Richards, 172-88. London: Longman.

Rickford, John R. 1974. The insights of the mesolect. Pidgin and
creole linguistics: current trends and prospects, ed. by David
DeCamp and Ian F. Hancock, 92-117. Washington: Georgetown
University Press.

Rickford, John R. 1975. Carrying the new wave into syntax: the
case of black English BIN. Analyzing variation in language, ed.
by Ralph W. Fasold and Roger W. Shuy, 162-83. Washington:
Georgetown University Press.

Rickford, John R. 1977. Processes of pidginization and creolization. Pidgin and creole linguistics, ed. by Albert Valdman,
190-221. Bloomington: Indiana University Press.

Rickford, John R. 1979. Variation in a creole continuum: quantitative and implicational approaches. Philadelphia: University of
Pennsylvania dissertation.

Rickford, John R. 1980. How does DOZ disappear? Issues in English
creoles, ed. by Richard Day, 77-96. Heidelberg: Julius Groos
Verlag.

Rickford, John R. 1983. What happens in decreolization.
Pidginization and creolization as language acquisition, ed. by
Roger Anderson, 298-319. Rowley, MA: Newbury House.

Rodney, Walter. 1970. A history of the upper Guinea coast,
1545-1800. Oxford: Oxford University Press.

Rosenthal, R., and L. Jacobson. 1968. Pygmalion in the classroom:
teacher expectation and pupils' intellectual development. New
York: Holt, Rinehart and Winston.

Ross, John R. 1969. Auxiliaries as main verbs. Studies in philosophical linguistics, ed. by William Todd, 77-102. Carbondale, IL:
Great Expectations.

Rousseau, Pascale, and David Sankoff. 1978. Advances in variable
rule methodology. Linguistic variation: models and methods,
ed. by David Sankoff, 57-69. New York: Academic Press.

Rueter, Grace S. 1975. Vowel nasality in the speech of rural middle Georgia. Atlanta: Emory University dissertation.

Rueter, Grace S. 1977. A dialect survey of rural Georgia: the progress. Papers in language variation: SAMLA-ADS collection, ed. by David L. Shores and Carole P. Hines, 33-43. University: University of Alabama Press.

Sanders, Sara L. 1978. The speech of Fairfax, South Carolina in its subregional context: selected phonological features. Columbia: University of South Carolina thesis.

Sanders, Willease. 1978. Selected grammatical features of the speech of blacks in Columbia, South Carolina. Columbia: University of South Carolina dissertation.

Sawyer, Claire Marie. 1961. Some aspects of the fertility of a tri-racial isolate. Catholic University of America Studies in Sociology 46. Washington: Catholic University of America.

Schane, Sanford. 1973. Generative phonology. Englewood Cliffs, NJ: Prentice-Hall.

Schneider, Edgar W. 1981. Morphologische und syntaktische variablen im amerikanischen early black English. Bamberger beitrage zur Englische sprachwissenschaft 10. Frankfurt: Peter Lang.

Schneider, Edgar W. 1982. On the history of black English in the USA: some new evidence. English World-Wide 3.18-46.

Schrock, Earl F., Jr. 1980. A study of the dialect of the blacks in Pope County, Arkansas. Fayetteville: University of Arkansas dissertation.

Scott, Jerrie. 1973. The need for semantic considerations in accounting for verb forms in black dialects of English. University of Michigan Papers in Linguistics 1.2.140-46.

Scott, Jerrie. 1981. Black language and communication skills: recycling the issues. Black English and the education of black children and youth, ed. by Geneva Smitherman, 130-45. Detroit: Harlo.

Selinker, Larry. 1972. Interlanguage. International Review of Applied Linguistics 10.201-31.

Shuy, Roger W. 1972. Speech differences and teaching strategies: how different is enough? Contemporary English: change and variation, ed. by David L. Shores, 331-45. Philadelphia: Lippincott.

Shuy, Roger W., Walter A. Wolfram, and William K. Riley. 1967. Linguistic correlates of social stratification in Detroit speech. Washington: U. S. Office of Education.

Shuy, Roger W., Walter A. Wolfram, and William K. Riley. 1968. Field techniques in an urban language study. Washington: Center for Applied Linguistics.

Sledd, James H. 1980. From black-white speech relationships to the ethnography of communication, or, who profits from research. ERIC Document 199 705.

Smith, Warren B. 1961. White servitude in colonial South Carolina. Columbia: University of South Carolina Press.

Smitherman, Geneva. 1977. Talkin and testifyin: the language of black America. Boston: Houghton Mifflin.

Smitherman, Geneva, ed. 1981. Black English and the education of
black children and youth: proceedings of the national invita-
tional symposium on the King decision. Detroit: Wayne State
University.

Speck, Frank G. 1915. The Nanticoke community of Delaware. Contributions from the Museum of the American Indian, Heye
Foundation, no. 2. New York.

Spindler, George, ed. 1982. Doing the ethnography of schooling.
New York: Holt, Rinehart and Winston.

Stein, Jess, ed. 1966. Random House dictionary. New York: Random
House.

Stein, Jess, ed. 1975. Random House college dictionary. Revised
ed. New York: Random House.

Stephenson, Jean. 1971. Scotch-Irish migration to South Carolina.
Strasburg, VA: Shenandoah.

Sternglass, Marilyn. 1974. Close similarities in dialect features of
black and white college students in remedial composition
classes. TESOL Quarterly 8.271-83.

Stewart, Sadie E. 1919. Seven folk-tales from the sea islands,
South Carolina. Journal of American Folklore 32.394-96.

Stewart, William A., ed. 1964. Non-standard speech and the
teaching of English. Washington: Center for Applied
Linguistics.

Stewart, William A. 1965. Urban Negro speech: sociolinguistic factors affecting English teaching. Social dialects and language
learning: proceedings of the Bloomington, Indiana, conference,
ed. by Roger W. Shuy, 10-19. Champaign: National Council of
Teachers of English.

Stewart, William A. 1966-1967. Nonstandard speech patterns.
Baltimore Bulletin of Education 43.2-4,52-65.

Stewart, William A. 1967. Sociolinguistic factors in the history of
American Negro dialects. Florida FL Reporter 5.2,11,22,24,26.

Stewart, William A. 1968. Continuity and change in American
Negro dialects. Florida FL Reporter 6.1,3-4,14-16,18.

Stewart, William A. 1969. Of the use of Negro dialect in the
teaching of reading. Teaching black children to read, ed. by J.
C. Baratz and R. W. Shuy, 156-219. Washington: Center for
Applied Linguistics.

Stewart, William A. 1970a. Historical and structural bases for the
recognition of Negro dialect. Linguistics and the teaching of
standard English to speakers of other langauges or dialects,
ed. by James E. Alatis, 249-57. Washington: Georgetown University Press.

Stewart, William A. 1970b. Toward a history of American Negro
dialect. Language and poverty: perspectives on a theme, ed.
by Frederick Williams, 351-79. Chicago: Markham.

Stewart, William A. 1970c. Sociopolitical issues in the treatment
of Negro dialect. Linguistics and the teaching of standard
English to speakers of other languages or dialects, ed. by

James E. Alatis, 215-24. Washington: Georgetown University Press.

Stewart, William A. 1971. Facts and issues concerning black dialect. English Record 21.121-35.

Stewart, William A. 1972a. Acculturative processes and the language of the American Negro. Language in its social setting, ed. by W. W. Gage, 1-46. Washington: Anthropological Society of Washington.

Stewart, William A. 1972b. Review of Black-white speech relationships, ed. by W. Wolfram and N. Clarke. Florida FL Reporter 10.25-26,55-56.

Stewart, William A. 1977. Ups and downs in comprehension across the Gullah-English continuum. Paper presented at first annual Language and Culture in South Carolina Symposium, Columbia.

Stoddard, Albert H. 1954. Folklore of the United States: animal tales told in the Gullah dialect. Library of Congress Division of Music, records AAFS 144, AAFS 145, and AAFS 146, ed. by Duncan Emrich.

Summerlin, Nan Jo Corbitt. 1972. A dialect study: affective parameters in the deletion and substitution of consonants in the deep south. Tallahassee: Florida State University dissertation.

Tayac, Turkey (Philip Sheridan Proctor). 1978. Tape-recorded interview. Mar. 21, 1978. Mt. Rainier, Md.

Taylor, Douglas. 1971. Grammatical and lexical affinities of creoles. Pidginization and creolization of languages, ed. by Dell Hymes, 293-96. New York: Cambridge University Press.

Thomson, Sarah Grey. 1980. On interpreting 'the indian interpreter.' Language in Society 9.167-93.

Tijerina, Juanita G. 1981. Black Seminoles' reunion set. Austin Light, Mar. 12.2(7).6.

Tinelli, Henri. 1981. Creole phonology. The Hague: Mouton.

Traugott, Elizabeth. 1972. Principles in the history of American English--a reply. Florida FL Reporter 10.1-2,5-6,56.

Traugott, Elizabeth. 1973. Some thoughts on natural syntactic processes. New ways of analyzing variation in English, ed. by C.-J. N. Bailey and Roger W. Shuy, 313-22. Washington: Center for Applied Linguistics.

Traugott, Elizabeth. 1974. Explorations in linguistic elaboration: language change, language acquisition, and the genesis of spatio-temporal terms. Historical linguistics I: proceedings of the First International Conference on Historical Linguistics, ed. by J. Anderson and C. Jones, 263-314. Amsterdam: North Holland.

Traugott, Elizabeth. 1976. Pidgins, creoles, and the origins of vernacular black English. Black English: a seminar, ed. by Deborah S. Harrison and Tom Trabasso, 57-94. Hillsdale, NJ: Erlbaum.

Trudgill, Peter. 1974. The social differentiation of English in Norwich. New York: Cambridge University Press.

Turner, Lorenzo D. 1945. Notes on the sound and vocabulary of Gullah. Publication of the American Dialect Society 3.13-28.

Turner, Lorenzo D. 1948. Problems confronting the investigator of Gullah. Publication of the American Dialect Society 9.74-84.

Turner, Lorenzo D. 1949. Africanisms in the Gullah dialect. Chicago: University of Chicago Press.

United States Bureau of the Census. 1971. General population characteristics. Washington: Government Printing Office.

Van Riper, William R. 1972. Shortening the long conversational dialect interview. Studies in linguistics in honor of Raven I. McDavid, Jr., ed. by Lawrence M. Davis, 177-85. University: University of Alabama Press.

Varenne, Herve. 1982. Jocks and freaks: the symbolic structure of the expression of social interaction among American senior high school students. Doing the ethnography of schooling: educational anthropology in action, ed. by George Spindler, 210-35. New York: Holt, Rinehart and Winston.

Vaughn-Cooke, Anna Fay. 1976. The implementation of a phonological change: the case of resyllabification in black English (parts I and II). Washington: Georgetown Unviersity dissertation.

Vaughn-Cooke, Anna Fay. 1979. Evaluating language assessment procedures: an examination of linguistic guidelines and public law 94-142 guidelines. Language in public life, ed. by James E. Alatis and G. Richard Tucker, 231-57. Washington: Georgetown University Press.

Viereck, Wolfgang. 1975. Lexikalische und grammatische ergebnisse des Lowman-survey von mittel- und sudengland. 2 vols. Munich: Fink.

Walker, John, ed. 1971. A critical pronouncing dictionary of the English language. London: G.G.J. and J. Robinson.

Wang, W. S.-Y. 1969. Competing changes as a cause of residue. Language 45.9-25.

Wang, W. S.-Y. 1979. Language change: a lexical perspective. Annual Review of Anthropology 8.353-71.

Wang, W. S.-Y., and C. C. Cheng. 1970. Implementation of phonological change: the Shuang-feng Chinese case. Papers from the sixth regional meeting Chicago Linguistic Society, 552-59. Chicago: Chicago Linguistic Society.

Ward, Martha C. 1971. Them children: a study in language learning. New York: Holt, Rinehart and Winston.

Wardhaugh, Ronald. 1970. The contrastive analysis hypothesis. TESOL Quarterly 4.123-29.

Warner, W. Lloyd. 1949. Social class in America. New York: Harper and Row.

Warner, W. Lloyd et al. 1960. Social class in America: the evaluation of status. New York: Harper and Row.

Warrior, William. 1982. The seminole indian scout. Laughlin Leisure Time, 19.

Washabaugh, William. 1975. Variability in decreolization on Providence Island, Colombia. Detroit: Wayne State University dissertation.

Weaver, Constance. 1970. Analyzing literary representations of recent northern urban Negro speech: a technique with application to three books. East Lansing: Michigan State University dissertation.

Weaver, P., and F. Shonkoff. 1978. Research within reach: a research-guided response to concerns of reading educators. St. Louis: CARMEL.

Webster, Noah. 1828. American dictionary of the English language. 2 vols. New York: S. Converse.

Weinreich, Uriel. 1953. Languages in contact. New York: Linguistic Circle of New York.

Weinreich, U., W. Labov, and M. Herzog. 1968. Empirical foundations for a theory of language change. Directions for historical linguistics, ed. by W. P. Lehmann and Y. Malkiel, 95-188. Austin: University of Texas Press.

Wentworth, Harold. 1944. American dialect dictionary. New York: Crowell.

Westerman, Diedrich. 1930. A study of the Ewe language. New York: Oxford University Press.

Whinnom, Keith. 1981. Non-primary types of language. Logos Semanticos 5.227-41.

White, Lonnie J. 1964. Politics on the southwestern frontier: Arkansas territory, 1819-1836. Memphis, TN: Memphis State University Press.

Whiteman, Marcia Farr. 1976. Dialect influence and the writing of black and white working class Americans. Washington: Georgetown University dissertation.

Whiteman, Marcia Farr, ed. 1980. Reactions to Ann Arbor: vernacular black English and education. Arlington, VA: Center for Applied Linguistics.

Whiteman, Marcia Farr. 1981. Dialect influence in writing. Variation in writing: functional and linguistic-cultural differences, ed. by Marcia Farr Whiteman, 153-66. Hillsdale, NJ: Erlbaum.

Whitley, M. Stanley. 1975. Dialectal syntax: plurals and modals in Southern American. Linguistics 161.89-108.

Williamson, Juanita V. 1961. A phonological and morphological study of the speech of the Negro of Memphis, Tennesse. Ann Arbor: University of Michigan dissertation.

Williamson, Juanita V. 1968. A study of the speech of Negro high school students in Memphis, Tennessee. Washington: U.S. Office of Education, Bureau of Research.

Williamson, Juanita V. 1969. A note on it is/there is. Word Study 45.5-6.

Williamson, Juanita V. 1970. Selected features of speech: black and white. CLA Journal 13.420-33.

Williamson, Juanita V. 1972. A look at the direct question. Studies

in linguistics in honor of Raven I. McDavid, Jr., ed. by Lawrence M. Davis, 207-14. University: University of Alabama
Press.

Witkop, Carl J. 1958. Genetics and dentistry. Eugenics Quarterly
5.15-21.

Wolfram, Walt. 1969. A sociolinguistic description of Detroit Negro
speech. Washington: Center for Applied Linguistics.

Wolfram, Walt. 1971. Black-white speech differences revisited.
Black-white speech relationships, ed. by Walt Wolfram and
Nona H. Clarke, 139-61. Washington: Center for Applied Lin-
guistics.

Wolfram, Walt. 1973a. Sociolinguistic aspects of assimilation.
Arlington, VA: Center for Applied Linguistics.

Wolfram, Walt. 1973b. Hidden agendas and witch hunts: which is
witch? Florida FL Reporter 11.1-2,33-34,45.

Wolfram, Walt. 1973c. Review of Black English, by J. L. Dillard.
Language 49.670-79.

Wolfram, Walt. 1974. The relationship of white southern speech to
vernacular black English. Language 50.498-527.

Wolfram, Walt. 1976. Levels of sociolinguistic bias in testing.
Black English: a seminar, ed. by Deborah S. Harrison and Tom
Trabasso, 263-87. Hillsdale, NJ: Erlbaum.

Wolfram, Walt. 1980a. Beyond black English: implications of the
Ann Arbor decision for other non-mainstream varieties. Reactions to Ann Arbor: vernacular black English and education,
ed. by Marcia Farr Whiteman, 10-23. Washington: Center for
Applied Linguistics.

Wolfram, Walt. 1980b. A-prefixing in Appalachian English. Locating language in time and space, ed. by William Labov, 107-42.
New York: Academic Press.

Wolfram, Walt, and Donna Christian. 1975. Sociolinguistic variables
in Appalachian dialects. National Institute of Education grant
no. NIE-G-74-0026 final report. Washington: National Institute
of Education.

Wolfram, Walt, and Donna Christian. 1976. Appalachian speech.
Arlington, VA: Center for Applied Linguistics.

Wolfram, Walt, and Donna Christian. 1980. On the application of
sociolinguistic information: test evaluation and dialect differences in Appalachia. Standards and dialects in English, ed. by
Timothy Shopen and Joseph M. Williams, 177-212. Cambridge,
MA: Winthrop.

Wolfram, Walt, and Nona H. Clarke, eds. 1971. Black-white speech
relationships. Washington: Center for Applied Linguistics.

Wolfram, Walt, and Ralph W. Fasold. 1974. The study of social
dialects in American English. Englewood Cliffs, NJ: Prentice-
Hall.

Wood, Gordon. 1971. Vocabulary change: a study of variation in
regional words in eight of the southern states. Carbondale:
Southern Illinois University Press.

Wood, Peter. 1974. Black majority: Negroes in colonial South Caro-
lina from 1670 through the Stone rebellion. New York: Knopf.
Woolf, Henry Bosley, ed. 1981. Webster's new collegiate diction-
ary. Springfield, MA: G. and C. Merriam.
Wright, Joseph. 1898-1905. The English dialect dictionary. 6 vols.
Oxford: Oxford University Press.
Wright, Joseph. 1905. The English dialect grammar. Oxford: Oxford
University Press.
Yap, Angelita C. 1961. The study of a kinship system: its struc-
tural principles. Catholic University of America Studies in
Sociology 45. Washington: Catholic University of America.
Yetman, Norman K. 1967. The background of the slave narrative
collection. American Quarterly 19.534-53.
Zwicky, Arnold M. 1978. Arguing for constituents. Papers from the
fourteenth regional meeting of the Chicago Linguistics Soci-
ety, ed. by Donka Farkas et al., 503-12. Chicago: Chicago
Linguistics Society.

Contributors

Guy Bailey is Assistant Professor of English at Texas A&M University, where he teaches language variation. He was formerly Assistant Editor of the Linguistic Atlas of Gulf States.

Marvin Bassett received his doctorate in English from Emory University in 1983 and was formerly Assistant Editor of the Linguistic Atlas of the Gulf States.

Charles E. Billiard is retired from Georgia State University, where he was Professor of Curriculum and Instruction and taught social dialects and education.

Harmon S. Boertien is Director of Graduate Studies and Associate Professor of English at the University of Houston Central Campus, where he teaches English linguistics.

Jeutonne P. Brewer is Associate Professor of English at the University of North Carolina at Greensboro. She has a long-term research interest in the ex-slave narratives and has recently investigated the speech of the Lumbee Indians in North Carolina.

Ronald R. Butters is Associate Professor and Supervisor of Freshman Instruction in the Department of English at Duke University. He edits American Speech.

Frederic G. Cassidy is Professor Emeritus of English at the University of Wisconsin. He is best known for his work on Jamaican Creole English and for his editing of the Dictionary of American Regional English.

Boyd H. Davis is Professor of English at the University of North Carolina at Charlotte. She is currently editing unpublished manuscripts of Ferdinand de Saussure and is continuing her study of the pragmatics of the language of adolescents.

George Dorrill is Visiting Assistant Professor of English at the University of South Carolina. His research interests are language variation, literacy, and language learning.

Crawford Feagin teaches sociolinguistics at the University of Virginia at Falls Church and is currently undertaking an instrumental analysis of the Southern drawl.

Glenn G. Gilbert is Professor of Linguistics at Southern Illinois University at Carbondale and is working on a book dealing with the history of creolistics.

Joan Hall is Assistant Editor of the Dictionary of American Regional English.

Ian Hancock is Professor of English and Linguistics at the University of Texas at Austin. His principal research interests are the Anglophone creoles and Romany.

Patricia Jones-Jackson is Assistant Professor of English at Howard University, where she teaches linguistics and writing.

Ceil Lucas, Assistant Professor of Linguistics at Gallaudet College, recently completed a study of language diversity in the elementary school classroom.

The late Raven I. McDavid, Jr., editor and fieldworker for the Linguistic Atlas of the United States and Canada, published widely on American English.

Virginia McDavid was formerly Professor of English at Chicago State University. She has been an editor for the Linguistic Atlas of the North Central States for many years.

Michael I. Miller teaches in the English Department at Chicago State University.

Michael Montgomery is Assistant Professor of English at the University of South Carolina, where he is editing a bibliography on Southern English. His main research interest is Appalachian English.

Patricia C. Nichols is Assistant Professor, Co-Director of the English Skills Center, and Coordinator of Teacher Training in the English Department at San Jose State. Her research interests are language and gender issues and Sea Island Creole.

Ruth A. Nix received her doctorate in Anthropology from Duke University in 1980 and now works in the private sector.

John R. Rickford is Assistant Professor of Linguistics at Stanford University. He edits The Carrier Pidgin and his research interests are pidgins and creoles and sociolinguistics.

Earl F. Schrock, Jr., is Professor of English at Arkansas Tech University, where he teaches linguistics, writing, and literature.

Jerrie Scott, Associate Professor of English at the University of Florida, is currently researching the relationship between language background and writing performance of college students.

Elisabeth Sommer is Associate Professor of English at the University of Central Florida.

Fay Boyd Vaughn-Cooke, Associate Professor of Communication Science at the University of the District of Columbia, is currently studying how children acquire locative constructions.

Walt Wolfram, Professor of Communication Science at the University of the District of Columbia and Director of Research at the Center for Applied Linguistics in Washington, has published widely on social dialects of American English.

Name Index

Subject Index

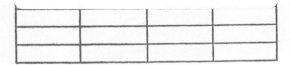